This Time We Knew

This Time We Knew

Western Responses to Genocide in Bosnia

EDITED BY

*Thomas Cushman and
Stjepan G. Meštrović*

New York University Press   NEW YORK AND LONDON

NEW YORK UNIVERSITY PRESS

New York and London

Copyright © 1996 by New York University

Library of Congress Cataloging-in-Publication Data
This time we knew : western responses to genocide in Bosnia / edited
by Thomas Cushman and Stjepan G. Meštrović.
p. cm.
Includes bibliographical references and index.
ISBN 0–8147–1534–6 (alk. paper)
1. Yugoslav War, 1991–   2. Genocide—Bosnia and Hercegovina.
3. World politics—1989–   I. Meštrović, Stjepan Gabriel.
II. Cushman, Thomas, 1959–   .
DR1313.T485 1996
949.702'4—dc2096-10071   96-10071
                                   CIP

New York University Press books are printed on acid-free paper, and
their binding materials are chosen for strength and durability.

Manufactured in the United States of America
10 9 8 7 6 5 4 3 2 1

To our daughters, who we hope will not see genocide again in their lifetimes.

Contents

Acknowledgments   *ix*

One   Introduction   1
        Thomas Cushman and Stjepan G. Meštrović

Two   The Complicity of Serbian Intellectuals in
        Genocide in the 1990s   39
        Philip J. Cohen

Three Bosnia: The Lessons of History?   65
        Brendan Simms

Four No Pity for Sarajevo; The West's
        Serbianization; When the West Stands In for
        the Dead   79
        Jean Baudrillard

Five Israel and the War in Bosnia   90
        Daniel Kofman

Six   The Politics of Indifference at the United
        Nations and Genocide in Rwanda and Bosnia   128
        Michael N. Barnett

Seven The *West Side Story* of the Collapse of
        Yugoslavia and the Wars in Slovenia, Croatia,
        and Bosnia-Herzegovina   163
        Slaven Letica

Eight Serbia's War Lobby: Diaspora Groups and
        Western Elites   187
        Brad K. Blitz

Nine   Moral Relativism and Equidistance in British
         Attitudes to the War in the Former Yugoslavia   244
         Daniele Conversi

Ten   The Former Yugoslavia, the End of the
         Nuremberg Era, and the New Barbarism   282
         James J. Sadkovich

Eleven War and Ethnic Identity in Eastern Europe:
          Does the Post-Yugoslav Crisis Portend
          Wider Chaos?   304
          Liah Greenfeld

Twelve The Anti-Genocide Movement on American
          College Campuses: A Growing Response to
          the Balkan War   313
          Sheri Fink

Thirteen Western Responses to the Current Balkan War   350
            David Riesman

Appendix 1 A Definition of Genocide   359

Appendix 2 Text of the United Nations Convention on
              the Prevention and Punishment of the Crime
              of Genocide   360

Appendix 3 Indictments by the International Criminal
              Tribunal for the Former Yugoslavia   363

              Contributors   *403*
              Index   *405*

Acknowledgments

The two coeditors of this volume were blessed with a nearly perfect working relationship. As social theorists and intellectuals, we share a number of theoretical interests, including postmodernism, critical theory, and an eclectic approach to theory. As friends, we shared our disbelief and outrage at the rationalizations, excuses, and obfuscations about the genocide that is still occurring in the Balkans. This blend of theoretical interests and reaction to current events led to our collaboration on this volume. It is our hope that the volume will provide an impetus for further exploration of Western indifference to genocide, not only in Bosnia, but in other parts of the world.

Each of us comes from otherwise different backgrounds, and acknowledges the assistance, inspiration, and encouragement of different individuals, but also of individuals common to both. Both editors thank the authors for working under pressure to meet deadlines. We are both grateful to the editors at New York University Press for their enthusiastic support of this project. Meštrović is especially grateful to David Riesman for his ongoing correspondence concerning the current Balkan War and for his encouragement in putting together this project. Cushman would like to thank Daniel Kofman, Michael Barnett, Sheri Fink, and Carol Hartigan for comments and advice on various stages of this project. Special thanks are due to James Petterson of the Wellesley College Department of French for providing superb translations of Jean Baudrillard's essays. The Wellesley College Committee on Faculty Awards provided generous financial assistance for all stages of this project. Finally, we are thankful to our wives and daughters for letting us spend too much time away from them working on this project.

ONE

Thomas Cushman and Stjepan G. Meštrović

Introduction

In the summer of 1995, Bosnian Serb attacks on UN-declared safe areas of Srebrenica and Žepa proceeded, as did previous onslaughts in Bosnia, under the watchful gaze of the West. In the ensuing violence, thousands of Muslims were driven from their homes or executed and buried in mass graves. In late November 1995, UN Secretary-General Boutros Boutros-Ghali reported that as many as 5,500 people are still unaccounted for in the wake of the Serbian attacks. At the time, no Western power intervened to stop the massacres. In the aftermath of the slaughter, however, the unexpected happened: Western powers seemingly decided that they had had enough of Serbian atrocities, war crimes, and genocide in Bosnia and made an apparent commitment to mobilize military power to protect other safe areas and to bring the Bosnian Serb leaders to the peace table. NATO air strikes commenced against the Bosnian Serbs, ostensibly to force them to remove their heavy weapons from the perimeter of Sarajevo.

This Western action was not agreeable to all the members of the NATO alliance. Yet it did occur, and the very fact that it did was remarkable, for the response of the West to the crisis in the Balkans prior to the air strikes had been weak, indecisive, and ineffective. One could even make the case that the nature of the Western response actually abetted genocide and

1

other crimes against humanity in the region by allowing the perpetrators to proceed with a guarantee that they would not be punished. Bosnian Serb forces pulled their weapons back, but fighting continued and ethnic cleansing and war crimes continued even as peace talks proceeded. In the northern territory near the city of Banja Luka, under threat of a concerted Croat-Muslim drive in 1995 to reconquer territory that was seized and ethnically cleansed three years ago, Bosnian Serb leaders reactivated concentration camps and their policies of mass terror and summary execution of civilians. Nonetheless, the West, weary of the conflict and perhaps guilty about its own silence in relation to it, continued to press for peace at any cost. Peace talks were held in Dayton, Ohio, and—despite Radovan Karadžić's pronouncement that, as a result of the peace talks, "Sarajevo will bleed for decades"—the parties in the conflict concluded a peace agreement in December, 1995. Questions of a "just peace" were put to the side in favor of settling the conflict, even at the cost of legitimizing ill-gotten Serbian territorial gains in Bosnia and at the cost of tolerating the nefarious deeds of indicted war criminals such as Radovan Karadžić or General Ratko Mladić (see appendix 2 for the text of the indictments against the latter by the International War Crimes Tribunal for the Former Yugoslavia). Events change daily in the Balkans, and one wonders, given the history of broken promises, just how stable the peace agreement will be.

The NATO objective of stopping the interminable siege of Sarajevo was apparently achieved. Yet at the same time hundreds and perhaps thousands more Muslims from northern Bosnia, from the area near the city of Banja Luka, were ethnically cleansed, some expelled to other parts of Bosnia, others summarily executed and thrown into mass graves. In spite of apparently more decisive action on the part of the West, the tragedies and atrocities continued. It is clear that peace in the former Yugoslavia is preferable to the continued loss of life. Yet even if peace is achieved there, a vivid memory of a form of barbarism unmatched in Europe since World War II will remain. Western scholars will try to explain that barbarism to themselves for a long time to come. They will seek answers to questions about the perpetrators of atrocities and war crimes. But at the same time, the nature of our response to the Balkan crisis will press us to explain another important aspect of the war: our own silence and irresponsibility. The German historian Leopold von Ranke once claimed, "history is." In the postmodern age of mass media we can agree with Ranke, but add that history is watched. For the last four years, the West has played an important role in the Balkan War: the role of voyeur. The West has been a silent witness to some of the worst atrocities and crimes against humanity to occur in Europe in this century. So, in addition to exploring the minds of the perpetrators—a usual approach in the social scientific study of genocide—we must also explore the mind of those who have watched the perpetrators. In a postmodern world, we continue to study the other, but it is also necessary to study those who watch the other.

In recent years we have seen a proliferation of books and articles on various aspects of the current Balkan War. But one important area that has been neglected thus far is the self-critical, reflective study of the role of the West in interpreting and responding to the war. We propose to remedy this lack of critical reflection by offering detailed sociological, political, and historical analyses of Western responses to the war. In particular, we focus on the response of Western elites—defined broadly as academics, public intellectuals, journalists, and policy makers—to the war. While many authors have made discussions of the Western response to the Balkans central in their historical examinations of the area, we offer an extended analysis from a variety of perspectives. In this respect, the present volume includes many essays by intellectuals who have brought to the interpretation of the issues at hand perspectives that are not necessarily present in the dominant Western discourse on the events in the Balkans over the last five years.

We begin with the observation that most writers use the terms "Balkan War," "war in the former Yugoslavia," and similar referents uncritically. To be precise, the wars that began in June 1991 against Slovenia and which were still raging in Bosnia as of this writing have *not* included a single hour's war in Serbia, Greece, Bulgaria, or other regions of the Balkans.[1] Until relatively recently, with the formation of a Muslim-Croat federation and the Croatian recapturing of territory occupied by armed Serbian rebels, the wars in question have been waged by proxies of the Belgrade regime and have been fought exclusively on the sovereign territories of the recognized nation-states of Slovenia, Croatia, and Bosnia-Herzegovina. The assessment given by Michael T. Kaufman in 1992 is the most accurate and still holds in 1995: "It is guns and ammunition supplied by Belgrade that are killing civilians in areas beyond the borders of Serbia.... Since the fighting started a year ago, not a single part of Serbia or its allied state of Montenegro has come under attack from a Croatian or Muslim force."[2]

In addition, while we mostly think of war as occurring between organized armies, these have not been wars among organized armies for the
most part, but mainly destruction inflicted by military and paramilitary
forces against civilians. This is significant because the deliberate killing
of civilians in wartime is considered a war crime. This was the situation
when Croatian Serbs, backed by Belgrade and the might of the Yugoslav
National Army, captured one-third of Croatian territory in an invasion in
1991, and it is especially the case in Bosnia, where, for almost four
years, Bosnian civilians were left defenseless against a Serbian military
juggernaut because of an arms embargo imposed on them by the West. It
was still the case as Serbian paramilitary units—led most notably by
the infamous Arkan—were imported from Belgrade to commence mass
killings and ethnic cleansing in northern Bosnia near the Serb stronghold
of Banja Luka, even as the sides prepared to make peace. Bosnian
government officials have regularly referred to the conflict as "slaughter,"
not war, an assessment reflected in David Rieff's 1995 book titled *Slaughterhouse: Bosnia and the Failure of the West.*

The central question that is the impetus for the present volume is why
so many Western intellectuals have been so unconcerned or ambivalent
about the genocide that has occurred in Bosnia for the last four years.
Again, let us attempt to be precise by noting that some sort of concern is
indicated by the existence of thousands of articles and books on the
events in Bosnia, to say nothing of the information that circulates along
the information superhighway on the internet. Yet such concern is only
partly characterized by strong statements advocating that this aggression
should be stopped, that genocide should be halted, that Bosnia has a
fundamental right to self-defense, and that territorial sovereignty of recognized European nations ought to be respected. Key elements of the rationalizations put forth by indicted war criminals have appeared with fre-
quency in the pages of the most well respected Western journals,
newsmagazines, and newspapers (indeed, in some cases the indicted war
criminals themselves have been given equal time in the press to argue
their cases). We cannot imagine that during World War II, the last time
genocide appeared as a state policy in Europe, Nazi leaders or their
acolytes in the West would have been interviewed on forums such as the
CBS newsmagazine *Sixty Minutes,* on National Public Radio, or in the
pages of large-city newspapers such as the *Houston Chronicle.*[3] More
astoundingly, we cannot imagine that some of the most well respected
Western intellectuals, both writers and policy makers, would reproduce

and agree with the views of leaders like Radovan Karadžić or Slobodan Milošević, whose actual and alleged deeds are so ignoble that any self-respecting thinkers should in their political decisions and in their writings immediately distance themselves from them.

In addition to these outright supporters, many Western intellectuals—despite their curdled indignation at the reported atrocities and genocide in Bosnia—have taken some variant of the ambivalent position that all sides are equally guilty (specifically, the Croats, Bosnian Muslims, and Serbs) and that peace at the price of ethnic partition or forgiving indicted war criminals is preferable to "more fighting." We see this as evidence of a significant change in the *habitus* of Western intellectuals; in contrast to an earlier age when intellectuals were inclined to choose sides and fight for a cause, the dominant disposition of the contemporary intellectual is to be ambivalent in relation to the dramatic conflicts that are emerging in the "new world disorder." Indeed, if in a previous age intellectuals were characterized by an almost overzealous degree of commitment to various causes, the present age is characterized by a stance of almost "aggressive ambivalence." It often seems that modern-day intellectuals, on both the left and the right, go out of their way to be "balanced" in their discourse on the Balkan conflict, even if such attempts at balance cause confusion about the historical record of just who is killing whom and why, or how many people have been killed. Balance is a necessary quality of intellectual life, except when it comes, as it has in the case of much analysis of events in the former Yugoslavia, at the cost of confusing victims with aggressors, and the failure to recognize those who are the perpetrators of genocide and crimes against humanity.

In 1936, George Orwell went to Spain to write about the Spanish Civil War and decided to remain there to fight against fascism. In his resultant chronicle, *Homage to Catalonia,* Orwell discusses many particulars of the war and his experiences of battle. But only in one short line does he give us some inkling of why he decided to stay and fight: "I had come to Spain with some notion of writing newspaper articles, but I had joined the militia almost immediately, because at that time and in that atmosphere, it seemed the only conceivable thing to do." For Orwell, and for many intellectuals of the day, there was little difference between holding a position and acting on it: one's beliefs and values necessarily led to action. In Orwell's case, his contempt for fascism served as a compulsion to act against it by supporting antifascists with his thoughts and, if need be, his life.

In the present day, it seems, a new kind of ethic seems to have emerged among intellectuals. This ethic champions a kind of cynical, detached, Panglossian ambivalence that not only leads to inaction, but actually celebrates it and seeks to justify it. Many of the articles in the present volume explore this ambivalence and the historical, social, and cultural reasons for its existence. As a way of contextualizing our discussion of ambivalence, however, we focus on the significance of this ambivalence as it is occurring fifty years after World War II.

From Auschwitz to Bosnia

Until now, the most common rationalization given by intellectuals for not stopping the Holocaust is "we did not know." This may or may not have been the case, since, even with regard to the Holocaust, one ought never to forget that the standard German cliché "we did not know" was more a rationalization than a truism. As Lucy Dawidowicz notes, the burning of corpses could be smelled in major population centers in Germany, and it is hard to imagine that Germans did not hear reports of atrocities and circulate them among themselves.[4] Still, the authentic shock registered on the faces of Allied troops as they liberated the death camps and more general Western responses to what we realized had happened in Auschwitz, Dachau, and elsewhere provide some evidence that we in the West did not know the true extent of the crimes being committed by the Nazis.

In relation to Bosnia, the globalization of information through the mass media has made available a great deal of information about the conflicts and crises set into motion by the Belgrade regime in the 1990s. As in World War II, when we watched and read about German troop movements, we knew of the invasion of Slovenia, Croatia, and Bosnia-Herzegovina as they happened. We also knew about ethnic cleansing, mass rapes, and genocide. In contrast to a previous age, Western observers have been literally bombarded with information about the most recent wave of genocide in Europe. Atrocities have been recorded in sound bytes of human history for all to see—every concurrent episode of atrocity can be seen, compared with the previous one, and filed away in physical archives and human memories.

The excuse that "we did not know" is thus not applicable to the present context; it might even be said that we "know too much." One might paraphrase the shift in collective attitudes to genocide in Europe over the span of fifty years as a movement from "we did not know" to "we are confused, or ambivalent" precisely because we know so much. This shift is the central focus of the present volume. With the advent of instantaneous forms of mass media in the early twentieth century, intellectuals were optimistic that these media would be an instrument of information in the service of democracy. In just a short time, we witnessed the loss of this optimism and the recognition that mass culture was preferable to learned discourse on the problems of the age. In what Mark Poster has called "the second media age" of the postwar era, the problem is similar, but of a slightly different order.[5] The new computer-based media such as electronic mail and the internet allow us to gain access to hitherto unimaginable amounts of information and to reform and reshape our thinking and our identities based on that information. For Poster, this reshifting of identity is what is most important about the new media, for we now have the power to resist conventional identities and to make ourselves, via the media, into new types of people and engage in new forms of political practice.

Yet it is questionable whether this new media age facilitates practical, moral intervention in the affairs of the so-called new world order. It may be that the Internet opens up the practice of "postmodern politics," and it may be, as activist Sheri Fink points out in this volume, that electronic media have enhanced the ability of activists to mobilize support for their causes. In this volume, however, we raise directly the uncomfortable question of whether there is any relationship between the degree or extent of public information and practical or moral engagement by those who receive it. Or, to put it another way, one might call into question whether the Holocaust would have been stopped had the world known what was then mostly a closely guarded secret. One thing is certain: the butchering of innocent people in Bosnia has gone on under the watchful gaze of the West. *This time, we know.*

We wish to make it clear from the outset that our references to the Holocaust are *not* intended to imply an equation between genocide in Bosnia and the Holocaust. Our position is that there have been and continue to be many sites of genocide, but that there was only one Holocaust. The Holocaust holds many social meanings, but in this discussion we make a careful and precise reference to the Holocaust as a site of genocide. We note with regret that many writers have invoked the Holocaust in a less careful and less precise manner. Nevertheless, there is a useful role for careful comparisons and contrasts. For example, Louis Gentile, a Canadian diplomat working for the United Nations in Bosnia-Herzegovina, writes in a letter to the editors of the *New York Times,*

> I wonder how many of your readers have seen Steven Spielberg's "Schindler's List" and how many have heard of Banja Luka.. . . To those who said to themselves after seeing "Schindler's List," never again, it is happening again. The so-called leaders of the Western world have known what is happening here for the last year and a half. They receive play by play reports. They talk of prosecuting war criminals, but do nothing to stop the crimes. May God forgive them. May God forgive us all.[6]

Even Steven Spielberg claimed that *Schindler's List* "speaks not only about the Jewish Holocaust, but of every Holocaust, by anyone's definition."[7] Anthony Lewis wrote a column entitled "Never Again" in which he contrasts Nuremberg with Bosnia.[8] Zbigniew Brzezinski makes a similar argument in "Never Again—Except for Bosnia."[9] Many Western intellectuals invoke this comparison and in the process remind us that it is sociologically useful to see formal similarities between historical events.

In the present volume, then, the Holocaust during World War II and the mass killing of Muslims in Bosnia are treated as European sites of genocide. Our precise aim is to compare and contrast Western intellectual responses to two different instances of genocide in Europe over the span of fifty years, one carried out deliberately and systematically against Jews and other peoples during World War II and the other carried out, also deliberately and systematically, against non-Serbs, primarily Muslims, in Europe in the 1990s. We shall refer below to the evidence that genocide has occurred and is occurring in Europe as of this writing. But the important point is that there is a sharp discrepancy between *what we know* and *what we do,* and this discrepancy has been neglected in most previous analyses. Yet this gap between knowledge and action is full of meaning for apprehending history as well as the present. In addition, this contrast causes us to rethink the success of the so-called Enlightenment project: the passive Western observation of genocide and other war crimes in the former Yugoslavia amounts to a toleration of the worst form of barbarity and gives us pause to wonder whether, behind the rhetoric of European progress and community, there is not some strong strain of irrationality that, if laid bare, would call into question the degree of enlightenment the civilized West has managed to attain at the century's end.

The neglected question that ought to be of concern to Western intellectuals—the main creators and purveyors of information—is, *How is it that genocide in Bosnia has been tolerated, given the information "superhighway" of the 1990s?* In a published response to an earlier work by Stjepan Meštrović on this issue,[10] philosopher Daniel Kofman offers a penetrating analysis of the importance of this question with regard to broad developments in social theory:

> How is genocide in Bosnia possible? But while putting it that way deliberately echoes the thought which has haunted the last half of our century—How was Auschwitz possible—Meštrović's work implies that the two questions, despite a superficial resemblance, are radically different. The question about Auschwitz addresses the sheer evil, the very depths of inhumanity, reached by the Nazis. It has spawned reflections in writers as diverse as Hannah Arendt, Horkheimer and Adorno, and Elie Wiesel. Theories have ranged from the blaming of "irrationality" and the incomplete nature of the Enlightenment project in Germany, to the triumph precisely of modern "instrumental rationality" as a moment of the "dialectic of the Enlightenment" (in Horkheimer's and Adorno's work bearing that title). What all these theories share, however, is a preoccupation with the minds of the perpetrators, and with the factors which led such minds to gain control of a modern state.
>
> With Bosnia the question which poses itself is rather different. It is not that the second time round on European soil we have moved from tragedy to farce, for despite the Serbian replacement of high tech gas chambers and crematoria with chain saws, knives, and everyday garden tools, the horror of genocide is never diminished by the bestial idiosyncrasies of its perpetrators. Rather, two factors have determined that on this occasion it is the onlookers—the Western powers in the main—and not the perpetrators themselves, who have become the chief focus of analysis. The first factor is that, as Meštrović puts it, the conflict in Bosnia has been given "massive coverage." If the Holocaust was high-tech genocide with low-tech reportage, genocide in Bosnia is just the opposite. And secondly, a factor alluded to throughout by Meštrović, precisely because we have been here before, we are supposed to have learned something. After all, "Never again!" had been turned into a pious slogan for an entire generation.[11]

It is the high visibility of genocide in Bosnia that distinguishes it from most other current as well as historical sites of genocide. Never has genocide been covered so much and so well. Bosnia has been referred to as "prime time horror"[12] in which, as one headline put it, "Serbs Shell Bosnian Capital as UN Monitors Watch."[13] Carla Anne Robbins wrote in

1994, "Despite two years of watching Bosnia's agony on TV, Americans seem remarkably disengaged."[14] Sarajevo journalist Zlatko Dizdarević noted, "Here in Sarajevo, hundreds of TV crews parade before our very eyes; dozens of foreign journalists, reporters, writers. Everything is known here, right down to the minutest details, and yet, nothing."[15] Roger Cohen quotes Simone Veil, a French minister and survivor of Auschwitz, who said regarding Sarajevo, " 'It's terrible, it's shocking' and then concluded that nothing can be done."[16] Elsewhere, Cohen writes: "The world is tired of Sarajevo. There has been too much killing, too many stories of suffering over more than 1000 days."[17]

For this reason, too, we reject the charge of Eurocentrism that some analysts have made regarding Western intellectuals' preoccupation with genocide in Bosnia. It is true that similar horrors in Cambodia, Rwanda, Kurdistan, and East Timor have not received the media attention that Bosnia captures. For whatever sociological reasons, Bosnia has been in the media spotlight, yet the information supplied by the media on genocide in Bosnia has not moved the West to put a decisive stop to it. For that very reason, it is a significant event in contrast to other sites of genocide. The Indonesian government, as Noam Chomsky has pointed out, has systematically killed thousands of East Timorese people, yet the media have remained relatively silent about these atrocities.[18] About this genocide, the world knew very little and, therefore, did very little. While this genocide is tragic, some can always say in self-defense that "we did not know." Yet Serbs have killed vast numbers of Muslims in the European country of Bosnia. About this, the world knows a great deal, and yet, until very recently with NATO air strikes (aimed primarily at bringing Bosnian Serbs to the so-called peace table rather than stopping or punishing genocide), the world has done very little. The visibility of this genocide leaves one with the troubling thought as to whether cognizance of genocide and moral condemnation of it even matter anymore.

Jean Baudrillard, in three essays especially translated for this volume, raises this haunting issue in his unique and provocative way: we do not respond because the portrayal of mass death is "hyperreal," a mere "simulacrum": in a world of manufactured violent images that coexist with the manipulated depiction of real violence, we have lost the ability to distinguish between real violence and simulated violence. Reality is confused with hyperreality, the world of the simulacrum. Western journalists and publics produce and consume the latter as if it were the "real world." And, should they ever be able to tell the difference, it would matter little, since, as Baudrillard tells us, there is no distinction between the Serbs and the West: the former's actions are a merely a reflection of the vicious tendencies that exist within us under the veneer of enlightened civility, which we imagine to be our dominant quality. The Serbs are us. The West's "Serbianization" (*serbissement,* in Baudrillard's terms) means that the issue of mass death and destruction will be little more than an afterthought, just as it is for those Serbs who have committed genocide and other atrocities; to acknowledge such genocide is to look in the mirror and see a face that looks remarkably like that of the perpetrator of mass violence and destruction.

To answer the question, "How is genocide in Bosnia possible?" we must examine the Western intellectual context in the 1990s, in which postmodernists have largely supplanted critical theorists as a frame of reference. The gap between George Orwell, the critic of evil, and Richard Rorty, the philosopher who has opened the way to seeing evil as just another vocabulary in a world where there are no final vocabularies, is vast. In Orwell's time, moral vocabularies were clearly defined and final; one acted on them. In the age of postmodernism, moral vocabularies are contingent and not final; our action in relation to them seems to consist in choosing what is best for ourselves and respecting the voice of the other, regardless of what that voice might be telling us.[19] This is not meant to suggest, of course, that all or even most Western intellectuals are postmodernists. Rather, we mean that until recently, most intellectuals shared the faith in the Enlightenment project expressed by critical theorists, including a faith in scientific facts and the taking of moral positions based on those facts. But postmodernism defines itself as rebellion against the Enlightenment project and revels in relativism, the questioning of the possibility of facts, and the celebration of ambivalence. And postmodernism has penetrated most disciplines and occupations with these attitudes and assumptions. Even if all intellectuals have not adopted relativism as a code for their conduct, they have encountered it and exist in it much the same way as fish exist in water. This is particularly the case with those who these days identify themselves with the "left." Many left positions nowadays (at least in the United States) are notable in their commitment to the ideal of "multiculturalism." Multiculturalism is a complex ideological position. At the very least, it calls for us to accept the possibility that every position (or, in Rorty's terms, every "vocabulary") is right. Yet it also proscribes the possibility of telling anyone that they are, or have done, wrong.

Many modern leftists working under the rubric of multiculturalism (and at least one of the editors of this volume would continue to classify himself as being a "modern leftist") have a difficult time identifying and condemning transgression. Many radical postmodernists actually celebrate transgression, since the object against which transgression is directed is usually some icon of modernist order that is seen as repressive. The calling of the modern leftist is not, as it was in George Orwell's time, to morally sound positions, but to the defense of all positions and the refusal to disavow some positions, even the positions of evildoers. Thus, the fact that genocide is occurring in Europe in the 1990s is not taken at face value, but is subjected immediately to the impulses of the postmodern age: disbelief, deconstruction, questioning, and ambivalence. Moreover, this kind of attitude makes it more likely that Western intellectuals cannot bring themselves to say, unequivocally, "The Serbs have done wrong." And if those words are uttered, then a corollary utterance is usually "Well, all of those Balkan tribalists have all done wrong." Or, in a more radically relativist vein, when confronted with evidence of genocide, some might even try to understand and even empathize with the perpetrators: "The Serbs have been victims of Muslims and Croats for centuries." Something, indeed, has happened when the perpetrators of genocide are seen by otherwise good and smart people as victims and when the genocide that they perpetrate is explained away by recourse to a lazy relativism that, in some varieties, assumes the form of empathy.

Postmodernism is a complex intellectual movement that is not amenable to easy characterization. Not all postmodernists would fit the generalization we make above, and postmodernism is difficult to define even among its adherents. A notable exception to our generalization is Jean Baudrillard, frequently referred to as *the* spokesperson for postmodernism (but who denies this label) and who clearly concludes that the Belgrade regime in Serbia is most responsible for the genocide under discussion here. It is, indeed, refreshing to see such a response, although it is an anomaly among those who would consider themselves adherents of Baudrillard's or others' postmodernist positions. Notwithstanding this ambiguity concerning postmodernism and intellectuals who see themselves as postmodernists, we hold that our generalization about postmodernism as a widespread social movement in the current *fin de siècle* holds overall. It is clear that there is not an absolute negative relationship between postmodernism and the proclivity to become morally engaged in the affairs of the world. Yet is also clear that there are cultural consequences of a generalized relativism that go far beyond the groves of academe and some of the petty battles that characterize that arena at present. We are at a point where fairness and the interests of seeing the world in terms of the other have come to include trying to understand the "plight" of the Serbs, who see themselves as victims of Ottoman repression, then Ustashe genocide, vanquished, but never victors, even as they annihilate Bosnia. In the press, we see the lionization of indicted war criminals like General Ratko Mladić: in a feature article by Roger Cohen in the *New York Times,* for example, the author seems less concerned to lay out the crimes for which Mladić is charged (and warn us about the future actions—the destruction of Srebrenica and Žepa could have been foreseen in the expressed character of the general) than he is in letting Mladić define himself as a heroic Serbian victim.[20] In a letter to the editor of the *New York Review of Books, New York Times* journalist David Binder, responding to a critical article about Mladić by Robert Block, writes, "I strongly wish to disassociate myself from his [Block's] assessment of the general as a crazed killer. Until compelling evidence to the contrary surfaces, I will continue to view Mladić as a superb professional, an opinion voiced by senior American, British, French, and Canadian military officers who have met him or followed his career and who are better qualified to judge him than either Block or I."[21] Writing on the war and those responsible for it is often not so much an act of objective reporting, or even moral engagement and advocacy, as it is a form of therapy or an occasion for paeans, a chance for the world to hear the case of war criminals and be given the option to decide that they may be justified or even lauded for what they are doing.

Genocide Is Occurring in Bosnia

The facts assembled by respectable fact-gathering organizations indicate very clearly the parties and individuals that are responsible for the current war of aggression and the commission of genocide in Bosnia. To be sure, one must look at the history of the entire area and the political actions of all the major players in the conflict. Even though we feel that the West has been intransigent in responding to the conflict, we do not feel that the West is responsible for it (even though many commentators insist that it is somehow Germany's fault for premature recognition of Slovenia and Croatia, as if the responsibility for genocide ultimately lies with those other than those who actually do the killing). Explanations of such things as the dissolution of Yugoslavia or the ethnic conflicts and genocide that have ensued must invariably begin with an analysis of events internal to Yugoslavia. To be sure, no parties in the current conflict are blameless in fostering interethnic conflict and very many accounts remind us, rightfully, that atrocities have been committed by all sides.

Such reports, however, very often fail to contextualize the actions of Croats, Bosnians, and Serbs. The Croatian recapturing of its Serb-occupied territory in the Krajina, for instance, is often seen as the same kind of "ethnic cleansing" as that engaged in by the Serbs. Seldom is any mention made of the fact that Croatia tried to negotiate with Serbs upon the breakup of the federation and then again during the Serbian occupation of the Krajina, a point noted by Slaven Letica in his paper in this volume. These negotiations were consistently met by Serbian aggression: in the early days of the conflict, by the rebellions of Jovan Rašković, amply described by Philip Cohen in his chapter on the complicity of Serbian intellectuals in genocide, and later by continued Serbian shelling of civilian targets in Croatia, in Vukovar, Dubrovnik, Zagreb, and other cities (one of the most memorable being the cluster bomb shelling of Zagreb in the spring of 1995, in which five civilians were killed and many more wounded). And, in contrast to the usual view that it was the revival of the Croatian currency unit, the kuna, or the Croatian coat of arms, the Sahovnica, that led Serbs to become ethnic cleansers, we feel compelled to point out that there is a difference between symbolic violence—the Serbs' taking offense at certain Croatian actions is quite understandable from a sociological view—and physical violence. Similarly, the West labeled as ethnic cleansing the exodus of Serbs in February of 1995 from areas under Bosnian Government control, even though the exodus was orchestrated by Serbian television and leaders, not by the Bosnian Muslims. Such capricious misuse of the term ethnic cleansing denatures its meaning and gives a false portrait of equal guilt among the three "warring parties."

Throughout the conflict, Serbs have complained that the West has failed to understand their case. They have complained that they have been demonized in the press (as if it takes the press to make demons out of those who have committed genocide). This may, in fact, be true, even though respectable news people have constantly offered the Serbs forums for their views. But what if the Serbs are right and their case has fallen on deaf ears? Why might that be so? One reason is that the West may not have, as yet, lost the capacity to recognize that there *is* no justifiable case to be made in defense of genocide. One might argue that after the commission of genocide, ethnic cleansing, and mass rape, the Serbs relinquished the right to be heard. Genocide committed by Serbian leaders in the name of Greater Serbia has nullified their right to be heard as an equal in the community of nations. *Verstehen,* the social scientific impulse to understand why people do what they do, is one thing, toleration and empathy are quite another. The practical consequences of the Serbian belief in their victimhood were atrocious, and such atrocities must be subject to moral and ethical adjudication if we are to avoid slipping down the slope from *verstehen* to relativism.[22]

The case against Bosnian Serb leaders as well as their supporters in Belgrade is so overwhelming that there is little need to be apologetic for sticking to the facts of the case. We do not agree that "all sides are equally guilty" of genocide, and therefore we do not need to defend against the perception of being polemical. We feel that it is vitally important to let the facts speak for themselves, particularly where genocide is involved. Moreover, the aim of the present volume is to offer a sustained critical assessment of the facts of the case and to offer a critical examination of why these facts seem to have been so egregiously ignored by many Western intellectuals and opinion makers. Indeed, all the articles in the present volume explain various facets of this inaction and ignorance in different ways. The central facts of the case are as follows:

1. According to a leaked CIA report, that the Belgrade regime is responsible for 90 percent of the atrocities committed in this war and 100 percent of the systematic killing (i.e., genocide).[23]

2. A UN-sponsored report over five thousand pages long, prepared under the direction of Cherif Bassiouni and released in 1994 is another key source of documentation that underscores Serbian official direction and responsibility for the vast majority of war crimes committed.

3. Reports prepared by Congress and the U.S. State Department likewise indicate that between 80 percent and 90 percent of the war crimes can be attributed to the Serbs.[24]

4. The reports by Helsinki Watch, *War Crimes in Bosnia-Herzegovina,* 2 vols. (New York, 1992–93) also confirm these other findings.

5. Other such reports exist, by the CSCE, the Red Cross, the news media—all of them remarkably consonant with one another.[25] For example, the United Nations concluded that Serbs committed the majority of rapes in Bosnia, and again, did so as an organized, systematic policy.[26]

6. It should be noted that during an election campaign in Serbia in 1993, Serb leaders openly accused each other of systematic war crimes outside Serbia: "This government consists of criminals, profiteers and the financial Mafia," shouts Vojislav Šešelj, former student of Frankfurt School critical theory, now ultranationalist leader of the Serbian Radical Party, and the coiner of "ethnic cleansing" as a concept and a policy . In return, Milošević's Socialist Party brands Šešelj, once a close ally, as a "war criminal." "The campaign is revealing in Serb leaders' own words that, first, Serbs from Serbia have indeed committed war crimes in Croatia and Bosnia and, second, that the goal of the Serbian authorities all along has been the creation of a Greater Serbia. And Belgrade newspapers have for the first time printed eyewitness accounts of Serb atrocities in Croatia and Bosnia."[27]

Genocide has occurred in Bosnia-Herzegovina and it has been perpetrated exclusively by the Belgrade regime and its proxies.[28] What is significant is that in the former Yugoslavia, as was the case during World War II in Europe, all sides have committed atrocities and war crimes, but only specific parties supported by and controlled by the Belgrade regime are responsible for genocide, which is a systematic and organized policy of mass murder with the intent to destroy, in whole or in part, a national, ethnical, racial, or religious group (see appendix 1 for specific definitions of genocide). To be sure, Croatian offensives against Bosnian Muslims in 1993, particularly in the city of Mostar, were contemptible and indefensible; those events should be publicly exposed and those responsible punished. The International War Crimes Tribunal has indicted seven Croats, including individuals directly and closely linked to Franjo Tudjman. Indictments of Bosnian Croats for war crimes is one indication that no side is without blemish in this conflict. In the late summer of 1995, Croatian troops recaptured the rebel-held Krajina area of Croatia, an area that had been seized and "ethnically cleansed" by Croatian Serbs four years ago with the aid of Yugoslav National Army troops. The European Commission on Human Rights, UN observers, Amnesty International, Helsinki Watch, and the Red Cross all reported that atrocities such as burning, looting, and the murder of a number of Serbs who remained in the region were committed by these Croatian troops upon the recapturing of the Krajina region. Subsequently, these very same Western fact-finding organizations have accused the Croatian government of deliberately covering up these atrocities. Franjo Tudjman stupefied the international community by promoting in the army a man who had recently been indicted by the International War Crimes Tribunal in the Hague. Presuming that the evidence for all these charges is accurate, we condemn those acts as we condemn any and all atrocities, whether committed by victims or aggressors.

Yet the central issue remains as to whether such Croatian actions—reprehensible and indefensible as they might be—constitute genocide as a policy. It is clear, as Norman Cigar has poignantly expressed it, that the systematic rounding up, torture, and murder of civilians have been a policy only of the Belgrade-sponsored Bosnian Serb aggressors in Bosnia-Herzegovina, whereas there is little evidence that the alleged atrocities in the Krajina proceeded as a result of state orders from Zagreb. In this event, small-scale acts of retribution by Croats have been given the same status as the large-scale, ongoing, and systematic atrocities and war crimes committed by Serbs in Bosnia; much of the mainstream media have been quick to use any act of violence on the part of Croats or Muslims as a pretext for morally equating all sides. Despite the fact that in the entire operation to liberate the Krajina only a few hundred civilians were killed, fewer than Bosnian Serbs slaughtered in an average hour of ethnic killing at Srebrenica, Žepa, and elsewhere, there is still no excuse for crimes and atrocities committed by Croatian forces, and the strident criticisms of Serbian actions that appear in this book should not be read as an apologia for Croatian misdeeds.[29]

This book, however, is about Western responses to the root cause of the Balkan War: the Serbian campaign of aggression and genocide. As the Cambridge historian Brendan Simms notes in this volume, "whatever opportunistic acts of Croat aggression may have taken place subsequently, the root cause of the war lies in a psychologically and logistically well prepared program of Serbian aggression." And perhaps no one has put the issue better than Patrick Moore of the Open Media Research Institute: "It is true, as in any war, that no one side consisted entirely of angels. But what made Serbian atrocities different from those committed by others was that they represented not an incidental development in the conflict, but a deliberate instrument of policy. The rapes, expulsions, burnings lootings, and massacres were a conscious and calculated means of setting up a Greater Serbia."[30]

Significantly, the Nuremberg tribunal differentiated between war crimes, of which all sides were guilty, and genocide, for which German defendants alone stood trial. We feel that it is important to examine critically an important assumption Western intellectuals make about the war in Bosnia, namely, that all sides are equally guilty for atrocities, war crimes, and genocide. All sides may have committed atrocities and war crimes, but all sides have not committed genocide. Our examination lays bare conventional wisdoms about "who has done what to whom" and offers evidence that challenges these conventional wisdoms. We feel this is important, since we are dealing with one of the most heinous of crimes—genocide. The facts of the case so clearly define the aggressor in this situation that some readers might be led to believe we are overtly partisan. This is not true, since, in addition to specifying the nature and causes of Serbian aggression, we acknowledge the existence of inter-ethnic conflicts between other parties in the region, particularly those between Croats and Muslims in 1993. It is certainly clear that Tudjman's actions on the eve of the Yugoslav break-up were perceived as provocations by many Croatian Serbs. Yet at the same time, such provocations were magnified and intensified by Belgrade and Pale propagandists who played on the fears of the Serbian minority and led them to take positions against the Croats that were not in keeping with the relatively peaceful state of Serbo-Croat relations in the post-World War II era. Serbian intellectuals could not really have believed that Tudjman was the reincarnation of Ante Pavelić and his Croatian Democratic Union (HDZ) a resurrection of the dreaded Ustashe. Nonetheless, as Philip J. Cohen, Brad K. Blitz, and Daniele Conversi point out in their articles for the volume, this was a central line of the propaganda created by Serbian intellectuals and promulgated in the Balkans and in the West and, in many cases, actually believed by many well-meaning Western observers, some who should have known better and all of whom should know about the dangers—both moral and logical—of the doctrine of collective guilt.

Unlike many Western intellectuals we do not consciously engage in moral equivocation or relativism in our assessment of responsibility for genocide or some of the most egregious war crimes committed on the European continent since World War II. It is one thing that the new Croatian government made Serbs aware of their minority status and displaced many of them from positions of government authority given to them during the Yugoslav period. It is quite another thing to agree that such actions warranted full military mobilization as a response or to agree with the dangerous principle of collective guilt as a pretext for mobilizing against a population. It is also quite another thing to agree that the appropriate response to symbolic political infelicities in Croatia was to unleash a military juggernaut against a civilian population, as the Serbs did in Slovenia, Croatia, and then Bosnia. When Western intellectuals find themselves aping the justifications and legitimations of the architects of Greater Serbia, when they find themselves nodding their heads in agreement with indicted war criminals who appear on *Sixty Minutes* or in interviews in the *New York Times Magazine,* then, we argue, we have reached a new stage in the moral de-evolution of the Western intellectual. Equivocation and relativism may have their place when the actions of each party can be equated, but in this case they cannot.

Yet what concerns us is the ease with which many Western intellectual observers of the events of the last four years engaged in equivocation and relativism in their judgments of the parties involved in the conflicts in the former Yugoslavia. This kind of equivocation is not new. Brendan Simms and Daniele Conversi, in their contributions to this volume, note that British government officials had previously equated victims with perpe-trators in the Balkans. History does not repeat itself, but it rhymes, as Mark Twain is reputed to have said. Conversi notes, without falling into the trap of historical determinism, that there is a long history of British Serbophilism that has had a direct impact not only on the conduct of the war, but in the toleration of war crimes and genocide in the region.

Such equivocation and relativism, we feel, obfuscate and obscure the realities of genocide, mass rape, and other atrocities and are, in our opinion, a central reason for the failure of Western intellectuals and political officials to respond adequately to these realities. Our own effort to respond responsibly is, therefore, grounded in a rather strident critique of our colleagues who have failed to do so and of those who see in every Serb action an equally bad and vile Croat or Muslim action.

As an important aside, we note that our treatment of genocide in Bosnia sidesteps intellectual arguments found in the literature as to whether a quantitative threshold has been reached to count as genocide in Bosnia; whether the UN definition of genocide is adequate; whether it is permissible to make any comparisons and contrasts between the Holo-caust and genocide, and so on (to repeat: our reply is that these events are not comparable to the Holocaust *per se,* but to the Holocaust as an instance of genocide). Following Emile Durkheim, our more sociological approach notes that respected fact-gathering organizations have deter-mined that genocide has occurred in Bosnia. In other words, even if the

UN definition is flawed, or some intellectuals are not satisfied that real genocide is occurring in Bosnia, or that others feel that "all sides" have committed genocide, or even if some believe that victims of genocide are simply getting what they deserve for past injustices, the fact remains: from the perspective of the social construction of reality, a respectable finding of genocide in Bosnia has been made and is largely ignored by Western intellectuals, politicians, and the public in general. And this fact calls into question the credibility of the United Nations, promotes cynicism among the general population in Western democracies, and hampers the development of the rule of law. The issue of the Western slide from the principles established at Nuremberg is described and analyzed in detail by James J. Sadkovich in his contribution to this volume.

The information media has noted and digested the findings above on several occasions. Regarding the practice of ethnic cleansing, the editors of the *New York Times* concluded that "the overwhelming responsibility for this practice lies with the Serbs."[31] The editors of the *Wall Street Journal* noted that "Serb forces were singled out in a UN report as the worst human rights violators in the Bosnian war."[32] And later, the same editors concluded that "UN investigators blame Serbs for the worst atrocities, from the creation of Nazi-like detention camps to forced deportations and systematic rape of Muslims."[33] Respected institutions such as the International Court of Justice in the Hague demanded in April 1993 that Serbia and Montenegro take preventative measures to prevent *genocide* from occurring in Bosnia. On February 13, 1995, the newly established International War Crimes Tribunal in the Hague charged a Serb with genocide and crimes against humanity. In April 1995 this same tribunal indicted the Serb leaders Radovan Karadžić and Ratko Mladić as war criminals who orchestrated genocide, but the United Nations continued to negotiate with them as peacemakers.[34] Commenting on many of these findings, Roger Cohen writes in the *New York Times* that "the overwhelming majority of crimes were committed by Serbs in an orchestrated campaign to eliminate Muslims from Serb-held territory."[35] Despite all these findings, as of this writing, the weapons embargo is still in place against Belgrade's primary victim, Bosnia-Herzegovina, the sanctions against Belgrade are openly violated, the United Nations in Bosnia and Croatia is accused of widespread corruption, and Belgrade-sponsored genocidal aggression continued unabated even as "peace talks" took place.[36]

Nevertheless, All Sides Are Deemed Equally Guilty

In the present context, knowledge abounds, but so, too, do rationalizations for nonintervention in Balkan affairs. Such rationalizations are scripted by political elites, circulated and reproduced by the mass media and by intellectuals, and consumed by the mass public, which is more or less trusting of expert systems of knowledge production and willing to abide by experts' judgments about domestic and international affairs. In sociological terms, such rationalizations can be seen as "frames" or "typifications" that guide the concrete policies of Western elites and mass publics.[37] In this case, such rationalizations, rather than fostering coherent policies, actually serve to mitigate against the formation of a coherent Western policy in the Balkans. The central rationalization in the West appears to be this: "We, as civilized Westerners, cannot do anything to stop the Balkan tribalists from slaughtering each other." The evolution of the main rationalization for non-intervention from "we did not know" to "we cannot do anything to stop them" represents an important transition in the mode of Western response to genocide and atrocities in modern Europe.

Thus, alongside the clear findings that Serbian leaders are responsible for genocide in Bosnia, we find the following examples of frames of reference that blame all sides equally: Margaret D. Tutwiler, former Department of State spokeswoman, pronounced that "No party is blameless for the current situation";[38] the European mediator Lord Carrington declared with regard to a broken cease-fire that "Muslim Slav fighters were at least as responsible as the Serbs and Croats for violations."[39] When the Serbs increased their shelling of Sarajevo in 1995, UN spokesperson Alexander Ivanko declared, "We're saying both sides were equally to blame for this fighting."[40] More recently, during the Serbian siege of the UN safe areas Srebrenica and Žepa—a time when the sheer horror of what was going on should have served as a clarion call for moral action by the West—we saw no reduction in the intensity of the equivocation and relativism in some of the leading organs of Western public opinion.[41]

Many Western intellectuals have either remained silent on the current genocide in Europe or, where they have become involved, have engaged in reproduction of some of the obfuscations, falsehoods, and other conventional wisdoms that circulate on the global information highway. However, we hasten to add that there are Western intellectuals and leaders of many political persuasions who have not hesitated to condemn Belgrade-sponsored aggression and who have called for a decisive, moral response to the genocide in Bosnia, including but not limited to Anthony Lewis, Jean Baudrillard, William Safire, Georgie Anne Geyer, David Rieff, William F. Buckley, Andrea Dworkin, Henry Siegman, Susan Sontag, Albert Wohlstetter, Catharine MacKinnon, Pope John Paul II, Elie Wiesel, George Will, Senator Robert Dole, and Zbigniew Brzezinski.[42] In her contribution to this volume, activist Sheri Fink offers an overview of anti-genocide campus grassroots activism in the United States and demonstrates convincingly that such activism exists and has had some positive effects.

Nevertheless, there are many different intellectual responses to the conflict and these responses are somewhat guided by the philosophical assumptions that underlie various Western intellectual positions. For instance, postmodern Western intellectuals who are guided by a spirit of ambivalence might find it difficult to act because to act would involve "choosing sides" and the relativism of postmodernism makes such choices difficult. Even some intellectuals who are committed to the modern project of Enlightenment (which some postmodernists challenge) have difficulty "choosing sides" in the conflict, since each side is viewed as "nationalistic" and therefore hostile to one of the central ideas of modernism, what we call "civilized federalism." On this view, scholars who take a stand against genocide, which in this case means taking a stand against the Serbian orchestrators of genocide, are often seen as deviant partisans or labeled "unbalanced" or "one-sided."

Indeed, it is also worth exploring the negative judgments of the phenomenon of nationalism among Western intellectuals: it is almost always seen as a negative force and as an antipode to Western civility. For example, the last U.S. Ambassador to Yugoslavia, Warren Zimmermann, writes that "Nationalism is by nature uncivil, antidemocratic and separatist because it empowers one ethnic group over all others."[43] Following David Riesman, our reply is that it depends on which nationalism and particular context is under discussion. As the great Czech statesman and sociologist Thomas Masaryk argued, nationalism can be a very constructive force, and there are many instances in which it serves as a firm basis for identity.[44] Liah Greenfeld, in a speech given to various national and international policy makers and reprinted in this volume, makes a distinction between civic nationalism and ethnic nationalism and points out the dangers of authoritarianism inherent in the latter. In a context in which nationalism is ritually and crudely blasted and vilified by Western intellectuals, Greenfeld reminds us, echoing Durkheim, that nationalism can, in fact, be an important basis of a civil or civic culture and, as such, can serve as an important basis for identity. While it is important to understand distinctions between the various types and degrees of ethnic nationalisms in the former Yugoslavia (and thus avoid what we have been critical of here, namely, the dangers of relativism in seeing all nationalisms as leading to the same consequence in the former Yugoslavia), it is also important to think about the ways ethnic nationalism can be made more democratic than it has often been so far in various postcommunist societies.

Proponents of neo-isolationism hold that "all sides in the former Yugoslavia have committed atrocities," so the West would be foolish to try to step in—the latter seldom differentiate war crimes from genocide, nor do they specify variations in the degree of guilt for war crimes. Western diplomats continued to negotiate with suspected war criminals (Slobodan Milošević) as well as indicted Serbian war criminals (Radovan Karadžić and Ratko Mladić) even as the United Nations threatened to put them on trial and even as strong evidence emerged that shows that Serbia continued to arm and supply Bosnian Serbs despite specific UN resolutions that prohibited such collaboration and even though Belgrade has emphatically declared that it did not:[45] "Even as the West courts Serbia's President in hopes of bringing peace to Bosnia . . . his military is secretly assisting the Bosnian Serbs."[46] Many journalists and editors, guided by a sense of realpolitik that seems strangely out of place in the world of journalism, nevertheless continue to argue that it is not in Western interests to intervene and that there is nothing else the West can do but let combatants fight it out or make an unjust peace to stop further killing. This view was promulgated forcefully by former secretary of state Lawrence Eagleburger: "Until the Bosnians, Croats and Serbs decide to stop killing each other, there is nothing the outside world can do about it."[47]

This, of course, neglects the central question of who started the killing, but this is rather normal in much discourse about the Balkans. Most policy makers are against lifting the weapons embargo that would enable victims to defend themselves, again, along the lines of the rationalization discussed above: all sides are potentially bad, so an increase in weapons would "escalate the violence." If Western weapons and troops are to be sent to Bosnia, it should be to protect the UN peacekeepers there, not the civilians. Indeed, in this volume, Michael N. Barnett has offered a theoretically and autobiographically informed discussion of the politics of indifference at the United Nations. He comes to the chilling conclusion that in Rwanda and Bosnia "the bureaucratization of peacekeeping contributed to [an] indifference to the suffering of the very people it is mandated to assist." As Barnett points out, the commitments of many UN personnel were primarily to the norms and goals of the organization, not the people that the organization had pledged to help. Such indifference is widespread, and in some cases it is actually proudly declared, as for instance by journalist Thomas L. Friedman, who notes, "I don't give two cents about Bosnia. Not two cents. The people there have brought on their own troubles. But I do feel loyalty to the Allies."[48] Such utterances are precisely what we find so problematic, not only because they are wrong (the Bosnian people did not bring their own troubles on themselves, but were brutally attacked by Serbs under the direction of Belgrade), but because they are so patently immoral. Can one imagine the outcry if one were to say that European Jews in Germany had brought on their own troubles?

But these and similar rationalizations really call into question how previous opinion makers and intellectuals rationalized World War II. During that war American, British, and Canadian servicemen all committed atrocities.[49] However, the understanding up to now has been that, unlike the Nazis, it was not Western government policy to do so in order to eliminate any ethnic or religious group. Moreover, despite the excesses of the Allies at Dresden, Hiroshima, and elsewhere, most intellectuals today are not prepared to say that Nazi Germany and the Allies were morally equivalent (that is, all equally guilty). But this argument is regularly made regarding Bosnia in the 1990s. They are also not prepared to say that it really does not matter who won the war. Yet these arguments are reversed with regard to genocide in Bosnia: all sides are treated as morally equivalent despite what the facts say, and the West behaves as if it does not matter who wins, so long as "peace" is achieved even at the cost of ethnic partition, which is the central outcome of the peace plan agreed on in Dayton in November 1995.

It seems unthinkable to most intellectuals today that Adolf Hitler might have been interviewed on television and allowed to defend his racist positions and heinous acts, yet Serb leaders and spokesmen get all the play they want on CNN and have been interviewed frequently by major media. Jimmy Carter is sometimes interviewed alongside them (and, in one instance, brought flowers to indicted war criminal Radovan Karadžić) and basically supports the rationalization that all sides are equally guilty and a "negotiated settlement" is the only option open to the West.[50] As Brad K. Blitz notes in this volume, Serbia's government agencies routinely disseminate propaganda advertisements as well as statements in the Western press—usually equating the Jews and Serbs as historical victims of Croats and Muslims, blaming all Muslims for their defeat at Kosovo in 1389, and insinuating that all contemporary Croats are Nazis.[51] Such propaganda, as Daniel Kofman points out in his criticism of Israeli-Serbian relations in this volume, seem to be accepted by many leading Israeli intellectuals, media figures, and politicians. In his essay, Kofman notes that while diaspora Jews have responded outstandingly to the crisis in Bosnia, many Israeli elites, including intellectuals, have been indulgent of Serbia.

But throughout the West, what is surprising is the number of intellectuals and scholars at conferences who mouth these clearly noncredible (and incredible) slogans. At the 1994 meetings of the American Association for the Advancement of Slavic Studies in Philadelphia, for instance, a panel on media coverage of the Balkan War included a presentation in which the presenter, a Serb, chastised the *New York Times* for its anti-Serb views, that is, for failing to point out that the Bosnian Serbs are allegedly victims of Croat-Muslim aggression. These very same views can also be found on elaborate home page displays on the internet's World Wide Web. If, in fact, the *New York Times* did take an unequivocal position against the Serbs and their genocidal practices, we would be heartened, since it would prove our arguments about the lack of intellectual response to be either exaggerated or just plain wrong. Yet many key elements of Serbian propaganda have been adopted to a large extent by intellectuals, diplomats, and journalists, and these serve as further rationalizations that mitigate the responsibility of intellectuals. For instance, an editorial in the *New York Times* notes that "Croatia's 20th century record of aggression and ethnic cleansing is every bit as bad as Serbia's. Memories of the atrocities committed by Croatia's fascist Ustashe regime against Serbs, Muslims, and Jews during World War II helped fuel the Serbian revolt in Krajina four years ago."[52] What is most striking about this statement is not only that it equates Croatian actions with those of the past, but that it so clearly resonates with the central themes of Serbian propaganda, which rely on the principle of intergenerational collective guilt as a legitimation for aggression.

Many other frames exist in the perceptions of this war; in our opinion, these frames have had a great deal to do with the inability of Western intellectuals to mount an effective response to genocide. A more detailed sociological study of these frames is needed, but we present here some of the central ones that are relevant to understanding the obfuscation of genocide in Bosnia in the West:

1. The fighting in Bosnia-Herzegovina is supposed to be a civil war.[53] Very often, the label "civil war" is applied without definition (there are many examples of this in scholarly literature on the conflict). All sides are viewed as warring parties who are equally responsible for the conflict. Consider, as a particularly drastic example, the following excerpt from an editorial by William Finnegan: "Basic values such as the rule of law, the inviolability of borders, and the safety of innocent civilians have been trashed beyond recognition by the war parties." This view and others like it ignore the history of Serbian expansion and aggression in the last two centuries, as well as the history of Serbian hegemony in the Yugoslav federation.[54] More important, it confuses victims with aggressors by presuming that all warring parties have committed the stated sins in equal measure.

2. Islamic fundamentalism is a threat to the West; Europe should not allow an Islamic nation (Bosnia) in Europe, since to do so provides a foothold for other, more aggressive fundamentalist regimes.[55] This rationalization presumes that there is little variation among Muslims in terms of degree of fundamentalism. It appears to be related to other Western "orientalist" assumptions of the kind that Edward Said has noted in his work on Western anti-Islamic prejudices.[56]

3. In World War II, all Serbs were on the Allied side—no Serbs collaborated with the Nazis. This is, in fact, not the case: the Serbian General Milan Nedić was a Nazi puppet ruler who collaborated with Nazi officials.[57] In the early days of Serbian aggression against Bosnia-Herzegovina, this frame served to legitimize Western Allied support for Serbs in spite of the fact that knowledge of what the latter were doing in Bosnia was abundant.

4. All Croats were Nazi collaborators in a homegrown Ustashe movement that was supposed to have been widely popular, and whose legacy still persists in Croatia.[58] This ignores overwhelming evidence that the Ustashe were not widely popular and that there was a strong resistance movement among Croats. As noted above, this frame is often invoked when authors try to rationalize and explain Serbian genocide, as if what a

small minority of Croatian thugs did in World War II is the root cause of Serbian-perpetrated genocide in the present.

5. Bosnia-Herzegovina is not a nation-state; it could never really exist as a nation-state because it never had been one.[59] Bosnia-Herzegovina, however, was a highly autonomous and defined area within the Ottoman Empire and was a republic within Tito's Yugoslavia, as were Slovenia and Croatia. The point has been rather glaringly made by historians of Bosnia, but generally ignored.[60]

6. The wars in Croatia and Bosnia-Herzegovina started because of premature Western recognition.[61] From the perspective of this frame, Western nations—in particular Germany—rather than the actual perpetrators of genocide are, at base, responsible for acts of aggression and genocide committed by Serbs in Bosnia.

7. Bosnian and Croatian Serbs commit atrocities out of generalized fear of Croats and Muslims.[62] While this may be true in the sociological sense that people act on their deeply held beliefs, the idea that contemporary Croats and Muslims are somehow genocidal by nature smacks of racism and essentialism. This view often relies on the doctrine of collective guilt, which holds that a whole group is guilty for the crimes of some of its members. On this logic, German reunification could have been used as a pretext for the invasion of Germany by former Nazi victims, an idea that is preposterous when thought of in the context of Western Europe, but that is invoked relatively unproblematically in explanations (and in some ways, justifications) of Serbian aggression in the Balkans. It is worth pointing out that Karadžić appeared on the CBS television newsmagazine *Sixty Minutes* in September 1995 and declared that Bosnian Serb aggression against the Croats was necessary to prevent the latter from doing to Serbs what they had done in World War II. He also noted that Europe would thank him and the Bosnian Serbs for protecting Europe from the threat of Islamic fundamentalism, presumably by killing Bosnian Muslims. As we have noted above, we find that these views resonate in the discourse of many Western intellectuals, and we are deeply troubled by this fact.

8. Bosnian Muslims often shoot themselves to gain sympathy. Very often, overt acts of aggression (shelling of Sarajevo marketplaces, bombing of schools) by one side are seen as potentially self-inflicted provocations by desperate victims (in this case the Bosnian Muslims). This type of equivocation recasts victims as villains. For example, Serbs massacred dozens of civilians in a Sarajevo marketplace in August 1995, and the

media dutifully reported the Serb claim that the Bosnian Muslims "had attacked their own civilian population today to arouse international sympathy and drag NATO into the war. 'This is a classic act of Islamic terrorism,' said Miroslav Toholj, a Bosnian Serb official."[63]

9. The leader of the Bosnians, Alija Izetbegović, is an Islamic fundamentalist. This is a variant of the more general orientalist theme rather than a comment on Izetbegović's own book, *Islam between East and West,* in which Izetbegović's admiration for the West is so great as to be pathetic, given how the West has rejected him.[64] In fact, Izetbegović takes great pains to show the distinctive identities of Bosnian Muslims as being "between East and West." Anyone even faintly familiar with the history of Bosnia would find the assertion that Bosnians are Islamic fundamentalists preposterous, given Bosnia's history of religious tolerance, pluralism, and cosmopolitanism. This frame is taken directly from Serbian propaganda, which uses a youthful work by Izetbegović, his so-called Islamic Declaration, in which he called for a "united Islamic community from Morocco to Indonesia," as the basis for present policy toward Bosnia.[65] The construction of Izetbegović as an Islamic fundamentalist has important ramifications for Western policy, given the historical relationship between Islam and the West.

10. If genocide is occurring in Bosnia, it is genocide with a small g— no big deal, and certainly not tantamount to that perpetrated against Jews (a point argued recently by former State Department official George Kenney in the *New York Times Magazine*).[66]

11. "Those people [in the Balkans] have been fighting each other for hundreds, if not thousands of years and conflicts are basically a result of age-old, tribal hatreds."[67] This rationalization might be said to be a "master frame" that circulates in intellectual and political circles and in the Western public sphere more generally.[68]

The Importance of Frames of Reference

These and other common rationalizations constitute "frames of reference" that condition thinking about events. Ongoing events are made to "fit" preexisting frames; this process ensures that conventional wisdoms and misperceptions are reproduced over time. Thus, if the Croats are defined as Nazis they cannot be victims of Serbs, since it is impossible for Nazis to be victims. If Serbs were Allies in World War II they cannot be enemies of the West at present, since the structure of Western alliances supersedes any other considerations, especially moral ones. If Bosnian Muslims are fundamentalists, this places them outside Enlightenment rationality and, as such, they either cannot be expected to act in a civilized manner or are an actual threat to Western civility. Serbian "ethnic cleansing" is thus conceptualized as a service to Europe since it guards against the persistent Islamic fundamentalist threat to modernity that began in Iran. And so on. Jean Baudrillard, in particular, poignantly exposes the direction of these and related frames of reference in his essays in this volume.

Genocide is a particularly sensitive issue that has been obfuscated in writings concerning the current Balkan War. To repeat: fact-finding organizations have definitely found that genocide has occurred and have laid all the blame for it on the Serbs (as explained above). But interestingly, the Belgrade regime has (1) claimed that its Serbian minorities in Croatia and Bosnia are and have been victims of genocide;[69] (2) made allusions to a Serbian Holocaust;[70] and (3) recast its genocide in Bosnia as a civil war in which Serbs are victims.[71] That these arguments have had their intended effect, including gaining widespread sympathy in Israel for the Belgrade cause even to the extent that some Israelis have offered military support for Serbia, is documented by Daniel Kofman in his essay in this volume.

Several issues ought to be examined in this regard. First, many Jews have rightly complained that efforts to compare the Holocaust with, say, the slavery of African Americans, the extermination of the Native Americans, and other sites of genocide are misguided because they cheapen the Holocaust. Serbian comparisons of their own plight with that of the Jews, in this sense, also debases the memory of the Holocaust. Second, what prevented Hitler from establishing his new order on the East European plains, including expelling the local population and replacing them with Germans, was the strong and effective resistance movements in these areas. Such resistance was and is championed by Western scholars and politicians and is regularly commemorated in celebrations of Allied victories in World War II. In the present context, the Bosnians, against all odds, without adequate weapons, and isolated by the West, have similarly fought back and resisted Serbian aggression and genocide. Yet this resistance goes unrecognized, except by a few prominent Western intellectuals who travel to Sarajevo to express solidarity with the Bosnians (but who, of course, are guaranteed exit from sniper fire, cluster bombing, and other acts of terror should the going get rough). And in late 1995, even as Bosnian forces recaptured territory and protected their people from further genocide, such acts were regularly seen as "opportunism" rather than as just reclamation of territory that was brutally seized and ethnically cleansed. As Jean Baudrillard notes in his contributions to this volume, the Western intellectual response is characterized by "harmless and powerless intellectuals exchanging their misery with those who are miserable, each sustaining the other through a sort of perverse contract." Did the Bosnian Muslims have to comply and avoid any resistance as they were being "cleansed" in order to conform to our notion of genocide victims? There was considerable criticism of the Jews after World War II that they were too passive and did not do enough to defend themselves. Third, one ought not to adopt a "bookkeeping" mentality on genocide. What is the numerical threshold of victims before genocide is reached? Is there one? Not according to the UN Charter, which focuses on the qualitative measure of efforts to destroy a group *in part or in whole*. Bosnia counts as an instance of genocide, not only because it has been determined by respected organizations to be genocide, but because by any scholarly or moral standard, the Bosnians have been isolated, dehumanized, and made fair game for elimination by government policy simply because individuals belong to a certain group and stand in the way of concrete policy goals, the main one being the establishment of a Greater Serbia.

One could argue also that people's willingness to respond to genocide is based on self-interest. That is why the international response to Bosnia has been weak. The world most likely would not have done much more in the case of the Holocaust at the time even if there was more information (the "we did not know" argument is useful ex post facto but probably irrelevant). One needs to recall that the Allies imposed a weapons embargo on the newly emergent state of Israel, right after the Holocaust, precisely because Israel's existence was perceived as a threat to British and French national interests in the Middle East. To a great extent, governments seek to rationalize situations by creating a model or image of the situation that is consonant with their policy interests when they do not want to intervene militarily, or for other reasons (cost, casualties, etc.). Hence the rationalizations listed above: civil war, eons of ethnic strife in the former Yugoslavia, no solution, Balkan quagmire, all equally guilty. This is self-evident. Much more problematic is the fact that many intellectuals and journalists follow in the wake of these rationalizations put forth by governments, and for the most part do not challenge them. Had these rationalizations been challenged effectively by intellectuals (as in the case of, say, the Vietnam War), governments would have had to respond in order to maintain proper public relations with their constituents. Indeed, it is interesting to note that during the Vietnam era, journalists were very adversarial to government's interventionist policy in Vietnam because they felt it was wrong, whereas in the present, they mostly appear supportive of the government policy of nonintervention in the Balkans to stop a situation that is wrong. Such a shift is definitely worthy of further study.

This book intends to do what intellectuals have been trained for—criticize, analyze, deconstruct—and our aim is to specify what should have been done on a large scale in relation to these rationalizations, which are clearly at odds with the findings of the world's most respected fact-gathering organizations. Specifically, the international community should have acted according to the rule of law championed by Senator Daniel Patrick Moynihan[72] and other political idealists to preserve the national sovereignties of Bosnia-Herzegovina and Croatia after these nations were recognized internationally; in accordance with Article 51 of the UN Charter, lift the illegal and immoral weapons embargo imposed on these nation-states at Belgrade's request;[73] and once a finding of genocide was established, take actions to prevent it, as specified in the UN Charter. This is the fulcrum of the volume: the critical examination of the tolerated discrepancy between the rationalizations and facts put forth by Western governments and organizations and the passive acquiescence of the West's intellectuals and policy makers, who, ideally, ought to be more willing to puncture such rationalizations. The various contributors to this volume not only puncture the rationalizations, but theorize on the reasons these rationalizations have persisted for so long.

Finally, we note that we are pleased to offer in this volume some commentary by David Riesman, one of the most eminent twentieth century American sociologists. Riesman has taken an active interest in the situation in the Balkans and has read the papers assembled here. We offer his observations and thoughts as an epilogue to this volume.

NOTES

1. We were reminded of this obvious fact by Slaven Letica during his presentation at a roundtable discussion chaired by Thomas Cushman, "Postcommunist Transformations," at the annual meetings of the American Sociological Association, Washington, DC, August 21, 1995.

2. *New York Times,* July 18, 1992, A1.

3. For instance, in September 1995, indicted war criminal Radovan Karadžić appeared on *Sixty Minutes.* An op-ed piece ostensibly written by him appeared in the *Houston Chronicle* the summer before that. During the Serbian conquest of safe areas in Bosnia in late summer 1995, Danielle Sremac, director of the Serbian American Affairs Office and the official Bosnian Serb representative in the United States, appeared often on Christian Science Monitor Radio to explicate the Bosnian Serbs' positions.

4. Lucy Dawidowicz, *The War against the Jews, 1933–1945* (New York: Holt, Rinehart, and Winston, 1975).

5. Mark Poster, *The Second Media Age* (Cambridge, Mass.: Polity Press, 1995).

6. *New York Times,* January 14, 1994, A16.

7. *New York Times,* April 7, 1994, B1.

8. *New York Times,* April 3, 1995, A11.

9. *New York Times,* April 22, 1993, A1.

10. Stjepan G. Meštrović, "Postemotional Politics in the Balkans," *Society* 32, no. 2 (1995): 69–77.

11. Daniel Kofman, letter, *Society* 32, no. 5 (1995): 7–9.

12. *Wall Street Journal,* May 28, 1992, A10.

13. Roger Cohen, *New York Times,* September 15, 1992, A3.

14. Carla Anne Robbins, "America's Inaction on Bosnia Stirs Critics to Debate and Despair: What Will Our Children Say?" *Wall Street Journal,* March 18, 1994, A1.

15. Zlatko Dizdarević, "What Kind of Peace Is This?" *New York Times Magazine,* April 10, 1994, 21.

16. Roger Cohen, "A Balkan Gyre of War, Spinning onto Film," *New York Times,* March 12, 1995, E1. Cohen adds, "No violence, real or fictional, is taken seriously any longer."

17. Roger Cohen, "A UN Peacekeeper Dies; Bosnia's Pain Does Not," *New York Times,* April 17, 1995, A3.

18. See Noam Chomsky, *East Timor and the Western Democracies* (Nottingham, England: Bertrand Russell Peace Foundation, 1979); and Edward S. Herman and Noam Chomsky, *Manufacturing Consent: The Political Economy of Mass Media* (New York: Pantheon, 1988), 284–85, 302.

19. For a discussion of Richard Rorty's views on "postmodern irony," the stance that a thinker "does not think that her vocabulary is closer to reality than others," see *Irony, Contingency, and Solidarity* (Cambridge: Cambridge University Press, 1989), esp. 73–74.

20. Cohen describes Mladić as "[a]stute, alternately ribald and boomingly defiant, this stocky general with bright blue eyes and a popular touch has been particularly effective in getting these messages across because he appears to

Serbs as a soldier's soldier, ready to take personal risks and repeating that his life is worth no more than that of any private in the trenches." In the next line, Cohen reports a UN figure who declares that Mladić "has charm . . . it's a little bestial, but it's there." *New York Times,* April 17, 1994, 12. One is reminded of journalists' laudatory discussions of the crazed killer in the Oliver Stone film *Natural Born Killers.*

21. David Binder, letter, *New York Review of Books,* December 21, 1995, 85.

22. This is something that the great progenitor of the idea of *verstehen,* Max Weber, managed not to do: for Weber, one could understand the world as it was perceived by the other, but not move from a position of understanding to empathy. One must imagine Weber as someone who could understand that subjective feelings led to the objective practice of genocide, but one can also imagine Weber having the ability, unlike many modern analysts of the war in the Balkans, to see the difference between symbolic perception and objective aggression.

23. Roger Cohen, "CIA Report Finds Serbs Guilty in Majority of Bosnia War Crimes," *New York Times,* March 9, 1995, A1:

> The report makes nonsense of the view—now consistently put forward by Western European governments and intermittently by the Clinton Administration—that the Bosnian conflict is a civil war for which guilt should be divided between Serbs, Croats and Muslims rather than a case of Serbian aggression.. . . . "To those who think the parties are equally guilty, this report is pretty devastating," one official said. "The scale of what the Serbs did is of a different order. But more than that, it makes clear, with concrete evidence, that there was a conscious, coherent, and systematic Serbian policy to get rid of Muslims through murders, torture and imprisonment."

24. United States Congress Commission on Security and Cooperation in Europe, *War Crimes and the Humanitarian Crisis in the Former Yugoslavia: Hearings before the CSCE in Europe,* 103d Cong., 1st sess., January 25, 1993 (Washington, D.C.: Government Printing Office, 1993).

25. The conference of the Commission on Security and Cooperation in Europe issued a statement on April 4, 1995, that quotes chairman Chris Smith, Republican Congressman from New Jersey, as noting that "the State Department human rights report refers to genocide in Bosnia." See also "Ethnic Cleansing—And a Cry for Help from Bosnia," *Newsweek,* August 17, 1992, 16–27; Tom Post, "A Pattern of Rape," *Newsweek,* January 11, 1993, 32–36; John F. Burns, "Bosnian Survivors Tell of Mass Ethnic Killings: Comparisons with Nazis Are Drawn as Attacks Rage in the Republic," *New York Times,* May 21, 1992, A28; Laura Silber, "The Street Was a River of Blood," *Washington Post,* May 28, 1992, A1; Roy Gutman, "Ethnic Cleansing: Yugoslavs Try to Deport 1,800 Muslims to Hungary," *Newsday,* July 3, 1992, 5; idem, *A Witness to Genocide* (New York: Macmillan, 1993).

26. "Serbs Implementing Policy of Rape, Says UN Study," *Dallas Morning News,* March 22, 1995, A12.

27. Roger Thurow, "Parliamentary Elections Dividing Serbs: Nasty Campaigns Reveal True Aims, Methods of War," *Wall Street Journal,* December 16, 1993, A5.

28. See also Norman Cigar, *Genocide in Bosnia* (College Station: Texas A& M University Press, 1995); Gutman, *Witness to Genocide*; "Serbian Genocide at Omarska," *New York Times,* February 15, 1995, A20; Roger Cohen, "Tribunal Charges Genocide by Serb," *New York Times,* February 14, 1995, A1; Catharine MacKinnon, "Turning Rape into Pornography: Postmodern Genocide," *Ms.* 4 (July-August 1993), 24–30; Jim Dyer, "Genocide in Europe, Again," *Lancet,* October 17, 1992, 965.

29. See, for example, Charles Krauthammer, "When Serbs Are Cleansed, Moralists Stay Silent," *International Herald Tribune,* August 12–13, 1995, 6.

30. Patrick Moore, "Milošević's War: The Tide Turns," *Transition: Events and Issues in the Former Soviet Union and East Central and Southeastern Europe,* 1, no. 20 (November 3, 1995): 5.

31. September 4, 1992, A16.

32. September 1, 1992, A1.

33. February 23, 1993, A1.

34. Roger Cohen, "Bosnia Plight for UN," *New York Times,* April 25, 1994, A1.

35. April 24, 1994, A1.

36. Christopher Wren, "UN Votes to Keep Its Troops in Balkans for Eight More Months," *New York Times,* April 1, 1995, A2; idem, "UN Ousts Russian from Croatia Post," *New York Times,* April 12, 1995, A8; Roger Cohen, "UN and Bosnia: Why Do the Peacekeepers Stay?" *New York Times,* April 20, 1995, A3; Anthony Lewis, "Nothing but Shame," *New York Times,* June 16, 1995, A13; William Safire, "Break the Siege," *New York Times,* June 1, 1995, A17.

37. Frame analysis in sociology focuses on the central ideas that are created by journalists, ways of seeing, and so forth. These frames then become rootless, circulating modes of perception. For an example of how frame analysis has been used in social analysis, see William A. Gamson, *Talking Politics* (Cambridge: Cambridge University Press, 1992). Also relevant to this discussion is William A. Gamson's presidential address to the American Sociological Association, "Hiroshima, the Holocaust, and the Politics of Exclusion: 1994 Presidential Address," *American Sociological Review* 60 (1994): 1–20. Gamson notes specifically the rationalization that "all sides are equally guilty" in the coverage of genocide in Bosnia.

38. *New York Times,* April 23, 1992, A4.

39. *New York Times,* July 23, 1992, A4.

40. *New York Times,* May 17, 1995, A4.

41. Again, see Krauthammer, op. cit., 21. Amazingly, Krauthammer does not mention the fact that the Croatian recapturing of the Krajina region was motivated by (1) the inability of Croats to make any progress after negotiating for three years for the return of their sovereign territory; (2) the Croatian efforts to guarantee Serbian autonomy in a Croatian state; and (3) the desire to stop further killing of Muslims and Croats in UN declared safe areas. Nor is mention made of the fact that while the West stood by, the Croat assistance of the Bosnians saved lives. Such historical context is rarely provided in such articles and, in this case, the standard line of "the Serbs were justified in invading and ethnically cleansing Croatia because of the Sahovnica and the kuna" takes precedence. Krauthammer is apparently unaware that his logic is exactly the same as that of indicted war criminals Radovan Karadžić and Ratko Mladić. A more in-depth study of this kind of relativism in major media is called for.

42. Many groups have also taken a moral stand on the slaughter in Bosnia, including the American Committee to Save Bosnia. Consider also advertisements such as the following: "In Memoriam: Our Commitments, Principles, and Moral Values. Died: Bosnia 1994. On the occasion of the 1000th day of the siege of Sarajevo." It was published in the *New York Times,* December 29, 1994, A6, and signed by Daniel Bell, Zbigniew Brzezinski, Hodding Carter, Leslie Gelb, Valéry Giscard d'Estaing, Bianca Jagger, Carl Sagan, Susan Sontag, and Simon Wiesenthal.

43. Warren Zimmermann, "The Last Ambassador: A Memoir of the Collapse of Yugoslavia," *Foreign Affairs,* March-April, 1995, 3–20. Zimmermann adds that "The Slovenes bear considerable responsibility for the bloodbath that followed their secession.... Tudjman [is] an implacable nationalist.... Unlike Milošević, who is driven by power, Tudjman is obsessed by nationalism.... It was the Slovenes who started the war." Slaven Letica provides a response to Zimmermann's article in this volume.

44. See, for instance, Thomas Masaryk, "Nationality and Internationalism" and "The Meaning of Our National Revival," in *Constructive Sociological Theory,* ed. Alan Woolfolk and Jonathan B. Imber (New Brunswick, N.J.: Transaction, 1994), 259–66 and 279–88. Indeed, Masaryk saw constructive nationalism as an antidote to the threat of communism. It is rare for Western intellectuals to see any constructive dimensions of ethnic nationalism.

45. See, for example, Raymond Bonner, "Embargoed Fuel Sent to Serbs via Albania," *New York Times,* April 2, 1995, A4; idem, "U.S. Acts to Prevent Oil Rigs from Reaching Yugoslavia," *New York Times,* April 8, 1995, A1; idem, "Leaky Embargo in the Balkans," *New York Times,* April 11, 1995, A3; idem, "Embargo against Belgrade Has a Major Leak," *New York Times,* April 15, 1995, A3; Raymond Bonner, "U.S. Asserts Greeks Avoid Yugoslav Ban," *New York Times,* April 30, 1995, A4; Stephen Engelberg and Eric Schmitt, "Western Officials Say Serbia Helps Bosnian Comrades," *New York Times,* June 11, 1995, A1.

This latter article asserts that Belgrade continues to supply the Bosnian Serbs with fuel and money, and that an air defense system remains linked to Yugoslav National Army computers in Belgrade.

46. *New York Times,* June 11, 1995, A1.

47. *New York Times,* October 1, 1992, A3.

48. *New York Times,* June 7, 1995, A19.

49. See, for instance, John Sack, *An Eye for an Eye* (New York: Basic Books, 1993).

50. Former President Carter traveled to Serb-occupied areas of Bosnia-Herzegovina on a peace mission. See the media coverage by Michael T. Kaufman, "Jimmy Carter, It Turns Out, Is a Poet, Too," *New York Times,* January 18, 1995, C9; "Merry Christmas, Mr. Karadžić," *New Republic,* January 9, 1995, 7; Roger Cohen, "Bosnia Foes Agree to a Four-Month Truce, Carter Reports," *New York Times,* December 21, 1994, A1; idem, "Bosnian Serb Leader Offers His Revisions to Peace Plan," *New York Times,* December 21, 1994, A14; idem, "Carter Is in Sarajevo, but No Progress Is Reported," *New York Times,* December 19, 1994, A12; Douglas Jehl, "Carter Takes Off for Bosnia on Broadened Peace Mission," *New York Times,* December 18, 1994, A1; Roger Cohen, "Carter Visit Instills Hope among Serbs," *New York Times,* December 18, 1994, A24.

51. Consider, for example, how some of these assessments are refracted in the following: Dan Morgan, "Haunted Serbia: My Journey Back in Time to a Self-Defeated Nation," *Washington Post,* June 19, 1994, E4, in which Morgan asserts that "Like the Jews, Serbs are unified by the memory of a glorious defeat"; Teddy Preuss, "Serbia, an Ally Spurned," *Jerusalem Post,* June 9, 1994, 6; Jo-Ann Mort, "Croatia's Festering Fascism," *Jewish Forward,* September 16, 1994, 7; Stephen Kinzer, "Pro-Nazi Legacy Lingers for Croatia," *New York Times,* October 31, 1993, A6; see also an editorial entitled "Ethnic Cleansing," *Boston Globe,* October 22, 1995, 78, which notes, "Much of what has been happening today in the Balkans cannot be understood outside the context of the ethnic cleansings of 50 years ago. In the Nazi puppet state of Croatia during World War II, Croats *[sic]* set about to cleanse Croatia of as many Serbs as they could." The author attributes to "Croats" in general the actions of the Ustashe minority, an obfuscation that implies collective guilt and that indirectly blames contemporary Croats for much of what is happening in the Balkans. No mention is made of the causes of the current genocide, which, as many authors in this volume point out, are to be found in the specific actions of Serbian intellectuals and leaders.

52. Reprinted in *International Herald Tribune,* August 9, 1995, 8.

53. See, for example, "A Balkan Quagmire Beckons," *Economist,* June 3, 1995, 41–42; Noel Malcolm, "Bosnia and the West: A Study in Failure," *National Interest* 39 (1995): 3–14; Stephen Kinzer, "Bosnian Muslims and Serbs Agree to Four-Month Truce," *New York Times,* January 1, 1995, A8; Paul Hockenos, "Bosnians Turn to Islam as War Grinds On into Third Year," *New Statesman and*

Society, March 10, 1995, 12; Roger Cohen, "Croatia Is Set to End Mandate of UN Force on Its Territory," *New York Times,* January 12, 1995, A4; idem, "A Fragile Truce in Bosnia," *New York Times,* January 19, 1995, A3.

54. The best documentation for this is found in Philip J. Cohen, *Serbia's Secret War: Propaganda and the Deceit of History* (College Station: Texas A&M University Press, 1996).

55. See Roger Cohen, "Bosnia Debate: Army as Defender of Islam or Multiculturalism?" *New York Times,* February 4, 1995, A4; Hockenos, op. cit, 12; Roger Thurow, "Muslims from Bosnia Find Refuge in Islam While Adrift in Europe," *Wall Street Journal,* September 6, 1994, A1; Roger Cohen, "West's Fears in Bosnia: 1. Chaos. 2. Islam," *New York Times,* March 13, 1994, A3; Robert D. Kaplan, "Ground Zero," *New Republic,* August 2, 1993, 15; John Kifner, "In Sarajevo: A Different Kind of Islam," *New York Times,* December 15, 1993, A20; Zachary T. Irwin, "The Islamic Revival and the Muslims of Bosnia-Herzegovina," *East European Quarterly* 17, no. 4 (1983): 437–58.

56. Edward W. Said, *Orientalism* (New York: Pantheon, 1978); idem, *Covering Islam: How Media Experts Determine How We See the Rest of the World* (New York: Pantheon, 1981).

57. The best documentation for this is found in Philip J. Cohen, op. cit.

58. See Roger Cohen, "Croatia Currency's Name Protested," *New York Times,* May 28, 1994, A3; Stephen Kinzer, "Croatia's Founding Chief Is Seen as Mixed Story," *New York Times,* August 5, 1993, A10; Robert D. Kaplan, "Croatianism," *New Republic,* November 25, 1991, 16; "Croatia, the Butcher's Apprentice," *New York Times,* July 8, 1992, A12; Kinzer, "Pro-Nazi Legacy Lingers"; Roger Cohen, "At a Womb of Horror, Croats Offer Ray of Hope," *New York Times,* May 9, 1995, A6.

59. This view was put forth most forcefully by Henry Kissinger, "Choosing among Evils," *Houston Chronicle,* June 11, 1995, 35A.

60. See, for instance, Robert J. Donia and John V. A. Fine, Jr., *Bosnia and Hercegovina: A Tradition Betrayed* (New York: Columbia University Press, 1994).

61. This charge is taken up and refuted by Albert Wohlstetter, "Creating a Greater Serbia," *New Republic,* August 1, 1994, 22–27; idem, "Embargo the Aggressors, Not the Victim," *Wall Street Journal,* June 28, 1994, A18; idem, "Genocide by Mediation," *New York Times,* March 3, 1994, A21.

62. See, for example, Bette Denich, "Dismembering Yugoslavia: The Nationalist Ideologies and the Symbolic Revival of Genocide," *American Ethnologist* 21 (May 1994): 367–90. Denich's article is perhaps the most glaring example of published pro-Serb sentiment in the American Balkan studies community. A further examination of such sympathies in this community is warranted.

63. *New York Times,* August 29, 1995, A1. This pattern of coverage began most prominently with the reporting of the shelling massacre in the crowded

Markale marketplace in northeastern Sarajevo on February 5, 1994. A prime example of the press's acceptance of the Bosnian Serb line in relation to this attack can be found in David Binder, "Anatomy of a Massacre," *Foreign Policy* 97 (winter 1994–95): 70–78. It is also worth stressing a point made above that Binder's own opinion of General Ratko Mladić, who has been indicted for war crimes against the people of Sarajevo, is that he is a "superb professional." See Binder, letter, 85.

64. Alija Izetbegović, *Islam between East and West* (Indianapolis: American Trust Publications, 1993).

65. See Alija Izetbegović, *Islamska deklaracija* (Sarajevo: Bosna, 1990).

66. George Kenney, "The Bosnia Calculation," *New York Times Magazine,* April 23, 1995, 42–43.

67. This phrase is found frequently, as in the *New York Times,* February 13, 1994, A10, which contains the phrases "These people are very afraid of each other" and "these people will fight on forever."

68. The power of this frame is gleaned from the frequent references to elected leaders in Bosnia, Croatia, and Serbia as "chiefs," as if they headed tribes, not nation-states. For example, see Steven Greenhouse, "Clinton Meets with Bosnian and Croatian Chiefs," *New York Times,* March 17, 1995, A5. See also Jacques Attali, "An Age of Yugoslavias," *Harper's,* January 1993, 20–22; Michael Barone, "Ethnic Tribes and Pandemonium," *U.S. News and World Report,* February 15, 1993, 55.

69. For example, "Serbian President Milošević called UN sanctions against his country an act of genocide." *Wall Street Journal,* November 9, 1993, A1.

70. A theme reproduced, for example, in an opinion piece, "Bosnian Serbs, Too, Have Vowed, Never Again," *Houston Chronicle,* March 16, 1995, A33.

71. See, for example, John F. Burns, "New, Virulent Strains in the Balkans and Beyond," *New York Times,* May 3, 1992, E3.

72. See, for example, Senator Moynihan's comments on the war in Bosnia in the *Congressional Record* regarding the Bosnia and Herzegovina Self-Defense Act of 1995, vol. 141, no. 117 (July 19, 1995); vol. 141, no. 121 (July 25. 1995); and volume 141, no. 122 (July 26, 1995).

73. An especially forceful analysis of this point is made by Albert Wohlstetter, "Genocide by Embargo," *Wall Street Journal,* May 9, 1994, A12.

Philip J. Cohen

The Complicity of Serbian
Intellectuals in Genocide in the 1990s

The war against Croatia and Bosnia-Herzegovina in the 1990s was planned by Serbian intellectuals and authorities long before the first Serbian attacks. In the fall of 1986, the Serbian Academy of Science and Art, representing Serbia's most prominent intellectuals, issued a memorandum demanding that the borders of Serbia be expanded.[1] The memorandum argued that the Serbs were the most mistreated and oppressed people in Yugoslavia, in spite of the fact that Serbs were the majority and in key positions in the Communist Party, the military, the police, diplomacy, finance and banking, and the legal and judicial systems. The 1986 memorandum advocated that all Serbs must live in one enlarged Serbia, a concept strikingly reminiscent of Hitler's own prewar rhetoric that all Germans must live in one country. This manifesto was, in essence, a blueprint for war. In 1987, the memorandum was circulated worldwide to Serbian émigré communities; it mobilized their support for Serbia's national and territorial goals, which were justified by the Serbs' alleged victimization in Yugoslavia, while making no mentions of the sufferings of other national groups at Serbian hands. In practical terms, the memorandum helped standardize the rhetoric by which the Serbian emigration would rally to defend Serbia once the war began.

Among the figures behind the 1986 memorandum was a Serbian Acad-

emy member with an impressive political pedigree, Vaša Čubrilović, then
nearly ninety years old. A surviving conspirator in the 1914 assassination
of Austrian Archduke Franz Ferdinand—the event that sparked the bloodshed of the World War I—Čubrilović reemerged as an advisor to the
royal Yugoslav government, from which position he authored the 1937
official government memorandum "The Expulsion of the Albanians,"
which began by citing Hitler's and Stalin's success in expelling Jews and
others as examples for Serbia to emulate. The document proposed that the
government render the lives of Albanians so intolerable and terror-filled
that they would flee en masse to Albania and Turkey, and it went on to
explain in detail how an "emigration psychosis" could be instilled among
the Albanians through a government-directed program of relentless persecutions.[2] After World War II, Čubrilović went on to hold several ministe-
rial posts in Tito's government (he was, for example, Tito's first minister
of agriculture)—a remarkable testimony to the moral flexibility of the
communist regime. Following Tito's death in 1980, Čubrilović turned his
energy toward reviving Serbian nationalism and played an essential role
in shaping the 1986 memorandum.[3]

Also among the principal authors of the memorandum was Dobrica
Ćosić, whose novels and political essays portrayed Serbs as the superior
nation of the Balkans, glorified Serbian militancy, and demanded "all
Serbs in one state."[4] Ćosić first articulated these views in 1968, when he
shocked a Communist Party meeting by proposing that Serbs rise to
destroy the multi-national Yugoslav state to fulfill "the old historical goal
and national ideal" of a Greater Serbia.[5] Ćosić later fanned the flames of
war in 1991, proclaiming that there was a "wild hatred against the Serbian
people," condemning Croats as "the most destructive force in Yugoslavia," and declaring that "pacifist rhetoric is senseless."[6] Promoting the
idea that Serbs were an eternally suffering people, whose martyrdom was
no less than that of the Jews in the Holocaust, Ćosić even proposed that
"The Serb is the new Jew, the Jew at the end of the twentieth century."[7]
In 1992, Ćosić became the ceremonial head of the rump federal Yugoslavia (Serbia and Montenegro) and added further intellectual imprimatur to
the war machine of Serbian president Slobodan Milošević, whom he
called "the best Serbian leader" in half a century.[8]

Serbia's maneuvering toward war took a decisive turn in March 1989,
when the Serbian government amended its constitution to impose control
over the two autonomous regions of Serbia: Vojvodina (with a substantial
Croatian and Hungarian population) and Kosovo (93 percent Albanian).

Under the Yugoslav Federal Constitution of 1974, these provinces, although technically part of the Republic of Serbia, operated in a manner virtually indistinguishable from that of the other Yugoslav republics. Vojvodina and Kosovo participated equally in the eight-member federal presidency, consisting of representatives of the six republics and two autonomous regions. Essentially, Vojvodina and Kosovo functioned as de facto republics. However, following Serbia's 1989 anschluss of the autonomous regions, Albanian leaders in Kosovo were arrested, and Serbia installed its own police, courts, and government officials. After unilaterally abolishing the autonomy of Vojvodina and Kosovo in explicit violation of the constitution, Serbia retained for itself their votes in the federal presidency. Since Serbia's ally Montenegro was by this time ruled by handpicked pro-Serbian politicians, and Montenegro characteristically voted in solidarity with Serbia, the Republic of Serbia came to effectively control four out of eight votes in the federal presidency—precisely the kind of imbalance of power that the Yugoslav Federal Constitution of 1974 had been designed to avoid. Months later, on June 28, 1989—the six hundredth anniversary of the Serbs' defeat by the Turks at Kosovo—Slobodan Milošević delivered a militant speech to the Serbs in Kosovo, reminding the crowd that "the Serbs throughout their history never conquered or exploited anybody else."[9] On the same day, with the encouragement of the Serbian government, the Serbs in the Croatian Krajina demanded their own autonomous province. This occurred nearly a year before Croatia held its first free elections, the event that Serbian propaganda would later claim had instigated the Serbs of Croatia to seek autonomy.

Also on the same day, the Serbian Orthodox Church issued its official national program, which echoed the 1986 memorandum of the Serbian Academy of Science and Art, as well as official documents of the Communist Party and the Yugoslav state apparatus. This manifesto, known as the "Proposed Serbian Church National Program," praised Serbia's decision to unilaterally terminate the autonomy of Vojvodina and Kosovo. Restating a central theme of the Academy's memorandum, the church document portrayed an aggrieved and oppressed Serbia, and it further praised Slobodan Milošević for beginning to right the alleged historical wrongs against Serbia:

> Since history and the future should now explain why Serbia had to suffer economic subservience, backwardness, partitions, and political inferiority in socialist Yugoslavia for almost half a century, one should now honestly

recognize certain merits and endeavors of the new Serbian leadership [Milošević] in resolving the Serbian question. The new authorities knew how to correctly use the great democratic energy and spiritual potential of the Serbian people, who have again begun to think with their heads and make decisions about their destiny. Therefore, some premises have been created for historical moves by leading men with participation of healthy forces of the nation for overcoming the many-years-long passivity and national neglect.[10]

The "Proposed Serbian Church National Program," like the earlier memorandum, demanded "a radical change" of the Federal Constitution of 1974. Replete with internal contradictions, the church document in one place supported the modern concept of the separation of church and state, but elsewhere emphasized that "there is no strong state without a strong church." The church's national program further advocated "a truly Christian Europe," raising the question of the church's commitment to religious tolerance. Thus, in 1989, the Serbian Orthodox Church positioned its archdioceses—both in Yugoslavia and in emigration—to function as conduits for an agenda primarily political in its substance and, in this sense, almost indistinguishable from that of the Belgrade regime. Moreover, the church contributed considerably to heightening tensions in Yugoslavia, as an American historian observed:

> Indeed, in Yugoslavia the Serbian Orthodox church has lately published a series of articles about the Second World War focusing exclusively on Serbian casualties at the hands of Croats and obscuring the fact that violence and intergroup conflict were common in wartime Yugoslavia, with serious casualties also among Croats, Jews, Muslims, Albanians and others. In the eyes of the Serbian Orthodox church, Serbia is the modern Job, and other nationalities are Job's tormentors.[11]

In August 1990, the first act of organized violence commenced in Croatia under the leadership of Jovan Rašković, the head of the recently formed Serbian Democratic Party. After confiscating weapons from a police station in Knin and murdering the Croatian police there, Rašković's followers blockaded the roads leading to the Krajina region to everyone except the Serbs. This was undertaken after consultation with Serbian president Slobodan Milošević, who promised that his republic would supply arms. To further reduce Croatia's defensive capability against military attack, the Yugoslav defense minister threatened to forcibly disarm Croatia's police and local militia. In January 1991, Croatian authorities acquiesced and disarmed these units themselves.[12]

In March 1991, Milošević stated that Serbia no longer recognized the power of the federal state, as Serbs crippled the functioning of the federal presidency. In early May 1991, Serbian irregulars in the town of Borovo Selo captured twelve Croatian police and several civilians, tortured them, gouged out their eyes, cut off their limbs and genitalia, and then murdered them.[13] In an act of calculated terror, the mutilated body parts were dumped in the middle of the town square. Several of these bodies had no heads. Although this violence had been directly encouraged by the Serbian government in Belgrade, the Serbian-controlled Federal Defense Ministry found this a convenient pretext to demand that it be allowed to intervene to "restore order." In mid-May, when the Croatian representative Stipe Mešić was due to assume the rotating post of president of the eight-member federal presidency, Serbs prevented him, in violation of constitutional procedure.[14] The next day the National Council of the Republic of Serbia, also in violation of the Yugoslav constitution, declared the Krajina region of Croatia an integral part of the territory of Serbia, although, notably, it shared no common border with Serbia.[15]

All these events occurred before Croatia held its plebiscite, also in May 1991, when the electorate overwhelmingly supported independence and confederation with other republics of Yugoslavia, while specifically guaranteeing "cultural autonomy and all civic rights to Serbs and members of other nationalities in Croatia."[16] Serbian propaganda has cited this independence plebiscite as having caused the Serbs to rise to arms, but the chronology of events shows clearly that covert Serbian preparations for the war against Croatia and Bosnia-Herzegovina had commenced years earlier, with armed actions against the legitimately constituted Croatian authorities and massacres of Croatian civilians. The June 25, 1991, independence declarations of Croatia and Slovenia did, however, serve as the pretext for the Yugoslav Federal Army's invasion, which commenced within two days.

In Slovenia, the Yugoslav Federal Army met a humiliating defeat by the Slovenian Territorial Defense Forces, partly because the army had underestimated Slovenian resolve and sent too few tanks, crewed primarily by inexperienced draftees, whose supplies of food and fuel were quickly exhausted.[17] Within a month, the Serbian leadership in the Yugoslav government conceded Slovenia's secession from Yugoslavia. Behind this decision were apparently several strategic considerations: Slovenia, 96 percent ethnically homogeneous, contained virtually no Serbian minority to organize a campaign of internal sabotage, as was possible in

Croatia and Bosnia-Herzegovina. Slovenia was also the only republic of Yugoslavia to share no common border with Serbia. Perhaps most significant, Slovenian territory had never been included in the maps of a Greater Serbia, dating back to 1844. To the contrary, Serbian ultranationalists had long viewed the Slovenes not only as parliamentary allies against Croatia, but as potential partners in the dismemberment of Croatia.[18] By permitting the secession of Slovenia, Serbia would have been left controlling four of seven votes in the federal presidency, guaranteeing absolute Serbian hegemony.

At the same time that the Yugoslav military was withdrawing from Slovenia, it was clear that Serbs were contemplating an intensified war against Croatia. General Blagoje Adžić, the army chief of staff, coldly assessed military plans for Croatia: "This rebellion must be terminated, even if it is going to generate a thousand deaths. The international community will be agitated a bit, but three days later everything will be forgotten and our objectives will be obtained."[19]

Tragically for the victims of Serbian aggression, General Adžić's assessment was largely correct, as the United States and the European Community continued to support the "integrity of Yugoslavia" for the next several months.[20] On July 5, 1991, the European Community, supported by the United States, imposed an arms embargo on Yugoslavia, notwithstanding that Serbia effectively controlled the entire Yugoslav Federal Army arsenal of tanks, ships, fighter planes, and heavy artillery.[21] Indeed, by freezing the military imbalance in favor of Serbia, the embargo did little more than abet Serbian aggression. By September 1991, Serbia's proxy guerrilla forces had seized over 30 percent of Croatia's territory. In that month, the Yugoslav government—practically, speaking only for Serbia—urged an international weapons embargo on Yugoslavia, transparently intended to preserve Serbian military superiority. On September 25, 1991, the United Nations Security Council unanimously granted the Serbian leadership's wish, adopting Resolution 713, which banned the sale of weapons to Yugoslavia.[22] Throughout the fall of 1991, Serbian forces on the ground executed a blitzkrieg of rape, looting, mutilation, and murder of unarmed civilians. However, in the world of news and information, especially for Western consumption, a barrage of Serbian propaganda cast these events in a heroic light, depicting the Serbs in Croatia rising to their defense, when endangered. In truth, however, fully 75 percent of the Serbian population of Croatia had resided without harassment in Croatian cities and towns outside the seized territory before the war.[23]

Since the beginning of hostilities in the former Yugoslavia, Serbian attacks have targeted primarily unarmed civilian populations of non-Serbs living in the lands coveted by Serbia.[24] Early in the war, there were reports that Croats and Hungarians living in Serbian-captured regions of Croatia were forced to identify themselves with armbands—a practice hauntingly reminiscent of the yellow star worn by Jews during the Holocaust. As early as 1991, there were reports that civilian prisoners of war were being tortured and killed in Serbian "labor" camps.[25] Also during 1991, there were extensive reports on the Serbian practice of mass deportation of non-Serbs from their homes and the systematic resettlement with Serbs.[26] When Serbian forces introduced the war into Bosnia-Herzegovina, they repeated the identical pattern of aggression and atrocities against non-Serbs, over a larger and more populated territory.[27] The goal remained the same: "ethnic cleansing," a euphemism invoked by the Serbs themselves to describe the process of creating ethnically pure Serbian regions through the methodical murder and expulsion of non-Serbs.[28]

Belying the hygienic sound of "ethnic cleansing" are the testimonies by survivors of Serbian-run camps such as Omarska in Bosnia-Herzegovina. There, atrocities were invented for the amusement of the Serbs. For example, prisoners were decapitated with chain saws, and one prisoner was forced to bite off the testicles or the penis of another. After the American embassy in Zagreb investigated reports of Serbian atrocities at Omarska, one top embassy official, speaking on condition of anonymity, commented, "The Nazis had nothing on these guys. I've seen reports of individual acts of barbarity of a kind that hasn't come up in State Department cable traffic in 20 years."[29]

In December 1992, the U.S. secretary of state Lawrence Eagleburger named suspected war criminals, which included the top Serbian leadership in Serbia and Bosnia-Herzegovina (see appendix 1). In early 1993, Tadeusz Mazowiecki, the rapporteur for the UN Commission on Human Rights, concluded, "The collected evidence leaves no doubt as to who is responsible for the horror: the Serbian political and military leaders in Bosnia-Herzegovina, supported by the authorities of the Serbian Republic."[30]

As of June 1993, the U.S. Department of State had submitted to the

United Nations eight reports on atrocities and war crimes in the former Yugoslavia.[31] Of the 347 incidents contained in the eight U.S. submissions, 304, or 88 percent, were attributable to Serbs, 7 percent to Bosnian Muslims, and 5 percent to Croats. The asymmetry in the number of victims is even more striking: the victims at the hands of Serbs numbered in the tens of thousands, while there were approximately 500 victims at the hands of Muslims and approximately 150 victims at the hands of Croats.[32] The most significant asymmetry, however, is that 100 percent of the acts of genocide, as defined in the UN Convention on Genocide, have been committed by Serbs alone—a finding confirmed by a highly comprehensive and secret CIA report.[33] There is little question that Serbia's policies constitute genocide, as understood in the Convention on Genocide, adopted by the United Nations General Assembly on December 9, 1948 (and entered into force on January 12, 1951). Article 2 of the Convention on Genocide defines genocide as

> Any of the following acts committed with intent to destroy, in whole or in part, a national, ethnic, racial, or religious group, as such: (a) Killing members of the group; (b) Causing serious bodily or mental harm to members of the group; (c) Deliberately inflicting on the group conditions of life calculated to bring about its physical destruction in whole or in part; (d) Imposing measures intended to prevent births within the group; (e) Forcibly transferring children of the group to another group.[34]

It is noteworthy that the post-World War II Nuremberg trials distinguished between war crimes (something the Allies also did) and crimes against humanity and genocide (something only the Nazis did). In executing a policy of genocide, the Serbs' methods are a matter of public record: deportations, torture, mutilations, death camps, rape/death camps, and mass executions.[35] The pattern of "ethnic cleansing" has been remarkably consistent, as one British journalist described:

> If you had to draw up a list of events that lead to killings here, it would go something like this: you get warnings on television and radio that Moslems are arming themselves; then arms being given out to local Serbs; from outside, Serbian paramilitaries arrive—people in uniform with names like White Eagles or the Tigers; you get local Serbs training in secret, outside the town; and, while all this is happening, there is a sudden inexplicable cooling in your relations with people who used to be your friends and neighbors.... After that, there is the bombardment from the hills, and the killing starts.... "[The Serbs] marched through the town and destroyed

houses.. . . I saw men lined up and shot with pistols. They . . . called for men, all Moslems, by name. There was a hall in the town; the women and the girls were brought there and raped."[36]

Mass rape as a Serbian method of terror has received considerable attention. Abundant documentary evidence demonstrates that Serbian forces engaged in the systematic rape of women, children, and men.[37] State-sponsored rape was an integral part of "ethnic cleansing" and was designed to accomplish several goals. Mass rapes destroy the victims' core social institutions, the family and community. Mass rapes instill terror, so that the victims will never seek to return to their homes and villages. Mass rapes instill interethnic hatred and undermine the possibility of continuing multiethnic community life. At the height of the aggression against Bosnia-Herzegovina, Serbian soldiers, as a routine practice, forcibly impregnated non-Serbian women held in rape camps, continued to gang-rape these pregnant women for months, and finally expelled them from Serbian-occupied territories when they were near term. In this way, the rape victims were forced to bear the children of their tormentors, thus compounding their personal suffering. Although severely traumatized, these rape victims often had little or no functioning support network. Other family members were often traumatized, separated, or dead. Mental health care was simply not available on the scale required. Forcibly impregnated rape victims have a tragically high incidence of suicide and infanticide. Mass rape, then, was an integral part of genocide.[38] Serbian forces told their rape victims that they were under orders to do so.[39]

The Serbian program of genocide was also carried out through a deliberate pattern of destruction of cultural monuments, houses of worship, and other institutions that define the collective identity of the targeted community. In areas designated for Serbian conquest, non-Serbian cemeteries and houses of worship are routinely destroyed, in order to erase any memory of the non-Serbian peoples and their culture. As is true for the preponderance of murders, tortures, expulsions, and rapes in Croatia and Bosnia-Herzegovina, Serbs are responsible for the overwhelming instances of destruction of cultural and religious monuments. For example, during 1993 in the Serb-occupied area of Banja Luka (the second largest city in Bosnia-Herzegovina after Sarajevo), Serbian authorities and armed forces destroyed 200 out of 202 mosques (99 percent) and destroyed or damaged 96 percent of Catholic churches. Six such mosques had dated to the sixteenth century and seven had dated to the seventeenth century.[40] Non-Serbian towns have been systematically renamed, or "Serbianized." For example, after driving the majority Bosnian Muslim population from the historically Muslim town of Foča in 1992, Serbian authorities renamed it Srbinje, to designate it as a Serbian town.

Within months of the Yugoslav Federal Army's invasion of Slovenia and Croatia in June 1991, Serbia was recognized and condemned as the clear aggressor by the United States, the European Community, the Helsinki Commission, and the United Nations, as well as the human rights organization Helsinki Watch.[41] By mid-1992, Western diplomats pointedly characterized the Serbian regime as "a lying, terrorist criminal organization," and the *New York Times* characterized Serbia's aggression as "a one sided war . . . reminiscent of the Nazis."[42] In April 1993, the International Court of Justice at the Hague ordered Belgrade to halt the genocide in Bosnia-Herzegovina.[43] The following month, prompted by the allegations against Serbian forces, the United Nations established a war crimes tribunal.[44]

The UN commission investigating war crimes bears an unwieldy title, the International Tribunal for the Prosecution of Persons Responsible for Serious Violations of International Humanitarian Law Committed in the Territory of Former Yugoslavia since 1991. This eleven-member commission was preceded by a five-member UN Commission of Experts, whose task it was to obtain preliminary testimony and establish the framework for the ensuing tribunal.

Before we consider the findings of the UN Commission of Experts, it is instructive to consider two known attempts to infiltrate the commission in order to subvert it to Serbian advantage. In the first instance, a Milwaukee attorney named David Erne volunteered his services to the UN commission. In March 1994, he submitted a fifty-nine-page document for the commission's consideration. It was entitled "Report on the Historical Background of the Civil War in the Former Yugoslavia," and a representative portion of this inaccurate, biased, and inflammatory document is quoted:

> Following Hitler's attack on the Soviet Union in June of 1941, the Independent State of Croatia declared war, and sent at least one military division to fight along side the Nazis on the Eastern Front. After Pearl Harbor, Croatia declared war on the United States and on Great Britain. . . .
>
> The first organized resistance against the Nazis originated in Serbia, led by Draža Mihailović, who tried to assemble what was left of the defeated Yugoslav army, which came to be known popularly as the Chetniks (*Cheta* is a term used historically for irregular Serb resistance fighters.) . . .

> In any event, a significant portion of the resistance fighters in both [Chetnik and Partisan] movements were Serbs.. . . Later, some Croatians joined both movements, and especially the Partisans, as did some Muslims in Bosnia, although most Muslims, like most Croatians, were part of the fascist Ustashi forces.

The astute observer will recognize the standard fare of Serbian propaganda: the thesis that Serbs during World War II were exclusively resisters and Croats were exclusively collaborators. This obfuscates the fact of significant Serbian collaboration with the Nazis, conceals the paucity of resistance to the Nazis in Serbia, ignores Mihailović's extensive collaboration with the Axis, and omits the prominent role of the Croats in the Partisan resistance.

This same document furthermore described the Bosnian Serb leader Radovan Karadžić in honorable and flattering terms as "a physician who trained in New York and practiced medicine in Sarajevo, and has published numerous books of poetry. He was elected primarily because he was a dissident during the communist regime in Yugoslavia."

This all-too-brief description omitted to mention, among other things, that Radovan Karadžić served prison time for real estate fraud and embezzlement, and for that reason was banned from the Communist Party.[45] As a practicing psychiatrist in Sarajevo, he indeed tried to establish himself as a poet, albeit without success. His poetry, however, with its emphasis on blood and destruction, revealed important aspects of his personality. The following excerpt is a typical example:

> I'm born to live without a tomb,
> this divine body will not die.
> It's not only born to smell flowers,
> but also to set fire, kill and
> reduce everything to dust.[46]

A closer look at Karadžić's background shows that he is the son of a convicted war criminal responsible for the massacre of Muslims during World War II.[47] His admiration for his friend and colleague Jovan Rašković is also informative, since Karadžić considered Rašković his main role model and philosophical inspiration.[48]

Jovan Rašković headed the psychiatry department at the Neuropsychiatric Clinic in Šibenik, Croatia, where he enjoyed the reputation of taking pleasure in administering electroshock therapy to Croats, especially Croatian women.[49] He developed his own psychoanalytic theory explaining the inferiority of Croats and Muslims and the superiority of Serbs, by which Serbs were destined to dominate and rule over the others. In 1990, Rašković advanced these theories in his book *Luda zemlja* (A mad country), which he began by reminding his readers of the Serbs' victimization by Croats during World War II:

> The Croats, feminized by the Catholic religion, suffer from a castration complex. That makes them totally incapable of exercising authority over others. They compensate their humiliation by their great culture. As to the Muslims of Bosnia-Herzegovina and neighboring regions, they are the victims, as Freud might have said, of anal frustrations, which incite them to amass wealth and to seek refuge in fanatic attitudes. Finally, the Serbs, the Orthodox, an Oedipal people, tend to liberate themselves from the authority of the father. From this spirit of resistance, they draw the courage of the warriors, who are the only ones capable of exerting real authority over the other peoples of Yugoslavia. It is no wonder that the situation of complete hatred and paranoia develops in this country.[50]

Thus, according to Rašković, Croats could not exercise authority or leadership, because they had a deep-seated fear of castration, were afraid of everything, and had to be led. Muslims were anal-erotic with a compulsion for acquiring money and property. Serbs, in contrast, were the only people qualified to exercise authority and dominate other peoples in Yugoslavia, because only the Serbs had overcome the Oedipus complex by symbolically "killing" the father. Upon its release, he promoted his book in newspapers and on television, gaining a substantial following among the Serbs of Croatia. Rašković also founded the Serbian Democratic Party in Croatia. The party's three leaders (Milan Martić, Jovan Opačić, and Suzana Zelenbaba) were his own psychiatric patients from the clinic in Šibenik. During 1990, Rašković organized many public meetings for Serbian audiences in Croatia, where he spoke of impending war.

In August, 1990, Rašković's followers (that is, members of the Serbian Democratic Party) attacked a police station in the town of Knin and confiscated the weapons, which were distributed to the local Serbian population. When the Croatian government responded by sending a troop of police officers to restore order, Rašković's followers killed them all and blockaded the roads to the region, forbidding all except Serbs to enter. Such incidents were repeated village by village and became the standard method of the Serbian leadership to incite local populations to violence. Observers of warfare will quickly recognize this method as a standard technique which could be found in textbooks on guerrilla warfare: the technique of "compromising the villages," as employed by the French Resistance, the Viet-Cong, and innumerable other guerrilla movements. This technique involves staging an incident—for example, shooting a carload of Croatian policemen outside a particular village—to invite a crackdown or reprisal, and then distributing arms to the villagers, telling them that the police are planning to attack them. When armed police do arrive, it is easy to spark off a gun battle; and suddenly a whole village, previously uncommitted, is now on the side of the insurgents.[51]

At each step of these actions, Rašković and his Serbian Democratic Party leaders closely consulted with Serbian president Slobodan Milošević. During early 1991, Rašković visited Bosnia-Herzegovina, where he created a Serbian Democratic Party there as well and placed Radovan Karadžić at its head. Together, Rašković and Karadžić held lectures throughout Bosnia-Herzegovina, where they incited the Serbian crowds to hatred and militancy.[52] In early 1992, Rašković made the following remarkably apologetic statement on Belgrade television:

> I feel responsible because I made the preparations for this war, even if not the military preparations. If I hadn't created this emotional strain in the Serbian people, nothing would have happened.
>
> My party and I lit the fuse of Serbian nationalism not only in Croatia but everywhere else in Bosnia-Herzegovina. It's impossible to imagine an SDP (Serbian Democratic Party) in Bosnia-Herzegovina or a Mr. Karadžić in power without our influence. We have driven this people and we have given it an identity. I have repeated again and again to this people that it comes from heaven, not earth.[53]

Shortly after this television appearance, Rašković died of a heart attack in Belgrade. Karadžić has carried on his mentor's work ever since. There is also a striking parallel between these war-promoting psychiatrists: Rašković's patients instigated the war from inside Croatia, while Karadžić's close friend and alleged former patient, Slobodan Milošević, orchestrated the war from Belgrade. Thus, David Erne's report to the UN Commission of Experts, describing Karadžić as simply a physician, dissident, and poet, was replete with deceptions by omission. In a similar vein, Adolf Hitler could be described as simply an artist, which, among other things, he was.

The UN Commission of Experts quickly recognized Erne's document as unreliable and of dubious value, or, more bluntly, as propaganda. For all practical purposes, it became a "dead letter" within the commission, since all submitted reports were confidential, and their disposition was solely in its hands. However, without the knowledge of the commission, and in direct violation of its protocols, this propaganda piece was quietly distributed to foreign officials and the press. It was misrepresented as an official UN document; its title page was typed on United Nations stationery. Moreover, the commission chairman's name was placed prominently on the cover, implying official imprimatur and adding the unmistakable dimension of fraud. What Erne neglected to reveal when he volunteered his legal services was that he happened to be a vice president of the Serbian Unity Congress, a Serbian American organization that has stalwartly supported the goals (and means) of the Belgrade regime.[54]

A second example relates to a lawyer named Tanja Petovar, who volunteered her services to the UN Commission of Experts and found herself engaged in the highly delicate task of taking testimony from Muslim women who had survived Serbian rape and death camps. The commission's protocol specifically required the presence of a witness when testimony was obtained, but Petovar often dispensed with that "detail." Her recorded testimonies, when double-checked, were significant for their rather consistent lack of fidelity. On at least one occasion, Petovar brought to the interview, without authorization, a man and woman, both recognizable as Serbs by their names and accents. Predictably, the Muslim survivor of rape found their presence intimidating and inhibiting. During an official commission briefing session held in Zagreb, Petovar identified herself as a human rights lawyer from Sarajevo, although her law practice was actually in Ljubljana and Belgrade. She also misrepresented her country of citizenship: from the outset, Petovar implied she was a citizen of Slovenia (her father was a Slovene), but the passport she carried at the time was from Yugoslavia. Perhaps most interesting of all, Petovar also neglected to reveal that in 1991 she helped organize a political rally in Belgrade for Vojislav Šešelj's militantly nationalist and racist Serbian Radical Party.

Fortunately, the work of the UN Commission of Experts was relatively unhampered by the activities described, and its report was issued in May 1994. Of 407 camps in Bosnia-Herzegovina investigated by the commission, nearly two-thirds were run by Serbs. While no policy or pattern of wrongdoing could be identified in the detention camps operated by Croats or Bosnian Muslims, the commission found that Serbian camps were instruments of state policy of "ethnic purification" through terror and genocide.[55]

Reminiscent of the Nazi camps a half-century earlier, the Serbian camps operated in clusters and networks and often specialized in rape, other torture, and murder. Characteristically, after a village or town was conquered, the local population was rounded up en masse, a process that entailed rape, other torture, and slaughter. Involved in the rounding up process were local civil servants, political leaders, and police. Prisoners (civilians) were forced to surrender their money and valuables, and they were interrogated about their political and religious beliefs and about the personal wealth and family connections of other prisoners. These interrogations almost always were accompanied by brutality and often by torture and murder. Prisoners were transported to camps in tightly packed buses and freight or cattle trains, in which they were often killed at random and denied food, water, and access to toilet facilities. When prisoners were unloaded at their destination, a few were often killed on the spot. Men between the ages of sixteen (or younger) and sixty were separated from older men, women, and children. These men, considered of military age, were transferred to larger, more heavily guarded camps, where tortures and murders were the rule. Within the camps, the selection of victims for atrocities appeared to follow a pattern, as Serbian guards consulted lists on their clipboards, and selected for torture those people who were wealthy, educated, and influential.

The critical fact is that Serbian war crimes and atrocities were systematized and centrally orchestrated, and they served as an instrument of state policy. According to a former prison guard from a Serbian camp in Bosnia, where about three thousand Muslims were murdered (Vlasenica), the confinement of the town's Muslim population was initiated by a unit of the Yugoslav Federal Army, based in Novi Sad, Serbia. Throughout the existence of this camp, the commander was an active-duty Yugoslav Federal Army major, which suggests the extent to which Belgrade authorities and the Yugoslav Federal Army centrally coordinated the "ethnic cleansing" campaigns in Bosnia-Herzegovina and, before that, in Croatia.[56]

The Serbian war crimes are genocidal in intent. In contrast, the crimes infrequently committed by the recently established Croatian and Bosnian forces have been sporadic and spontaneous, rather than the result of a political program of genocide. The UN Commission of Experts concluded emphatically that there is no "moral equivalency" between the Serbs, Bosnian Muslims, and Croats as perpetrators of war crimes. Nevertheless, many Serbian intellectuals in Serbia and in emigration and other apologists for the Belgrade regime have repeatedly invoked this argument of "moral equivalency" to obfuscate the Serbs' responsibility for the overwhelming preponderance of war crimes.[57]

From the outset, the goal of the war in Bosnia was the creation of Greater Serbia. This has been true of all of Serbia's wars for more than a century. For years before the onset of war, the Belgrade regime covertly supplied arms, funds, and personnel for the Serbian irregulars (Chetniks), who were training to fight a guerrilla war in Croatia and Bosnia-Herzegovina. Six months before the war "officially" began with the June 1991 invasion of Slovenia and Croatia, barbed wire and posts were already erected in some sites that would become Serbian concentration camps.[58] When the war began, Chetnik militias initiated their campaign of massacres, terror, torture, and rape, proceeding systematically from village to village. The Chetniks' victims were consistently unarmed non-Serbian civilians, as well as the occasional antiterrorist Serb who would have been made into a public example. Not infrequently, the Chetniks' victims were neighbors and acquaintances, even friends. To ensure their success, the Serbian-dominated regular army actively assisted in the Chetnik attacks, when needed.[59] In official posturing, however, the Chetniks maintained the thinly veiled pretext of operating independently of Belgrade, while the army maintained the pretext of neutrality.[60] This well-established strategy of using Serbian irregulars, covertly supported by the state, to execute a state policy of genocide may be termed the "Chetnik subterfuge." Indeed, the thinly veiled subterfuge was reported in the *Washington Post* in the very first month of the war in Croatia:

> There is ample evidence that Serbian fighters are receiving clandestine support and equipment from Serbian officers in the Yugoslav Federal Army. The officers corps in the Yugoslav Federal Army are *[sic]* dominated by Serbs. At camp headquarters, the commander reads positions from detailed, Yugoslav Army topographical maps. Soldiers wear crisp, new camouflage uniforms . . . identical to those worn by the special forces of the federal army. Local officials say they were provided by federal army officers.[61]

Thus, the "Chetnik subterfuge" has reemerged as an important component in a war as yet unnamed, but which may be accurately termed the Greater Serbian War. Since 1991, Serbia's war effort primarily targeted unarmed civilians in Croatia and Bosnia-Herzegovina, although brutal repression of Albanians, which began in 1989, has never remitted, and a quiet campaign of ethnic purification has been undertaken in Vojvodina as well. Characteristically, the victims have been non-Serbs living in areas designated for Serbian ethnic purity or annexation to Serbia or both.

What has been especially disturbing is that the Serbian intellectuals, especially since the mid-1980s, have resurrected the attitudes, plans, and methods responsible for their forebears' genocidal behavior for over a century. Dobrica Ćosić, as a principal ideologist of the 1986 memorandum, was not alone among politically active intellectuals who worked to advance Serbia's war agenda. For example, psychiatrist Jovan Rašković, who advanced his racial theory of the superiority of Serbs over Croats and Muslims in *Luda zemlja,* also played an important behind-the-scenes role in forging the 1986 memorandum. During its drafting, Dobrica Ćosić consulted extensively with Rašković at his home in Croatia.[62] Although Rašković was not a member of the Serbian Academy of Science and Art at the time of the drafting of the memorandum, he was later inducted into this body of Serbia's leading intellectuals in 1990, the year he organized and led the Serbian Democratic Party in Croatia, which was responsible for the first of many Serbian guerrilla attacks against Croatia.

The coauthors of the memorandum included the internationally regarded Serbian philosophers Svetozar Stojanović and Mihailo Marković, both prominent in the Belgrade political establishment as defenders and promoters of Serbian war policy (ironically, both have remained members in good standing of the Academy of Humanism, based in Buffalo, New York).[63] Stojanović, a former copresident of the International Humanist and Ethical Union and a professor of philosophy at the Universities of Belgrade and Kansas, served in 1992 as the chief advisor to Dobrica Ćosić, president of rump Yugoslavia. Similarly, Mihailo Marković, for years a member of the American Philosophical Association, was the vice president of the Serbian Socialist Party of Slobodan Milošević and one of its principal ideologists. In 1990, Marković declared the Serbian Socialist Party's "extreme resoluteness in defending all threatened parts of the Serbian people in the other republics," a signal for war.[64] In February 1991, Marković, interviewed on Radio Belgrade during the Persian Gulf War, condemned the role of the United States and described the American political system as "totalitarianism."[65] More recently, a similar, distinctly uncritical view of Milošević was offered by Marković's philosophy student Zoran Đinđić, the president of the Democratic Party in Serbia at the time of this writing. A former "liaison officer" to the notorious Baader-

Meinhoff terrorist group in Germany during the 1970s, Đinđić described Slobodan Milošević in May 1994, as "a skillful, realistic, self-confident politician who knows what he wants. He is not a direct competitor to us. We are not unreal, we are not megalomaniacs. Our competitors are at much lower levels."[66] Comment on Milošević's policy of genocide was of no interest to this student of philosophy.

Further evidence of the complicity of intellectuals in genocide and their foreknowledge of events emerges in the testimony of Predrag Finci, a professor of philosophy from the University of Sarajevo, who happened to be of Jewish origin. From London, he wrote of the strange disappearance of his Serbian colleagues from Sarajevo, immediately preceding the Serbian attacks on the Bosnian capital:

> I was a witness in Sarajevo (where I spent the first 6 months of the war) how many of my colleagues of Serb origin left Sarajevo silently few days before the war broke out. They all found jobs in Serbia, where, like all polite guests, [they] silently approve of every deed of their hosts. One of them, an expert on Kant, is a minister in the Serb Republic.. . . I am pleased to say that my Sarajevo colleagues were not caught in the web of daily politics, even in the most difficult of times. They did not become (at least a majority of them) the propagandists of the war ideology, they remained the advocates of freedom and fighters for a multicultural and multiethnic society, instead.[67]

As they did in World War II, a critical mass of Serbian intellectuals have willingly embraced and promoted Nazi-like ideology, exerted political leadership, and mobilized the masses to a genocidal campaign. With the backing of Serbia's intelligentsia—among whom there is precious little dissent—the Belgrade regime has fostered the "emigration psychosis" advocated by Vaša Čubrilović in the 1930s.[68] Tragically, five decades after the Holocaust and Nazism, Čubrilović's ideas have remained alive in Belgrade.

NOTES

1. The memorandum by the Serbian Academy of Science and Art (known by its Serbian acronym, SANU) was issued on September 29, 1986, and distributed to the Serbian emigration in 1987. See Serbian Academy of Science and Art, *Nacrt memoranduma Srpske akademije nauka u Beogradu* (Framework for the memorandum of the Serbian Academy of Science and Art in Belgrade) (Srpske

narodne odbrane [Serbian National Defense], 1987). For a version in the Latin alphabet, see " 'Memorandum' SANU (grupa akademika Srpske akademije nauka i umetnosti o aktuelnim društvenim pitanjima u našoj zemlji)," in *Izvori veliko-srpske agresije* (The roots of Greater Serbian aggression), ed. Bože Čović (Zagreb: August Cesarec and Školska knjiga, 1991), 256–300. A typewritten English translation is available from the Library of Congress, "Suppressed Memorandum of Members of Serbian Academy of Arts and Sciences SANU September, 1986," published by the Serbian Literary Association. See also "The SANU 'Memorandum' (a Group of Members of the Serbian Academy of Arts and Sciences on Topical Social Issues of Yugoslavia)," in *Roots of Serbian Aggression,* ed. Bože Čović (Zagreb: Centar za strane jezike, 1993), 289–337.

2. For the full Serbian text, see Vasa Čubrilović, "Iseljavanje Arnauta" (The expulsion of the Albanians), in *Izvori velikosrpske agresije,* ed. Čović, 106–24, which cites as its source the Military-Historical Institute (Belgrade), Archive of the Royal Yugoslav Army, file 2, document 4, box 69. For an English translation, see Vasa Čubrilović, "Deportation of Albanians," in *Roots of Serbian Aggression,* ed. Čović, 114–34.

3. See Zvonko Ivanković-Vonta, *Hebrang* (Zagreb: Bibliotheca Scientia Yugoslavica, 1988), 25; Čović, *Roots of Serbian Aggression,* 21 n.18; Mark Almond, *Europe's Backyard War: The War in the Balkans* (London: Heinemann, 1994), 194–95.

4. See Roy Gutman, "Serb Author Lit Balkan Powder Keg," *Newsday,* June 28, 1992, 1.

5. Ibid. It is notable that Ćosić was not censured for his ultranationalist remarks. To place this in perspective, even mild expressions of "nationalism" among non-Serbs was severely punished by the Yugoslav regime. For example, the mere possession of a "Croatian" dictionary—rather than a "Serbo-Croatian" dictionary—was reason for imprisonment in Yugoslavia.

6. Ibid.

7. Almond, op. cit., 206.

8. Ibid.

9. Foreign Broadcast Information Service, "Celebrations Highlight Kosovo Battle Anniversary," *Eastern European Daily Report,* July 3, 1989, 83. See also Almond, op. cit., 197.

10. "Vidovdanska poruka *Glasa Crkve:* Predlog srpskog crkvenonacionalnog programa" (The St. Vitus Day message of *The Voice of the Church:* The proposed Serbian Church National Program), *Glas crkve* (The voice of the church) (Valjevo, Serbia) 17, no. 3 (1989): 5–6 (entire document spans pp. 3–11). For excerpts in English, see Foreign Broadcast Information Service, "Commentary on Serbian Church Reform Document," *Eastern European Daily Report,* August 4, 1989, 42–44.

11. Sabrina Petra Ramet, "Priests and Rebels: The Contributions of the Chris-

tian Churches to the Revolutions in Eastern Europe," *Mediterranean Quarterly: A Journal of Global Issues* 2, no. 4 (fall 1991): 108.

12. Blaine Harden, "Croatia Charges Army Shadows Its Officials: Police Arming for Showdown with Serbia," *Washington Post,* January 19, 1991, A10; idem, "Croatia Agrees to Demobilize Police: Showdown with Yugoslav Army Averted by Compromise," *Washington Post,* January 27, 1991, A14.

13. An understated and dispassionate account of this and numerous other massacres during 1991–92 appears in a useful and rather comprehensive volume of testimony and documentation prepared by the Croatian government. See Ivan Kostović and Miloš Judaš, eds., *Mass Killing and Genocide in Croatia 1991–92: A Book of Evidence* (Zagreb: Hrvatska sveučilišna naklada, 1992), 225.

14. Jim Fish, "Serbia Keeps Croatian from Top Post: Deadlock of Collective Presidency Adds to Yugoslav Turmoil," *Washington Post,* May 16, 1991, A27; Celestine Bohlen, "Rotation of Yugoslav Leaders Blocked by Dominant Region," *New York Times,* May 17, 1991, A1.

15. The Krajina is a sparsely populated rural region containing 4 percent of the population of Croatia, according to the Yugoslav census of March 1991. Seventy-five percent of the Krajina population (roughly 193,000) was Serbian, and 75 percent of the Serbs of Croatia lived outside the Krajina. For the official 1991 Yugoslav census figures, see Jasna Crkvenčić-Bojić, ed., *Popis stanovništva, domaćinstava, stanova i poljoprivrednih gospodarstava 31. ožujak 1991* [Census of Population, Households, Apartments, and Farms, March 31, 1991] (Zagreb: Republicki zavod za statistiku Republike Hrvatske, 1992).

16. During the Croatian plebiscite of May 19, 1991, 86 percent of eligible voters participated and 94 percent decided that Croatia "as a sovereign and independent country which guarantees cultural autonomy and all civic rights to Serbs and members of other nationalities in Croatia, may with other republics join a confederation of sovereign states." See Chuck Sudetic, "Croatia Votes for Sovereignty and Confederation," *New York Times,* May 20, 1991, A3.

17. Jim Fish, "Yugoslav Army Upended in Slovenia: Takeover Begun Leisurely Becomes Albatross for Privileged Force," *Washington Post,* July 2, 1991, A1; Blaine Harden, "Slovenia Nears Independence as Croatia Faces Civil War: Slovenes See Army Pullout as Key Step to Freedom," *Washington Post,* July 20, 1991, A1.

18. The ideology of an ethnically homogeneous Greater Serbia was codified in 1844 by Ilija Garašanin (1812–1874), an influential minister in the Principality of Serbia under the crown of Prince Aleksandar Karadjordjević. His official memorandum, *Načertanije* (Outline), was a blueprint for the creation of Greater Serbia through the conquest of lands inhabited by Bulgarians, Macedonians, Albanians, Montenegrins, Bosnians, Hungarians, and Croats. *Načertanije* first appeared in unabridged published form in M. Vučković, "Program spoljne politike Ilije Garašanina na koncu 1844 godine" (Foreign policy program of Ilija

Garašanin at the end of 1844), *Delo* (Work) (Belgrade) 38 (1906): 321–36. See Paul N. Hehn, "The Origins of Modern Pan-Serbism: The 1844 Načertanije of Ilija Garašanin: An Analysis and Translation," *East European Quarterly* 9, no. 2 (1975): 153–71. In June 1941, Stevan Moljević, an advisor to Chetnik leader Draža Mihailović, issued a plan for an ethnically homogeneous Greater Serbia, with an expanded Slovenia, rewarded with Croatian territory. See Stevan Moljević, "Homogena Srbja" (Homogeneous Serbia), in *Izvori velikosrpske agresije,* ed. Čović, 141–47, esp. Moljević's original map reproduced on 146. For an English translation, see Stevan Moljević, "Homogeneous Serbia," in *Roots of Serbian Aggression,* ed. Čović, 151–58, esp. map on 157.

19. Gian Paolo Rossetti and Gigi Zazzeri, "Here Are the New Warlords" (in Italian), *Europeo* (Italy), no. 29 (July 19, 1991): 22.

20. Chuck Sudetic, "Yugoslav Battles Rage on Eve of Talks," *New York Times,* November 5, 1991, A3; Laura Silber, "Serbs, Croats Press War of Words, Guns," *Washington Post,* November 6, 1991, A26; David Binder, "Unified Yugoslavia Goal of U.S. Policy," *New York Times,* July 1, 1991, A6; idem, "U.S. Voices Regret on Yugoslav Crisis: Plans to Ignore the Secession Attempts by Croatian and Slovenian Republics," *New York Times,* June 27, 1991, A10.

21. Alan Riding, "European Community Freezes Arms Sales and Aid," *New York Times,* July 6, 1991, L4.

22. John M. Goshko, "UN Imposes Arms Embargo on Yugoslavia," *Washington Post,* September 26, 1991, A1; Marian Houk, "UN Backs Yugoslav Call for Embargo," *Christian Science Monitor,* September 27, 1991, 4.

23. See John Tagliabue, "Serbs in Croatian Cities Are Quiet and Invisible," *New York Times,* September 6, 1991, A14. For the official 1991 Yugoslav census figures for the Republic of Croatia, see Crkvenčić-Bojić, op. cit.

24. The first hostilities were initiated by Serbian authorities in 1989 in the Albanian-populated province of Kosovo. Overlooking these events, however, some observers date the war to the 1991 invasion of Slovenia and Croatia by the Serbian-led Yugoslav National Army. For a chronology of Serbia's preparations for war in the 1990s, see Patrick Moore, "Former Yugoslavia: Prospects and Problems," *RFE/RL Research Report,* 1, no. 50 (December 18, 1992): 32–37.

25. Amnesty International, *Yugoslavia: Torture and Deliberate and Arbitrary Killings in War Zones* (New York, 1991); idem, *Yugoslavia: Further Reports of Torture and Deliberate and Arbitrary Killings in War Zones* (New York, 1992).

26. Stephen Engelberg, "Serbs Settle In Where Croats Decided to Retreat," *New York Times,* November 30, 1991, A4; Blaine Harden, "Observers Accuse Yugoslav Army: Report Charges Campaign of Violence Designed to Drive Out Croats," *Washington Post,* January 17, 1992; idem, "Serbia Plans Resettlement of Croatian Region," *Washington Post,* November 25, 1991, A14; John F. Burns, "The Demographics of Exile: Victorious Serbs Repopulate Croatian Villages," *New York Times,* May 10, 1992, A3.

27. Amnesty International, *Bosnia-Herzegovina: Gross Abuses of Basic Human Rights* (New York, 1992); idem, *Bosnia-Herzegovina: "Rana u duši": A Wound to the Soul* (New York, 1993); idem, *Bosnia-Herzegovina: Rape and Sexual Abuse by Armed Forces* (New York, 1993); Helsinki Watch, *War Crimes in Bosnia-Hercegovina,* 2 vols. (New York, 1992–93).

28. "The Situation of Human Rights in the Territory of the Former Yugoslavia Submitted by Mr. Tadeusz Mazowiecki, Special Rapporteur of the Commission on Human Rights," UN Security Council document S/25341, February 26, 1993, 7; Stephen Engelberg, "Muslims Tell of Serbs' 'Ethnic Cleansing,' " *New York Times,* July 31, 1992, A3.

29. Roy Gutman, *A Witness to Genocide: The 1993 Pulitzer Prize-Winning Dispatches on the "Ethnic Cleansing" of Bosnia* (New York: Macmillan, 1993), 93.

30. Tadeuz *[sic]* Mazowiecki, "Witness to Horror: 'Ethnic cleansing' Threatens the Concept of Human Rights Everywhere," *Washington Post,* November 29, 1992, C7.

31. Each of eight submissions is a Security Council document entitled "Former Yugoslavia: Grave Breaches of the Fourth Geneva Convention . . . in Accordance with Paragraph 5 of Resolution 771 (1992) and Paragraph 1 of Resolution 780 (1992)." The U.S. submissions are dated September 23, 1992; October 22, 1992; November 5, 1992; December 7, 1992; January 26, 1993; March 1, 1993; April 9, 1993; and June 17, 1993. Under the Geneva Conventions, the prosecution of "grave breaches" is mandatory.

32. Data analyzed by Henry L. de Zeng IV, historical researcher, Orlando, Florida. See also Gutman, *Witness to Genocide,* 169.

33. Roger Cohen, "CIA Report on Bosnia Blames Serbs for 90% of the War Crimes," *New York Times,* March 9, 1995, A1.

34. The UN Convention on Genocide was adopted as UN General Assembly Resolution 260A (III), December 9, 1948. See Lawrence J. LeBlanc, *The United States and the Genocide Convention* (Durham: Duke University Press, 1991), 245–49. For a text of the definition of genocide, see appendix 1 in this volume.

35. Peter W. Galbraith and Michelle Maynard, "The Ethnic Cleansing of Bosnia-Hercegovina," Staff Report to the Committee on Foreign Relations, U.S. Senate, Washington, DC, August 1992; " 'Ethnic Cleansing'—And a Cry for Help from Bosnia," *Newsweek,* August 17, 1992, 16–27; Tom Post et al., "A Pattern of Rape: A Torrent of Wrenching First-person Testimonies Tells of a New Serb Atrocity: Systematic Sexual Abuse," *Newsweek,* January 11, 1993, 32–36; idem, "Bosnia: Getting Tough at Last," *Newsweek,* May 10, 1993, 18–31; "Shame in Our Time, in Bosnia" (editorial), *New York Times,* May 21, 1992, A28; John F. Burns, "Bosnian Survivors Tell of Mass Ethnic Killings . . . Comparisons with Nazis Are Drawn as Attacks Rage in the Republic," *New York Times,* June 21, 1992, A1; idem, "Bosnian Strife Cuts Old Bridges of Trust: Ancient Ties of

Coexistence Are Broken by 'Ethnic Purification,' " *New York Times,* May 22, 1992, A1; Laura Silber, " 'The Street Was a River of Blood': Twenty Die in Sarajevo Shelling: EC Votes Yugoslavia Sanctions," *Washington Post,* May 28, 1992, A1; Gutman, "Serb Author"; idem, " 'Ethnic Cleansing' Yugoslavs Try to Deport 1,800 Muslims to Hungary," *Newsday,* July 3, 1992, 5; idem, "Prisoners of Serbia's War: Tales of Hunger, Torture at Camp in North Bosnia," *Newsday,* July 19, 1992, 7; idem, "Croats Deported in Freight Cars: Witnesses Report Some Deaths," *Newsday,* July 21, 1992, 4; idem, "If Only They Could Flee: Muslims, Croats Held in City," *Newsday,* July 26, 1992, 4; idem, "Death Camps: Serbs Imprison Thousands for Slaughter, Starvation," *Newsday,* August 2, 1992, 5; idem, "Gulag: The War against Muslim and Croat Civilians: Former Inmates of Serbian Forces Describe Atrocities," *Newsday,* August 3, 1992, 4; idem, "Serbs' Death Camps: How the Guards Chose the Victims," *Newsday,* August 5, 1992, 4; idem, "Bosnia Rape Horror," *Newsday,* August 9, 1992, 4; idem, "Mass Rape: Muslims Recall Serb Attacks," *Newsday,* August 23, 1992, 5; idem, "Deadly Transfer: Many Reported Killed, Missing in Move from Serb Camp," *Newsday,* August 26, 1992, 3; Roger Cohen, "Ex-Guard for Serbs Tells of Grisly 'Cleansing' Camp," *New York Times,* August 1, 1994, A1; idem, "Bosnian Camp Survivors Describe Random Death," *New York Times,* August 2, 1994, A1; Steve Coll, "In the Shadow of the Holocaust," *Washington Post Magazine,* September 25, 1994, 8. See also Gutman, *Witness to Genocide.*

36. Quoted from Melanie McDonagh, "My Last Drink with Condemned Men," *Evening Standard* (London), February 23, 1993. See also Noel Malcolm, *Bosnia: A Short History* (New York: New York University Press, 1994), 217.

37. Amnesty International, *Bosnia-Herzegovina: Rape and Sexual Abuse*; Gutman, *Witness to Genocide*; idem, "Mass Rape"; idem, "Bosnia Rape Horror"; Post et al., op. cit., 26–30.

38. That the rape conducted by Serbian forces is genocidal has been eloquently argued; see Catharine A. MacKinnon, "Rape, Genocide, and Women's Human Rights," *Harvard Women's Law Journal* 17 (spring 1994): 5–16; and Gutman, *Witness to Genocide,* 68. As the experience of women during the Holocaust provides insight into the genocidal rape of the 1990s, the reader is referred to the thoughtful, pioneering work of Joan Ringelheim, cited in Carol Rittner and John K. Roth, *Different Voices: Women and the Holocaust* (New York: Paragon House, 1993), 373–407.

39. See Gutman, *Witness to Genocide,* 68; Post et al., op. cit., 32–36.

40. András Riedlmayer, "The War on People and the War on Culture," *New Combat: A Journal of Reason and Resistance* 3 (autumn 1994): 16–19; idem, "Erasing the Past: The Destruction of Libraries and Archives in Bosnia-Herzegovina," *Middle East Studies Association Bulletin* 29, no. 1 (July 1995): 7–11; Helsinki Watch, "War Crimes in Bosnia-Hercegovina: UN Cease-Fire Won't Help Banja Luka," *Human Rights Watch/Helsinki* 6, no. 8 (June 1994): 15–16; Council

of Europe, Parliamentary Assembly, "Information Report on the Destruction by War of the Cultural Heritage in Croatia and Bosnia-Herzegovina," reports 1–5 (February 2, 1993–April 12, 1994) available as Assembly Documents, nos. 6756, 6869, 6904, and 7070, from the Secretary, Committee on Culture and Education, Conseil d'Europe, B.P. 431, Strasbourg Cedex F-67006, France. For an earlier report of the Serbs' systematic destruction of non-Serbian religious monuments, see Roy Gutman, "Unholy War: Serbs Target Culture, Heritage of Bosnia's Muslims," *Newsday,* September 2, 1992, 3. See also Robert Fisk, Waging War on History: In Former Yugoslavia, Whole Cultures Are Being Obliterated," *Independent* (London), June 20 1994, 18.

41. Chuck Sudetic, "Observers Blame Serb-Led Army for Escalating War in Croatia," *New York Times,* December 3, 1991, A8; Blaine Harden, "EC Withdraws Ambassadors from Belgrade: Serbia Rebuked Again on Bosnian War," *Washington Post,* May 12, 1992, A14; idem, "U.S. Joins EC in Recalling Envoy from Belgrade: Serbian Aggression in Bosnia Cited as International Countermeasures Take Shape," *Washington Post,* May 13, 1992, A25; Jeri Laber and Ivana Nizich [of Helsinki Watch], "Milošević's Land Grab," *Washington Post,* May 25, 1992, A25.

42. Blaine Harden, "The Enemy around Us: A Serb View: State Media, Age-Old Traditions Fuel Sense of Victimization," *Washington Post,* May 7, 1992, A33; "The World Watches Murder" (editorial), *New York Times,* June 24, 1992, A20.

43. Order of the International Court of Justice, April 8, 1993, concerning "Application of the Convention on the Prevention and Punishment of the Crime of Genocide (Bosnia and Herzegovina v. Yugoslavia [Serbia and Montenegro])," Security Council document S/25686, dated April 29, 1993; Stephen Kinzer, "Belgrade Is Urged to Control Serbs: World Court Asks Yugoslavia to Work against Genocide by Its Allies in Bosnia," *New York Times,* April 9, 1993, A5; Eugene Robinson, "World Court Orders Belgrade to Prevent 'Genocide' in Bosnia," *Washington Post,* April 9, 1993, A19.

44. The legal basis for the establishment of the tribunal, its jurisdiction, and its organization is defined in UN document S/25704, dated May 3, 1993, entitled "Report of the Secretary-General Pursuant to Paragraph 2 of Security Council Resolution 808 (1993)." By Resolution 808 of February 22, 1993, the Security Council decided that "an international [war crimes] tribunal shall be established for the prosecution of persons responsible for serious violations of international humanitarian law committed in the territory of the former Yugoslavia since 1991."

45. See Roger Cohen, "Tribunal to Cite Bosnia Serb Chief as War Criminal," *New York Times,* April 24, 1995, A1.

46. As cited in Patricia Forestier, "Genocide! How the Barbarities of 'Ethnic Cleansing' Were Spawned by Psychiatry," *Freedom,* May 1993, 11.

47. Ibid.

48. Ibid.

49. Ibid.

50. Mirko Grmek, Marc Gjidara, and Neven Šimac, *Le nettoyage ethnique: Documents historiques sur une idéologie serbe* (Paris: Fayard, 1993), 312.

51. Malcolm, op. cit., 217.

52. Forestier, op. cit., 11.

53. Ibid., 6, 11, 34.

54. See the chapter by Brad Blitz in this volume.

55. "Final Report of the Commission of Experts Established Pursuant to Security Council Resolution 780 (1992)," UN Security Council document S/674, May 27, 1994, 51–55.

56. The testimony of Pero Popović, a former guard of the Sušica camp in Vlasenica, is of particular value for establishing the chain of command to the Belgrade leadership. He has been granted political asylum in the United States and given immunity to prosecution in exchange for testimony to the War Crimes Tribunal in the Hague. See Cohen, "Ex-Guard for Serbs"; idem, "Bosnian Camp Survivors."

57. Two apologists for the Belgrade regime deserve special mention: former UNPROFOR General Lewis MacKenzie and European Community "peace talks" negotiator Lord David Owen. For their own respective reasons, both have emphasized the moral equivalency of victim and aggressor. MacKenzie, after leaving his post in Sarajevo, emerged on a speaking tour in the United States and Canada paid for by the Serbian lobbying organization SerbNet. See the chapter by Brad Blitz in this volume. Owen actually instructed Cherif Bassiouni, the chairman of the UN Commission of Experts, to "go easy" on the Serbian leadership and to find all sides equally guilty, so that the "peace negotiations" could go forward. See R. C. Longworth, "Peace vs. Justice: DePaul Professor Fears UN Sabotaged his Inquiry into Yugoslav War Crimes," *Chicago Tribune,* September 2, 1994, 1. Bassiouni's testimony of April 4, 1995, before the CSCE (Helsinki Commission) makes clear that UN authorities systematically attempted to sabotage his investigations.

58. Testimony of Serbian death camp survivors, as given to the Rape/Genocide Law Project, Hamden, CT.

59. Norman Cigar, "The Serbo-Croatian War, 1991: Political and Military Dimensions," *Journal of Strategic Studies* (London) 16, no. 3 (1993): 297–338.

60. Mary Battiata, "Serbian Guerrilla Camps Operate inside Croatia: Serbs Train inside Croatia for Civil War," *Washington Post,* July 22, 1991, A1; Stephen Engelberg, "Serbia Sending Supplies to Compatriots in Croatia," *New York Times,* July 27, 1991, A3; John Kifner, "Yugoslav Army Reported Fighting in Bosnia to Help Serbian Forces," *New York Times,* January 27, 1994, A1.

61. Battiata, op. cit.

62. Forestier, op. cit., 8.

63. *Free Inquiry* (quarterly journal of the Council for Democratic and Secular Humanism) 13, no. 2 (spring 1993): 2, 67.

64. Radovan Čolević, "Socijalisti: Akademik Mihailo Marković: Angažman je danas etički imperativ" (The socialists: The academician Mihailo Marković: Engagement is an ethical imperative today), *Stav* (Attitude) (Novi Sad, Serbia), November 16, 1990, 9.

65. Mihailo Marković and Nikola Milošević, "Mogu li zajedno slobodna i jednakost" (Can freedom and equality exist together), *Nedeljna borba* (Sunday struggle) (Belgrade), February 23–24, 1991, 6.

66. Ljiljana Habjanović-Đurović, "Revolucionar u ruralnoj kontrarevoluciji: Zoran Đinđić, jedna beogradska prica" ([A revolutionary in a rural counterrevolution: Zoran Đinđić, a Belgrade story), *Duga* (Belgrade), May 28–June 10, 1994, 17.

67. Predrag Finci, *Proceedings and Addresses of the American Philosophical Association* 68, no. 2 (November 1994): 84–85.

68. Čubrilović, "Iseljavanje Arnauta," 106–24; idem, "Deportation of Albanians," 114–34.

Brendan Simms

Bosnia: The Lessons of History?

> And so it came that the high priests, scribes and phari-
> sees assembled at a town they called Geneva and they
> held council there on how they could best abandon the
> nation of Bosnia. They were led by Thorwald and by
> David, Lord of the fantasy land of Owenia. And the
> Bosnian presidency saw that its hour had struck and
> spake: "My soul is sad unto death." And they said unto
> the men assembled: "Truly, truly I say unto you, one of
> you here will betray me." But they were wrong, for not
> one, but all of them would betray Bosnia. And behold!
> Britain whispered to David, Lord of Owenia, "Betray it
> and the Nobel peace prize will be yours." Germany and
> the United States said: "What has it done, we can find
> no fault with it?" Britain and France however said: "It is
> better for a whole nation to die, than that we would all
> be dragged into a hellhole." And they let it be bound
> and handed it over so that it should be crucified.
> — Brendan Simms, "Bosnian Passion"

Until comparatively recently, the idea that one could learn from history
was axiomatic. "Histories," Francis Bacon once wrote "make men
wise." But the closer we get to the present the more skepticism takes
over. From Hegel's familiar, almost clichéd dictum, "The one thing one
learns from history is that nobody ever learns anything from history," it is
but a short step to Alan Taylor's pessimistic belief that all we learn from
the mistakes of history is how to make new ones. In our day it is
customary for historians to play safe, to insist that history may inform or
edify us, but never provide us with lessons for the future. The intellectual
credentials for this attitude are impressive. Jacob Burckhardt tells us that

history makes us not clever for today, but wise forever. Sir Herbert Butterfield questioned whether historians were "any wiser than the rest of their contemporaries on political matters." Indeed, Butterfield saw real danger in the manipulation of history to provide "patterns which we can immediately transpose into the context of contemporary politics."[1]

And yet, if we scratch the surface, we find that the notion that history has much to teach us is a persistent one. In *The Use of History,* A. L. Rowse writes that "Though you may hardly say that there are historical laws of the regularity and exactness of the laws of physical science, there are generalizations possible, of something like a statistical character." Rejecting the idea that "history never repeats itself," he went on to say that "there is no one rhythm or plot in history but there are rhythms, plots, patterns, even repetitions. So that it is possible to make generalizations and to draw lessons."[2] Similar views can be found among professional historians. In *The Practice of History* the late Sir Geoffrey Elton writes, "Its lessons are not straightforward didactic precepts, either instructions for action (the search for parallels to a given situation) or a universal norm." "Nevertheless," he continues, "a sound acquaintance with the prehistory of a situation or problem does illumine them and does assist in making present decisions; and though history cannot prophesy, it can often make reasonable predictions."[3] Historians of international relations are particularly prone to drawing lessons from history. Norman Rich even subtitled his book about the Crimean wars *A Cautionary Tale.* Nor did he leave any doubt at whom his work was directed: to "the future leaders of the world—in other words, to students—in the hope that they and all others interested in international affairs will find this cautionary—as did the author."[4]

In short, the case for and against the lessons of history is fairly finely balanced. Perhaps the last word among the authorities should be left to the great high priest of whiggery, G. M. Trevelyan. Trevelyan, who had a great deal more sense than he is often given credit for, once said, "History repeats itself and history never repeats itself are about equally true. The question in any given case, is which part of history is going to repeat itself."[5]

This goes to the heart of the matter. What is important is not whether history is repeating itself in Europe today, but *which part* of history is doing so. Of course, one could still criticize my argument on the a priori basis that there are no lessons to be drawn from history. But if one accepts that historical analogies can be helpful, then the proof of the pudding will be in the eating. In that case the question must be, do the analogies convince? It is only after hearing out the comparisons that one will be able to judge whether this essay does more than convert the precious metal of historical understanding into the dross of political polemic.

• • •

But before going on to discuss the historical parallels to the Bosnian horrors, we should call to mind the various interpretations of the war and the facts on which they are based.

1. The first is the Serb view. It is that this is a war of self-defense for a Serbian people haunted by a fear of a repeat of the genocide suffered at the hands of the Croat puppet fascist state during World War II. On this reading the Serbian people are the victims of a long-thought-out Croat-German-Vatican-Muslim plot to destroy the old Yugoslavia and erect in its place either a Fourth Reich, a rerun of the genocidal Croat puppet fascist state, an Iranian-style Muslim theocracy, or some bizarre combination of all three.

2. The second view is the standard view of Western governments and more specifically, the view of the British government. This is that the conflict in Yugoslavia is essentially a civil war, though an unusually tragic and vicious one, for which all sides are more or less equally to blame. While there is general agreement that the Serbs have committed the most atrocities, there is also a broad consensus that the conflict involves no vital Western interest and thus does not justify the use of Western troops to check Serbian aggression.

3. The third view is one that I share. This view holds that, whatever opportunistic acts of Croat aggression may have taken place subsequently, the root cause of the war lies in a psychologically and logistically well prepared program of Serbian aggression.

• • •

In the face of the greatest European upheaval since 1945, involving an enormous displacement of population (at least 2.5 million at the latest tally), more than 100,000 deaths, most of them not battle casualties but in consequence of deliberate terror accompanying the practice of ethnic cleansing, mass rape, expulsion, concentration camps, and integral nationalism run riot, it is hardly surprising that commentators have resorted to historical analogy in an effort to find their bearings.

Predictably, the specter of the Third Reich, the Holocaust, and appeasement was frequently invoked. Lady Thatcher warned in December 1992
of the risk of a second holocaust. Mark Thompson speaks of the "final
solution" of Bosnia-Herzegovina.[6] The deportation of the Muslim population in railway boxcars led the American journalist Roy Gutman to speak
of "Third Reich practices." He compares the fate of Muslims to that of
the Armenians and Milošević to Hitler. Citing George Santayana's dictum
that those who disregard the past are bound to repeat it, Gutman argued
that the lesson of World War II is that there must never be genocide in
Europe again.[7] Elie Wiesel made the link between the two crimes clear
when in an address at the opening of the Holocaust Memorial in Washington, D.C., he rebuked Clinton for his inaction over Bosnia. The Labour
M.P. Malcolm Wicks made the same point in April 1993 when he wrote,
"Yesterday in Washington the Holocaust Memorial was opened. The
timing could not have been more momentous. Will its opening challenge
us to prevent a Bosnian holocaust, or mock our pretensions that we have
learned this century's most important lesson?"[8] Perhaps the most plain-
tive of such calls was that of Brenda Katten, chairman of the Zionist
Federation: "As Jews, we are quite horrified at what is going on: we lost
a lot of our people in the 1930s because the gates were closed on us.
What is sad, is that we don't learn from history."

This analysis was not shared by the majority of commentators, though
their sense of historical analogy was no less acute. Instead, they argued
that history showed that only nation-states "worked," that Bosnia was
unviable on this count and was thus doomed to fail. Others argued that
history had shown intervention always made things worse; that it led to
open-ended commitments, ended in Vietnam traumas, and achieved no
purpose. Others still evinced a deep-seated abhorrence for all things
Balkan, and adapted Bismarck's bon mot to argue that the Balkan peoples
were not worth the bones of a single British grenadier. Above all, these
pundits rejected analogies with the Third Reich, Hitler, the Holocaust,
and appeasement. "Comparisons with Hitler are intoxicating and should
be avoided," wrote Conor Cruise O'Brien. He went on to state, indisput-
ably, that "It was by seeing Nasser as Hitler that Anthony Eden got Britain
into Suez."[9] In the *Sunday Telegraph* Frank Johnson argued that history
taught us to stay out of the Balkans.[10] Allan Massie saw similar dangers
in intervention.[11] "Russia," he wrote, "might abandon sanctions against
Serbia and come to the defense of its traditional ally: shades of 1914."
Before his conversion to the cause of intervention, Andrew Marr in

the *Independent* spoke of the pro-interventionists as "Mr. Gladstone's inheritors," referring to the Bulgarian agitation of 1876;[12] more of this presently. One of those warning of a new Vietnam was the war photographer Don McCullin: "What most people seem to forget about Bosnia is rule one: read history. Certainly it's got the makings of another Vietnam where you just tie up thousands of troops and lose in the end."

Other more imaginative parallels can be drawn. If Timothy Garton Ash spoke of the period 1989–90 as a rerun of 1848, another "springtime of the nations," the years 1991–93 can be compared to 1849–50 with the unsettling discovery of incompatibility of liberal revolutionary national aims in Transylvania, Posnania, and elsewhere. Another persuasive parallel might be with the immediate aftermath of World War I. The post-hegemonic chaos of the years 1918–23, in which the smaller European and Near Eastern states struggled for the Habsburg, tsarist, and Ottoman inheritances, bears a close resemblance to the struggle for the Soviet succession we are witnessing today. Once again we have turmoil in Moscow, breakaway movements on the former Soviet periphery and in the Balkans. We have a host of new countries with recondite currencies. We have, once again, worrying signs of an American withdrawal from Europe, a hint of neo-isolationism even. Disturbing though these signs may be, the essential message of such a comparison is a comforting one. Because though there was much unpleasantness in the years 1918–23, things eventually sorted themselves out. Then as now the lesson seems to be not to get involved, for the two most spectacular interventions after World War I, the expeditions to Russia and the Chanak crisis, were notorious failures. So perhaps it should hardly surprise us to find the Greek-Turkish population exchanges of the 1920s, which involved millions of people and enormous human suffering, being touted in UN circles as a model for Bosnia.

But numerous though the possible historical parallels may be, it is the Balkan crisis of 1876–78 and the events of the 1930s to which commentators and politicians return again and again.

• • •

In 1875 the peasants of Bosnia rose against their Ottoman rulers. Against the hopes and expectations of the British government the Turks were unable to put the insurrection down quickly. During the following year, the revolt spread to Bulgaria. If the struggle in Bosnia had shown scant regard for humanity, the Bulgarian insurrection soon degenerated into massacre, as Turkish irregulars, the so-called bashi-bazouks, were loosed on the largely defenseless Christian population. This provoked an outcry in Britain where a vociferous section of the public, led by the prime minister, William Gladstone, began to demand intervention, or at least an end to the traditional pro-Turkish and anti-Russian policy of Disraeli's Conservative administration. The parallels with the present day are compelling. It is more or less the same geographic area that is at issue, although the roles of victim and perpetrator in the public mind have been neatly reversed. If in 1876 it was the hapless Orthodox peasantry being raped and massacred by bestial Turkish soldiery, today it is the Muslim civilians who were at the mercy of crazed Serbian Chetniks. The reaction of the British government and the Foreign Office is also similar.[13] In 1876 they urged the Turks to stamp out the revolt quickly and their misgivings about Turkish policy stemmed not from the casualties involved but from the length of time the Ottomans were taking to get to grips with the insurrection. Today such feelings are more subterranean but they are nonetheless widespread in government circles. As for the Foreign Office, the scarcely concealed desire that the Serbs should "get on with it" in Bosnia is attested by many leaks and the general thrust of British policy.[14] There is another striking parallel, namely, the efforts of the British government to establish some kind of moral equivalence between victim and perpetrator. In 1876 the undersecretary at the Foreign Office, Bourke, spoke of the insurrection as being "fomented by foreigners (i.e. the Russians)" and "how sanguinary were the intentions and acts of the insurgent Christians." The *Daily Telegraph* spoke of the "wholesale massacre of Moslems whenever found, and they did not fail to ill-treat both women and children.. . . They point to their bleeding little ones—did they remember humanity when they fell upon the Turk? Their villages are in flames, and they protest, yet they cheerfully set Ottoman hamlets in a blaze." Much in the same way the Foreign Office and the British government have wasted no opportunity today in drawing attention to the fact that there are no innocent parties in the Yugoslav conflict.[15] At the popular level this argument was an effective one, for nobody likes to be accused of gullibility or failing to understand what is, in another classic Foreign Office phrase, a "very complex situation." In the media this view found expression in headlines such as "No Nice Guys Left [in Bosnia] as Patience Runs Out" or "They Are All Baddies at Odds in Bosnia."[16]

But perhaps the most arresting similarity between the two phenomena lies in the extraordinary public debate generated by the massacres and the response of the British government to such pressures. If the Bulgarian agitation was, in Richard Shannon's words, "by far the greatest and most illuminating revelation of the moral susceptibility of the High Victorian public conscience," then the Bosnian agitation of 1992–93 is the nearest equivalent in modern times, the closest our jaded and compassion-fatigued age will ever get to the moral fervor of Gladstonian liberalism.

Unsurprisingly, there is also a sense of déjà vu about the anti-interventionist camp. If in 1876 Disraeli and others pointed to the British interest in upholding Turkish power in Europe against the Russians, today Hurd, Hogg, and Rifkind justify their passivity in terms of the absence of any vital British interest in the stability of the Balkans.[17] There is the same defiance, almost willful cynicism in the face of the outrage of what they regard as the chattering classes, the strictures of facile utopians ignorant of the realities of power politics. Nor is this all. There is also the same strange specter of alliances cutting right across the whole party-political and cultural spectrum. In 1876, for example, strong support for the Bulgarian agitation came from Gladstone and many Liberals, from the Welsh, Anglo-Catholics (Puseyites), anti-Ultramontane Catholics (pro-Newmanites, anti-Manning and Wisemanites), from nonconformist ministers, and from a selection of newspapers and journals, including the *Methodist,* the *Church Review,* and the *Daily News.* Opposition to the agitation came from the *Daily Telegraph,* the Conservative Party, low church evangelicals in the Church of England (except Lord Shaftesbury), the pope and the English Roman Catholic church, Ireland, the Jewish community, and the poet Swinburne. Today, support for intervention in Bosnia has been expressed by Lord Callaghan, Michael Foot, and Lady Thatcher, writers such as Malcolm Bradbury, trade union grandees such as Bill Morris (general secretary of the Transport and General Workers' Union, Britain's biggest union), the trenchant anti-Marxist and political guru Edward Heath, and also Bruce Kent (vice president of the Campaign for Nuclear Disarmament), the Reverend Ian Paisley, Dennis Skinner, Tony Benn, Max Hastings, and Alan Clark. Then as now interventionist rhetoric has been seen as merely a vehicle for a political comeback. Thus Disraeli accused Gladstone, who had come out of retirement to lead the Bulgarian agitation, of "taking advantage of such sublime sentiments" and applying them "for the furtherance of their sinister ends." The *Times* spoke of Gladstone's "rhetorical inebriation."

Much the same has been said of Margaret Thatcher's sensational interview in April 1993, when she accused the British government of "complicity in genocide." It was then that Malcolm Rifkind dismissed her charges as "emotional nonsense." Finally, perhaps the Bosnian question will follow the nine days' wonder of the Bulgarian agitation into oblivion. Doubtless the British government takes comfort from the fact that the agitation fizzled out after the failure of the Straits conference of 1877 and was utterly negated by the surge of popular anti-Russian and pro-Turkish jingoism that followed the outbreak of the Russo-Turkish War of 1877–78.

But only perhaps. What if the Balkan crisis of today is more than just a flash in the pan? What if there is a clear Western and thus British national interest to be defended in the former Yugoslavia? [18]

• • •

Of course, there are obvious ways in which the current situation does not resemble the 1930s. First of all, Milošević is no Hitler. Though he may possess a fairly highly developed murderous instinct, it pales in comparison to the sheer scale of Hitler's crimes. Second, Serbia does not possess even a fraction of the strength, cohesion, and talent that made the Germans such a formidable threat to European peace in the 1930s and 1940s. Similarly, the horrors inflicted on the Muslim and Croat peoples of the former Yugoslavia cannot be equated with the planned and industrialized destruction of a whole people we call the Holocaust. Horrific though it is, "ethnic cleansing" is not strictly speaking "genocide" in the sense we mean when referring to the Third Reich, Cambodia, or Stalin's Russia. And yet the lack of an indisputable equivalence with the 1930s and 1940s should not surprise us. For if the parallel were *that* obvious, this paper would be redundant, for in that case we should be doing nothing else in Western Europe than discussing the Serbian threat night and day. In short, I am not saying that the drive for a Greater Serbia corresponds exactly to Nazi expansionism. What I am saying is that the Balkan massacres are, if not of genocidal dimensions, then easily the *nearest thing to genocide* in Europe we have witnessed since World War II. Similarly, the political culture and behavior of present-day Serbia are, if not the pure Nazism of Hitler's Germany, then at least the most frightening example of expansionism and integral nationalism run riot that we have seen for fifty years. Perhaps even more significant, the response of the West to this phenomenon bears more than a passing resemblance to the policy of appeasement adopted in the face of the German threat.

• • •

The Abyssinian war that began in 1935 has a strangely familiar air about it. As in the case of Bosnia, it was argued that Abyssinia should never have been admitted to the League of Nations in the first place. When the crisis blew, a British government review swiftly established that there were insufficient British interests at stake to justify resistance to Italian aggression; Britain, in particular Douglas Hurd and Malcolm Rifkind, take exactly the same line on Bosnia today. Then as now, comparatively few people in authority seemed to make the point that it was collective security, not the individual country, that was ultimately at issue.

As for the Spanish Civil War, the scope for comparison with contemporary events is practically unlimited. Franco's rebellion broke out in July 1936. Within a month France and Britain had imposed an arms embargo on both sides, much in the same way as the United Nations did in Yugoslavia at the end of 1991. In both cases the West treated the recognized and democratically elected government of an embattled state on an equal footing with the rebels. In both cases the effects were far from evenhanded, for in the Spanish instance Italian and German weapons were supplied to the rebels in an abundance that the Soviet Union did not match for the government side, while in Yugoslavia the embargo directly favored the Serbs who, having planned the war well in advance, had already helped themselves to most of the old federal armory. And in both cases the British and French governments have celebrated their policy as the height of responsibility. There are further similarities. For example, in April 1993, when Western governments still put on a pretense of concern for the Bosnian Muslims, a common argument advanced against a lifting of the arms embargo was that it would enable the Russians to supply the Serbs, as if they had not enough arms already. This was very redolent of the logic of Arthur Greenwood, deputy leader of the Labour Party in the 1930s, who said that for every weapon sent to Spain, the Germans and Italians would send fifty to the insurgents. He rather overlooked the fact that the Axis countries were already sending as much as they could. In 1936 the deputy speaker of the Spanish parliament made an impassioned appeal to the Labour Party conference to allow Spanish democrats to defend themselves; surely this was not too much to ask? In the same way, the Bosnian prime minister Haris Silajdžić became a familiar and forlorn figure on Western television, arguing that if the west was unwilling to defend the Bosnians against aggression and massacre they should at least allow them the opportunity of defending themselves.

Moving forward a couple of years to the Sudeten crisis of 1938, the parallels between the roles of Konrad Henlein and Radovan Karadžić as the respective leaders of a nationalist irredenta are obvious, although one may credit the latter with a much greater autonomy from his puppet master. Once again the British government was quick to state that there were no British interests at stake. In the words of the permanent undersecretary at the Foreign Office, Alec Cadogen "(the foreign policy) committee is unanimous that Czechoslovakia is not worth the bones of a single British grenadier. And they are quite right too." After the Czechs were abandoned to their fate it was not long before the customary vilification of the victim followed. According to Sir Thomas Inskip, minister for the coordination of defense, Czechoslovakia "was an unstable unit in Central Europe," and he "could see no reason why we should take any steps to maintain such a unit in being." The chancellor of the exchequer, Sir John Simon, pronounced that "Czechoslovakia was a modern invention, a very artificial creation with no real roots in the past." All this is highly redolent of the anti-Bosnian rhetoric of Western statesmen today: Bosnia has no historical justification (never mind its medieval statehood), is not a nation-state and thus not viable (never mind the Swiss example), should never have been recognized, and so on. It may be that these critics had a point, but only in the same way they would have had a point about Czechoslovakia in 1938. After all, the national composition of the Czech state in 1938 was as follows: approximately six million Czechs, three million Germans, two million Slovaks, and well over half a million Hungarians. This is not so very different from the ethnic breakdown in prewar Bosnia: with just over 40 percent Muslims, 39 percent Serbs and about 18 percent Croats. If it is right to abandon the Bosnian state today on the ground of its "unviability," it was certainly the height of realism for Chamberlain to throw the Czechs to the wolves in 1938.

The Czech parallel also helps us understand one of the more distressing aspects of the Bosnian War, namely, the conflict between the Bosnian government and Croat separatists. For after Czechoslovakia had been abandoned by the West in 1938, both the Poles and Hungarians stepped in to claim their share of the carcass in Teschen and southern Slovakia, respectively. Predictably, the failure of the West to uphold international law triggered a frantic scramble for territory at the expense of the victim; it would, however, be absurd to claim that the opportunist behavior of the

Poles and Hungarians put them on par with the original aggressor, Nazi Germany. The opportunist behavior of the Croats in Bosnia should be seen in the same light. This conflict was eagerly seized on by the British government as evidence of the moral equivalence of "all sides" and the inherent "complexity" of the situation. Yet the Croat-government split, which in Bosnia was effectively a Croat-Muslim split, was substantially a response to the Western policy of nonintervention against the original Serb aggression. If there was to be no salvation from the West, the Croats argued, then why not grab what was left of Bosnia, before the Serbs took everything? This conduct was immoral, shortsighted, and—as it turned out—suicidal, but to argue that it makes for a moral equivalence with the original Serb aggression is to accept the logic of the appeasers.

But the parallels do not end there. We find the same schizophrenia over the role of the League of Nations, or in our case, the United Nations. Then as now Western governments made the international body responsible for the implementation of collective security. This meant effectively—and the aggressors of the 1930s and of today were not slow to figure this out for themselves—that collective security was being upheld by nobody. When Britain and France said the invasion of Abyssinia was a matter for the League of Nations, this was a green light for further aggression. In the same way, when the West abdicated responsibility for Bosnia to the European Community and then to the United Nations they issued an open invitation to the Serbs to press their advantage. But there are yet more parallels. There is the same stress on retrenchment and the need for financial stability. Once again there is no stomach for the additional financial burden resulting from a rigorous defense against aggression. Another similarity lies in the strange alliance of pacifist fundamentalists and conservative timeservers created by fear of military involvement. In the 1930s the appeasers were men such as Chamberlain and Baldwin, but also Labour grandees such as the strongly pacifist Ponsonby and Lansbury. Today, it is men of such diverse views as Malcolm Rifkind and Tony Benn who have set their faces against Balkan involvement. Likewise, in the 1930s such political opposites as Churchill and Bevin preached the gospel of resistance, much in the same way as Margaret Thatcher, Paddy Ashdown, and Michael Foot call for intervention today.

We hear the same risible rhetoric to cover up our own inadequacy. Just after the Munich agreement Chamberlain wrote to the archbishop of Canterbury that he was sure that "some day the Czechs will see that what we did was to save them for a happier future." How familiar this must sound to the Bosnians who were told that the arms embargo and Western neutrality were "in their own best interests." To intervene or to supply arms, ran and still runs the British government's argument, would simply be to "prolong the agony." The sheer nonsense and insolence of this argument are obvious. After all, what if the British government had been refused aid against the Nazis in 1940 on the grounds that it might prolong our agony?

There is one last parallel. In November 1937 Hitler's adjutant Friedrich Hossbach drew up a document that set out the Führer's intention to wage aggressive war against his neighbors. In September 1986 the Serbian Academy of Sciences in Belgrade formulated a memorandum that provided the blueprint for Serbian expansionism. Of course, unlike the Hossbach protocol it was not an official government document, still less was it a detailed politico-military plan with a timetable attached. But we may assume that such timetables and plans were devised in due course, for the Greater Serbia envisaged in the memorandum was henceforth singlemindedly pursued by Milošević. In fact the authors demanded the creation of a new and vastly expanded Serbian republic out of the ruins of the old Yugoslavia. This was to include Serb settlements in Croatia, much of Bosnia, the whole of Kosovo, and Vojvodina. This phase in the creation of Greater Serbia has almost been completed. It remains to be seen whether Milošević or his successors will now call it a day, or whether they will be emboldened to carry the war into Macedonia and beyond.

• • •

In the last analysis, of course, any objections to such comparisons will probably be political, not historical. If one does not share my belief that Serbian expansionism is a threat to the security of Europe as a whole, then one can hardly be expected to be persuaded by my historical analogies. Yet if I am in danger of turning into a kind of modern-day Churchillian Don Quixote, charging at the windmills of supposed threats to peace, might my critics not be in peril of slipping into the complacency and misjudgments of the 1930s? This is the lesson of history I see being ignored so fatally in our own time. Because in disputing whether there is British interest at stake in the Balkans today we are effectively disputing *which part of history,* to recall Trevelyan's formulation, is repeating itself. Are we back in 1876–78 or in 1938? The question is the more dramatic because in 1938 Chamberlain's "peace with honour" were the same words that Disraeli had brought back in triumph from the Congress of Berlin and to which he added his own immortal and infamous gloss, "I believe it is peace for our time." One could not help being reminded of this in May 1993 when, after obtaining the entirely worthless signatures of Karadžić and Milošević to a Bosnian peace accord, David Owen announced that "now is the time to talk of peace," just days before his hopes were trashed by the Bosnian Serb parliament. Similarly, one could not help but have an eerie feeling about the choice of words Warren Christopher, the new American secretary of state, used to describe the Bosnian crisis in early summer 1993. It was, he said, "a humanitarian crisis a long way from home, in the middle of another continent." Ever since Neville Chamberlain spoke of German aggression against Czechoslovakia as "a quarrel in a faraway country between people of whom we know nothing," one never thought to hear such a formulation from the lips of a Western politician again.

NOTES

This piece started life as a paper presented to various audiences in Britain and the former Yugoslavia. I am particularly grateful to Dražen Katunarić for enabling me to address the Croatian Writers' Festival in Zagreb in December 1994. I also thank Anita Bunyan, Stjepan Meštrović, Michael Foot, Jill Craigie, and Alain Finkielkraut for their useful comments. Needless to say, they are not responsible for any shortcomings this piece might have. For reasons of space, notes have been kept to a minimum.

1. Herbert Butterfield, *History and Human Relations* (London: Macmillan, 1951), 161, 173.

2. A. L. Rowse, *The Use of History* (London: Hodder and Stoughton, 1946), 17, 20.

3. G. R. Elton, *The Practice of History* (London: Methuen, 1967), 7.

4. Norman Rich, *Why the Crimean War? A Cautionary Tale* (Hanover, N.H.: University Press of New England, 1985), xix.

5. G. M. Trevelyan, "Stray Thoughts on History (1948)," in *An Autobiography and Other Essays* (London: Longmans, 1949), 84.

6. Mark Thompson, *A Paper House: The Ending of Yugoslavia* (New York: Pantheon Books, 1992), 314.

7. Roy Gutman, *A Witness to Genocide: The 1993 Pulitzer Prize-Winning Dispatches on the "Ethnic Cleansing" of Bosnia.* (New York: Macmillan, 1993), 178.

8. *Independent,* April 24, 1993.

9. *Independent,* February 2, 1993.

10. *Sunday Telegraph,* February 14, 1993.

11. *Sunday Telegraph,* November 12, 1992.

12. *Independent,* December 2, 1993.

13. See Richard Shannon, *Gladstone and the Bulgarian Agitation, 1876* (Hassocks: Harvester Press, 1975), passim.

14. See the critique by Mark Almond, *Europe's Backyard War: The War in the Balkans* (London: Heinemann, 1994), 321.

15. See insightful comments in Thompson, op. cit., 326.

16. Victoria Clark and Michael Ignatieff, *Observer,* January 31, 1993.

17. See some of the evidence marshaled by Almond, op. cit., 307, et passim.

18. I have attempted to make the case for a strong British interest in Conservative BOW Group paper P610 "The Case for Intervention" (May 1993); M706 "The Last Chance" (July 1993); P725 "Why the Americans Are Right" (October 1994); M739 "The National Interest" [with Alexander Nicoll]; and in a number of newspaper articles.

Jean Baudrillard

Editors' note: The following three articles from the Paris newspaper Libération *appear here in translation for the first time. At the time of the publication of this volume, the siege of Sarajevo by Bosnian Serbs has gone on for over a thousand days and has been covered intensely by the Western media. In much of his previous work, the prominent French social theorist Jean Baudrillard has written critically of the voyeuristic tendencies of postmodern society. One of his most notable contributions is his discussion of the world of "hyperreality," a world characterized by the detachment of symbols from their social contexts and references. The currency of the world of hyperreality is the "simulacrum," that is, the image created as a representation of the real world. Increasingly, as Baudrillard informs us, audiences have lost the ability to distinguish simulacra from the real world phenomena they are meant to represent. This might explain some of the Western inaction in Bosnia: images of atrocities, death, and destruction do not seem real because they are simply placed in and among a wider universe of unreal images in which audiences exist. Lack of action proceeds, then, from the fact that the mediated images of the world are mere representations that lend an air of unreality to the things they represent.*

Baudrillard's criticisms of Western media and intellectuals, contained in the following essays, cause us to move from thinking only about the perpetrators of genocide to thinking about those who stand passively by or engage in self-serving forms of ineffective action while genocide proceeds. Just as media watchers lose touch with reality—even as they are presented with its most evil manifestations—so, too, have many Western intellectuals lost the ability to differentiate effective moral intervention from other kinds of symbolic action. The result has been the transformation of Western intellectuals from effective moral agents into postmodern voyeurs, aggregates of radical individualists whose voyeurism and individualism feed on televised images of evil. Baudrillard is not afraid to name and confront evil, or to name the aggressor in Bosnia. Nor is he afraid to suggest what many might consider heresy: that the new Europe, by refusing to confront aggression and genocide in Bosnia, has proven itself a sham. Baudrillard reminds us in his own provocative way that the case of Bosnia informs us as much about our Western selves as it does about the nature of evil in the present fin de siècle.

No Pity for Sarajevo

What was striking about "The Corridor for Free Speech" (the December 19, 1993, simultaneous broadcast between Strasbourg and Sarajevo, on the Arte channel) was the exceptional status and absolute superiority conferred by misery, distress, and total disillusion. It was this disillusion that enabled the citizens of Sarajevo to treat the "Europeans" with contempt, or at least with a sarcastic sense of freedom, in sharp contrast with the remorse and hypocritical regrets of their counterparts. They had no need for compassion, and pitied our own dejection. "I spit on Europe," one of them said. One is in fact never more free or sovereign than when one's contempt is not only justified, but directed at those good consciences basking in the sun of solidarity, rather than at the enemy.

They certainly have seen their share of such good friends. Most recently, it was Susan Sontag who came to Sarajevo to stage *Waiting for Godot*. Why not bring *Bouvard et Pécuchet* to Somalia or Afghanistan? Worse than such cultural soul boosting, however, is the condescension and the inability to distinguish positions of strength from positions of weakness. They are strong, and we, who look to them for something, anything, to revive our strength and our lost sense of reality, are weak.

Our sole reality is indeed at stake, and we must save it, even if through the most pitiful of slogans: "Something should be done. We can't just do nothing." Yet to do something simply to avoid doing nothing has never been a valid principle for action or liberty. It is, at the most, a form of self-pity and a way of absolving one's own powerlessness.

The people of Sarajevo are not faced with such questions. Given where they are, what they do is out of absolute necessity. They do what they have to, without deluding themselves about the outcome, and without self-pitying self-indulgence. This is the meaning of being real, and of being in reality. Their reality has nothing to do with the "objective reality" of their misery—which *should not exist,* and which elicits our pity. Their reality exists "as is," as the reality of action and fate. This explains why they are alive, and why we are dead. It also explains why we sense reality must be salvaged from war, and why we must impose this "pitiful" reality on those who, in the midst of war and misery, suffer from it without truly believing in it.

Susan Sontag admits that the Bosnians do not really believe in the suffering that surrounds them. They end up finding the whole situation unreal, senseless, and beyond their understanding. It is hell, but a somewhat hyperreal hell, made even more so for their being harassed by the media and humanitarian agencies, who simply reinforce the incomprehensibility of the world's attitude toward them. Thus, they live amid a type of spectral war—luckily so, since they could never bear it otherwise. I should mention that these are not simply my words, but theirs.

But, of course, Susan Sontag is from New York, and she must have a better idea than they of what reality is, since she chose them to incarnate this reality. Perhaps it is simply because this reality is what she and the Western world most lack. To re-create reality, one must go where the blood flows, and all these "corridors" we have opened for our food and "cultural" shipments are really emergency lifelines along which we import their life blood, and the energy of their misery ... yet another unequal exchange. These people, who are absolutely disillusioned with reality, and who no longer even believe in the rule of political rationality that is very much a part of the European reality principle, have found an alternative source of courage, founded on surviving in a senseless situation. These are the people Susan Sontag wants to convince of the "reality" of their suffering, by acculturating it, of course, and by putting it on stage, so that it may serve as a useful reference point within the theater of Western values (which includes solidarity).

Susan Sontag is not, however, the issue. She is merely the high-society instance of what has become a generalized situation, where harmless and powerless intellectuals exchange their misery with those who are miserable, each sustaining the other through a sort of perverse contract. This parallels the way political classes and civilian societies exchange their respective misery: the one offering up corruption and scandals, the other artificial convulsions and inertia. Not so long ago, for example, Bourdieu and Father Pierre were the offerings in a televisual holocaust, the one exchanging the language of pathos for the other's sociological metalanguage on poverty.

In the guise of ecumenical pathos, our society as a whole is literally on a path of "commiseration." It is as though we were in the midst of a moment of immense repentance, shared by intellectuals and politicians alike, and linked to the panic of history and the twilight of values. We must therefore replenish the preserve of our references and values. By way of that smallest of common denominators known as world suffering, we must restock our preserves with artificial game. "It is presently impossible to show anything else than suffering on television newscasts." (David Schneidermann). Ours is a victim-society, and I surmise society is simply expressing its own disappointment and remorse faced with an impossible, self-inflicted violence.

The New Intellectual Order follows, in every way, on the heels of the New World Order. Everywhere we look distress, misery, and suffering have become the raw goods of the primitive scene. The victim status of human rights is the sole funereal ideology. Those who do not directly exploit it do so by proxy, and there is no dearth of middlemen skimming a financial or symbolic profit along the way. As with global debt, deficits and suffering are negotiable and have resale value on the futures markets—here, the intellectual-political markets—which are the present-day equivalents of the military-industrial complex of the sinister old days.

The logic of suffering governs all commiseration. Even if we mean to confront suffering, our very reference to it gives suffering an indefinite base of objective reproduction. Clearly, to combat anything, one's starting point must be the evil underlying suffering.

Sarajevo is truly the theater where evil is in evidence. It is the repressed cancer cell that rots all else, the virus whose most blatant symptom is now the paralysis of Europe. The belongings of Europe are salvaged through the GATT negotiations, only to be thrown into the flames of Sarajevo, which, in a way, is a good thing. Bogus Europe, undiscovered Europe, and the Europe squandered in the most hypocritical of dealings is a flop in Sarajevo. Thus, the Serbs could almost be hailed the demystifying tool and the savage analyzer of this phantom Europe, born of the techno-democratic policies that are as triumphant in their discourses as they are decrepit in their deeds. The disintegration of Europe keeps pace with the burgeoning discourses of a united Europe (exactly as the weakening of human rights keeps pace with the proliferation of speeches on human rights). The fine point of the story is the following: in carrying out ethnic cleansing, the Serbs are Europe's cutting edge. The "real" Europe in the making is a white Europe, a bleached Europe that is morally, economically, and ethnically integrated and cleansed. In Sarajevo, this Europe is victoriously in the making. In a sense, what is happening there is not at all an incidental occurrence along the way to a nonexistent, pious, and democratic Europe, but a logical and ascending phase of the New European Order, itself a branch of the New World Order, whose global characteristic is white fundamentalism, protectionism, discrimination, and control.

Some say that if we let this happen in Sarajevo, it will be our due later on. We are, in fact, already there, since all European countries are on the road to ethnic cleansing. This is the true Europe, slowly in the making in the shadows of national parliaments, spearheaded by Serbia. Invoking some undefined sense of passivity or inability to react is useless, since we are dealing with a logically implemented program, of which Bosnia is merely the new frontier.

Why do you think Le Pen has all but vanished from the political scene? He has vanished because the substance of his ideas has in every way infiltrated the political class in the form of "French particularity," the sacred union, the Euro-nationalist reflex, and protectionism. Le Pen is no longer of any use, since his victory was not political, but viral, winning over people's way of thinking. Why should this be limited to Sarajevo, since the same thing is at stake everywhere? Displays of solidarity will change nothing. The miraculous end will be at hand only when the exterminations come to an end, and when the borders of "white" Europe have been drawn. It is as if all European nationalities and policies had acted in concert to take out a contract for murder with the Serbs, who have become the agents of the West's dirty jobs—just as the West had taken out a contract with Saddam Hussein against Iran. The problem is, if the killer goes overboard, he too must be eliminated. The operations against Iraq and in Somalia were relative failures for the New World Order, but the Bosnian operation bodes well for the New European Order.

The Bosnians know all this. They know they owe their accursed fate to the international "democratic" order, and not to some vestige or monstrous excrescence of fascism. They know they are scheduled for extermination, exile, or exclusion, as are all heterogeneous and rebellious elements throughout the world. I do not wish to upset the hypocritical guilty consciences of Western democrats and humanitarians, but there can be no appeal to this process, since it is the unswerving path of progress. Clearly, modern Europe will rise from the eradication of Muslims and Arabs— unless they survive as immigrant slaves. The strongest objection to the offensive led by guilty consciences, and as displayed in happenings such as the one in Strasbourg, is that it perpetuates the image of the alleged weakness of European policies, and the image of Europe's conscience supposedly torn by its own powerlessness. It thereby covers up entirely what is really going on, by granting this reality the benefit of spiritual doubt.

Of course the people of Sarajevo who appeared on the screens of Arte seemed disillusioned and without hope, but they did not look like martyrs in waiting. Rather, they displayed their objective misery, whereas the true suffering of false apostles and voluntary martyrs, was on the other side. Then again, it is written, "the voluntary martyr will not be recognized in the hereafter."

Libération, January 7, 1993
Translated from the French by James Petterson

The West's Serbianization

At the price of a superhuman effort, after three years of massacre, and, above all, after the humiliation of the forces of the international community (finally something unbearable), international opinion seems to have recognized, though grudgingly and with strong reservations, that the Serbs are the aggressors. This recognition might also seem to demonstrate that we are being as firm and lucid as possible. In fact, it simply brings us to the war's starting point. Even those who long ago contradicted the official doctrine of the "belligerents" and denounced Serb aggression now welcome this change of position as a victory. They naively hope that, from now on, the only possible conclusion will be that the Western powers end this aggression. This, of course, will not happen. This rather platonic recognition of the executioners as executioners does not imply that the victims will be recognized as victims. To be fooled in this respect is to buy into the evangelical idealism of those who suggest that the "depths of ridicule and dishonor" have been reached, and who call on a sudden reaction from the international powers and from a "suicidal" Europe, without for an instant being surprised by the uselessness of their efforts (which are certainly a match for the unending hypocrisy of politicians). Recrimination goes hand in hand with the crime, and the two proliferate through an unending orchestration of events. Since the West's conscience takes it upon itself to mourn this situation, and since it simultaneously monopolizes hypocrisy and good intentions, there is no reason that the criminal will not maintain his monopoly over arrogance and crime. In fact, neither the grotesque gesticulations of the international powers nor the sickened outcries of the stewards of good causes can have any real effect, since the decisive step has not been taken. No one dares nor wants to step up to the final analysis, to recognize that the Serbs are not only the aggressors (this is a bit like breaking down an open door), but are our objective allies in this cleansing operation for a future Europe, freed of its bothersome minorities, and for a future world order, freed from all radical challenges to its own values—based on the democratic dictatorship of human rights and on free markets.

What is at stake is the question of evil. By denouncing the Serbs as "dangerous psychopaths" we pride ourselves for having put our finger on this evil, without questioning the innocence of our democratic intentions. We suggest our job is done once we have declared the Serbs the "bad guys," but not the enemy. With good reason, since from a world perspective, we Westerners, we Europeans, are fighting exactly the same enemies as the Serbs are: Islam, the Muslims. Everywhere, in Chechnya with the Russians (the same shameful, deadly intolerance); in Algeria, where we denounce the military powers, all the while giving them major logistical support. (By some quirk of fate, the good souls who discredit the official doctrine of the "belligerents" in Bosnia use this doctrine's language when speaking of Algeria: state terrorism against fundamentalist terrorism—equally matched evils—while we remain the helpless victims of this barbarity. As if state terrorism were not *our* terrorism, administered in homeopathic doses on the home front). The short of it is that we will bomb a few Serb positions with smoke-mortars, but we will never really intervene against them, since their work is basically our own. If it were necessary to end the conflict, we would rather break the backs of the victims, since they are far more irritating than the executioners. If Bosnian Muslims make an attempt at defending themselves, then you will see that it is they the International Rapid Reaction forces will have to neutralize and liquidate. In the event of a powerful Muslim offensive, the international forces will become efficient.

These are the real reasons for this unending war. Appearances to the contrary (which, by their very ambiguity, speak for themselves), without this deep-rooted complicity, and without this objective alliance (which was not necessarily willed or deliberate), there is no reason this war should still be going on. The scenario is the same as with Saddam Hussein: in our battle against him, we deployed a great deal of media and technology. In the final analysis, however, he was, and is, our objective ally. Reviled, denounced, and discredited in the name of human rights, he remains our objective ally against Iran, against the Kurds, and against the Shiites. This is why the Gulf War never really took place: Saddam was never our true enemy. This is also the case with the Serbs. By banishing them from the human community, we are actually protecting them and continuing to let them carry out their work.

The trick lies in convincing the Bosnians that they are responsible for their own misery. If this goal is not obtained through diplomacy, already two years in the works, it will have to be reached through force. Maybe we should take a look behind this gigantic trompe l'oeil, behind the rote speeches of the humanitarians, the diplomats, and the military. In any conflict, the political dimension of war implies a distinction between what is fought against and what is sacrificed. Though it is seldom admitted, the main stake and the ultimate objective of war is not necessarily the defeat of the adversary, but what is truly swept away and liquidated. During the Algerian War, for example, we fought against the Algerian military, but what was really sacrificed was the Algerian revolution—this sacrifice was (and still is) carried out with the Algerian military. In Bosnia, we are combating (not excessively) the Serbs in the name of a multicultural Europe, but what is being sacrificed in the process is precisely the other culture, the one that, through its values, opposes an indifferent world order lacking in values. We are carrying out this sacrifice *with* the Serbs.

Imperialism has changed faces. What the West wants to impose on the world, from here on out and in the guise of universals, are not completely disjointed values, but its lack of values. Where any particularity, any minority, any specific idiom, any passion or irreducible belief, and, above all, any antagonistic worldview survives or persists, an indifferent order must be imposed—as indifferent as we are to our own values. We generously distribute the right to be different, while secretly and inexorably working to produce a pale and undifferentiated world.

This terrorism is the result not of fundamentalism, but of an unfounded culture. It is the integrationism of emptiness, whose stakes are beyond any political forms or vicissitudes. There is no longer a front or a balance of power, but a transpolitical fault line that, for the most part, presently runs through Islam—but also through the heart of each so-called civilized and democratic country, and certainly through each of us.

Libération, July 3, 1995
Translated by James Petterson

When the West Stands In for the Dead

The West's military inability to react to Serb aggression is equaled by its inability to put the life of a single soldier at risk. Accordingly, these soldiers were hostages long before the Serbs actually took them as hostages. Their life must be spared above all else, and the body count must be zero: this is the leitmotif of a clean war, and the decisive factor of a perfect war: a flawless, athletic performance.

We already witnessed this during the Gulf War, where all fatalities among Western soldiers were attributed to accidents. At least this war was pawned off on us through a technological demonstration that gave the illusion of power (virtual invincibility). Bosnia, on the other hand, exemplifies total weakness. Even if this weakness, which gives the Serbs a free hand, corresponds to the war's unavowed objective, it is, nevertheless, the equivalent of the symbolic castration of the West's war machine. Poor Western powers! If only they could swiftly and victoriously accomplish their mission to establish a World Order (by liquidating all pockets of resistance). Instead they must watch helplessly, from the depths of their torn consciences, as this dirty little job (with international status) is carried out by intermediary mercenaries. The West has to watch helplessly as it is humiliated and disqualified.

This military paralysis is not surprising, however, since it is related to the mental paralysis of the civilized world. It might seem that the West's inability to put a single soldier's life at risk is the highest expression of civilized society, where even the military heeds the humanitarian call and respects the sacred right to life. Yet quite the opposite is true. No longer even a soldier, this virtual soldier's fate is the same as civilized man's. The latter's stakes and collective values have, for the most part, disappeared, and his existence can be sacrificed to nothing—something we do not value cannot really be put at risk.

The individual we have produced, and glorify, is absolutely concerned with himself. This individual, whose weakness we protect through the entire judicial system of human rights, is the last man mentioned by Nietzsche. He is the final user of himself and of his own life. He is the terminal individual, without hope of descendant or transcendence. He is without return, devoted to hereditary sterility, and counting down. Merchandise without return—environment without return—raw goods without return—atmosphere without return: this man is the cycle's end.

His sole final task is to try desperately to survive, by becoming spectralized, fractalized, pluralized, by becoming his own creature and his own clone. Thus, this last man cannot be sacrificed, since he is the last. No one any longer has the right to put his life at risk, since it has been reduced to use-value and to real-time survival. This is the fate, or lack thereof, of the last man. These are the consequences of his weakness, which are also those of the civilized nations that cannot even risk saving face.

The following two aspects are profoundly linked: on the one hand, eliminating any foreign culture and any singular minorities, in the name of ethnic cleansing; on the other hand, eliminating the singularity and irreducible fact of death itself, eliminating death, as the most singular of all singularities, in the name of protecting ourselves and surviving at any cost. In a way, our life is also cleansed—ever more sheltered from death in its virtual shell, just as the virtual soldier of the United Nations forces goes about in a technical shell. Being taken hostage does not make this soldier any more real. He simply serves as exchangeable matter in the trompe l'oeil potlatch of complicities and divergences between the West and the Serbs. He is the exchangeable item in this unlikely chain of watered down collusion and cowardice, in this military masquerade, where the virtual soldier replaces the tomb of the unknown soldier. This soldier does not die, but is paralyzed and immobilized, a stand-in for the dead. Thus death, in all its forms, is redeployed, precisely where we no longer expected it.

Consider UNPROFOR or the Rapid Reaction Force: in the Bosnian conflict they immediately stood in for (and fervently defended!) the dead. Behind our television screens, even we secretly stand in for the dead. The Serbs, the assassins, are alive in their own way, whereas the victims of Sarajevo are on the side of real death. We, however, are in a strange place, neither dead nor alive, but stand-ins for the dead. In this sense, the Bosnian conflict is a global challenge; everywhere in the present world, the West stands in for the dead.

Certainly, we tried everything possible to avert this situation. We almost managed the Swiss trick, whose secular ruse was to furnish mercenaries to all of Europe and to shelter themselves from war. This is what all rich countries are doing today, furnishing weapons the world over, thus managing to exile, if not violence, then at least war from their territory. But this is a hopeless attempt. Where we had thought to hem death in, death pops up again through all our layers of defense and even in the depths of our own culture.

This is what all our humanitarian and ecological ideologies are about: the human species and its survival. This is the difference between humanitarianism and humanism. The latter was a system of strong values, related to the concept of humankind, with its philosophy and its morals, and characteristic of a history in the making. Humanitarianism, on the other hand, is a system of weak values, linked to salvaging a threatened human species, and characteristic of an unraveling history. The only, necessarily negative, outlook for humanitarianism is the optimal management of waste that is by definition nondegradable. From the point of view of survival—life superstitiously prolonged and sheltered from death—life itself becomes a waste product we can no longer rid ourselves of, one that falls under the spell of infinite reproduction.

In Bosnia we are witnessing this infinite reproduction, this macabre parody, and this sinister confusion of history unraveling. We are witness to the face of history where the military and the humanitarian converge.

History reproducing itself becomes farce.
Farce reproducing itself becomes history.

Libération, July 17, 1995
Translated by James Petterson

FIVE

Daniel Kofman

Israel and the War in Bosnia

Israel is neither the most important nor the guiltiest of the industrialized states with regard to the war in former Yugoslavia. Moreover, if any nation ever appeared to have a legitimate plea of extenuating circumstances, it would seem to be Israel. Beset by problems with its own peace process, shaken by unprecedented waves of terror unleashed in a seemingly mindless and fanatical response to its commitment to make far-reaching concessions—not excluding the creation of a Palestinian state, as its government ministers had increasingly hinted—and rent by internal division about how next to proceed, Israel would appear to be the last country to bear a burden of blame for a war in far-off Bosnia. And if that were not exculpatory enough, it is also a fact that Israel's Foreign Ministry did offer Bosnia mutual recognition from 1993, while the Bosnian government—dependent on aid from Muslim countries, including Iran—reluctantly delayed acceptance of the Israeli offer. Nor will one fail to notice that the same Iran has been a spiritual and material supporter of the Palestinian groups claiming responsibility for terrorist attacks on Israeli civilians. In light of all this, even to discuss whatever shortcomings Israel's Balkan policy might have, let alone to dwell on them at book chapter length, might appear captious at best, and at any rate of little interest to those whose chief concern is the people of Bosnia.

In fact, as I will attempt to demonstrate in what follows, Israel's failings have been significant and for reasons at most only indirectly and partially related to any of the above. Moreover, these failings reveal a good deal about the nature of Serbian propaganda, its method of dissemination, and at least something about its receptivity in some circles in the West.

We may begin by noting that the debate in Israel about the war in Bosnia was in the first three years somewhat unusual.[1] In most countries, discussion focused on what, if anything, should have been done by Western powers. Opinions ranged from advocacy of some form of military intervention and/or a lifting of the arms embargo on Bosnian government forces, to continuing the policy of nonintervention (if an embargo on victims of genocide can be called nonintervention). Among advocates of the latter were those, to be sure, who minimized Serbian guilt and attempted as much as possible to blur the distinction between main aggressor and main victim. The most notorious case was that of the former U.N. commander in Bosnia, retired Canadian Major General Lewis MacKenzie, who, it was revealed in June 1993, had received payments from the Serbian American lobby group SerbNet. MacKenzie was the best known and most outspoken opponent of Western military intervention, a view he often justified with the claim that all parties were to blame for the war. (Another case in point was Lawrence Eagleburger, who became a personal friend of President Milošević during his years as U.S. ambassador to Belgrade, and since maintained close business ties with Serbia.)[2] And British cabinet ministers, in particular Malcolm Rifkind, invoked the claim from time to time when international pressure mounted to react to Serb aggression. Such cases notwithstanding, however, at least the essential facts about the conflict—despite its frequent mischaracterization as a purely "civil war"—were for the most part not in great dispute in most of the West, and the usual line of "noninterventionists" was that a "Balkan civil war" was nothing over which it was worth risking such and such nationality's lives. In short, the debate is mainly over values, or policy, not facts.

In Israel by contrast, the debate departed from this norm in two crucial respects: on the question of who was the main aggressor, and relatedly, on the assumed relevance of World War II to the conflict. Among politicians as well as newspaper columnists, the notion that Serbs were the main aggressors was rarely accepted in the first three years of war. On the contrary, the opinions expressed by government officials and regular columnists tended to range from the view that all sides were more or less equally to blame, to the not infrequently voiced position that the Croats, Muslims, and on some versions also the Slovenes were the real culprits, whether for having had the audacity to break up the federation, or simply by virtue of having been Croats, Muslims, and Slovenes. This latter view was expressed by well-known right- and left-wing commentators, as well as by prominent figures from the center of the political spectrum, most notably ex-mayor of Jerusalem Teddy Kollek.

The case merits interest for a number of reasons. Since the start of the war, Serbia has had a major stake in invoking World War II memories in an effort to cash in on the reputations of the respective ethnic groups and their putative war loyalties. Winning over the opinion of the group whose members were the Nazis' quintessential victims—the Jews—has therefore been seen as a paramount propaganda objective, heightened all the more by the common belief in Serbian ruling circles that "the Jews [exert] a vast influence worldwide."[3] On the whole, diaspora Jews have overwhelmingly spurned Serbian overtures; as Alain Finkielkraut put it, "the Nazis in this story are trying to pass themselves off as Jews." In Israel, by contrast, a highly motivated Serbian lobby, the perceived interests of state, and other related factors led to what might be called an "imagined affinity"[4] with Serbia during the first three years of war.

I will return to an analysis of these factors at the end. I begin, however, with a few representative descriptions of the war by international observers, journalists, and human rights groups. These will then be contrasted with the debate in the Israeli press. This will be followed by discussion of some aspects of Israel's political relations with the former Yugoslavia, including evidence of military support to Serbia, after which I will conclude with a few comments on Israel's general demeanor in light of Serb-perpetrated genocide in Bosnia.

The War in Bosnia

José Maria Mendiluce, career official with the United Nations High Commissioner on Refugees (UNHCR), arrived in the east Bosnian town of Zvornik just as it was overrun by the notorious Serb irregular unit called the White Eagles. He recounts,

> I saw kids put under the treads of tanks, placed under there by grown men, and then run over by other grown men.... Everywhere people were

shooting. The fighters were moving through the town, systematically killing all the Muslims they could get their hands on.[5]

Mendiluce further comments,

These people had a coherent strategy. The whole point was to inflict as
much terror on the civilian population as possible, to destroy as much
property as possible, and to target as much of the violence as possible
against women and kids. After the irregulars had done their work, the
established authorities—the J.N.A [the federal army of the former Yugoslavia which since the breakup has been in the service of Milošević of Serbia]
or Karadžić's forces, or the local police—would come in, ostensibly to
restore order. But of course, that would mean that the ethnic cleansing of
that particular place had been successful, and the White Eagles could move
on.

This seems to have been the scenario in dozens if not hundreds of
Bosnian towns and villages. The Amnesty International report of October
1992 entitled *Bosnia-Herzegovina: Gross Abuses of Basic Human Rights*
describes similar events in Bosanski Novi, Blagaj, Modrica, Doboj, and
others. In Zaklopaca, near Vlasenica, according to the same Amnesty
International report, eighty-three Muslims, including men, women, and
children, were massacred by uniformed Serbs, as described by surviving
eyewitnesses. As early as April 1 and 2, 1992, before the United States
had recognized Bosnia (sometimes cited as a "cause" of the war), Serbian
paramilitaries under the command of Zeljko Raznatović, the notorious
"Arkan" who in 1993 scored a significant success in Serbia's parliamentary elections, killed twenty-seven mainly Muslim civilians in Bijeljina,
registering the first of what was to be a long campaign of such massacres.
Amnesty's news release of January 21, 1993, describes eyewitness reports
from the town of Bosanski Petrovac of the "descent of the town from
tension to terror," as Serbian paramilitaries seized control of the town,
shooting and abducting Muslims at will; the terror ended only with the
final exodus of the few thousand surviving Muslim residents. Roy Gutman, cowinner of the 1993 Pulitzer Prize for his dispatches to *Newsday*
from the war zone, describes similar events in many other Bosnian cities.[6]
In villages such as Liplje, according to Melika Kreitmayer, chief gynecologist of a rape investigation at Tuzla Hospital Gynecological Institute,
"practically every woman in the village was raped."[7] One can easily
multiply these reports from dozens of other villages.[8]

As former Pentagon analyst Norman Cigar has shown in the most detailed analysis so far of Serbian ethnic cleansing, the operational procedure tended to follow a systematic pattern, despite variations, which relied on a "symbiotic relationship" between heavily armed Serbian forces and more lightly armed militias. The former would first take control of an area, thereby creating a "safe environment in which the more lightly armed Serbian militias and local Serbian activists were able to engage in ethnic cleansing. Often, Serbian militia units were attached directly to regular Army units for this specific purpose."[9] As Cigar points out, this recalls the procedure implemented by the Nazis, according to which "heavily armed Wehrmacht combat forces [would secure] ... an area, thereby enabling lighter forces [made up of *Einsatzgruppen* and locally raised auxiliaries] to operate with relative impunity."[10] The early stages of ethnic cleansing relied primarily on mass terror against the civilian population. Later, Serbian authorities found it more convenient to employ other methods: "The restriction on food and fuel supplies, in particular, became a key tool to pressure the civilian population, with the reduction of food supplies to near-starvation levels."[11] This would typically proceed in tandem with the arrest and execution of the educated Muslim elite and community leaders. Thus "in the Kozarac area of northwest Bosnia-Herzegovina, prominent local Muslims were identified, separated, arrested, and earmarked for elimination according to prepared lists." Religious leaders were particularly targeted: "Thus in Bratunac the local Muslim cleric reportedly was tortured in front of the townfolk, who had been rounded up in the soccer stadium, was ordered to make the sign of the cross, had beer forced down his throat, and then was executed."[12] Elsewhere children of Muslim clerics were impaled on spikes in front of their parents and townspeople.[13]

It has now been clearly established that some detention camps could aptly be described as death camps. The Omarska camp was located in a large mining complex. As Gutman describes it,

> According to former detainees, the killing went on almost everywhere: Inside the huge hangarlike building that houses earth-moving equipment, armed guards ordered excruciating tortures at gunpoint, sometimes forcing one prisoner to castrate another. The tarmac outside was an open-air prison where 500 to 1000 men had to lie on their bellies from dawn to dusk. Thousands more packed the offices, workshops and storage rooms. . . . All were on starvation diets.
>
> The most feared locations were small outbuildings some distance from the main facilities: the "Red House," from which no prisoner returned

alive, and the "White House," which contained a torture chamber where guards beat prisoners for days until they succumbed.[14]

Prisoners reported having to remove sometimes five or ten, sometimes as many as thirty or forty corpses daily in a small yellow pickup. The U.S. embassy in Zagreb investigated the massive atrocities at Omarska for a special UN war crimes panel. A top embassy official, speaking on condition of anonymity, remarked, "The Nazis had nothing on these guys. I've seen reports of individual acts of barbarity of a kind that hasn't come up in State Department cable traffic in 20 years."[15] Atrocities ranged from decapitating prisoners with chain saws to forcing one prisoner to bite off the testicles of another. This latter atrocity resurfaces in other parts of Bosnia: David Rieff quotes a UNHCR official as willing to "stake his reputation" on the truthfulness of testimony taken from a Muslim in Bosanski Petrovac in western Bosnia, that he was forced by his Serb captors to bite off the penis of a fellow Muslim.[16] In another incident at Omarska a prisoner died of massive blood loss after his testicles were tied by wire to a motorcycle that took off at high speed. Another was burned alive after being doused with gasoline. Prisoners were beaten to death daily, or had their heads smashed against radiators. "You'd see pieces of flesh or brain there the next day," related one survivor.[17]

Omarska was only one of several such camps run by Serbs in Bosnia. The Keraterm tile factory near Prijedor, where grisly accounts of mass slaughter exceed those of Omarska, and Trnopolje, Brčko, and Manjaća were among the worst. At Brčko, nine-tenths of the inmates were eventually killed. After that, camp guards turned on the remaining townspeople who had not been captured. According to one of the few survivors of the town, prisoners were forced to drive the bodies to an animal feed plant, where they were apparently cremated for animal feed. During the cremations "the air in Brčko would stink so badly you couldn't open the window," reported a traffic engineer, one of the town's few survivors.[18] The Helsinki Watch report of August 1992 entitled *War Crimes in Bosnia-Herzegovina* cites a special UN memorandum as listing other Serb-run camps in Bihać, Cazin, Velika Kladuša, and Bosanska Dubica. The Manjaća camp in particular continued to run for many months while all attempts at inspection by international representatives, including former Polish prime minister Tadeusz Mazowiecki, who visited the area on behalf of the United Nations, were denied. Elie Wiesel was finally invited to visit the camp by Serbian authorities attempting to counter horrifying international reports. Somewhat later the prison was closed down in a highly publicized gesture by Serbian political leaders, including Radovan Karadžić, and the prisoners were said to have been handed over to the Red Cross. Wiesel himself, however, was soon writing in the *New York Times,*

> But last month there came terrible news: not all the prisoners had been freed. Some 500 remained unaccounted for. Most disturbing to me was that many of those I had interviewed had been singled out for special punishment and transferred to an even worse camp, Batković.
>
> The very men we came to help were hurt in the process, an action of deceit that poses a morally painful dilemma: how can humanitarian efforts be continued if the victims end up paying the price?[19]

"Atrocities on All Sides"

Before turning to the Israeli arena, it is necessary to take a short excursion through one of the most widely disseminated motifs of Serbian propaganda in Israel, namely, the claim that all sides in the conflict are guilty of atrocities. Taken in that form and with strict literalness, the claim is of course true, but also vacuous, since there has never been a war fought among civilian populations, especially when involving large numbers of irregular infantry, that did not witness abuses by all sides. This was the case in World War II[20]—not necessarily regarded as an overall moral stalemate—and it is no doubt the case in the conflict in the former Yugoslavia. As mentioned at the start, there have been those throughout the West, notably retired Canadian General Lewis MacKenzie, and increasingly Secretary of Defense Malcolm Rifkind and Prime Minister John Major of Britain, who resorted to this argument in order to justify maintaining the arms embargo—and consequent critical deficit of heavy weaponry—on the Bosnian government. In Israel, however, constant repetition by politicians and the powerful Serbian lobby brought the argument early on to critical mass, such that it became an obligatory piece of conventional wisdom without an incantation of which one could not speak publicly about the war. The claim, in fact, like that about Muslims firing on their own people to gain world sympathy, originated in Serbian and Bosnian Serb official circles, and became their favorite fallback position each time international observers revealed incontrovertible proof of systematic Serbian atrocities. As Cigar has pointed out, "a Serbian public relations campaign sought to promote the idea that what was happening was the unavoidable result of warfare or that all sides were equally guilty."[21] In Israel, the Embassy of the Federal Republic of Yugoslavia, as it is officially known, made a concerted effort to propagate the "atrocities on all sides" argument; its chargé d'affaires, Mirko Stefanović, was indefatigable in defending the fallback line: "The tragedy and the sufferings of the Yugoslav peoples are impossible to explain if one tries to blame only one of them for all the events. There are no 'good' or 'bad' parties, no 'aggressors' or 'victims' in the ongoing war. All those involved are responsible for atrocities."[22] The expression "there are no good or bad in the Yugoslav civil war" had already become a Hebrew cliché by the late summer of 1992. It was repeated to me by environment minister Yossi Sarid, Knesset Foreign and Defense Committee chairman Ori Orr, and Israel's new representative in Belgrade (as of May 1995) Tsvi Rav-Ner, and it has been a constant media refrain. The findings of scores of international observers, human rights organizations, independent reporters, the Bassiouni Commission, and even the State Department and the CIA, to the effect that there is no comparison between the systematic campaign of "ethnic cleansing," as Serbian officials themselves dubbed it, and the handful of sporadic abuses committed by isolated units, in or nominally under control of the Bosnian Army, have gone virtually unmentioned in the Israeli press.[23] Already in late 1992, the U.S. State Department had compiled a list of war crimes, of which eighteen, or a mere 6.3 percent, were attributed to Muslim-dominated forces.[24] By 1995 this percentage had, if anything, declined. A CIA report attributed "at least 90 percent" of atrocities to Serbian forces, in the words of one of the officials who leaked the report. No information was publicized about the remaining 10 percent or less, but it is almost certain that the majority were the responsibility of the Croatian HVO. The proportion committed by Bosnian government forces or those nominally under their control is thus infinitesimal by the historical standards of the paradigm case of a morally just war against aggression, the Allied cause in World War II. The CIA report was based on aerial photography and what one senior official called "an enormous amount of precise technical analysis."[25] While acknowledging incidents of war crimes by other parties, the report stated that the Serbs "were the only party involved in a systematic attempt to eliminate all traces of other ethnic groups from their territory." Significantly, the report stated that "the systematic nature of the Serbian actions strongly suggests that Pale and perhaps Belgrade exercised a carefully veiled role in the purposeful destruction and dispersal of non-Serb populations." It added that there was "specific evidence" that "Bosnian Serb leaders—including Radovan Karadžić—knew of the concentration camps through which many Muslims and Croats who had been evicted from their homes in 1992 were processed." One of the officials commented, "To those who think the parties are equally guilty, this report is pretty devastating. The scale of what the Serbs did is so different. But more than that, it makes clear, with concrete evidence, that there was a conscious, coherent, and systematic Serbian policy to get rid of Muslims, through murders, torture, and imprisonment." The leaked CIA report was classified "at an obscene level," according to one official, apparently to prevent embarrassment to the Clinton administration's policy of "nonintervention" and maintaining the embargo. In fact, it merely corroborated the by then massive evidence that, as Cigar put it, Serb-perpetrated ethnic cleansing "followed a premeditated strategy" according to "a pattern which suggests adherence to general top-down policy guidance and a degree of coordination across the republic and, apparently with unofficial and government circles in Belgrade."[26]

The Serbian attempt to divert attention from the implementation of their plan has included a host of stratagems, from outright denial to what Cigar calls "damage control."[27] This has ranged from blaming the victims in various ways, to accusations that Serbian civilians have been equally victimized by opposing forces. International organizations and observers have repeatedly attempted to investigate Serbian claims. The aforementioned Helsinki Watch report, for instance, refers to Serbian allegations of abuses, but then notes: "Although some of their concerns have proven correct, others have been wildly exaggerated and, in some cases, falsified."[28] For example, the report continues, after Serb forces were unable to take the village of Sijekovac, they alleged that Serb civilians there had been massacred. However, on the basis of interviews with approximately twenty Serb villagers who had fled the area, it emerged that "those Serbs who were killed in Sijekovac were armed combatants engaged in hostilities or were civilians who were killed by cross-fire." The report concludes that "Helsinki Watch representatives could not find evidence to substantiate claims of excessive force."[29]

Similar cases crop up throughout the reports with regard to Serb allegations[30] (which is not to say that there have been no abuses by the other parties to the conflict). By contrast, as David Rieff observed, "The most lurid tales the Bosnian Muslims had told about the process of ethnic cleansing—stories dismissed as exaggerations during the spring and summer of 1992—turned out to have understated the slaughter."[31] He relates the story of an Italian journalist shown a room in a recently conquered Muslim village. The local Serb commander himself stated that two hundred Muslims had been slaughtered there: "The wooden flooring, [the Serb commander] said, had been so saturated with blood that he ordered it ripped out and burned. 'My men could not be expected to function properly,' he said, 'with that kind of stench in the air.' "[32] That Serbian atrocities have been uniquely systematic and highly organized is again evident with regard to the mass rape of Muslim and other non-Serb women. A special report on mass rape in *Newsweek* stated that while a direct order from the top of Serbian leadership has as yet not been discovered,

> there does seem to be a widespread pattern of on-the-ground commanders encouraging—or even ordering—their men to rape. The testimonies of so many victims and witnesses, and of some captured Serb perpetrators, have a consistency that cannot be accidental. "It's hard to believe that all these Serbian men, no matter how animalistic you think human nature is, would suddenly get it in their heads to find a 7-year-old girl and rape her," says the lead State Department researcher. Rape is an integral part of ethnic cleansing, of eradication of entire areas of their historic Muslim populations through brutal intimidation, expulsion and outright murder.[33]

Melika Kreitmayer, chief gynecologist at Tuzla of an investigation into mass rape by Serbian forces, reported cases of some young women who were abducted and taken to a house, but released without being raped after having been instructed to tell others they had been.[34] The implication is that the men were under order to rape, and wished to protect themselves from punishment. Kreitmayer's rape study group included Slovene and Serb doctors who concurred with the findings.[35] The terror in Foča, including the notorious rape camp at the Partizan sports hall in the center of town, was apparently organized by three of Radovan Karadžić's closest aides, Velibor Ostojić, Vojislav Maksimović, and Petar Cancar. Ostojić traveled frequently for consultations with Karadžić at the height of the terror. A minister in Karadžić's government, he was once fired as a high school teacher for "sexually deviant behavior toward young female students." He is said to have directly ordered the rape of Foča's Muslim women. Some women were raped repeatedly, sometimes in front of all others at the stadium.[36] On an earlier occasion (August 23, 1992) Gutman reported from Tuzla that

Serb forces in northern Bosnia systematically raped 40 young Muslim women of a town they captured early this summer, telling some of their victims they were under orders to do so, the young women say. Statements by victims of the assault, describing their ordeal in chilling detail, bear out reports that the Serb conquerors of Bosnia have raped Muslim women, not as a by-product of the war but as a principal tactic of the war.[37]

The Israeli Response: The Media

When news of concentration camps and ethnic cleansing broke in reports around the world, Israeli newspapers duly carried the stories. Indeed, the more tabloid-style papers outdid each other with front-page tales of gore. Thus, under the by-line "N.Y. Times Publishes Horrifying Testimony from Yugoslavia," *Yediot Aharonot* flashed this banner headline: "After She Was Raped, the Mother Requested to Breast-Feed Her Baby. The Rapist Cut Off the Baby's Head and Handed It to her."[38] Somewhat less lurid is the headline over an article by veteran journalist Ron Ben Yishai: "The Women and Children Were Separated from the Men, and Then Shots Were Heard."[39] Around the same time, *Ma'ariv* carried one of Roy Gutman's world-shattering dispatches under the headline "Witnesses from the Death Camps: 'Ten Men Were Laid in a Row—Their Noses and Testicles Cut Off.' "[40] And in the same paper a week later: "Even Journalists Are Fleeing Sarajevo, City of Terror."[41] The article by Emmanuel Rosin and Yossi Aloni, *Ma'ariv* correspondents in Sarajevo, describes the Serb-inflicted terror on the besieged city, while an accompanying article from Reuters recounts incidents of gang rape of Muslim women. In short, even someone whose reading was restricted to local Hebrew papers could not claim to lack access to the facts.

The Israeli departure from the international norm begins, however, with the daily columnists and commentators. Among many, especially those of Serbian origin, which includes several prominent journalists, there was a distinct sense of unease about the reports, and a compelling impulse to respond. Leading the way was Yosef "Tommy" Lapid, an editor and columnist of *Ma'ariv,* and a permanent fixture on the widely watched television show *Popolitika.* A right-winger with a reputation for not mincing his words, Lapid comes from Novi Sad in the Serbian province of Vojvodina. In a moment of candor he revealed his true credo: "We must support the Serbs no matter what they do. In my eyes they are my tribe."[42] This loyalty was still unshaken in June 1995, when he stated on *Popolitika,* "We owe the Serbs our absolute support. The Jewish heart is with the Serbs." As early as June 1, 1992, he set the tone for his future comments on the war with a piece in *Ma'ariv* entitled "A War of the Cameras." The theme, reminiscent of some commentators' complaints about media coverage of Israel's 1982 invasion of Lebanon, is that the war is mainly media hype, not reality. He begins by complaining that media influence is responsible for bringing the Security Council to impose sanctions on Serbia, an imposition he apparently resents. He next explains that Sarajevo "is not Beirut": it hasn't been destroyed, but only damaged, mainly from fires (implying that Serbs are perhaps not directly responsible for the ensuing damage). "The cameras of CNN and SKY [News] naturally focus on the same damaged houses. It is the Yugoslavs' misfortune that a camera happened to be present . . . when shells from a Serb mortar fell on a bread line in Sarajevo, killing seventeen." He goes on to explain that the photos of this bloodbath led to the imposition of sanctions. By "Yugoslavs" he obviously means the Serbs who will suffer from the sanctions, apparently the chief victims of this "war of the cameras." Nor does he deprive readers of a more general explanation of what he considers Western bias:

> Western journalists arriving in Zagreb and Ljubljana at the beginning of hostilities sympathized with the Croats and Slovenes because they were more Western, more civilized, more liberal, and more Catholic than the Serbs. The Serbs failed completely in their efforts to explain their cause, which is no less just than that of the British in Northern Ireland, the Spanish in the Basque province, or the French in Corsica.

Whether Western journalists also found the Muslims "more Catholic than the Serbs" Lapid does not say. Or perhaps they sympathized with Muslims out of sheer anti-Serb inertia spawned by their initial falling in love with the Slovenes and Croats. As for Northern Ireland, the Basque province, and Corsica, I do not recall those regions having declared independence after their populations voted for it in referenda, but such trifles are not Lapid's concern.

On August 9, 1992, when photographs of emaciated Muslim detainees and new tales of unspeakable horrors were again electrifying front pages, Lapid fired off another of his Let-The-Truth-Ring-Out columns, declaring,

> As of this moment: In Bosnia and Herzegovina no extermination camps *[machanot hashmada]* and no proof of mass murder have been found, things which the Croats and Muslims have accused the Serbs. The Serbs

have offered to turn over all prisoner camps which they have set up to UN supervision. [For the facts, see first section above.] It seems that another chapter in the war has been completed, in which the Serbs are the victors at the military front while their rivals are the victors at the propaganda front.

It is perhaps not inappropriate to bear in mind that this comment was made in a cultural environment in which denial of a genocide of fifty years ago is considered a heinous crime.[43] Lapid's piece goes on to lambast Knesset member Yossi Sarid for planning a trip to Sarajevo, cites Germany's and Austria's leaders as "the real culprits" for having encouraged the breakup of Yugoslavia (a familiar line from Serbian official circles), and interestingly enough, praises foreign minister Shimon Peres in the last paragraph for "having acted wisely when he expressed regret at the suffering of the peoples of Yugoslavia and condemned acts of brutality—without citing names and without taking a position."

Lapid's representation of Peres's stance is the only correct statement in the piece. In fact, he might just as well have praised Yossi Sarid, who had then also refused to "cite names or take a position" regarding war crimes in Bosnia, or the former Yugoslavia in general; at the time of his planned trip to Sarajevo, aborted when the United Nations could not guarantee his safety, he stressed that his reasons were purely humanitarian. (In a telephone conversation on January 15, 1994, Sarid reiterated to me that he sees "nothing to choose between the warring factions in ex-Yugoslavia." Three weeks later, however, he did sharply criticize in the Knesset the "genocidal" *(retsach am)* shelling of Sarajevo on February 5, 1994, an attack that led to a temporary toughening of Western policy and an easing of the siege on Sarajevo.)

Lapid may possibly be dismissed as a far-right crank unworthy of serious attention, despite his well-entrenched position in the media establishment. The evidence indicates, however, that his views have been not at all unrepresentative of the rest of the Israeli political spectrum, as he correctly implied through his praise of Peres. Even commentators on the left and far left adopted a similar stance, albeit with the necessary rhetorical changes.

A case in point is Raoul Teitelbaum, who writes in the daily *Yediot Aharonot* under the pen name Yisrael Tomer and who became senior Knesset reporter of the paper in 1994. A Serbian immigrant to Israel and former member of Maki (the Israeli Communist Party) who still occasionally employs the Party rhetoric, Teitelbaum became one of the leading spokespersons for the pro-Serbian lobby, appeared publicly on the serious television show *Moked* (which has often hosted prime ministers, cabinet ministers, and army generals), and a guest lecturer at public symposia on the war. In his appearances on *Moked* and at a Hebrew University symposium, he ran through the regular litany of official Serbian accusations, beginning with his quotation of Bosnian president Alija Izetbegović's so-called Islamic Declaration—written in 1970 when he was a youthful anticommunist dissident—which called for a "united Islamic community from Morocco to Indonesia." Whatever Izetbegović might have meant by that—and do not many Jews call for a united Jewish community from New York to Jerusalem?—Teitelbaum neglected to mention that his declaration was without standing in the present Bosnian government. In the symposium at the Hebrew University, June 7, 1993, Teitelbaum repeated the twenty-five-year-old quotation, and heaped scorn on the notion that Muslims could be a nationality, employing rhetoric reminiscent of orthodox Marxists' traditional antagonism to the notion of Jewish nationality or peoplehood. He referred to the World War II SS division organized in Bosnia and Herzegovina with the help of the Palestinian Mufti, a staple of pro-Serbian propaganda both abroad and especially in Israel. He omitted to mention, as always in that context, that despite the mufti's considerable efforts the division managed to enlist a mere fraction of 1 percent of the population, while many times that number of Muslims fought alongside Tito's Partisans against the fascist occupiers; also unmentioned was the fact that Serb Chetniks were responsible for the deaths of thousands of Jews in areas in which they operated,[44] while "in the Sandjuk and south Serbia, Chetniks slaughtered Muslims to try to create a homogenous Serbian population."[45] Estimates of Muslim victims of Chetnik terror run in the tens of thousands, to which must be added thousands of Partisan victims of all nationalities, slaughtered according to the doctrine of revenge as a "sacred duty."[46] Teitelbaum concluded his remarks with the bald assertion that the Muslims were holding their own militarily, when they had already been reduced to a mere 10 percent of Bosnian territory, most of it then under a yearlong siege.

The pro-Serbian lobby in which Teitelbaum is active is grouped around the Federation of Yugoslav Immigrants (Hitachdut Olei Yugoslavia). Reflecting the composition of the Israeli Yugoslav community itself, the organization is largely Serbian-dominated and has adopted an avowedly pro-Serbian stance from the start. When Israel decided in February 1993 to take in eighty-two Bosnian Muslim refugees (then in transit camps in Croatia) partly to offset the stream of international condemnation of the expulsion of some four hundred alleged Islamic activists from the Occupied Territories, a spate of letters appeared in Israeli newspapers opposing the gesture. Two were published together on February 2, 1993, in *Ha'aretz*. The first saw fit to delve deeply into the history of Bosnia's Muslims, pointing out that they are descendants of either Turks who conquered the area in 1463, or else Christians "who converted to Islam for reasons of convenience and have remained Muslim to this day." (Presumably, had these ancestors converted out of any genuine faith, the writer might not oppose so vehemently the granting of asylum to today's refugees.) If the presumption of transgenerational collective guilt was insufficiently clear, the next paragraph made the obligatory reference to the World War II Bosnian SS division, then asked dramatically, "Who can guarantee that the same 101 *[sic]* refugees are not children or grandchildren of those Bosnians who killed Jews 48 years ago?" The letter concludes, "The absorption of Vietnamese refugees [in the 1970s] was a humanitarian act. The absorption of Bosnian refugees is an act of propaganda, lacking any justification." The following letter made the same reference to the SS division, and concluded with the same supposed contrast with the Vietnamese refugees, indicating that the letters were perhaps part of an orchestrated campaign. It was signed by "Gershon Kaponi, National Chairman, Federation of Yugoslav Immigrants." That organization has been a hotbed of pro-Serbian sentiment; the handful of Sarajevo Jews who have arrived in Israel since the start of the war have told me they stay clear of it.

The Jewish community of Serbia was by World War II already highly assimilated, as Yosef Levinger points out in his introduction to *The History of the Holocaust: Yugoslavia*.[47] Thus it is perhaps not so surprising that many of them have adopted the ultranationalist sentiments that have swept through Serbia in the last few years, taking in their wake even intellectuals of the dissident socialist *Praxis* publication, among others. Those of them inclined toward notions of collective national guilt may be further motivated to blame the entire Croat nation for crimes of the Ustashe regime, notwithstanding the fact that Harvard historian Aleksa Djilas (son of the famous Montenegran dissident Milovan Djilas; neither is considered overly sympathetic to Croatia) was able to sum up the conclusions of "Yugoslav and other scholars" that the Ustashe "never had the support of the majority of the Croatian people."[48] And Jovan Zametica—when still in his former avatar as independent scholar John Zametica before becoming Bosnian Serb leader Karadžić's official spokesman—admitted that the Ustashe regime "was no more that a Nazi puppet state, and had little support among the Croats."[49] And those living in Israel might tend to filter their perceptions of the war in Bosnia through yet another prism of prejudice, namely, their fear of and antipathy toward Muslims in general. Thus by the time the light of events has passed through these interpreters, it has taken on the opposite colors of the spectrum.

What *is* astonishing is that these perceptions have been embraced almost wholesale by so many prominent Israeli commentators. These have included well-known figures of the left, like the "new historian"[50] Yehoshua Porat, who runs through the familiar arguments about Muslims not being a real people (without mentioning the Bosnian independence referendum of February 29–March 1, 1992, passed with near-unanimous support from Muslims, Croats, mixed ethnics, and some Serbs, while the official Serb community boycotted it),[51] the editorial board of *Ha'aretz,* left-wing columnist of *Kol Ha'ir* Haim Baram, and many others too numerous to cite. Indeed, it is simpler to list the handful of *dissenters* who have appeared sporadically on op-ed pages. One is Hebrew University philosophy professor Igor Primoratz, who appeared opposite Raoul Teitelbaum in the aforementioned television broadcast of *Moked* (alongside Army Radio's Itai Engel), and who published several op-ed pieces in *Ha'aretz* and the *Jerusalem Post.* Shlomo Avineri also published op-ed comments urging Israeli support for Bosnia, albeit in part "to prevent a [Bosnian] jihad against the West," duly given prominence in a bold takeout by *Ha'aretz.* (This argument has been invoked by Western friends of Bosnia on occasion, but the notion that such an eventuality could come to pass in Bosnia makes about as much sense as the possible recrudescence of Crusader activity in Western Europe. By any available standard, Bosnian Muslims are among the most secular peoples in Europe.) Itai Engel's direct reports from the war zone in 1992 for Army Radio were on a high professional level, and there have also been Gidon Levi's dispatches from Sarajevo to *Ha'aretz* in the fall of 1993, which compared what he witnessed to the Warsaw Ghetto. Until the end of 1993 that was about the sum total of Israeli printed commentary that was either unambiguously sympathetic to the victims of the Serb campaign or at least tried to depict their victimization as accurately as possible. From the electronic media one could add the Saturday night international news television program *Viewing the World,* which has had consistently good segments. By the summer of 1995, the television news had become generally in line with foreign coverage, and Michal Yaniv and Nitsan Horowitz had written sympathetically in *Ha'aretz.*

Haim Baram is by his own frequent self-description a "genuine leftist." He is perhaps Israel's best representative of what Marcuse called a "lefter than thou" attitude, as he brings his weekly strictures against prominent figures of the moderate left, from Amos Oz to A. B. Yehoshua. Virtually alone among Israeli commentators in opposing the Gulf War, Baram denounced the self-righteousness of Israelis who gloated over the bombing of Baghdad while scorning Palestinians dancing on rooftops as Scud missiles fell on Ramat Gan. At the aforementioned 1993 Hebrew University symposium on Bosnia, Baram castigated the American media for portraying the Balkan conflict in a one-sided manner. His presumption seemed to be that if the American media say X, then X must be false, and furthermore its utterance a consequence of the darkest reactionary motives. In the present case, the media still sympathized with the Croatian fascists and harbored lingering Cold War antipathy to Serbian communism. His solution to the conflict? None other than the complete restoration of the Federal Republic of Yugoslavia within its previous borders. Thus, a self-proclaimed "genuine leftist," wielding a wholly different discourse, arrived at a result exceeding in pro-Serbian nationalism the fanatical ethnic cleansers Šešelj and Arkan, who were by then at least willing to concede the independence of Slovenia and perhaps part of Croatia. Baram told me a year later that he now regarded the reconstitution of Yugoslavia as "utopian" and accepted Avineri's argument that while "no side is better than the other" the military forces were so unbalanced that it was necessary to help the weaker party, the Muslims. (For both Avineri and Baram there seems no difference in principle between the Bosnian aspiration to a democratic multiethnic state and the Greater Serbian campaign of ethnic cleansing via siege, terror, and murder.) After the fall of the first UN-declared "safe area," Srebrenica (July 1995), in the wake of which the entire town was ethnically cleansed by means perfected in 1992, including rape of young girls, the apparent murder of thousands of men, and mass deportations, Baram wrote that the Serb attack was "provoked by a Muslim atrocity eight months earlier." (It would be interesting to elicit Baram's views on the German government's claim in 1938 that the orchestrated anti-Jewish pogroms known as

Kristallnacht were "provoked" by the shooting of a German diplomat in Paris by a German Jewish refugee.) Baram also ridiculed a planned demonstration (which never materialized) in support of Bosnia by the "Young Guard" of the Labour Party and the Palestinian Authority.[52]

And then there is the case of former Jerusalem mayor Teddy Kollek, who in an offhand remark to a *Boston Globe* reporter revealed much about the prejudices besetting Israeli society. In a discussion of why, in the then mayor's view, Israel must retain sovereignty over all Jerusalem, he explained, "Deep down in Arab philosophy is the conquest by war and not a peaceful conquest." Interviewer: "So that if you were to give them East Jerusalem, they'd still declare war? That's your feeling?" Kollek: "I'm convinced of that. They don't want East Jerusalem. Look, they still want Granada and Cordoba and half of Spain—it belongs to them. 'The *Dawlet el Islam,* the land of Islam that we once ruled, we will rule again.' You can observe that again about Bosnia. That is basic Islam. I make it difficult for myself [saying this] but I have to see that, too."[53]

Why Kollek thought he made things difficult for himself is not clear. The remark about Bosnia in particular, at least in the Israeli context, was certainly at the time not terribly out of synch. Indeed, it recalled a familiar dilemma: evil never presents itself naked on the stage of history; it always appears dressed up as itself the victim, the defender, the perhaps misunderstood struggler for survival (as observers of Serbian statements frequently point out). Thus the leaflets of the Black Hundreds never proclaimed: "We are pogromists, and have come to rape, pillage, and murder defenseless Jews." Rather, they exhorted, "Mother Russia is in peril. The Jews are bringing it to its knees. Come save Mother Russia." The message was between the lines, but nonetheless clear: Disregard the actual facts on the ground; a Jew is always a Jew and Mother Russia must be defended. Similarly, when the affable cultured (ex-)mayor says, "You can observe that again about Bosnia. That is basic Islam," he doesn't mean that you can observe it literally as much as he means, "Disregard the actual facts on the ground. A Muslim is always a Muslim." One better than Arendt, it is the sheer civility of evil that is squarely beneath our gaze.

The Kollek interview was reprinted in the *Jerusalem Post* editor's column.[54] Editor David Bar-Illan regarded Kollek's views as deeply insightful; he similarly reprinted for its presumed merits Uri Elitsur's *Yediot Aharonot* column which argued, "Maybe the terrible stories of ethnic cleansing, genocide, and rape of tens of thousands of women are mainly war propaganda by Bosnian spokesmen, for whom the free press has volunteered to be their trumpet."[55] The column ends with a reminder that the Serbs were on our side in World War II, while "the Bosnians were on the side of the Nazis." *Post* editor Bar-Illan's lone complaint was that Elitsur had omitted to mention the Bosnian government's hiring of a public relations firm in the US to spread this "war propaganda."[56]

The *Jerusalem Post* actually distinguished itself throughout the war by running what could only be called straight Belgrade propaganda repeatedly in its op-ed pages, while disallowing responses. (However, its foreign news editor, Tom O'Dwyer, was permitted to condemn Serbian aggression in a number of unsigned editorials, and a few pieces by Igor Primoratz and others were also tolerated, albeit with commissioned responses. The op-ed balance was roughly six to one in favor of Serbia, a tilt probably unparalleled in Western newspapers outside Greece and Israel.) Typical articles included "The Coming of the Sword" by Alfred Sherman.[57] The title refers to the sword of Islam again threatening civilization, this time in Bosnia. As the author puts it, "There are good reasons for Jews in general and Israelis in particular to identify with the Serbs. We have several common enemies: German expansionism, Moslem fundamentalism; Catholic clerico-fascism; and the so-called 'international community' — a disguise for great-power egoism and manipulation."[58]

Another characteristic sample was aptly titled "Don't Cry for Bosnian Moslems."[59] Its crankish author, Yohanan Ramati, has had at least eight pieces in the *Post* on Bosnia since the start of the war. This one compressed over a dozen familiar Serbian charges particularly popular in Israel: Islamic fundamentalism, German responsibility, the Bosnian Muslims "supported the Holocaust," and so on. (A response by the present author was not allowed by the editors. Ramati's article of April 17, 1995, reports matter-of-factly that the shell on the Sarajevo market of February 1994 was actually a bomb, "probably" planted by Muslims.) Similar contributions were made by retired Israeli diplomat Zvi Locker on May 5, 1992, "Hillel Flesch" (possibly a pseudonym) on January 2, 1994, and several letters by the rump-Yugoslav *chargé d'affaires,* on, for example, February 14, 1994. But no doubt the Israeli publication surpassing all others, even the *Post,* in its service to Karadžić and Milošević has been the formerly Histadrut-owned *Davar,* purchased in early 1995 by private interests, after which Ron Ben Yishai became editor. Two of its staff,

Pazit Ravina and Teddy Preuss, have traveled back and forth between Israel and Belgrade since the beginning of the war, bringing to Israeli readers the latest explanations and insights. (It would be interesting to confirm whether Belgrade has paid for the numerous trips of Ravina, Preuss, and Ramati.) Every horrible shelling of Sarajevo brought a column from one of the two revealing special evidence that it was really Muslims who were responsible, or that the real issue was still the Ustashe-run Jasenovac concentration camp in World War II. Thus on February 18, 1994, Ravina cited an unnamed "senior Israeli ballistics and explosives expert" who concluded, from his special vantage point in Israel, that the explosion in the Sarajevo marketplace couldn't have come from a shell, but was probably caused by the type of device used by the Hezbollah in Lebanon and the Mujaheddin in Afghanistan. "There are at present several hundreds of Mujaheddin in Bosnia" (another staple of Israeli reportage), Ravina ominously reminds readers. Ravina is a regular pundit on Kol Yisrael's daily international news radio program, her Belgrade connections and willingness to serve Serbian propaganda apparently never having been judged by the editors as detracting from her objectivity or "expertise."

Preuss published some twenty rambling pieces in *Davar,* the *Jerusalem Post,* and even *Ha'aretz,* making claims so hysterical it is doubtful that they could have been published in most Western newspapers, again outside Israel and Greece. He exceeded even Serbian propagandists in his charges of "Nazism" against not only Tudjman but also Izetbegović. A local Israeli Bosnian support group was equally labeled "pro-Nazi" after it presented "An Evening for Bosnia" at the Jerusalem Cinematheque (April 6, 1994). A previous article (March 19, 1994), ostensibly a critique of the evening, was accompanied by a huge photo (indicating editorial collusion) of victims of Jasenovac. It seems unnecessary to add that while cranks like Preuss exist throughout the West, the free access to the media granted them in Israel—not to mention the near immunity from rebuttal—is an almost unique feature of the Israeli debate about the war; one must look to Greece and Russia for possible comparison.[60]

A final example worth mentioning is the Israeli reaction to the February 1994 shelling of the old market in Sarajevo. While most of the world was calling for force finally to be used to break the siege of that unfortunate city, Israeli pundits knew better. A case in point was Israel Television's David Witstom, whose earlier claim to notoriety derived from his long

interview with one of Panama strongman General Noriega's last supporters, his Israeli military advisor Michael Harari. (The interview was widely
perceived as a whitewash of Harari, who it was later discovered, was a
relative of David Witstom.) Now Witstom took to the printed media in an
effort likely to endear him anew to elite circles here.[61] People think that
it's "one bang and we're all done," he ridiculed. What is needed, rather,
is to "act wisely," by which he meant—as the remainder of the article
made clear—a continuation of the policy that had led thus far to 200,000
deaths.[62]

To sum up the public discussion in Israel: in contrast to that of the rest
of the world, the basic facts about who is the main aggressor were in the
first three years rarely acknowledged outside actual direct reports, especially those picked up from foreign news agencies. When debates were
held, either in the media or the universities, organizers generally saw fit
to "balance" the speakers so that at least half viewed the Serbian cause as
unjustly maligned. This was quite at odds with the situation in most
Western countries, where expression of sympathy for the Serbs was
generally confined to the occasional op-ed piece or interview with a Serb
official, some exceptions notwithstanding. And it has been even more at
odds with the reaction of many diaspora Jews, especially in the US and
France, who have taken the lead in urging their governments to use force
to stop the slaughter. In Israel, it was sympathy with the Bosnian Muslims
that was only occasionally voiced in a rare op-ed article. Frequently the
content of debate almost immediately turned to World War II in an effort
to establish which nation, in general, was the collectively guilty party. In
this way Israel has resembled much more the killing fields of the former
Yugoslavia than the West. As David Rieff observed,

> Everywhere in former Yugoslavia, even on battlefields where the corpses
> are still fresh, it is almost easier to get a history lesson than to get a straight
> answer about what happened in this place where one is standing with one's
> interlocutor. He or she is more likely to talk about the massacre of the
> Serbs by the Croat Fascists in the Second World War, or the dream of
> Greater Serbia, which dates back to the nineteenth century and beyond,
> even to the Battle of Kosovo of 1389, that holiest of days in Serb folk
> mythology.[63]

It seems difficult to deny that Israel shares with its cousin just north of
the Mediterranean an obsession with history reminiscent of Amos Elon's
phrase about Jerusalem, "In the high noon of the ghosts, the human
dimension is lost."[64]

The Israeli Response: The Political Level

Until July 1995, all official government pronouncements had remarkably reflected the unwillingness of public commentators to attribute blame. Indeed, as Yerach Tal observed in *Ha'aretz* in 1992, it was the express policy of the government not to take sides in any of the conflicts in the former Yugoslavia.[65] The first explicit condemnation of Serbian atrocities in the name of the government came only after the fall of Srebrenica (more than three years after the commencement of the Serbian onslaught in Bosnia), when Prime Minister Rabin, speaking by telephone on a live Jordanian television broadcast, was pressed by the moderator to state his position, whereupon he declared that he "condemned Serbian atrocities against Muslim civilians."[66]

Until that moment, that is, throughout the first three years of war, Israeli officials had insisted on maintaining official neutrality at best, and sometimes overt pro-Serbian sympathy. Nevertheless, during the height of Serbian atrocities in the summer of 1992, the legacy of the Holocaust obviously weighed on the consciences of politicians. Thus, as news of death camps, ethnic cleansing, mass atrocities, enforced ghettoes, and deportations made reaction unavoidable, officials began to utter peculiar statements in which they condemned the atrocities, but scrupulously refrained from naming the perpetrators, rather like a schoolteacher who scolds, "Whoever threw that piece of chalk while my back was turned had better stop." In August 1992, Yerach Tal cited government "sources" as saying that they can't take sides because "there is a lack of clarity about what is going on there, since according to information in [government] hands, no side is innocent of atrocities in Yugoslavia." A hint about the nature of the "information in [government] hands" can perhaps be gleaned from a report in the *Jerusalem Post* two days earlier, on August 5, 1992. Peres had "expressed deep shock" at reports of concentration camps, saying, "Such actions anger us deeply, and I call on *the peoples of Yugoslavia* to stop" (emphasis added). The article stated that he then "called on the parties in Yugoslavia to resolve their differences through negotiations." By transposing the remarks, *mutatis mutandis,* to, say, Eastern Europe in 1942, one can fully appreciate their political significance. But especially revealing is that the article went on to describe the interview with Budimir Kosutić, rump-Yugoslavia's ambassador-designate in Israel, himself a possible candidate for war crimes.[67] He is quoted as follows:

> The concentration camps in Bosnia-Hercegovina were set up by the Cro-
> ations *[sic]* and the Moslems, and they are the ones who approached the
> world media. In areas controlled by the Serbian people, there are no
> concentration camps. The Serbs have been the victims of the travesty in
> Yugoslavia, not the aggressor.

It is difficult not to wonder why Kosutić was granted an interview on
Israeli radio's *Eight in the Evening* program the night before, and whether
this was not the "source" of the "information in [government] hands"
leading to a "lack of clarity about what is going on," since by the first
week of August there was no parallel lack of clarity in corroborated
reports from the Red Cross, *Newsday,* UNHCR, and Helsinki Watch. A
week later, Peres was again quoted as saying it was impossible to take a
position on the claims of the three warring entities, Serbs, Bosnians, and
Croats. "But we can take a stand on tortures and concentration camps."[68]
Again, it is somewhat like saying in 1942, We cannot take a stand on the
claims of the warring factions, Germans, Jews, and Poles, but we do
condemn concentration camps.

Not all politicians were content with this noncommittal policy. According to the *Jerusalem Post,* several Knesset members

> charged the government was not doing enough to protest against the
> reported Serbian atrocities.
>
> MK Rafi Elul and law committee chairman Dedi Zucker (Meretz) also
> accused the Knesset presidium and speaker Shevah Weiss[69] of hindering
> their efforts to raise the issue in the plenum. . . .
>
> Elul said the reported Serbian atrocities were being conducted "ac-
> cording to the horrible practices of the Nazis during the Holocaust, and the
> world is silent. Israel must not be silent," he declared.
>
> Zucker criticized the government for not following the lead of most
> European countries and severing diplomatic ties with Yugoslavia.
>
> "We must not only take pragmatic considerations into account; the
> moral consideration is also very powerful," he said.[70]

What some of those pragmatic considerations might have been can perhaps be pieced together from various clues appearing in scattered sources
about possible Israeli-Serb arms deals. There is now no doubt that Israeli
arms — and arms, not necessarily Israeli, but supplied by Israeli dealers —
are being sold to Serbia; the only question is the extent, if any, of
Israeli government involvement. Its spokespeople naturally deny such
involvement, as it no doubt would even if it did exist. The duty incumbent
upon morally responsible people, therefore, bearing in mind the signifi-

cance that such arms sales to Serbia would have, is to analyze as objectively and carefully as possible the available facts. They are the following:

In June 1993, in the *European,* Roger Faligot reported that, in the wake of an operation to take out hundreds of Jews from ex-Yugoslavia in November 1992, "Western intelligence agencies have told journalists that the Jewish refugees were allowed to leave only after a back door deal that involved supplying arms in breach of UN sanctions."[71] The writer provides no further information about which intelligence agencies were involved, nor what their own sources were. However, other evidence, both Serbian and Israeli, indicates that at least until late 1991,[72] high-level military relations were maintained, including, on one account, at least one major arms deal. Thus Dobrila Gajić-Glišić, former secretary of the Belgrade War Minister's office, writes in a recent book, "Certainly one of the biggest deals was closed by Jezdimir Vasiljević in October 1991 in Israel. At that time, for understandable reasons, the details of that deal with the Jews were not made public. It was a complicated and difficult deal. But it was made successfully."[73] The same Jezdimir Vasiljević, prominent banker and old crony of Serbian president Milošević,[74] arrived in Israel in February 1993. Though not Jewish, he announced his intention of staying in the country for a lengthy period, received considerable media attention, and was apparently still in the country by the end of the year. From the Israeli side, there was a statement in November 1992 by Ari Ben Menashe (former Mossad agent) on Belgrade radio B-92 that Serbia and the Federal Republic of Yugoslavia were acquiring arms from Russia and Israel (according to the Serbian wire service Tanjug, November 23, 1992, and picked up by several dailies throughout the former Yugoslavia). After describing some details of the arms deals, Ben Menashe replied to questions about Israel's interests in Yugoslavia. "Ben Menashe reminded listeners that in the eighties the Serbs in the federal government helped the Jews, and that brought the setting up of 'close personal relations between the people involved; thanks to those relations, the arms trade is functioning so well today.' "[75]

Peculiar about the quotation from Ben Menashe is his reference to Serbs helping Jews in the eighties. Jews in Yugoslavia were at that time free to travel wherever they wanted (as were all Yugoslavs), so it is not clear to whom he is referring. Possibly he is simply conflating the commencement of military cooperation between the two sides, which may have occurred in the eighties, with the ideological pretext for such relations in Israeli circles, namely, that "Serbs are friends of the Jews," reverting back to World War II. Alternatively, he may be conflating the same initiation of relations with the alleged deal cited in the *European* of taking Jews out beginning November 1992 in exchange for arms.

In any case, we have so far three separate sources—Serbian, Israeli, and Western intelligence—claiming that there were arms deals between the two countries. Though scant by themselves (and Ben Menashe is not generally considered the most reliable source), these reports gain credence against the particular political background in which they occur. In mid-July 1994 Ori Orr, who heads the parliamentary committee overseeing Israeli arms sales abroad, led an official Israeli delegation to Belgrade and met with (in his own words) "all of the top leadership of Serbia with the exception of President Milošević, who was out of town" (telephone conversation with author, July 1994). This visit was a follow-up, according to Orr himself, of a meeting six months earlier between Israeli foreign minister Shimon Peres and his Yugoslav (Serbian) counterpart (the latter who, according to Reuters and AP, visited Israel in February 1995, at least the third ministerial-level meeting between the two countries within less than a year). The visit by Orr worried the American administration enough that, according to one Israeli report,[76] Vice President Al Gore summoned the Israeli ambassador and officially "warned Israel not to establish any relations with the Serbian regime in Belgrade" (an official of Israel's foreign office told me that the meeting with Gore was simply for purposes of gaining a "clarification" about the visit of the Israeli delegation). In a telephone conversation, Orr denied that Israel was selling arms to Serbia, but then proceeded to run through virtually all the usual elements of Serbian and Israeli-Serbian arguments in an effort to convince me that Israel had good reasons to be on the Serbian side.[77] (Specifically, he mentioned World War II, Iranian and Hezbollah aid to Bosnia, and Croatian president Tudjman's anti-semitism. An Israeli "Foreign Ministry spokesman" made a similar remark to the *Jerusalem Report,* adding, "You may draw the conclusion where our sympathies lie.")[78] And indeed, Orr addressed his Belgrade hosts accordingly:

> Because of history and World war II, the Israelis support the Serbs. . . . We have not forgotten that we fought together. We have a good memory. We know what it is to live under sanctions and boycott. . . . Every UN resolution against us was adopted by a two-thirds majority, often with Yugoslavia voting against us. But we should think of a better future. The first step was the recent meeting between minister Jovanovic and Peres in Bucharest. We here are the second.[79]

Orr also stated, according to the same report, that "Israel should help the Serbs to improve their relations with the international public." As an official responsible for approving or withholding permission for any arms sale abroad, Israel's guardian of sanctions against Serbia—one may be forgiven for suspecting—was much like the proverbial fox in charge of the chicken coop. (Since the assassination of Prime Minister Rabin, Orr has pursued his pro-Serbian policy in his new portfolio of deputy minister of defense.)

It has also been confirmed on Israeli television that Bosnian Serb forces used Israeli-made munitions.[80] Well-known television personality Yaron London interviewed an Israeli aid worker in Bosnia, who related that at the request of a UN official, he had identified the Hebrew writing on the casing of a shell recently fired into Sarajevo as indicating that it was a standard Israeli military issue, complete with serial number. He also reported having seen Israeli-made arms in Serbian hands, including Uzi rifles. It is of course true that Israeli munitions could have reached Bosnian Serbs in any number of ways. It is the totality of the evidence, however, that while not absolutely conclusive, is certainly ample cause for concern.

A possible further piece of earlier evidence is the report in *Ha'aretz* that an Israeli transport ship loaded with twenty military trucks and Kalashnikov rifles was detained off the coast of Sicily, and its captain arrested for illegal transport of weapons in Italian territorial waters.[81]

But the most reliable report yet has been provided by the government-owned Israeli television itself. Veteran correspondent Hanan Azran reported on the evening news of August 2, 1995 (barely weeks after the joint Israeli-Jordanian airlift), that "private Israeli dealers," in collaboration with French arms merchants, had closed a deal to provide Serbia with American-made LOW missiles. Private arms deals, in Israel as elsewhere, require government approval. Of course, the prevalence of arms entrepreneurs in Israel—some with dual citizenship—renders supervision difficult. On the other hand, it is also the case that Israeli governments have long used nominally private dealers to trade arms with unsavory or disgraced regimes, for example in Latin America, where plausible deniability of government involvement was desired. Whatever the case, it is entirely possible that the token but highly publicized planeload of Israeli-Jordanian humanitarian aid may end up treating victims of the same LOW missiles supplied by Israeli merchants to Serbia in defiance of international sanctions.

Israel and Serbia: A Cozy Relationship?

Environment Minister Yossi Sarid stated to me in 1994 that there were then no arms sales to Serbia, but declined to deny or confirm that there had been any in the past.[82] But even assuming his statement is correct, the overall picture appears to be one of a cozy relationship that has developed between the military and diplomatic elites of Serbia and Israel since the late 1980s, and which has taken on its own dynamic, as Ben Menashe's statement seems to testify.[83] This relationship has ramified, and now manifests itself in the fact that Serbia's legal advisor in the World Court is Israeli law professor Shabtai Rosenne,[84] the presence in Israel of Milošević's former crony and arms trade negotiator Jezdimir Vasiljević, the easy and frequent access to the Israeli media by pro-Serbian sentiment, including by officials of the rump-Yugoslav embassy (officially not recognized but still issuing visas and giving the impression of carrying on business as usual), the frequent top-level meetings between the respective foreign ministries, and especially the official policy of neutrality the Israeli government has generally pursued (with the exception of Rabin's statement on Jordanian television).

In accounting for the discrepancy between Israeli and diaspora Jewish reactions to the war, it seems that six principal factors can be singled out. First, the influential Serbian-Jewish lobby, backed by the concerted efforts of Serbia itself (for reasons mentioned at the beginning), has operated in a political culture preoccupied with daunting local problems: the peace process and its persistent obstacles, continuing terrorism, regional insecurity, and so on. A highly motivated lobby backed by foreign resources and appealing to ostensible national interests was thus able to get an early "jump" on other potential commentators. This lead dissipated somewhat with the July 1995 brutal fall of two "safe areas," with Jordanian friendly persuasion, and with the rise of some local pro-Bosnian activity.

Second, the competition with Iran for zones of influence seems to have been taken seriously by some government officials, including Ori Orr. Rather than compete with Iran by supplying Bosnia with sufficient arms to render Iran's contribution dispensable, Israel seems to have opted for the easier solution of joining a Serbian-Greek-Russian regional alliance. (Recent Israeli military agreements with Greece have been reported on in the Israeli press, while trade with Russia of all sorts appears to be flourishing.)

A third factor is the legacy of World War II, reinforced by anti-

Semitic remarks by Croatia's President Tudjman, and the all-too-ready exploitation of these by a Serbian lobby operating in an arena much more congenial to the expression of anti-Croatian and anti-Muslim sentiment than, say, the United States or France.

Fourth is a lingering suspicion of Islam, as Teddy Kollek's remarks reveal. Even Foreign Ministry officials not taken in by charges of fundamentalism may be wary of having one more potential UN vote against Israel down the road, especially if a weakened Bosnian state remains dependent on Muslim countries.

Fifth, there is the interesting phenomenon of an instinctual feeling of solidarity with another pariah state, as evidenced by Ori Orr's remark in Belgrade: "We know what it is to live with sanctions and boycott." One often encounters an Israeli reaction along these lines: Well, we have been accused of these same things—ethnic cleansing, defying the international community, not respecting human rights. We know about the United Nations and the international media.[85] All these have fed on each other and generated relations between respective national elites now exerting independent force.

In general, then, it seems that, far from having a double standard of morality applied to it, Israel has actually fallen somewhat short of the international standard on this issue. Whatever the extent, if any, of government involvement in the arms trade, the overall indulgence of Serbia—evidenced again in June 1995 by Israel's rush to renew direct flights with Belgrade, and the refusal of government officials to condemn Serbia and its proxies publicly through the first three years of war—has remained an ongoing concern. This is especially true as Serbia attempts to use Israel to regain its standing in the international community.

Beyond paltry international standards there is much that Israel could have done, and could still do after the Dayton Accord, assuming that Rabbi Hillel's dictum that where there are no humans one should strive to be a human has application also to those collectivities of humans known as states. Israel seems fated to have become a significant arms producer, and it is unlikely that the breaking out of peace in the Middle East will lead to large-scale Israeli conversion from military to civilian production in the near future.[86] But this does not mean that its selection of clients cannot become more circumspect in a post-Cold and Arab-Israeli War era. The inclusion of moral considerations in foreign policy decisions may itself dovetail with new political interests, as Israel seeks to develop ties with Muslim and Third World nations emerging from the Cold War. Like

Israel in 1948, Bosnia is a UN-recognized fledgling state threatened with annihilation by more numerous and powerful enemies. Israel has the potential to play the role for Bosnia that Czechoslovakia filled for Israel in 1948, that is, to be a source of desperately needed arms. To be sure, while the embargo was maintained on Bosnian forces (leaving them with about 45 tanks against 400 for the Bosnian Serbs and 2,800 against the gamut of Serb forces), Israel did not risk violating it for the nebulous chance of befriending a beleaguered Muslim ministate, whether or not the same risk was already taken for the established ally Serbia. Nevertheless, with the embargo lifted, and if Israel and Bosnia were to establish diplomatic relations (which would be at some risk to the Bosnians, who have relied by default on military support largely from Muslim countries), the beginning of an important relationship could develop, which would in turn reinforce Israel's ties to Turkey, Albania, and the Muslim former Soviet republics. The case of South Africa provides a precedent for Israel's overnight reversal of policy following an American congressional decision; if the United States lives up to its commitment made at Dayton to arm the Bosnian government, a similar about-face should be possible.

Nor is the appeal of Serbia overwhelming. Unlike other pariah states supported by Israel in the past, Serbia's claim on Israeli allegiance is less than unshakable. Latin American dictatorships, as well as Indonesia and UNITA forces in Angola, were viewed by some Americans as loyal allies in the Cold War. Arming them not only filled immediate requirements, but also ingratiated Israel to significant segments of the American defense community, itself hampered by congressional and domestic media scrutiny. Serbia, which has been described with some accuracy as the last bastion of communism in Europe, holds out little for Israeli long-term interests, since few among the Western elites would be enamored with Israel's indulging of Serbian needs. There is every reason to believe that even if some settlement is reached with coercive help of NATO countries, Serbia will remain quite isolated. Its own economy will require years to recover, while its strongest ally, Russia, is itself floundering economically and in a quagmire politically. Moreover, as the full story of the Bosnian horrors becomes increasingly well known, it is likely that the perception of Serbia as pariah will persist among both Western and Muslim publics for years to come. For all these reasons it will be in Israel's interest to distance itself as much and as soon as possible from its erstwhile client, and to establish a positive record with the emerging Bosnian state.

NOTES

This version has been updated to August 1995, except for minor revisions in 1996. Other versions were presented at the International Conference on Responses to Genocide and Holocausts, Hebrew University of Jerusalem, December 30, 1993, and the International Conference on Bosnia and Herzegovina, Bilkent University, Ankara, April 1995. Another version appeared in the Journal of Mediterranean Studies, summer 1996. I wish to thank Roy Gutman for his warm encouragement and advice, and Igor Primoratz for generous help.

1. Official pronouncements of some Western states with troops serving in UN forces in Bosnia—Britain, France, and Canada—have sometimes resembled Israeli statements of extreme caution and neutrality. Among nations *without* troops on the ground, Israeli official statements were matched in their coddling of Serbian sensitivity only by Greece, Russia, China, and perhaps some other former republics of the Soviet Union and former Soviet bloc states. It is also noteworthy that in the three Western countries mentioned above there has been sharp opposition to government policy not only by much of the respective media, but also by some leading politicians, sometimes of the governing party itself. In Britain, for instance, the policy set down by John Major and Douglas Hurd of maintaining the arms embargo on the Bosnian government and not using force against Serb forces was harshly criticized by former prime minister Margaret Thatcher and Social and Liberal Democrat leader Paddy Ashdown, as well as some stalwarts of the Labour Party left. There was little parallel in Israeli politics. As for the media, Israel was again distinct from all Western nations other than Greece, which continued to guard its traditional ties to Serbia. Despite some problems with Western media coverage, there was a general tendency at least to sympathize with the Bosnians, and often to criticize Western foreign policy makers. *New York Times* editorialists, to take a nontrivial example—from Safire on the right, to Gelb in the center and Anthony Lewis on the left (but excluding A. M. Rosenthal)—have excoriated both Bush and Clinton administrations on Bosnia. *Le Monde* and the *Guardian* have similarly lambasted their respective governments' inaction toward Serbian aggression. Again, there is no parallel in Israel, where analogous comment is a very rare exception.

2. MacKenzie admitted to having received a large sum from the Serbian lobby group for a two-day speaking tour in Washington. SerbNet later confirmed that he had been paid $15,000 plus expenses for his efforts on the organization's behalf. Roy Gutman, "Serbs Bankroll Speeches by Ex-UN Commander," *Newsday,* June 22, 1993. Reprinted in Gutman, *A Witness To Genocide* (New York: Macmillan, 1993), 168. For a discussion of Eagleburger's Serbian connections, see p. xii.

3. The quotation is from the Krajina Serbian parliamentary session, as re-

ported in the now defunct Croatian opposition weekly *Danas,* March 10, 1992. For fuller quotation and surrounding circumstances, see note 67 below.

4. The allusion, of course, is to Benedict Anderson's celebrated definition of a nation as "an imagined political community." *Imagined Communities* (London: Verso, 1983, 1991), 6. Anderson gives the impression of wanting to protest too much against reductionist views—especially of a Marxist variety—that disparage nationalism as ideology or illusion. However "creative" imagination can be, an underlying assumption lingers that there is a "real" substratum of nationless individuals, over against which one "imagines" the mental construct of national identity. But one would have to imbibe a heavy dose of materialism—whether Marxist or liberal—to take nationless individuals as less "imaginary" than the thickly described and self-identifying people we know. But the point is well taken if it means merely that national belonging can be imagined in a variety of ways. It is this point that I would broaden to international relations against the traditional "realism" of that field, proffering Israel's imagined affinity with Serbia—however "ideological" and distorted—as a case in point.

A good example of someone who slides easily from moderate to extreme readings of "imagination" is Michael Ignatieff. Without credit to Anderson, he discovers that "You can never know the strangers who make up a nation with you," so "A nation, therefore, is an imagined community." *Blood and Belonging* (New York: Vintage, 1994), 109). But he is soon taking to describing his Ottawa boyhood "illusions" and "phantoms" of "Frenchies" lying in ambush behind cemetery gravestones as having "shaped my imagined Canada" (112). With such loose usage, little wonder that Quebec, Croatian and even Bosnian (e.g., p. 188) varieties of the "new nationalism" get lumped together with the Serbian: all are guilty of "tearing apart" federal systems based on a "civic" principle according to which individuals and not ethnicity count.

5. Quoted in David Rieff, "Original Virtue, Original Sin," *New Yorker,* November 23, 1992, 82–88.

6. For instance, Gutman, *Witness to Genocide,* notes atrocities in Kozluk (20–22), Kljuc (31), Sanica Gornja (31), Kozarac (37, 41), Bosanski Novi (38), Brezovo Polje (68), Novo Selo (78), Bratunac (78), Prijedor (38, 44, 109 ff.), Skender Vakuf (85, 86), Biscani, Zečovi, Carakovo, Sredeci (sites of mass slaughters, 86), Višegrad (21, 24), and others.

7. Ibid.

8. For instance, see the two books published by Helsinki Watch, *War Crimes in Bosnia-Herzegovina,* 2 vols. (New York, 1992, 1993).

9. Norman Cigar, *Genocide in Bosnia: The Policy of "Ethnic Cleansing"* (College Station: Texas A&M University Press, 1995), 53, 55.

10. Ibid., 55.

11. Ibid., 58.

12. Ibid, 59. Cigar cites the U.S. Department of State, *Submission,* second submission (October 1992).

13. Gutman, *Witness to Genocide,* 41.

14. Ibid., 90.

15. Ibid., 93.

16. David Rieff, *Slaughterhouse: Bosnia and the Failure of the West* (New York: Simon and Schuster, 1995), 87.

17. Ibid., 96.

18. Gutman, *Witness to Genocide,* 50.

19. February 25, 1993.

20. Istvan Deak, for instance, went so far as to argue recently that the Allied policy of holding all Germans collectively responsible actually prevented an effective German resistance to the Nazis from coalescing. He further states that "the doctrine of collective guilt, although never officially promulgated, was made clear to all through the Allied policy of carpet bombing German cities and the murderous behavior of the advancing Red Army toward German civilians. Ultimately about two million German civilians were killed and twelve million were expelled from East Central Europe as well as from what used to be Germany east of the Oder-Neisse line. *New York Review of Books,* January 13, 1994.

21. Cigar, op. cit., 93.

22. *Jerusalem Post,* February 14, 1994.

23. My article in *Ha'aretz,* July 30, 1995, and Igor Primoratz's review of Norman Cigar in *Ha'aretz,* June 1995, are about the only exceptions I know of.

24. Gutman, *Witness to Genocide,* 169.

25. Roger Cohen, *New York Times,* March 9, 1995.

26. Cigar, op. cit., 47.

27. Ibid., 90.

28. Helsinki Watch, 45.

29. Ibid.

30. In some cases not only have Serbian claims subsequently been falsified, but it turned out that it was actually Serbian forces who massacred non-Serbian civilians at the time and place where the opposite had been alleged. Thus the Helsinki Watch report of January 21, 1992, addressed to President Milošević and Defense Minister Adžić, states,

Reports by the news agency Tanjug accused Croats of having committed war crimes against Serbs in the areas near the town of Grubisno Polje in Croatia. The allegations were investigated by members of the European Community (EC) monitoring commission who found that Serbian forces, not Croatian forces, were guilty of summary executions and destruction of civilian property in the area. The EC report concludes: "We established evidence of crimes which were committed by the [Serbian forces] during the two- and three-month period that they controlled that particular zone. Our team did not find evidence of killings later, nor of the systematic destruction of Serbian property by the Croatian National Guard or Croats from the area." The EC report also found that Czechs and Croats were killed in 16 villages visited by the mission, homes were destroyed and residents were terrorized. (pp. 4–5)

Cases of this kind arise in the reports uniquely with respect to Serbian allegations. It is also worth noting that the U.S. State Department, while acknowledging that all sides in the former Yugoslav republic had been guilty of atrocities, stated that "the atrocities of the Croats and Bosnian Muslims pale in comparison to the sheer scale and calculated cruelty of the killings and other abuses committed by Serbian and Bosnian Serbian forces against Bosnian Muslims. The policy of driving out innocent civilians of a different ethnic or religious group from their homes, so-called ethnic cleansing, was practiced by Serbian forces in Bosnia on a scale that dwarfs anything seen in Europe since Nazi times" (State Department, January 1993).

31. Rieff, op. cit., 94.

32. Ibid.

33. *Newsweek,* January 11, 1993.

34. Gutman, *Witness to Genocide,* 69.

35. Ibid.

36. Ibid., 161.

37. Ibid., 68.

38. December 14, 1992.

39. *Yediot Aharonot,* August 6, 1992.

40. *Ma'ariv,* August 3, 1992.

41. *Ma'ariv,* August 10, 1992.

42. Quoted in the religious paper *Yeted Hane'eman,* August 14, 1992.

43. For instance, Franjo Tudjman's minimizing of the number of Jews killed in the Holocaust and shifting of blame to them were understandably condemned by many Jews and Israelis, and have even been cited by Israel's Foreign Ministry as grounds for not establishing relations with Croatia (known in Israel as "the Waldheim principle" in reference to the freezing of relations with Austria during Waldheim's presidency). But it seems almost too obvious to mention that unlike the denial, however ignominious, of a past genocide, the denial of an ongoing genocide can have an actual effect on it, and on the readiness of politicians to urge intervention to stop it. Needless to say, comparison between the two denials does not presume identity between the genocides. Among differences, French historian Jacques Julliard cites two in his powerful book *Ce fascisme qui vient* (Paris: Seuil, 1994) worth repeating here: (1) in the Bosnian and Croatian case,

"barely are [atrocities] there committed when the reports of them can be found in all the best libraries" (102) (or, one might add, on CNN and other networks; indeed, the unprecedented simultaneous documentation of this ongoing genocide gives it claim to its own uniqueness); (2) "Germans, had they protested [the Holocaust], risked losing their lives. We risk losing an evening" (103).

44. For an extensive discussion of Serbian collaboration in the Holocaust, see the forthcoming book by Philip Cohen, as well as Philip Cohen, "Holocaust History Misappropriated," *Midstream* 38, no. 8 (November 1992).

45. Phyllis Auty, *Tito: A Biography* (New York: McGraw-Hill, 1970), 235.

46. See the subchapter of chapter 7, called "Chetnik Terror," of Jozo Toma-sevich, *The Chetniks* (Stanford: Stanford University Press, 1975). For the doctrine of revenge as "sacred duty," see 261. With this history in mind, one can imagine how a Muslim must feel to hear the claim sometimes made, not only by Serbian nationalists (I heard it from the organizer of a conference on the Holocaust), that what is happening to the Bosnian Muslims is revenge for what *they* did to the *Serbs* in World War II. One might as well say that what Ukrainian collaborators did to Jews in World War II was revenge for what the *Jews* did to *them* in 1919. After Jews and Gypsies, Muslims had the greatest proportional losses in Yugoslavia during World War II, roughly 8.1 percent. See Noel Malcolm, *Bosnia: A Short History* (New York: New York University Press, 1994), 192.

47. Menahem Shelach, et al., *History of the Holocaust: Yugoslavia* (Hebrew. Toldot HaShho'a: Yugoslavia) (Jerusalem: Yad V'shem, 1990).

48. Aleksa Djilas, *The Contested Country: Yugoslav Unity and Communist Revolution, 1919–1953* (Cambridge: Harvard University Press, 1991), 124.

49. John Zametica, *The Yugoslav Conflict* (London: Brassey's, for International Institute for Strategic Studies, 1992), 8.

50. The "new history," as it is referred to in Israel, questions many assumptions of earlier Zionist and Israeli historiography. In particular, the notion that Palestinian refugees fled in 1948 because Arab leaders had instructed them to do so has been decisively rejected by historians like Benny Morris. In general the works show a sensitivity to the plight of Palestinians, but other controversies have also been given new attention, such as the treatment of Oriental Jews in Israel, and Zionist policy during the Holocaust. The major contributors to this stream, in addition to Morris and Porat, have been the late Simha Flapan, Tom Segev, Avi Shlaim, and Ilan Pappe.

51. "The Villain Is No Villain," *Ha'aretz,* August 14, 1992.

52. *Kol Ha'ir,* July 21, 1995.

53. *Boston Globe,* November 29, 1992.

54. December 11, 1992.

55. March 2, 1994.

56. *Jerusalem Post,* March 4, 1994.

57. *Jerusalem Post,* March 23, 1994.

58. Ibid.

59. *Jerusalem Post,* August 11, 1993.

60. The *Ha'aretz* newspaper has come closest to meeting international standards. Though its editors have toed the familiar Israeli line, it has run foreign commentary sympathetic to Bosnia. A series on Sarajevo by foreign writers was carried weekly from December 1993 to February 1994 and other foreign articles of note, including one by Fouad Ajami in the *New Republic,* have also been reprinted. Its European correspondents Michal Yaniv and Nitsan Horowitz became increasingly sympathetic to the victims of Serb aggression, especially after the fall of Srebrenica and Žepa in July 1995. However, frequent contributors such as Yehuda Nadav and Teddy Preuss continue to stamp the unmistakable Israeli logo on the opinion section.

61. *Yediot Aharonot,* February 1995.

62. At the same time, the Israeli Foreign Ministry declared, "Israel hopes that the wave of violence plaguing the region of former Yugoslavia, which reached a peak with the terrible killing in the Sarajevo market, will quickly come to an end. Israel expresses its regret for the deaths of innocent civilians, and expresses the hope that the efforts to find a peaceful settlement of the conflict will soon bear fruit." Quoted in *Ha'aretz,* February 7, 1995. The statement was criticized in a letter to the paper published February 15 (admittedly penned by this author) and signed by thirty academics.

63. Rieff, op. cit., 87.

64. *New York Review of Books,* August 17, 1989.

65. August 7, 1992.

66. Rabin's phone call to the station was a follow-up to Jordanian King Hussein's direct call to him a few days earlier. According to the initial report in *Ha'aretz* (July 18, 1995) based on Rabin's own account to the Knesset Defense and Foreign Relations Committee, Hussein proposed that the two leaders undertake a joint project of aid to Bosnian refugees and residents, but the prime minister rejected the offer on the grounds that "the wealthy European countries" should bear responsibility for Bosnia's victims. Nevertheless, perhaps on the advice of Foreign Ministry officials concerned to limit the damage, Rabin called the open line show a few days later, issuing his condemnation, pledging $3,000 of his own money to their telethon, and announcing a joint Israeli-Jordanian airlift of humanitarian aid.

67. Kosutić had been Serbian vice premier during the ethnic cleansing of the Krajina, and had been nominated for president of the self-declared Serbian state of Krajina. According to the protocols of the Krajina Serb parliament, reported in *Danas* (March 10, 1992), it was decided that "due to the vast Jewish influence worldwide," a more important post awaited him: ambassador to Israel. Thus Milan Martic, himself eventually indicted for war crimes, became the Krajina chief. Nevertheless, the Serbian speaker presiding over the parliamentary session

concluded, "That does not mean that he [Kosutic] will not one day be President" of the Krajina Republic. Alas, as of this writing (August 1995), it appears Kosutić will have to miss this career opportunity.

68. *Jerusalem Post,* August 12, 1992.

69. Himself a Holocaust survivor, Weiss's own position marks an interesting evolution. As he became aware of the actual details of the Serbian campaign, he became increasingly critical both of Serbian aggression and of Western inaction in stopping it, and he issued a harsh condemnation of Bosnian Serb forces after the shelling of Sarajevo's old market in February 1994. A few weeks later he spoke openly about the change, in the *Jerusalem Post,* February 18, 1994: "At the beginning of the Yugoslavian crisis, the majority of Jews [*sic*] automatically had sentiments with the Serbs ... I remember that the Serbs had a unique place against Fascism and Nazism, but today, with such a cruel regime in Serbia, I've changed my feelings."

70. August 6, 1992.

71. June 3–6, 1993.

72. When the right-wing Likud was in power; it was ousted by a left coalition in June 1992.

73. *Iz kabineta ministra vojnog: Srpska vojska* (Cacak: Marica and Tomo Spasojevic, 1992), 23.

74. Serbian strongman Milošević rose up through the ranks of Yugoslavia's central bank, Beobanka. His influence over this institution was a chief factor in his ability to plunder the Yugoslav federal reserves in 1991 and redirect them to his base in Serbia. Aside from the repressive measures against Albanians in Kosovo, this single act did more than any other to undermine confidence among the republics in Yugoslav prime minister Ante Marković's economic reform plan, and thus in the federation as a whole. As one commentator put it, "In fact, Milošević's theft had already wrecked the economic plan for 1991, by making off with no less than half the entire primary emission of money set aside for all six Yugoslav republics for that year. . . . Indeed, the Marković plan was already a failure by the time it was touted in the West as Yugoslavia's salvation." See Jonathan Eyal, *Europe and Yugoslavia: A Lesson from a Failure* (Royal United Services Institute for Defence Studies, 1993). Vasiljević had a falling-out with his erstwhile colleague after being accused of embezzling state funds. His prolonged presence in Israel is nevertheless of interest, especially in light of Gajić-Glišić's claim regarding his role as arms negotiator with Israel.

75. *Vecernji list* (Zagreb), November 23, 1992.

76. *Yediot Aharonot,* July 19, 1994.

77. Television conversation with the author, July 1994.

78. *Jerusalem Report,* January 26, 1995.

79. Cited in the Belgrade daily *Politika,* July 18, 1994.

80. Channel 2, December 2, 1994.

81. August 27, 1993.

82. Telephone conversation, January 15, 1994.

83. An article in the Tel Aviv weekly *Ha'ir* (July 7, 1995) paints a picture of shadowy Israeli businessmen in Belgrade bragging behind a cover of anonymity of their connections with Mossad and other security agencies, and reiterating the standard justifications of Jewish-Serbian friendship.

84. See "Serbs, in World Court, Deny Guilt" by Stephen Kinzer, *International Herald Tribune,* Friday, August 27, 1993:

> Lawyers for the remnants of Yugoslavia told the World Court on Thursday that their government had no territorial ambitions in Bosnia Herzegovina and was not supporting any militia forces fighting there. "Yugoslavia cannot be held responsible at all for the course events have taken on the territory of the former Yugoslav Republic of Bosnia Herzegovina, nor for an *[sic]* crimes including the crime of genocide," said Miodrag Mitic, chief legal officer of the Yugoslav Foreign Ministry. "The Federal Republic of Yugoslavia has no paramilitary of any kind, either within or out of its territory."
>
> Asked about this during a break in the courtroom arguments, a senior legal adviser to the Muslim-led Bosnian government, Francis A. Boyle, replied: "It's a total lie. You know it and I know it. . . ."
>
> "The court is being invited to take political decisions to substitute itself for the will of other countries and organs," said Shabtai Rosenne, an Israeli law professor who is a legal adviser to the Yugoslav government. "This is far beyond the competence of the court, which had in the past repeatedly refused to substitute its judgment for that of communities and states," he said. "The court should not attempt to dictate to the republics of the former Yugoslavia, and perhaps to other states participating in the Geneva negotiations, how they should proceed and how they should negotiate," Mr. Rosenne said. "It would exacerbate the conflict."

85. Thus a cartoon in the *Jerusalem Report* (January 26, 1995): Frame 1: "The media has decided that the Serbs are the bad guys." Frame 2: "Just like they decided the Israelis were the bad guys." Frame 3: "Remember when reporters were supposed to report . . . and it was the job of the public to make the judgments?!" Frame 4 (second interlocutor, sarcastically): "No. . . . And just how old are you?"

Of course, in terms of moral reasoning, implied arguments like Orr's or the above are devoid of sense. Whether critics of Israel have been right, wrong, or alternately both, that has no bearing on the probity of claims against Serbia, nor is it clear how the media can report a genocide without making its perpetrator look bad. But beyond these obvious points, the underlying guilty conscience apparently revealed by this identification with a pariah has an added tragic dimension. In the wildest dreams of neither Israel's staunchest supporters nor harshest detractors has Israel committed anything like the crimes of Serbia and proxies in this war. Critics (or alternatively guilt-ridden Israelis) may seek to compare the flight/expulsion of Palestinians in 1948 with Serbian ethnic cleansing. But the 1948 war began with the attempt to expunge at birth the new UN-declared partition state of Israel, as Serbia has attempted with Bosnia. Thus both the evil attempted by the Arab states and the evil subsequently committed by Israel are incarnated in Serbia's policy toward Bosnia. But there is also no comparison between the "ethnic cleansing" of Palestine and of Bosnia. In the former, there really were atrocities committed by both sides on a rather similar scale. Moreover, that scale doesn't approach what Bosnian Serb forces did in a few days alone around Srebrenica. The largest massacre in 1948 was at Deir Yassin, where 242 Palestinians were killed. Three days later Arabs killed seventy-seven Jewish doctors and nurses en route to the Hadassah hospital at Mount Scopus. A handful of smaller massacres occurred on both sides, including a terrorist bomb in Jerusalem that claimed fifty-five mainly Jewish lives. Awkward as it is to point out, the victims on both sides are in the same ballpark—which is scarcely Little League size for even two days of serious Serbian cleansing. Israeli internalization of decades of demonization by the Soviet bloc and Arab states thus presents a fascinating case study for social psychology.

86. Aside from genuine security requirements, there are also the self-perpetuating dynamics of Israel's military-industrial complex, analyzed in Shimshon Bichler, "The Economics of Israeli Military Production" (Ph.D. diss., Hebrew University).

Michael N. Barnett

The Politics of Indifference at the United Nations and Genocide in Rwanda and Bosnia

In April 1994 genocide erupted in Rwanda. By the time the carnage had run its course in this country of eight million, roughly five hundred thousand people fell victim to a premeditated genocidal campaign that was designed by Hutu extremists to cleanse the country of the minority Tutsis. The Security Council's initial response to the violence was not to expand the size and responsibilities of the UN operation but to call for its reduction. Only a month later did the Security Council deliver its proposed response to the genocide, and it was not until a UN-authorized French operation arrived in late June that the United Nations offered some sort of protection for civilians in Rwanda. The United Nations eventually returned in the fall, but this was long after the genocide had run its course and a modicum of stability had returned.

The overwhelming response by the international community to the genocide was one of silence and a decided lack of urgency. To be sure, there were those who implored the United Nations to match the international response to the moral imperative, but by all accounts there was comparatively little of that. Still, many commentators have noted in disbelief that the United Nations, the symbol and representative of the international community, could remain idle while such horrors were occurring before its very eyes. The United Nations defends itself against such criticism because it is, to quote its secretary-general, merely a servant of the member states and is obligated to carry out the mandates of the Security Council and no more. The subtext, then, is that the United Nations' failure to respond forcefully to genocide was the preference of its member states. The United Nations' indifference is an indicator of the member states' indifference; nothing more, nothing less. Conversely, the United Nations could have been an effective agent against genocide had only the member states desired as much. So the failure resides with states. At the end of the day, states calculated that their own citizens cared very little about genocide, or at least they did not care enough to place their men and money on the line.

While there is much to this argument, this is only part of the story. As state and UN officials framed and discussed how to respond to genocide, they rarely approached the topic in such a callous manner; rather, their responses were shaped by and filtered through the organizational culture and bureaucratic interests of the United Nations. I come to this conclusion from personal observations and experiences. Beginning in September 1993 I was a political officer at the U.S. Mission to the United Nations. This opportunity arose through a fellowship from the Council on Foreign Relations, which offers to place academics like myself somewhere in the foreign policy bureaucracy so that we can, in theory, carry out a research project but, in practice, become part of the policy process. When I first arrived at the U.S. mission I worked on Somalia, but soon thereafter the United States announced its withdrawal, and my responsibilities were shifted from Somalia to other peacekeeping operations. By January 1994 I was the political officer for various parts of sub-Saharan Africa, including Rwanda. Among my duties as a political officer (sometimes referred to as an "action officer") were reading cable traffic on my issue, writing talking points for the ambassadors, covering my issue in the Security Council and writing cables on its proceedings, and generally acting as a conduit between Washington and the United Nations.

Consequently, I was well-positioned as both an observer and a participant when genocide erupted in Rwanda in April 1994. Although horrified by the Security Council's failure to take even the most minimal steps to alleviate the suffering, I justified the lack of action with the assumption that anything short of a massive and dramatic intervention would have stopped the genocide, the knowledge that no states were offering troops for such a campaign, and the belief that another "loss" after Somalia would jeopardize the United Nations' future. When I left the U.S. mission in June 1994 and returned to academic life I began to put these thoughts to paper, and wrote on peacekeeping and its future, highlighting the policy implications of Rwanda and other peacekeeping operations. An important conclusion was the need to protect the United Nations' resources and to better define the limit and scope of potential UN operations in order to salvage its reputation and to place on a firmer footing the basis of member states' support. When asked to discuss the United Nations' failure to respond to the genocide in Rwanda, I would argue that there was no effective basis for intervention, that throwing peacekeepers into dangerous situations to demonstrate the international community's concern needlessly exposes them to violence and undermines the United Nations' future, and that the Security Council's decision reflected a welcome learning process concerning when the conditions are ripe for peacekeeping to be effective.[1]

Although I still have strong doubts whether there was an effective basis for UN intervention in Rwanda, as I reflect on the Security Council's debates and my stance I am increasingly struck by how the concerns for the organization overshadowed, drove, and framed the debate, how easily member states and UN officials were able to conclude that the needs of the organization overrode the needs of the victims of genocide. The concern for the organization overshadowed and dominated much of the debate in the Security Council over whether or not to intervene, and I, too, framed the issue in these terms. There is little evidence, for instance, that the Secretariat or any member state vigorously petitioned the international community to assemble an intervention force, and most were much more exercised by the need to restrain the United Nations from any further involvement. Indeed, I now pose the issue in a more brutal manner: that the United Nations had more to lose by taking action and being associated with another failure than it did by not taking action and allowing the genocide in Rwanda. The choice was straightforward: genocide was acceptable if the alternative was to harm the United Nations' future.

I am increasingly drawn to the conclusion that the bureaucratization of peacekeeping contributed to this indifference to the suffering of the very people it was mandated to assist. As I, for one, more closely identified with the United States and the United Nations, it became easier for me to remain indifferent to the occasional evil because of the overarching needs of the organization. My intuition is that this narrative is as applicable to Bosnia as it is to Rwanda. Why did I justify UN inaction in Rwanda because of concern for the United Nations' reputation and future? How were I and others able to strike a comfortable moral equation between the reputation of the United Nations and the victims of the genocide in Rwanda? Why were the United Nations and NATO motivated to act in Bosnia only to save their reputation rather than to protect the victims of ethnic cleansing and the residents of safe havens? In this article I want to explore the possible connection between the discourse of acting in the best interests of the United Nations and the international community, the bureaucratization of peacekeeping, and the production of indifference in Rwanda and Bosnia.[2]

Peacekeeping and the Production of Indifference

To understand what makes this moral equation possible, I borrow the concept of the "production of indifference" from Michael Herzfeld's *Social Production of Indifference: Exploring the Symbolic Roots of Western Bureaucracy.*[3] Herzfeld opens with a succinct concern: "how and why can political entities that celebrate the rights of individuals and small groups so often seem cruelly selective in applying those rights?" How is it, he asks, that "Western" bureaucracies, which are supposedly rooted in a democratic culture, be so unaccountable to, and demonstrate such little concern for, those they represent? Why do citizens of a democratic society come to accept, if not expect, such arrangements? While I cannot do justice here to the complexity and breadth of Herzfeld's provocative argument, he offers the following observations that inform my discussion of the relationship between peacekeeping and indifference.

First, bureaucracies are not only instruments of domination, they also are symbolic markers of boundaries between peoples and are expressive of the cultures that produced them. As symbolic instruments of the nation-state, bureaucracies differentiate citizens from noncitizens, separating the community of believers from the community of apostates. All bureaucracies, in short, are expressive of a community and exhibit criteria that define who is a member of the community and who is not. Second, bureaucracies will selectively apply rights even among the community of believers. Not all members of the community are treated equally or receive the same privileges; some are, if you will, more equal than others. Although part of the reason derives from material considerations, identity also figures centrally in determining who is a "core" member of the community, and, therefore, who is more likely to receive its benefits and protection. Simply stated, while those with political or economic power are routinely given greater care and consideration by the state, those who are identified as possessing the defining qualities and characteristics of the community, including race, religion, and gender, will also receive better treatment than those who do not.

Third, identity is linked to the production of difference and indifference. Bureaucracies are connected to the identity of the community, differentiate between members of the community and nonmembers, and are expected to attend to members while ignoring nonmembers. "Compactly expressed . . . indifference is a rejection of those who are different."[4] The identity of the bureaucracy, in other words, represents the emotional and cognitive mechanism for creating threats and producing apathy. Bureaucrats, as members of the nation-state, use identity to determine who will receive their attention and who will not. The most intuitive and straightforward marker, of course, is citizenship, and it is expected that bureaucrats will attend to citizens and be indifferent to noncitizens.

Yet bureaucrats also are known to disregard some who are citizens of the nation-state. This leads to the fourth observation: the same process that produces indifference to outsiders can also generate indifference to some members of the community. Why? One reason is that bureaucrats are more likely to attend to members of the community who exhibit its defining characteristics and qualities. Again, while some groups in society are seen as core members, others are defined as peripheral; those who are core are more likely to receive the bureaucrat's attention than are those who are peripheral. Another reason bureaucrats have selective attention is that they identify not only with their fellow citizens but also with their bureaucracy. Bureaucrats, in this respect, have something of a dual identity: as members of a particular community they draw symbolic boundaries between themselves and those outside the national state, and as members of a bureaucracy they draw boundaries between the organization and the community. Simply stated, bureaucrats will often privilege the needs of, and take their identity from, the bureaucracy rather than the community. Bureaucrats pursue not only a bureaucratic agenda but also a personal one. Successful bureaucrats are able to manipulate their culture to achieve their specific and personal goals.

Herzfeld offers a fourth reason bureaucrats will exhibit indifference toward members of the community. As Western bureaucracies developed and deepened, supposedly in response to the growing needs and demands of their constituents, they were able to remain indifferent to the plights of the individual because of the guise of universalism. The bureaucrat, as a representative of the state, is supposed to represent the collectivity; therefore, s/he can dismiss the needs of the individual on the grounds of the universal. To explain this development Herzfeld forwards the concept of "secular theodicy,"[5] which originates from Weber's discussion of how religious systems account for the "persistence of evil in a divinely ordered world." The basic idea is that because moral principles transcend time and space, they allow the individual to maintain a belief in the transcendental notwithstanding the existence of the occasional evil. By transferring the concept from the religious world to the secular world of nation-states, Herzfeld is suggesting that state officials can themselves explain the presence of evil (and even justify their own indifference) with reference to abstract moral principles. More to the point, both religious and secular theodicy are founded on a "principle of identity; the elect as an exclusive community, whose members' individual sins cannot undermine the ultimate perfection of the ideal in which they all share. Both posit a direct connection between the community of believers and the unity of the ideal."[6] Therefore, the notion that actions occur with reference to and are embedded within the larger community allows bureaucrats and other members of the community to accept disappointments if not evil. Such indifference "permits genocide and intracommunal killings, to be sure, but it also perpetuates the pettier and less sensational versions of the same logic."

To be sure, bureaucrats will seldom present their indifference and self-interest in a public manner. One way that bureaucrats excuse their indifference and failure to respond is through buck-passing, red tape and bureaucratic rules, and so on. Yet bureaucrats will also feign concern and use the rhetorical device of the common good and the community's needs to cover their unwillingness to act and to further their own self-interest. In other words, they will frequently argue that their inability to act is not due to the limits of their bureaucratic responsibility and organizational rules but rather because these rules and practices are designed to protect the community's interests and aspirations. Sometimes this is simply a rhetorical device designed to allow state officials to excuse their personal indifference and to pursue their own self-interest. Yet, at another level, it allows them to live with themselves while acting indifferent and permitting injustices; they begin to effect the understanding that they are representatives of organizations that are, in turn, representative of the common good, allowing them to become indifferent to the individual under the discursive cloak of community. Such indifference is a testimony to the dominance of the needs of the organization over those of the individual, a testimony to the primacy of the universal over the particular.

Peacekeeping and Indifference

Herzfeld's discussion guides my narrative of the United Nations' actions regarding Rwanda and Bosnia by drawing attention to how: (1) the United Nations is a symbolic marker of the boundaries of the community; (2) the United Nations will selectively apply the rights of the community among its members; (3) identity helps produce difference and indifference by differentiating members of the community from nonmembers; and (4) UN and state officials will frequently identify with and protect the United Nations' interests and reputation and will evoke the discourse of universalism while ignoring the plights of the individual. These developments, I want to suggest, coincide with and are largely a function of the bureaucratization of peacekeeping that has occurred since the end of the Cold War.

To begin, a complex and contested feature of the United Nations is its constituency and articulated definition of the community: does the United Nations represent the "peoples" or states of the world? In the opening sentence of the Charter and throughout its fifty-year history, the United Nations has claimed that it represents the peoples of the world, and claims that there exist universal rights and principles that envelop state boundaries. In other words, the United Nations embodies a set of moral principles that are transcendental, existing across time and space, and the existence of state sovereignty can do little to abrogate or silence such principles. Indeed, various groups, including women, minorities, and native peoples, have used the United Nations to place their grievances on the world's agenda and to hold states accountable for how they treat their populations; their ability to do so is dependent on the discursive power of these claims and the vision articulated in the Charter.

Yet the UN Charter also observes that a cornerstone of international society and the United Nations is sovereignty and the principle of noninterference. The United Nations is an intergovernmental organization, its membership is limited to states, only states have the right to be part of the General Assembly and the Security Council, and states alone can determine what sorts of policies and actions the United Nations can espouse. Throughout its history the United Nations has generally promoted and honored the principle of sovereignty, which means that any tension over the its constituency has been resolved in favor of states.

This development is evident in the UN peacekeeping operations during the Cold War. Peacekeeping forces and military observer missions were designed with an eye to the politics of territorial restraint and juridical sovereignty. Although peacekeeping is seen as an invention of the Cold War and superpower conflict, it was originally designed to insure that decolonization, which potentially unleashed questions and conflicts over the state's territorial boundaries, and juridical sovereignty moved in tandem.[7] Conversely, these UN operations did not concern issues of human security, the protection of human rights, or the goal of humanitarian intervention, reflecting the general insistence of the newly emerging states that state sovereignty be duly respected.[8] Throughout the Cold War the United Nations favored states over peoples; accordingly, the focus was on the security of states rather than the security of peoples.

The end of the Cold War, however, shifted the United Nations' concern from state security to "human security." One of the interesting features of the United Nations' leap into the fray was a shift of representation: it was to protect not only the community of states but also the community of peoples. If prior to 1988 peacekeeping concerned interpositioning lightly armed UN troops between two states that had agreed to a cease-fire, they were now involved in a myriad of activities associated with nation building and humanitarian assistance. The UN involvement in Namibia, Cambodia, and El Salvador involved domestic and ethnic conflict resolution and facilitating the difficult transition from civil war to civil society. "Operation Provide Comfort," the UN assistance to the Kurds of Iraq, inaugurated a new chapter in humanitarian intervention, and Somalia and Bosnia stirred further promise of the United Nations' humanitarian instincts. Many UN officials with whom I spoke recall a sense of excitement and exhilaration during these first post-Cold War days; not only were they unshackled from the Cold War but their activism was directed at helping people rather than states. "There are greater rewards," recalled one official, "from helping the victims of political turmoil than its instigators." To be sure, there were some who feared that the United Nations had gone too far and was now treading on state sovereignty, but others championed this more ambitious agenda and cosmopolitan outlook, which suggested a United Nations that was on the verge of fulfilling its initial but long delayed promise. In any event, the United Nations, as exhibited through its peacekeeping operations, was shifting away from state security and toward "comprehensive" security.

As the United Nations became increasingly concerned with the security of peoples, it still dealt and thought in state-centric terms: human security meant "saving failed states."[9] In doing so, the United Nations was signaling that while it was shifting its constituency, it was also provocatively suggesting who is considered a core member of the community. To save a failed state was to save a member of the international community. What does it take to be a member of the community? A necessary condition is that the state be granted juridical sovereignty by the community of states. Yet not all sovereign states are created equal. Although material considerations contribute to the currency of power, also present in shaping the defining qualities of core membership are ideational forces. Said otherwise, some types of states are worthy of emulation and come to define the highest aspirations of the community. As states and nonstate actors began to debate who was considered a "civilized" and responsible member of the international community, and as the United Nations began to actively consider what kind of states it wanted to create, considerable emphasis was placed on domestic order in general and democracy in particular. In other words, while the community of states was still interested in the state's external behavior, an increasingly important element was the state's domestic behavior and identity. The international community, in short, was interested in fashioning and encouraging the development of democratic states.[10] One reason for this desire and concern for the state's internal attributes was the growing belief that domestic threats to the state and domestic instability undermine international order; domestic stability, which is best secured through democratic principles, fosters international order. Still, all roads pointed to democracy. To belong to the elect, a state must be democratic.

Peacekeeping operations are a direct extension of the view that domestic stability in general and democracy in particular are related to international order and define membership in the international community. Nearly all post-Cold War operations concern the transition from civil war to civil society; for instance, the operations in Namibia (UNTAG), Cambodia (UNTAC), El Salvador (ONUSAL), and Haiti (UNMIH) all aspired to end civil war and forward democracy. Indeed, as the United Nations looked to end an operation it used the symbol of a "free and fair" election. Peacekeeping operations, in short, are designed with the purpose of helping to rehabilitate fallen members of the community by instilling them with democratic features and characteristics.

This highly ambitious security agenda overwhelmed a bureaucratically and organizationally underequipped United Nations. In response to its observed shortcomings and associated failures, there emerged a flurry of peacekeeping proposals and reforms that were designed to professionalize, institutionalize, and make more efficient and effective UN peacekeeping. Contact groups were established, conferences held, the Department of Peacekeeping Operations was reorganized and expanded, a Situation Room, Department of Humanitarian Affairs, and Electoral Assistance Unit were inaugurated, standby arrangements for military forces were planned, and so on. These reforms and developments were absolutely essential if an antiquated and inefficient organization was to meet the challenges of the day and carry out its mandated responsibilities.

The bureaucratization also encouraged individuals and states to develop a vested interest in peacekeeping and the United Nations. For some the incentive was interest-based; they benefited materially and financially from their involvement in UN peacekeeping operations, and, therefore, championed their continuation. For others the benefits were not simply material but also cognitive; they came to believe that peacekeeping represented an important instrument of the international community for interstate and intrastate conflict resolution. Still others, however, came to identify with the idea of the United Nations and to see it as a symbol that transcended power politics. The common denominator of all three, however, is an identification with the United Nations, its interests, and its future. Inside and outside the United Nations, public officials and private citizens alike came to support and benefit from UN activities; the result was that a cadre developed who identified with the needs and interests of the organization.

An additional feature of the bureaucratization of peacekeeping was a greater consideration and elaboration of the conditions when an operation was likely to be successful, and, relatedly, should be approved. In the first days after the Cold War it seemed that no operation was too small, large, or complex to deserve UN attention; the United Nations was anxious to prove its promise, and the great powers, who now discovered the United Nations to be a useful place to dump intractable conflicts, encouraged that direction. These and other factors contributed to an explosion of peacekeeping operations. While there were eleven operations prior to

1988, subsequently there were twenty-four. Indeed, the Security Council appeared so quick to authorize a proposed operation that many quipped that "the UN never met an operation it didn't like." By the fall of 1993, however, many state and UN officials grumbled that such automatic authorizations were leaving the United Nations stretched thin and increasingly ineffective; it was time, they said, to exhibit greater self-restraint. The sobriety was partially a response to "failures" in Somalia and Bosnia, and the Security Council now began to incorporate a list of considerations to inform its decision to approve or extend a peacekeeping operation, including whether there is a genuine threat to peace and security; regional or subregional organizations can assist in resolving the situation; a cease-fire exists and the parties have committed themselves to a peace process; a clear political goal exists and is present in the mandate; a precise mandate can be formulated; and the safety of UN personnel can be reasonably assured.[11] In many respects, the United Nations was returning to its traditional tenets that peacekeeping was dependent on the consent of the parties and strict neutrality, a growing belief that its functions were to compel and encourage—not coerce and force—stability. In any event, there was growing sentiment that the future of peacekeeping depended on the Security Council elaborating a tighter set of conditions for the authorization or extension of an operation.

The emergence of these criteria, however, contributed to the production of indifference. The bureaucratization of peacekeeping, both in terms of its means and the conditions for its deployment, was couched in terms of the organization's needs. To be sure, there was an emerging pragmatism that demanded that the United Nations' activities match the willingness and resources of its member states, but in the wake of Bosnia and Somalia there was considerable fear that any more UN "failures" would spell the end of the United Nations. Much discussion at the United Nations revolved around how to better publicize "success stories," how to portray so-called failures as successes (or at least to demonstrate that the United Nations was not to blame), and how to ensure that the United Nations was not saddled with operations that had little chance of success. And many of the same individuals who now supported and had a stake in peacekeeping also were clamoring for greater sensitivity to the question of when peacekeeping was effective, and exhorting the Security Council to reject those proposed operations that did not satisfy these conditions.[12] In short, there occurred an important shift in the discourse of peacekeeping as officials in and around the United Nations were now taking greater care to protect the organization's interests, reputation, and future. Select wisely became the adage, because the next selection may be your last.

The concern for the United Nations' reputation and interests affected the operations that were selected. Perhaps the first instance in which the needs of the organization were explicitly cited and used to justify inaction was the Security Council's decision not to intervene in Burundi in October 1993, when nearly one hundred thousand died in ethnic violence. Living in the immediate shadows of Somalia, many members of the Security Council argued against intervention on the grounds that there was "no peace to keep" and that the United Nations needed to avoid obvious quagmires. Many UN officials and delegates breathed a sigh of relief when the Security Council opted to abstain from the conflict, observing that the United Nations had to conserve its energies for "winners." Burundi symbolized a shifting sentiment at the United Nations concerning the feasibility and desirability of humanitarian intervention. After all, such crises are a by-product of wars, wars are defined by instability, and a modicum of stability is a precondition for effective peacekeeping. The United Nations, in effect, was stepping away from its previous move toward human security and back toward state security. There was, if you will, a belief that the occasional evil could be tolerated so long as it did not damage the greater collective good.

By the fall of 1993, then, there were three related and highly important shifts in the discourse and practices of peacekeeping. First, there was greater concern for the United Nations' organizational needs, reputation, and future. As peacekeeping received greater attention and resources, various groups and individuals came to have a vested interest in its activities and future. The desire by UN officials and member states to pick winners and avoid failures meant that the United Nations was less interested in human security than its own well-being. Second, the desire to identify the conditions under which peacekeeping was effective meant that it was less likely to be deployed during instances of humanitarian crises or severe domestic turmoil. The United Nations could be effective only when there was a "peace to keep," and was best utilized for nurturing democracy. Effectiveness, in other words, was now being defined as creating the conditions for domestic order and democracy.

Third, whereas once UN officials routinely noted that they had a responsibility to help those who could not help themselves, they were now suggesting that the United Nations could help only those who were willing to help themselves. The language that began to creep into nearly all Security Council statements as a consequence of Somalia indicated that the Security Council would maintain an operation only so long as the parties of the conflict demonstrated a resolve to work toward political progress; in doing so, the Security Council emphasized, for instance, how "the people of Somalia bear the ultimate responsibility for achieving national reconciliation and for rebuilding their country."[13] Such statements are highly defensible; the United Nations, stretched thin and facing a nearly inexhaustible number of potential crises, must decide who deserves its attention, and one reasonable criterion is the active support of those it is helping. Yet the shift in language represented a search not only for accuracy but also for political expediency, to shift the criticism away from the United Nations and onto Somalia. Many UN officials and member states were now routinely claiming that "the people had to take control of their lives" as a way of deflecting criticism away from the organization. Indeed, whereas once they recognized that "the people" were the victims of violence and needed the protection of the international community, these same officials were now, for all intents and purposes, using the failure of "the people to take control of their lives" as a justification for inaction. Who were "the people" in Bosnia? in Somalia? in Rwanda? By and large "the people" no longer meant the victims of violence but those who controlled the means of violence. The United Nations had decidedly stepped away from its initial post-Cold War concern for human security and returned to the traditional tenets of peacekeeping that stressed the need for stability as a precondition of deployment.

The bureaucratization of peacekeeping was producing indifference. This had a number of components. To begin, the great powers used the United Nations to give the appearance of being involved, concerned, and engaged at minimal cost. This had already become cruelly evident in Bosnia. By hiding behind the UN flag, in other words, member states were able to mask their own indifference. Moreover, UN officials and member states became much more concerned with preserving the reputation and furthering the interests of the organization, and this meant ensuring that the United Nations became involved only when the probability of success was reasonably assured. Conversely, those moments when the United Nations was most needed, for instance, during a humanitarian crisis, it was less likely to get involved because of the fear that such involvement might jeopardize its interests and reputation. Yet moving toward indifference is not to be taken lightly or adopted without well-developed defense mechanisms; to justify the failure to act, UN and state officials developed a battery of defenses and devices, among which were the needs of the organization and the unfortunate necessity of ignoring the occasional evil in order to justify the continuance of the organization (which is equated with the community's interests).

Rwanda

These developments imprinted the UN response to genocide in Rwanda. The genesis of this tragic chapter of Rwanda's history can be briefly told. Beginning in the late 1980s mainly Tutsi refugees who had fled Rwanda to neighboring Uganda established an independence movement, the Rwanda Patriotic Front (RPF). From Uganda they launched a civil war in 1990 against the Hutu-led Rwandan government; because of the RPF's battlefield successes, a French-led force intervened to support its longtime Hutu allies. This represented only a temporary lull in the civil war, for the violence continued until the summer of 1993 when the RPF and the Rwandan government concluded the Arusha agreement that offered the promise for an end to the civil war and national reconciliation. On October 5, 1993, the Security Council, though with some concerns regarding whether the peace was possible, authorized a peacekeeping operation to oversee the Arusha agreement.

If the Security Council was concerned, it was for good reason. Early reports warned that Arusha would be difficult to implement because of the objections of extremist Hutu elements. Obstacles to implementation began almost as soon as the ink was dry on the agreement, and the initial December deadline came and went without the establishment of the transitional government. There was still no government when UNAMIR came up for renewal in early April, and many on the Security Council, increasingly aggravated by the heel dragging of the Hutu-led Rwandan government, were intent on using the renewal debate to send a message to the government that the United Nations might withdraw unless progress was made in the near future. How strong these signals should be and how serious should be the threat to close the operation were principal points of contention during these negotiations over the mandate's extension. The United States was quite insistent that the Rwandan government be told that unless it quickly established the transitional government the UN operation would be closed. Its stated justification for doing so was, first, to use whatever carrots and sticks were available to move the political progress forward, and, second, to signal to present and future operations that the existence of a peacekeeping operation was tied to political progress. Although the Clinton administration might have had the future of the United Nations in mind as it formulated its policies, it also incorporated its own political future in that decision: it was intent on demonstrating that it could be tough on peacekeeping to a Congress that was fairly hostile to the United Nations. Such "toughness," suggested some administration officials, would benefit the United Nations because the administration would better shield it from further congressional attacks. "Tough love," offered one U.S. official. In any event, the Security Council approved an extension just as the mandate expired, satisfied that its concerns were communicated to the Rwandan government (which happened to be a member of the Security Council).

No sooner had the Security Council approved the mandate extension than on April 6 the plane carrying Rwandan president Habyarimana, who was returning from Tanzania where he was rumored to have put the final pieces in place for the transitional government, crashed as it approached the Kigali Airport. In a swift, preplanned, and highly coordinated operation, the extremist forces within the military executed moderate Hutu and Tutsi politicians. With only five thousand lightly armed peacekeepers scattered throughout Rwanda, UNAMIR was ill-prepared to confront the wave of terror unleashed by Hutu extremists against Tutsis and Hutu moderates. UN troops were instantly confronted by two increasingly untenable tasks: protecting the lives of innocent civilians and defending themselves. The tension between these two goals became immediately apparent when ten Belgian peacekeepers were brutally murdered as they tried to protect moderate Hutu politicians during the first days of the violence; the remaining Belgian troops were widely believed to be marked for assassination. If the non-Belgian peacekeepers were not at immediate risk from Hutu forces, they were running dangerously low on fuel, water, and food; moreover, resupplying or rescuing them was becoming increasingly questionable as the airport became a major battleground, raising the real possibility that any approaching aircraft might suffer the same fate as Habyarimana's. To make matters worse, the RPF was now assembling and preparing to march on Kigali. Therefore, the meager and badly supplied UN forces were confronted by two wars: the Rwandan government's terror campaign against its "enemies" and the brewing civil war between the RPF and the government.

Back in New York the Security Council had to decide quickly on the future of UNAMIR and the UN response to the growing violence. While the Secretariat generally maintains some say over the future of peacekeeping operations by structuring the debate in the Security Council through its reports and recommendations, in this instance its ability was heightened because few if any member states had independent sources of information and had come to rely on the Secretariat and UNAMIR for intelligence on the conditions on the ground. Yet the Secretariat shied away from taking this leadership responsibility and opportunity to imprint the Security Council's debate on the future of UNAMIR, leaving the impression that it was either overwhelmed to the point of paralysis or insensitive to the dead peacekeepers and the escalating violence. As I met with my contacts at the Department of Peacekeeping Operations (DPKO) and attempted to ascertain what might be their thinking and recommendations, I became increasingly alarmed by their "business-as-usual" approach. Few I encountered displayed much urgency.

Two other incidents reinforced this impression of a distant Secretariat. In the first days of the crisis there was a meeting between the troop contributors to Rwanda and the UN Secretariat. Many troop contributors bitterly complained that they were unable to receive any information on the whereabouts or safety of their troops; they could not even get DPKO to return their phone calls. As those attending the meeting departed they mumbled that they could not afford to place the lives of their people in the hands of a cavalier United Nations. One story making the rounds was that a member of the Secretariat said that the United Nations need not be overly concerned with their troops since "they are not our boys." In the United Nations' world, according to the delegate who told me the story, jeeps are more valuable than people. Although I cannot say that the incident ever occurred, it sounded plausible to me, and, more important, very plausible to others.

Boutros-Ghali also emanated indecision to the point of paralysis if not complacency. He happened to be in Europe in early April, and elected to keep to his schedule and declined to return to New York. In the view of many Security Council members, this decision was irresponsible and nearly inexplicable, a troubling abdication of responsibility and leadership. A more disturbing episode concerned a reported conversation between the secretary-general and the former Belgian foreign minister William Claes. With ten peacekeepers already dead and its remaining soldiers at risk, the Belgian government was debating whether to withdraw its troops. Claes called Boutros-Ghali to ascertain the Secretariat's thinking and how Belgium's decision might affect the future of UNAMIR. According to an authoritative source, despite the urgency of the situation, Boutros-Ghali responded by saying that he would "get back to him in four or five days."

The Secretariat's performance in the Security Council was equally removed and noncommittal, as it provided little input into or direction for the debate.[14] Its reports during the first, highly critical days were always sketchy, insistent that it was not in a position to present definite options to the Security Council on the future of UNAMIR. At the time I attributed their lack of direction to "not being up to the task" of crisis management. Yet a highly authoritative and exhaustive report on Rwanda suggests not amateur but rather instrumental and strategic behavior.[15] The Secretariat was receiving definite options and instructions from its Force Commander General Romeo Dallaire, who was cautiously optimistic that a limited military intervention could halt the bloodshed. The Secretariat, however, failed to pass on UNAMIR's observations and recommendations to the Security Council. I can only speculate on why the Secretariat would fail to enter the force commander's observations into the Security Council's debate, but one very real possibility is that the Secretariat was fearful of becoming further embroiled and mired in an ethnic conflict that spelled little possibility of success and only danger and failure.[16] By taking a highly noncommittal position, the Secretariat conveyed the image that it was either opposed to any further involvement or completely over-whelmed by events.

While the motives are unknown, the consequences of the Secretariat's actions are more certain: the Secretariat's failure to offer any concrete options, let alone the possibility of a successful intervention, played directly into the hands of those Security Council members who demanded UNAMIR's immediate withdrawal. Many of the permanent members argued forcefully for withdrawal on the grounds that UNAMIR's mandate to oversee the Arusha accords was over, no country was willing to send its troops into an increasingly chaotic environment, access to the airport was progressively precarious, the Security Council's responsibility was to protect its peacekeepers, and keeping a symbolic force in Kigali would not only expose the peacekeepers to needless danger but also threaten the United Nations' future.[17] Many of the nonpermanent members of the Security Council, however, argued for increasing UNAMIR's size and handing it more responsibility, including the protection of civilians. Those advocating this position, however, had little ammunition: the Secretariat, which would be responsible for carrying out the mandate, was silent, and silence was widely interpreted as disapproval; in addition, no troop contributors were volunteering for an expanded force.

After nearly two weeks of endless and circular debate, on April 21 the Security Council decided to withdraw the bulk of UNAMIR and to leave in place those that might help General Dallaire fashion a cease-fire agreement between the RPF and the government. Because this outcome was consistent with the stated U.S. position, many argue that the United States bent the Security Council to its will. Yet persuasion and not coercion is what won the debate, and those who were arguing for withdrawal had the silence of the Secretariat and the discursive power of the United Nations' interests to give weight to their arguments. By the end of the debate there was a general consensus that peacekeepers, unprotected and exposed, could do little good and much harm to themselves and the United Nations' reputation and future; even those states who initially argued for expanding UNAMIR's size and mandate chose to vote in favor of rather than abstain from the resolution.[18] Moreover, the decision to maintain a token presence was consistent with the Security Council's desire to preserve the United Nations' reputation. Expanding or completely withdrawing UNAMIR might easily tarnish the United Nations' reputation; the former because it might hand the United Nations another failure, the latter because it would make the United Nations appear morally bankrupt and wholly unavailable when it was most needed. By maintaining a presence, the United Nations was able to symbolize its continued concern. In general, those who argued for reducing UNAMIR's presence couched their claims in terms of the organization's needs, and frequently did so to mask their self-interest. At the end of the day, prudence on the side of the United Nations carried the debate.

After the Security Council voted to reduce UNAMIR's presence, the discussion somewhat ironically returned to the United Nations' possible response to the genocide. In fact, the secretary-general now began to take a visible lead in using his bully pulpit to formulate options and to urge the Security Council and the member states to respond vigorously to the continuing massacres. When the Secretariat finally unveiled its long-awaited plan in late April, it was greeted by the Security Council with considerable enthusiasm. Yet the enthusiasm was arguably less for its potential effectiveness as an antidote to genocide and more for its "impression management," that is, to try and recover the United Nations' moral standing.[19] Simply put, while this proposal proved merely symbolic and highly impractical—it proposed to dispatch five thousand troops to

Kigali, acknowledged that the forces might not be located for months (if ever), and confessed that it had no real idea what they would do once they arrived—it did generate the impression that the United Nations was poised for action. Consequently, most members of the Security Council quickly embraced this unworkable scheme. The United States, however, rightly criticized the plan as little more than smoke, demanded that the United Nations and the Security Council design a realistic proposal, and circulated its own suggestions for providing relief to and protecting the growing number of refugees. The U.S. decision to oppose the Secretariat's plan exposed it to much media criticism, but the basis of its opposition threatened to expose the Security Council's Potemkin village.[20]

During these first weeks and the enfolding genocide the Security Council remained "seized of the matter," in almost constant session for updates from the Secretariat and to outline options for future action. Sitting through these lengthy meetings could be tortuous: officials could have distributed information as easily without convening the Security Council, and there were no concrete proposals for action. Why, then, the endless stream of meetings? One reason was to give all members the opportunity to express their moral outrage. At the end of the day's debate the president of the Security Council would announce to the press that the Security Council was alarmed by the violence and would continue to follow events closely. Indeed, there was a nearly rhythmic quality to the deliberations during these first weeks. On one day hours would be spent exchanging information and extolling the need for concrete action; pleased that now they had expressed sufficient concern, delegates would hold a highly abbreviated meeting the next day. This pattern repeated itself during the height of the crisis throughout April and into May.

Another reason was that having Rwanda on the Security Council's agenda meant giving the international community the appearance that it cared, enabling it to veil its indifference. While member states were unwilling to assemble an intervention force, they also did not want to appear heartless and indifferent to genocide. By filling the halls of the United Nations, remaining in constant session, and generating endless documents and statements, the Security Council could give the facade of action when in fact few if any states wanted anything of the kind. The very presence of the United Nations enabled states to cloak their indifference (though perhaps not very effectively). This suggests that one function of the United Nations is to distribute accountability to the point that it becomes irretrievable. Who was to blame for the lack of response to Rwanda? Everyone. The mere presence of the United Nations allows states (and the Secretariat) to shield themselves from responsibility, to point fingers in all directions, to mask their inaction in the name of a greater good.

Third, these meetings also provided the members of the Security Council with an opportunity to remind themselves that they had a responsibility not only to Rwandans but also to the United Nations. A defining subtext to the debate was the need to preserve the United Nations' future and to reject the intervention temptation. The dominance of the organization's needs became particularly stark as it became undeniable that genocide was transpiring. During the debate Security Council members were reluctant to utter the word "genocide," fearing its discursive ability to command action. Indeed, on those rare occasions when a member implored action because of genocide, the discussion slowly descended on the recognition that little could be done, that the Security Council had to protect UN interests, and that on no uncertain terms should the president of the Security Council use such irresponsible and highly inflammatory language when he met with the press. During these first few weeks the Security Council continually reminded itself that its course of action, regardless of its tragic consequences for those on the ground, was the only responsible and feasible option.

Maintaining a loyalty to the United Nations was facilitated by two other factors. First, those who were responsible for and oversaw Rwanda (and other operations) were "experts" in the way that I was an expert on Rwanda; expertise derived from my bureaucratic roles and responsibilities rather than my intrinsic knowledge. My expertise concerned the U.S. foreign policy process and UN operations, not Rwanda; my colleague had spent a career at the U.S. mission covering Africa but had never stepped foot on the continent. Our expertise, then, derived from our knowledge of the United States and the United Nations rather than those countries that were part of our "portfolio." Being able to elevate the United Nations' organizational needs over the events in Rwanda was also facilitated by scale, that is, the fact that discussions were occurring among UN officials and member states in New York while the tragedy was occurring in Rwanda. Herzfeld suggests that as the distance expands between the bureaucrat and those s/he is expected to serve it becomes more difficult for the bureaucrat to conceptualize them as residing within the same conceptual space.[21] This facilitates a sense of indifference. While those in New York expressed genuine anguish for what was occurring in Rwanda, it was easier to identify with those with whom one interacted on a daily basis. In contrast to the "civilized" confines of the diplomatic world, the reports from Rwanda suggested barbarism and cruelty unimaginable and of a different world. It was almost certain that I and others would more easily identify with our state's interests and the organizational needs of the United Nations than the interests of those who lived in a country that was conceptually and strategically removed. That Rwanda was a member of the Security Council during this period did not help bridge the cultural gap; he was a Hutu, a member of the ruling coalition, and therefore linked to the architects of genocide. His presence did not help overcome the sense of indifference; rather, it acted as a reminder that the international community would have to tolerate the occasional evil, but that was a small price to pay to maintain the community's central international organization.

Little was done in Rwanda until it was too late and relatively safe. The stark truth is that while many states called for action, few if any stepped forward to volunteer their own services for any intervention force. Yet the bureaucratization of peacekeeping, in my view, shifted the dynamics and debates in consequential ways. One counterfactual that I occasionally ask myself is, would the United Nations have responded more vigorously to Rwanda had it occurred, for instance, in April 1993 rather than in April 1994? If possibly yes, can the unwillingness to rush in be understood as simply a result of the fact that UN officials had learned when peacekeeping is most effective? If no, then we are left with the very real prospect that the bureaucratization of peacekeeping shaped the decision not to respond. Moreover, as the member states and the Secretariat debated what should be done, they could not in good conscience confess that their self-interest dictated that they ignore genocide. Rather, the United Nations loomed large in two respects as they formulated their nonresponse. Member states used the United Nations to mask their own indifference. To be sure, that indifference was not completely camouflaged, but it was shielded from direct view. And as they debated the potential consequences of action they forwarded the United Nations as a possible casualty. Any more peacekeeping fatalities, argued many in the halls of the Security Council, would undoubtedly mean more criticism and fewer resources for the United Nations. This was the moral equation and the justification for inaction.

Bosnia

If indifference accurately characterizes the international community's and the United Nations' response to the genocide in Rwanda, it is perhaps unfair and somewhat uncharitable to offer a direct parallel to Bosnia. The contrasting places of Bosnia and Rwanda in the Western imagination are brought into stark relief when it is recalled that in mid-April 1994, as the genocide in Rwanda was picking up full steam, Western media attention shifted dramatically from Rwanda to Bosnia due to a Serb assault on the safe haven of Gorazde. Arguably because of its contiguity to Europe, its echoes of the Holocaust, the potential implication of great power strategic interests, and the fit-and-start attention of the media and the Western public, Bosnia has intermittently commanded front-page news, many intellectuals, state officials, and private organizations lobbied long and hard for the West to respond appropriately to the ethnic cleansing and concentration camps. The United Nations has been present and active in the former Yugoslavia since the conflicts there first began, and there is now the International Force (IFOR) designed to stitch together political reconciliation. The indifference that defines Rwanda, therefore, does not wholly or accurately capture Bosnia. Yet systematic neglect instead of a forceful response to ethnic cleansing and war crimes better characterizes the Security Council's and the United Nations' response. Various features of the UN involvement in Bosnia are suggestive of the relationship between the bureaucratization of peacekeeping, the concern for the organization's interests, and the production of indifference.

The United Nations began its peacekeeping presence in the former Yugoslavia with Security Council Resolution 743 of February 21, 1992, when the United Nations Protection Force (UNPROFOR) was mandated to deploy to certain areas of Croatia where Serbs were a substantial minority, and to monitor the cease-fire between Serb and Croat forces. Before long, however, the consequences and conflicts associated with the disintegration of Yugoslavia spread to Bosnia, and when the United Nations became formally involved on July 13, 1992 (Security Council Resolution 764), its mandate differed from this initial operation in two respects. First, this second resolution was more narrowly humanitarian, designed "to ensure the security and functioning of Sarajevo airport and the delivery of humanitarian assistance." Second, whereas Resolution 743 operated with the consent of the parties, the mention of Article 25 in

Resolution 764 suggested that the Security Council might require the host states to accept the operation and its humanitarian mission whether they liked it or not.[22]

There is little evidence, however, that either the Security Council or the Secretariat was eager to jump into the fray of ethnic cleansing in Bosnia. Marrack Goulding, then UN undersecretary-general for political affairs, argued in an internal memo that the United Nations should keep its distance from Bosnia until it could operate with the consent of the parties and there was stability on the ground,[23] a stance that not only reflected a traditional view of peacekeeping but would also suspend the United Nations' moral involvement. And while Boutros-Ghali's staff was working on *The Agenda for Peace* as the Security Council was debating Bosnia, his vision of a United Nations that was running complex and multidimensional peacekeeping operations did not immediately extend to combating ethnic cleansing and liberating concentration camps. The Secretariat's general recommendations were to proceed slowly and cautiously.

The Security Council, however, disregarded this advice and chose to assign the United Nations the task of protecting the delivery of humanitarian assistance. The Security Council's actions, however, were not motivated solely by humanitarian concerns. As is well known, because of a combination of symbolic boundaries and strategic calculations, neither Europe nor the United States saw itself as having just cause for intervention. Still, total disregard of the ethnic cleansing and the camps was both morally callous and politically unwise. By turning to the United Nations, the West could give the appearance of engagement and offer some limited assistance without having to become fully implicated in the conflict.[24] Adam Roberts and Sir Brian Urquhart openly questioned whether this was not a cynical use of the United Nations; the former queried whether the West was using the United Nations "as a substitute for a real policy," and the latter suggested that the West found the United Nations a good place to dump intractable and unwanted conflicts.[25] The subtext to their observations and the Security Council's deliberate decision to find a middle road between disengagement and involvement is that the West used the United Nations to mask its indifference. The history of the West's role in Bosnia continued this initial pattern.

While UN and Western officials feared that by deploying peacekeepers they would be inviting "mission creep," the overall record is that the United Nations and the Security Council studiously avoided any involvement that would mean the use of force to either deliver humanitarian assistance or protect civilians. The UN mandates included enforcing no-fly zones, protecting the seven regions that became known as "safe havens," delivering humanitarian assistance, making Sarajevo free from heavy weapons, and other demands in over one hundred Security Council resolutions over the last four years.[26] The United Nations had the authority to enforce these resolutions and protect civilians: it could use "all necessary means." Yet these mandates were intermittently implemented at best, and, at worst, ethnic cleansing, war crimes, and other atrocities were carried out by Serbs in full view of the United Nations without much response.

How do we explain such indifference? There are arguably a multitude of explanations, including a lack of will on the part of the member states, Russia's place on the Security Council and willingness to veto any robust action (because of its alliance with the Serbs), and the Security Council's failure to allocate the resources and apply the diplomatic muscle required for the job.[27] By and large many identify the primacy of state interests as the reason for the United Nations' refusal to come to the defense of the civilians it was mandated to protect.

While these arguments have some merit, an organizational culture and bureaucratic interests also are present and contribute to indifference. Many journalists covering the war incredulously asked how intelligent, thoughtful, and internationally minded UN officials could articulate, through their actions and occasional statements, the view that ethnic cleansing had to be allowed to continue.[28] How could they believe that they could remain morally uncompromised by their position? How were they able to maintain a distant stance, even while recognizing that their actions might implicate them in these atrocities?

One explanation is that UN officials insist that peacekeeping is most appropriate and most effective when it operates with the consent of the parties and the United Nations maintains neutrality and impartiality. These principles of peacekeeping generate the stance that enforcement actions are unproductive and are not what the United Nations is about. Although in the first moments after the Cold War the United Nations debated whether it should become involved in peace enforcement and collective security, the opinion of longtime hands was that the United Nations should be wary of this departure from its traditional organizational mission. Although Boutros-Ghali was an early advocate of a more muscular United Nations, he began to rethink this initial position and the wisdom of the United Nations' traditional approach after Somalia and other peacekeeping setbacks.[29] Simply put, these peacekeeping travails reinforced the view that the United Nations should avoid enforcement actioɪ operate with the consent of the parties, and adhere to strict standards oɪ neutrality. This broad organizational and bureaucratic culture defines what the United Nations is, what it is able to do, and how its interests are best served. Such organizational principles shaped the United Nations' actions in Bosnia.

The United Nations' operating principle of consent underlines its general reluctance to use force to deliver humanitarian assistance. An ongoing saga of the UN mission to provide humanitarian relief was the necessity of having to negotiate with and obtain the consent of the very forces that had caused this humanitarian crisis. UN officials had to constantly obtain permission from Serb authorities to use the Sarajevo airport and the roads to the safe havens, and quite often found their way blocked or were forced to endure numerous hardships and humiliations because of Serb intransigence. Although the United Nations was authorized to use force through the "all necessary means" provisions of the Security Council resolutions, on few occasions did UNPROFOR elect that option, preferring instead negotiation and consent. UN officials defended their decision to use persuasion rather than coercion on the argument that they could operate effectively only with the consent of the parties, and that force could be used but once (or that it might trigger a war it neither wanted nor was authorized to fight).[30] The UN insistence on avoiding force derived not only from the negative lessons of Somalia and Bosnia but also from the positive lessons of Cambodia: the United Nations was most effective when employing its powers of persuasion and not its (rather limited) powers of coercion.[31] The secretary-general's special representative Yasushi Akashi, who had come to the former Yugoslavia from Cambodia, championed the principle of consent. After watching what occurred in Somalia after the United Nations chose to operate through force rather than persuasion, UNPROFOR Commander Michael Rose vowed not to cross the "Mogadishu line" and become "helpless."[32]

The UN peacekeeping ethos also claims for itself impartiality and neutrality, and these principles inform the United Nations' unwillingness to militarily defend the safe havens.[33] In this view, the United Nations' power derives from persuasion rather than coercion, which, in turn, is dependent on its moral authority. And, the argument goes, its moral standing is founded on its impartiality. All parties must be treated equally and not be shown favoritism or partiality. Therefore, in the moral calculus of the United Nations, to protect civilians might very well require taking sides, an act that would compromise the organization's neutrality and future effectiveness. For instance, some UN officials would concede that Bosnia had the clear moral imperative, but would also claim that as administrators of a peacekeeping operation they must remain impartial.[34] UN officials, in other words, would have to tolerate the occasional evil if they were going to be able to remain effective not only in Bosnia but elsewhere.

Impartiality, therefore, flowed into indifference. Sometimes this meant rejecting the call to defend the safe havens. Responding to President Clinton's suggestion that the United Nations become more active in peace enforcement and battling the Bosnian Serbs, UNPROFOR Force Commander Michael Rose said, "If someone wants to fight a war here on moral or political grounds, fine, great, but count us [the United Nations] out. Hitting one tank is peacekeeping. Hitting infrastructure command and control, logistics, that is war, and I'm not going to fight a war with painted tanks."[35] At other moments maintaining impartiality meant ignoring or distorting the casualties of war crimes.[36] And at still other times it meant representing the interests of the aggressor rather than protecting the victim. For instance, in the spring of 1994 after the safe haven of Gorazde came under attack from Bosnian Serbs, NATO requested retaliatory air strikes. "But instead of ordering air strikes, [UNPROFOR Commander for Bosnia Michael Rose] asked the Bosnian government to make a 'goodwill gesture' to encourage the attackers to pull back . . . an act of capitulation requested neither by NATO nor by the UN Security Council."[37] The predictable, violent, and sad conclusion of this culture of impartiality was the Serb conquest of the safe haven in Srebrenica in the summer of 1995, when Dutch peacekeepers stood by and watched war crimes being committed by Serbian troops.[38] In general, UN officials could remain indifferent to crimes they were witnessing because of the principles of the consent of the parties and impartiality.

Yet the UN insistence on consent and impartiality might represent not only organizational culture but also self-interest. To become more fully involved in Bosnia, particularly when it could not be fully certain whether it had the diplomatic and military backing of the Security Council or NATO, might leave the United Nations on a limb and susceptible to greater criticism. By arguing that it had to adhere to the principles of consent of the parties and impartiality, the United Nations could avoid further involvement and (hopefully) provide some cover from future criticism. No doubt these concerns intensified after the United Nations came under greater fire from its critics for its performances in Bosnia and Somalia in 1993. Moreover, when the United Nations was castigated for not protecting civilians, Boutros-Ghali and others would emphasize the importance of the humanitarian mission. In doing so, the United Nations could transform a moral failure into an organizational victory: if UNPRO-FOR was judged according to how well it protected civilians, then its activities were a failure; if, however, it was judged by its delivery of humanitarian relief, then it could be judged a qualified success. And, by emphasizing the delivery of humanitarian relief rather than the protection of civilians, UN officials could shift responsibility from themselves to the participants of the conflict. The United Nations could not be blamed for what the parties brought on themselves.

Yet there were moments when the United Nations and NATO punished the Serbs for their actions and for violating the Security Council resolutions. We must recognize, however, that the deployment of force was designed not to defend the safe havens but rather to protect peacekeepers and to rescue the reputation of NATO and the United Nations. To begin, there were frequent disagreements within NATO, within the Secretariat, and between NATO officials and the Secretariat over whether to retaliate against Serb attacks. Yet the impetus for the use of force was frequently the need to protect peacekeepers, not the residents of safe havens. For instance, the Serb assault on the safe haven of Gorazde in the spring of 1994 unleashed a storm of controversy over the United Nations' rejection of NATO's request for air strikes. In defending the UN decision, the undersecretary-general for peacekeeping operations, Kofi Annan, argued that the rationale for the air strikes is "to protect lives—not just of the handful of UN soldiers who might be threatened by a given attack but the thousands of lightly armed peacekeepers and hundreds of unarmed relief works, military observers and police monitors whose lives could be threatened by precipitous military action."[39] Missing from Annan's list of groups to be protected were the residents of the safe havens. Yet before one fully applauds NATO's stance, recall that "NATO governments . . . insisted that the air strikes [be] used to protect a handful of UN personnel, not the 65,000 residents of Gorazde."[40] New York frequently chastised and overruled the military commanders in the field for ostensibly over-stepping their authority and the mandate when they recommended the use of force. One famous incident was when Force Commander General Cot publicly criticized the Secretariat for failing to approve his requested air strikes in January 1994. Yet he based his arguments on the need to revenge the "humiliation of the international community's force" and the need to make military threats credible.[41] Simply put, NATO and the United Nations seemed more willing to use force to protect UN troops than it did to protect civilians; UN forces were most outraged when they were personally humiliated, not by acts of ethnic cleansing.[42]

The United Nations and NATO also employed force to retrieve their reputation. In other words, the stimulus of this slide toward military confrontation was not moral indignation but rather impression management. Such moments generally occurred after the Bosnian Serbs launched a well-publicized attack against civilians, which would trigger a debate among the Security Council and the West over the proper response. The subtext to these debates, however, frequently turned on the reputations of NATO and the United Nations. For instance, in the spring of 1995 the Serbs assaulted the safe havens and Sarajevo and kidnapped peacekeepers. These developments left many openly asking not how to save Sarajevo but how to secure the United Nations' and NATO's future; commentators began clamoring that if NATO did not draw a line in the sand and stand firm, then NATO would unequivocally demonstrate its irrelevance to the post-Cold War order. After a lengthy debate, the United Nations authorized the deployment of a Rapid Reaction Force of ten thousand in June 1995. Yet the impression management intent of the force became painfully obvious as its mission was downgraded from opening the airport and delivering humanitarian relief to protecting peacekeepers, dramatizing that the growing involvement of NATO and the United Nations was designed to rescue their reputation and not to protect civilians.[43] Similarly, President Clinton intimated that the real threat unleashed by the Serbian attack on Srebrenica was to the "integrity of the mission."[44] In the Senate hearings on the possible U.S. deployment of soldiers to monitor any possible peace agreement, Secretary of State Warren Christopher and Secretary of Defense William Perry argued that the issue at stake was the future of NATO and the Western alliance.[45] In general, Bosnia mattered not because of the moral tragedy but because the Western alliance was on the line. The United Nations' use of force was not to protect civilians in Sarajevo or the safe havens but rather the organization's interests. UNPROFOR acted to protect its reputation and peacekeepers and not the civilians who the peacekeepers were deployed to protect.

While it is difficult if not somewhat uncharitable to label as indifference the United Nations' multibillion-dollar, multiyear, and multidimensional operation in Bosnia, the general evidence suggests that the West used the United Nations as a place to mask its indifference and to avoid having to respond fully to the horrors of Bosnia. Yet UN officials had little trouble playing that part, and, indeed, sometimes excelled at it beyond what the Security Council and NATO officials expected or desired. Indeed, because both the Security Council and the Secretariat operated in a way that generally furthered the war aims of the Serbs, many of UNPROFOR's harshest critics conclude that the UN role in Bosnia suggests not indifference but rather active complicity.[46] In any event, as representatives of the international community's central international organization, they represent the common good; as representatives of the common good they are able to remain indifferent to the individual because of the discursive cloak of community.

Conclusion

One of the central post-Cold War debates has been how to make the United Nations a more effective and useful instrument for international security. After a first wave of tremendous enthusiasm and promise, the high expectations for the United Nations were dashed as it became barraged by criticism and condemnation. These criticisms largely derived from the United Nations' reported performance in Somalia, Rwanda, and Bosnia, where it failed to fulfill its mandates and expectations. One response offered by many of the United Nations' defenders is that the answer is not less of the United Nations but more. The United Nations requires more tools and capabilities for crisis management and prevention; the capability to intervene before the crisis explodes; and the ability to deploy its forces as soon as the Security Council authorizes the operation rather than after the lengthy delays it currently experiences. For instance, in the aftermath of Bosnia and Rwanda there is much talk that the United Nations should have an international "fire brigade," early warning indicators, and other preventive measures that will enable it to act before it is too late.

There are many merits to these and other proposals, but the Security Council's and the United Nation's performance in confronting the genocide in Bosnia and Rwanda suggests that bureaucratization does not translate into action or intervention. First, an assumption of the search for early warning indicators and the proposal for a UN standing army for preventive deployment suggest that knowledge brings action. There is an unwritten belief that with knowledge the international community will act. Yet it was not the lack of knowledge that halted action in either Bosnia or Rwanda—it was politics. In both cases state and UN officials knew of but chose to ignore the war crimes that were being committed. In both cases UN forces were on the ground and were eyewitnesses to acts of ethnic cleansing and genocide, and in both cases the rules of engagement prevented UN forces from coming to the active aid of civilians. More technologies and capabilities are no elixir and no substitute for a politics of engagement.

Second, while the professionalization of peacekeeping was absolutely necessary if peacekeeping was to have a future, this professionalization produced bureaucratization, and with bureaucratization individuals come to have a stake in and identify with the bureaucracy, begin to evaluate strategies and actions according to the needs of the bureaucracy, and, accordingly, begin to frame discussions and justify policies through a different mentality. As I became part of this bureaucratization process, I, too, altered how I judged and evaluated UN peacekeeping. Sometimes this meant I had a heightened awareness of the complexities of issues involved and the stakes of the game. Yet, at other times, this involved a shift in what I thought was desirable and valuable; I became more interested in protecting the bureaucratic and organizational interests than I was in employing the organization to help those it was supposed to serve.

This suggests that while the United Nations might be above power politics it is not above politics. The ideal is that the United Nations represents a nobler vision of global politics; indeed, the mere presence of the United Nations reminds states and individuals that they have an obligation not only to themselves but to each other, that they should avoid stark self-interested policies and pursue more enlightened strategies that reflect a cosmopolitan ethic. While there is truth to these observations, absent is a consideration of the United Nations as an organization that attends to its own interests, reputation, and future. UN officials were able to portray their self-interested policies as being in the best interests of the international community.

The United Nations is more than an arm of the international community; it is one of its most important symbols. It represents aspirations and values that are assumed to be common to states and transcend state boundaries and historical periods. In this respect, it is the international community's singular organization that embodies transcendental values and moral principles. The United Nations allows individuals and states to maintain a belief in the transcendental, even in the face of the occasional evil that exposes the sins of the members. That actions occur with reference to and are embedded within the larger community, in other words, allows bureaucrats and other members of the international community to accept disappointments if not evil. Officials in and out of the United Nations were able to explain the evils of Rwanda and Bosnia and their indifference by pointing to the secular religion of the international community and its cathedral, the United Nations.

NOTES

I want to thank Michael Herzfeld, Victoria Shampaine, and Hakan Yafuz for their comments.

1. I develop this autobiographical angle and tie it more directly to the bureaucratization of peacekeeping and the production of indifference in Michael N. Barnett, "The Politics of Indifference at the United Nations: The Professionalization of Peacekeeping and the Toleration of Genocide" (paper presented at the workshop "Culture and the Production of Insecurity," University of Minnesota, October 27–29, 1995).

2. I want to offer the following caveats. First, I am representing my personal reflections after a year's time, and I am attempting, as best as possible, to represent and interpret the events unfolding around me; I have no doubt that others who also were there would tell a different tale. Relatedly, I observed these events from the U.S. mission to the United Nations, and I expect that those residing in Rwanda, the United Nations, or other delegations would offer a different view. Second, while I will argue that the bureaucratization of peacekeeping helps produce indifference, I came to respect the integrity and values of many of those with whom I worked; these were highly dedicated individuals who worked long hours and labored under difficult conditions, and who were pained and disturbed by these tragedies and the failure of the international community to respond commensurate with the moral imperatives.

3. Michael Herzfeld, *The Social Production of Indifference* (Chicago: University of Chicago Press, 1993).

4. Ibid., 33.

5. Ibid., 5–7.

6. Ibid., 10.

7. Brian Urquhart, "The UN and International Security after the Cold War," in *United Nations, Divided World,* ed. A. Roberts and B. Kingsbury (New York: Oxford University Press, 1993), 91–92.

8. Harold Jacobsen, "The United Nations and Colonialism: A Tentative Appraisal," *International Organization* 1 (winter 1972): 47.

9. See Gerald Halman and Steven Ratner, "Saving Failed States," *Foreign Policy* 89 (winter 1992–93): 3–20.

10. See, for instance, Boutros Boutros-Ghali, "Democracy: A Newly Recognized Imperative," *Global Governance* 1, no. 1 (winter 1995): 3–12.

11. S/PRST/1994/22, May 3, 1994.

12. See, for instance, President Clinton's address to the 1993 General Assembly. Reprinted in *Dispatch* (U.S. Department of State) 4, no. 39 (1993).

13. S/Res/923, May 31, 1994.

14. "The [Security] Council received blurred, sanitized summaries from Boutros-Ghali's staff depicting mutual and chaotic killing." Julia Preston, "Rwandans Confound UN Security Council," *Washington Post,* May 8, 1994, A25.

15. Howard Adelman and Astri Suhrke (with Bruce Jones), *Early Warning and Conflict Management: Genocide in Rwanda,* Study 2 of the OECD-sponsored project on "Evaluation of the Emergency Assistance to Rwanda" (January 1996).

16. Dallaire ignored instructions from the Secretariat that asked UNAMIR to remain in its barracks rather than roaming the streets and attempting to protect civilians. Preston, op. cit. Later Boutros-Ghali took an unequivocal stand in favor of humanitarian intervention and blamed donor fatigue for the lack of a response. See his interview with Ted Koppel on ABC News *Nightline,* May 4, 1994.

17. There is little doubt that after Somalia the United States wanted to avoid involvement in another humanitarian operation in Africa. The United Nations provided a highly useful device to this end, for it could appear engaged without having to become so. In a response to a question concerning the role of U.S. leadership, State Department spokesman Michael McLurry said that "this situation will be under the review at the United Nations, and that's appropriately the place where that discussion will occur." Elaine Sciolino, "Peacekeeping Under Stress," *New York Times,* April 15, 1994, A5.

18. Parenthetically, Boutros-Ghali did not distinguish himself at this moment either: when he finally recommended to the Security Council that UNAMIR forces be reduced, he hinted that his hand was forced by Belgium's inexplicable decision to withdraw its forces. The Security Council, uniformly outraged, rallied to Belgium's defense.

19. See Erving Goffman, *The Presentation of Self in Everyday Life* (New York: Anchor Books, 1959), chap. 6.

20. Part of the reason for the U.S. stance can be attributed to its desire to forward its proposal that would immediately dispatch troops to the borders of Rwanda to help with the emerging refugee crisis—but no more.

21. Herzfeld, op. cit., 68–69.

22. Adam Roberts, "Humanitarian War: Military Intervention and Human Rights," *International Affairs* 69, no. 3 (1993): 442.

23. David Rieff, *Slaughterhouse: Bosnia and the Failure of the West* (New York: Simon and Schuster, 1995), 163.

24. As George Kenney, one of the State Department officials who resigned over Bosnia policy, wrote, "The goal from the beginning was not good public policy, but good public relations." "See No Evil, Make No Policy," *Washington Monthly,* November 22, 1992, 33.

25. Roberts, op. cit., 442; Brian Urquhart, "Who Can Police the World?" *New York Review of Books* 41, no. 9, May 12 (1994): 33.

26. However, many of these resolutions were designed to cover up past policy failures and to overcome the demand for more concerted action. For instance, Senator Biden (D-DE) argued that the very need to create these safe havens resulted from the United Nations' acquiescence to ethnic cleansing and the desire to avoid any greater involvement. See Joseph Biden, Jr., "More UN Appeasement on Bosnia," *New York Times,* June 7, 1993, A15.

27. The contributions to this volume speak eloquently to the issue of identity. Other commentators have also wondered whether the UN response would have been different if the religious identity of the attacker and the victim were reversed, or, even more cynically, if the Bosnians had been dolphins. Edward Luttwak, "If Bosnians Were Dolphins . . ." *Commentary* 96 (October 1993): 27–32. The issue of identity and difference is also evident among UN officials. In *Slaughterhouse,* David Rieff offers various episodes in which UN officials created symbolic markers between themselves and the Bosnians.

28. See, for instance, Rieff, op. cit., 170, 193.

29. Julia Preston, "UN Officials Scale Back Peacemaking Ambitions," *Washington Post,* October 28, 1993, A40.

30. Another possibility is that UN officials believed that while the Serbs had instigated atrocities, the war had been won and the Bosnians had to recognize realities; consequently, their refusal to admit defeat delayed the possibility of a peace agreement, prolonged UNPROFOR, and made the United Nations' life more difficult. Rieff, op. cit., 127. In the reasoning of UN officials, UNPROFOR was there to protect the delivery of humanitarian assistance, fighting made it more difficult to accomplish this objective, and the Bosnian refusal to concede defeat was ultimately responsible for this end. Ibid., 139.

31. "UN Peacekeeping Missions: The Lessons from Cambodia," *Asia Pacific Issues,* Analysis from the East-West Center, no. 11 (March 1994): 5.

32. Interview by Renaud Girard, *Le Figaro,* February 28, 1994; cited in Norman Cigar, *Genocide in Bosnia* (College Station: Texas A&M University Press, 1995), 189.

33. Rieff, op. cit., 170. Fred Cuny, one of the revolutionaries of humanitarian relief and a frequent organizer of humanitarian assistance to Sarajevo, who died while on a mission in Chechnya in 1995, liked to comment that "if the UN had been around in 1939 we would all be speaking German." Quoted in Rieff, op. cit., 140.

34. Ibid., 166.

35. Roger Cohen, "UN General Opposes More Bosnia Force," *New York Times,* September 29, 1994, A7.

36. See Rieff, op. cit.; Noel Malcolm, "The Whole Lot of Them Are Serbs," *Spectator,* June 10, 1995, 14–18.

37. Carol Williams, "UN's Hollow Threat," *Los Angeles Times,* May 29, 1994, A5.

38. See the arresting article by David Rieff, "We Hate You," *New Yorker,* September 4, 1995, 41–46.

39. Kofi Annan, "The UN's Power in Bosnia," *Washington Post,* March 28, 1994, 21.

40. Bruce Clark, "UN Exposed by Debacle in Gorazde," *Financial Times,* April 18, 1994, 2.

41. Roger Cohen, "Dispute Grows over UN's Troops in Bosnia," *New York Times,* January 20, 1994, 8. Another infamous incident occurred when Bosnia Force Commander General Phillipe Morillon went to Srebrenica to compel the Serbs to stop their shelling; he was lambasted by the Secretariat for exceeding the mandate. Rieff, *Slaughterhouse,* 169.

42. John Pomfret, "UN Finds Good Intentions Don't Feed Beset Bosnians," *Washington Post,* January 21, 1994, A1.

43. John Pomfret, "Reaction Force for Bosnia Is Fading Away," *Washington Post,* July 1, 1995, A1.

44. Michael Dobbs and John Harris, "Clinton Cites Challenge to UN Force in Bosnia," *Washington Post,* July 14, 1995, A26. Clinton resisted these calls to end UNPROFOR, however, because it might lead to an "Americanization of the war." Michael Dobbs, "Serbs May Have Dealt Death Blow to UN Peacekeeping," *Washington Post,* July 12, 1995, A15. Clinton's statement revealed how the United Nations was being used to shield the United States from greater involvement.

45. Norman Kempster, "Christopher Links NATO's Future, U.S. Role in Bosnia," *Los Angeles Times,* October 4, 1995, A16; Eric Shmitt, "Senators Query U.S. Role in Bosnia," *New York Times,* October 18, 1995, A1.

46. See the cover story of the *New Republic,* "Accomplices to Genocide: The Consequences of Appeasement in Bosnia," August 7, 1995. Rieff pulls no punches when he expresses his view that the United Nations was morally complicit in helping the Serbs carry out the genocide: "By providing a humanitarian

fig leaf for what was really taking place in Bosnia, and pretending that their interests were not the parochial ones of a moral and intellectually bankrupt organization that had been forced by the Security Council to take on a task it was quite incapable of coping with honorably, UNPROFOR and the Department of Peacekeeping Operations became accomplices to genocide." See Rieff, *Slaughterhouse,* 189.

SEVEN

Slaven Letica

The *West Side Story* of the Collapse of Yugoslavia and the Wars in Slovenia, Croatia, and Bosnia-Herzegovina

Editors' note: This chapter was written as a response to an article published by Warren Zimmermann in the prestigious journal Foreign Affairs. *The article is a reflective piece in which Zimmermann considers the personalities and political personae of the various Balkan leaders and speculates on the causes of the country's breakup. As the last U.S. ambassador to Yugoslavia, Zimmermann was obliged to hold to the official American position, which was unequivocally in favor of maintaining the federation. In discussing the issue with his diplomatic colleagues in Belgrade, Zimmermann reports that "the worse case [scenario] we could think of was the breakup of the country." Zimmermann favors the preservation of a loose federation under the leadership of the new prime minister, Ante Markovich (a Croat), and expresses disdain for "naked nationalism" and the nationalistic leaders who were gaining popularity in the constituent republics of the former Yugoslavia.*

Zimmermann's analysis is a remarkable document both as an autobiographical account of a committed American diplomat and as an example of American diplomatic thinking about the Balkans. While his strongest distaste is reserved for Slobodan Milošević (whom he characterizes as cynical and mendacious, but not wholly responsible for the aggression he unleashed) and the leader of the Bosnian Serbs, Radovan Karadžić (who, he says, "invites comparison with a monster from another generation, Heinrich Himmler"), he also provides rather strident critiques of other republics and leaders of the former Yugoslavia. Zimmermann wisely points out that the failure of Western resolve in the early days of the war allowed the Serbs to "push about as far as their power could take them."

Only part of Slaven Letica's response published below was published in Foreign Affairs. *This response was written as a rejection of the idea that all sides (and all Balkan leaders) were equally guilty either for the breakup of Yugoslavia or for the resulting aggression. We print the response in its entirety here, together with an excerpt (attached as an appendix) from Letica's diary of events surrounding his visit, as national security advisor to Croatian president Franjo Tudjman, to the White House on September 25, 1990, and his meeting with Henry Kissinger. Letica's observations demonstrate that the Bush administration was adamantly opposed to the idea of nationhood for the former republics of Yugoslavia and supported federalism in spite of the fact that war might be the result of a commitment to federalism. Kissinger's position, as understood by Letica, is an indication of the realpolitik attitude of many Western intellectuals, an attitude strengthened by strongly held negative and often prejudicial attitudes about the various ethnic groups involved in the Balkan conflict. Kissinger's position on the Balkan crisis could best be described as cautious and appears to be grounded in a view that all sides are more or less to blame for the crisis there. In an editorial in the* New York Post *in which he urges caution in defining the role of U.S. peacekeeping troops in Bosnia, Kissinger writes, "While the Serbs initiated the present round of slaughter, they would no doubt hearken back to comparable depredations inflicted by Croats and Muslims. Early resistance by the West to ethnic cleansing might well have stopped the outrage, but too many brutalities have been wrought by all groups to envision coexistence under a single government as a realistic option."* [1] *In another passage, he notes that "The three ethnic groups have in effect been separated by the revolting ethnic cleansing they have practiced."* [2] *Such attitudes—namely, seeing all parties as somehow guilty for the devastation of Yugoslavia—might explain Kissinger's earlier response to new leaders of a small nation such as Croatia.*

Letica's article is included here as a "perspective from within," a response from one of the elites deeply involved in the affairs of the reformation of postcommunist Yugoslavia. Such a perspective is often lacking in favor of some of the convenient frames of analysis that are

*imposed on the Balkan crisis, many of which are discussed in the intro-
duction to this volume. His essay should be read as part of a more
general phenomenology of the birth of new nations in Eastern and Central
Europe.*

W arren Zimmermann's article "The Last Ambassador: A Memoir of
the Collapse of Yugoslavia," published in *Foreign Affairs,* is a
remarkably interesting account written by a man with an undeniable
literary talent.[3] At the same time, it is an important historical document
because it was not written by just any casual voyeur of Balkan postcommunist democratic revolutions and wars, such as a journalist or a scientist,
but by one of the few foreign diplomats who had a hand in creating
history, and had a real opportunity to change its course, because he was
the last American ambassador to Yugoslavia, from 1989 to 1992.

Since I myself played a similar—although not so important—role as
witness to and participant in the events described by the former U.S.
ambassador, it seems logical for me to present the story from my perspective. (I was the personal advisor to the Croatian president from April 1990
to March 1991. I resigned when I learned that Franjo Tudjman was
planning a meeting with Slobodan Milošević, and that his advisors had
been ordered to make maps for the division of Bosnia and the "humane"
transfer of populations.)

It must be said from the outset that Zimmermann's "Memoir" is a
typically American view of the disintegration of Yugoslavia and the
causes of the conflict, but it is also an interesting account of his experiences with the key protagonists in this tragic event. The "American"
aspect of the story is patent insofar as the author assesses Balkan vicissitudes through the lens of what Robert N. Bellah calls the (American)
"habits of the heart"[4] or "American civil religion," and what has been
called the "American social character" by other authors.[5] In practice, this
means that Warren Zimmermann observes all processes, people and
events in the former Yugoslavia through the lens of a political "religion"
that firmly upholds sacred ideals such as individualism, federalism, the
rule of law, liberal democracy, and cultural tolerance, and sincerely de-
spises any form of racism, xenophobia, nationalism, authoritarianism, or
"Balkanization." This is why Zimmermann's memoir is a kind of "American mirror," or the *West Side Story* of the Croatian, Slovenian, Bosnian,
and Serb consciousness and reality in the period between 1989 and 1992.

It is a *West Side Story* in the sense that the United States has romanticized and oversimplified the complex realities of the former Yugoslavia by portraying all parties as simply members of competing gangs.

All the key figures in that reality—Slobodan Milošević, Vuk Drašković, Franjo Tudjman, Radovan Karadžić, Vojislav Šešelj, Alija Izetbegović, Kiro Gligorov, Ante Marković, and the author himself— were known personally to Zimmermann, who gained, as he believed, an almost psychoanalytical insight into their social-psychological being.

For the U.S. ambassador, love is the justification for his outspoken and sincere account—sometimes not very considerate of the protagonists' feelings—of the leaders, peoples, and events that have been rocking Europe and the world for five years. At the beginning of his article, he says of Lawrence Eagleburger and himself that they "shared a love of the country [Yugoslavia] and its people."[6] As far as his love of Yugoslavia and the "Yugoslav people" is concerned, I can confirm the following: everyone who has met and known him can testify that his love for the people and sights of the former Yugoslavia was deep and sincere (I had the pleasure of meeting him several times: we dined together three times, in the company of President Tudjman, and we also took part in a VIP tennis tournament at Rogla, Slovenia, in 1990, after which the Serb press accused us both of having conspired to break up Yugoslavia under the guise of playing tennis).

The U.S. public and even Croatian readers will regard with sympathy his sincere albeit belated admission, no longer of any avail to all the victims of Serb aggression, that at the time of the destruction of Vukovar and the shelling of Dubrovnik, nobody, including himself, had done anything (such as urging the use of force) to prevent the suffering or to halt it once it had begun: "Yet no Western government at the time called on NATO's military force to get the JNA to stop shelling Dubrovnik, although NATO's supreme commander, General John Galvin, had prepared contingency plans for doing so. The use of force was simply too big a step to consider in late 1991. I did not recommend it myself—a major mistake."[7]

Unfortunately, this laconic sentence, "I did not recommend it myself— a major mistake," hides the missed opportunity to create a different, happier history that would have put a definite end to the JNA (Yugoslav Federal Army) aggression toward Croatia and prevented all the atrocities of the war in Bosnia-Herzegovina. Unfortunately, Warren Zimmermann's real—but blind and platonic—love for "Yugoslavia" and the "Yugoslavs" was not only for the natural beauty and the people, but also embraced the state and the political system, which Zimmermann believed were worthy of not only his personal love, but also the love of the United States. He obviously thought that for Tito's Yugoslavia, which he knew well, to be worthy of general (i.e., Serb, Croat, Slovenian, American, Albanian, etc.) love, it only needed true Westernization or Americanization, that is, democracy, true federalism, true protection of human rights, and a true market economy. I would like here to repeat his words: "a [second] major mistake."

In the early 1990s, and in 1995, Warren Zimmermann saw the vision and reality of such a federalist, multicultural, democratic, and market-oriented Yugoslavia only in the personality and reformist project of Ante Marković. In his story, Ante Marković is the only positive, albeit naive and tragic, figure.

In general, it can be said that the key to understanding all Zimmermann's sound judgments as well as his preconceived ideas, errors, and mistaken views (and wrong decisions) regarding the events and people in the former Yugoslavia is to be found in his attitude to nationalism: "Nationalism is by nature uncivil, antidemocratic and separatist because it empowers one ethnic group over all others."[8]

With his deeply ingrained American "civil religion," discussed above, which is aware only of separatist nationalism (and which attaches an a priori negative meaning to the very notion of confederalism, let alone secession), Warren Zimmermann could not understand, and still does not seem to understand, the essence of Greater Serbian postcommunist nationalism. This nationalism is basically "federalist" and "antiseparatist," that is, its goal is either absolute national domination (based on the dogma of the superiority of the Serb people) or military conquest.

Zimmermann's culturally imposed or learned inability to grasp the expansionist, imperialist, and criminal nature of Greater Serbian national-ism (which logically led to concentration camps, ritual and mass murder, rape, and the destruction of all material signs of the historical presence of non-Serb populations in the conquered territories) affects his judgment throughout the article. Since he is not aware of and does not recognize "federalist" (i.e., "expansionist") nationalism, Zimmermann does not see Slobodan Milošević as a nationalist: *"Milošević is an opportunist driven by power rather than nationalism."*[9] Throughout Zimmermann's article we see this reduction of nationalism to separatism and the unawareness of the fatal fact that in the case of Milošević we are faced with the worst form of militant national socialism.

Comparing the Serbian and Croatian presidents, Zimmermann says, "Unlike Milošević, who is driven by power, Tudjman is obsessed by nationalism."[10] In general terms, Zimmermann sees no nationalism in Serbia, but only "Milošević's aggressive tactics."[11] While he sees various forms of "naked nationalism" in Slovenia and Croatia, in Serbia he sees only a form of power politics.

Zimmermann calls Slovenian nationalism "Garbo nationalism" and describes it in the following words: "They just wanted to be left alone. Their vice was selfishness. In their drive to separate from Yugoslavia they simply ignored the 22 million Yugoslavs who were not Slovenes. They bear considerable responsibility for the bloodbath that followed their secession."[12] At another point, he notes, strangely, that "Contrary to the general view, it was Slovenes who started the war." There is no doubt that he saw the position and role of the Slovenes and Slovenia through the prism of the American Civil War, in which the separatist South (in this case the secessionist northwest) was cast as the bad guy.

However, Croatian nationalism is definitely the worst kind of nationalism in his story: "Croatian nationalism is defined by Tudjman—intolerant, anti-Serb, and authoritarian. These attributes—together with an aura of wartime fascism, which Tudjman has done nothing to dispel—help explain why many Serbs in Croatia reject Croatian rule, and why the core hostility in the former Yugoslavia is still between Serbs and Croats."[13] Only pages later does he generously concede, "Albanian nationalism was, like Croatian nationalism, to some degree a reaction to Milošević's aggressive tactics."[14]

"Serbian nationalism" as a phrase appears only once in his article: "During 1990, Serbian nationalism under Milošević became even more aggressive."[15] It is quite obvious that Zimmermann is unaware of it as a cultural and political phenomenon in its own right. There are only individual Serb leaders who may be fanatical, extreme, and monstrous nationalists. Some of them are "fanatic nationalists like Vojislav Šešelj," others, such as Vuk Drašković, are "pro-Serbian extremists," yet others, like Radovan Karadžić, are "monsters"—but "Serbian nationalism" does not exist as a collective evil. In Zimmermann's consciousness, it cannot exist, because he knows and recognizes only separatist nationalism.[16]

All Zimmermann's views on the key protagonists of these events stem from his utterly negative attitude toward any form of separatist national-ism and his benevolent attitude toward "federalist" nationalism (in Slavic languages, this form of nationalism is encompassed by the notion of "unitarism," which has very negative connotations), even when it is based on a racist and militarist ideology of the all-Serbs-in-one-state type and the method of genocide called "ethnic cleansing."

Thus, Radovan Karadžić and Ante Marković are seen as representing opposite poles, Karadžić as the epitome of the bad guy, and Marković as his antipode, with all other figures situated somewhere in between. The position and labels attributed to Radovan Karadžić correspond to his true demonic nature and the crimes he has ordered or tacitly condoned, but they also reflect the author's system of values. For Zimmermann, Rado-van Karadžić is both a war criminal and a "separatist nationalist" aspiring to break up Bosnia-Herzegovina, which is seen by Zimmermann as the surrogate of the ideal state: federalist, democratic, multicultural. Here is how Zimmermann describes Karadžić: "He was the architect of massacres in the Muslim villages, ethnic cleansing, and artillery attacks on civilian populations. In his fanaticism, ruthlessness, and contempt for human values, he invites comparison with a monster from another generation, Heinrich Himmler." [17]

Although Zimmermann's use of the metaphor "architect of massacres" is questionable—since the concepts of ethnic cleansing and territorial conquest had already been established in Serbia—all his other judgments on Karadžić are quite sound. Karadžić can be called only the high priest and practitioner of massacres, not its architect, since that label would imply that he was the intellectual creator of the idea of such evil (that he worked out the technique and timing of the crimes, and probably ordered them to be committed). The following descriptions and opinions are also valid: "his disdain for the truth was absolute" and "his apartheid philoso-phy was as extreme as anything concocted in South Africa." [18]

On the other hand, the author presents Ante Marković as the absolute opposite of the demonic Radovan Karadžić. In a way, Marković is the ideal (but quite unrealistic) expression of the American "Yugoslav dream," which is based on the belief in human rights, democracy, federal-ism, and the "melting pot of nations." Describing Ante Marković, Zim-mermann describes and justifies himself and the American policy that, even after the destruction of Vukovar and the attack on Dubrovnik, kept their faith in the last Yugoslav prime minister: "Marković still departed as a symbol of everything his country needed: a modern, stable economy, the rule of law, ethnic tolerance. He had treated Yugoslavia like a patient with a serious cancer—nationalism. A semi-heroic, semi-tragic figure, Marković failed, but at least he had fought the cancer instead of adjusting to it. He had aspired to be Yugoslavia's savior. Instead, he turned out to be the Yugoslavian equivalent of Russia's last leader before the Bolshevik deluge, Aleksandr Kerensky."[19] The literary phrase "he had fought the cancer instead of adjusting to it" unerringly suggests that in the eyes of the last ambassador, Marković is some kind of mythical, unquestionably tragic hero, who is aware of the futility of his tragic sacrifice, but consciously chooses his fate. Unfortunately, Ante Marković is, like Warren Zimmermann himself, more of a loser. I myself can testify that he deeply believed he would win the polls in Bosnia and ultimately defeat Slobodan Milošević, Milan Kučan, and Franjo Tudjman.

By describing Ante Marković as a tragic figure, Zimmermann shows not only a sad ignorance of the personality of the last Yugoslav prime minister, but also his ignorance of tragedy as an art form. According to the ancient Greeks, tragedy is a lofty form of drama in which the fate of the chief protagonist is always determined in advance. In a series of tragedies, history had cast Ante Marković in a marginal and farcical role. His "dramatic" scenario for building a "new kind of socialism" was halfway between a historic farce and a provincial comedy: while the JNA was concocting plans for a military coup and the scenario for the salvation of communism, he was planning to set up a reformist party. Of course, he had his chance to change his role into a semiheroic, semitragic one. If he had stood before the tanks setting out to destroy Vukovar and said something along the lines of "Take or kill me but let this wonderful town and its inhabitants live in peace—they have not done anything wrong!" Ante Marković would have earned the description of hero or tragic figure. There is no doubt that Aeschylus and Shakespeare would have written such a role for him before bestowing on him the aura of tragic figure or hero.

Instead, he sat on quietly in Belgrade until the last moment, when nobody, as Zimmermann himself says, even noticed his "protest" resignation. After this, he settled in Vienna, probably convinced that his project was noble and unworthy of the barbarians living southeast of that city. Thus, Ante Marković was not, and could not be, even a semihero or a semitragic figure because he was by nature an opportunist, bureaucrat, and careerist, who in his pre-Zimmermann career played the role of a communist apparatchik, and in the Zimmermann period switched to the role of an opportunistic "democratchik." Instead of taking on the role of "divider" of Yugoslavia himself (brilliantly played by Vaclav Havel a few years later), he took on the role of "tragic" savior, thrust upon him by the U.S. administration (including Warren Zimmermann). To use Zimmermann's metaphor, we could say that this was an example of "Garbo federalism" and that, as far as responsibility was concerned, Marković himself and the administration represented by Warren Zimmermann "bore considerable responsibility for the bloodbath that followed Marković's reformism."

Instead of a strategy of gradual delegitimization of the Socialist Federal Republic of Yugoslavia (SFRJ), which could have begun in the autumn of 1990 (or at least after Franjo Tudjman's visit to the White House; my commentary on this visit is appended to this article), the chimeras of "reformism" and "federalism" were encouraged, which enabled the JNA and Serbia to prepare for aggression undisturbed. The moment the aggression began, the U.S. administration introduced an additional means of punishing the victims by imposing an arms embargo. Warren Zimmermann's article clearly reveals how the Bush administration's policy, mediated and/or suggested by the ambassador himself, was wrong from the beginning.

Especially interesting is the honesty with which the last ambassador rationalizes what is arguably the biggest foreign policy and diplomatic mistake committed by the U.S. State Department this century: "Eagleburger and I agreed that in my introductory calls in Belgrade and the capitals of the republics, I would deliver a new message: Yugoslavia no longer enjoyed the geopolitical importance that the United States had given it during the Cold War."[20] The Yugoslavia to which Zimmermann refers is not so much a state as a corridor, a geopolitical corridor. And this is where the error lies: even though the fall of communism and the creation of democratic and free-market institutions were the most important strategic interests of the United States and Western civilization, at the brink of a possible "democratic revolution" in the Balkans, Zimmermann openly proclaimed that this corridor no longer had any geopolitical interest for the United States. In terms of the power relations in the former Yugoslavia, Slobodan Milošević and the leadership of the JNA understood this message in only one way: You can do whatever you want!

The oft-quoted message delivered by James Baker in Belgrade on June 21, 1991, was "read" in a similar way. Warren Zimmermann views Baker's statement in a very positive light: "Listening to Baker deal with these complex and irascible personalities, I felt that I had rarely, if ever, heard a Secretary of State make a more skillful or reasonable presentation."[21] For us who lived in the former Yugoslavia with the awareness that the JNA was fully prepared to attack Slovenia and Croatia, James Baker's statements that he supported the unity of Yugoslavia and that only the reformist Ante Marković had the backing of the U.S. administration were taken as a go-ahead to the JNA to attack Slovenia.

The lay psychological descriptions of other key protagonists of this tragedy, which Zimmermann offers his reader, include many lucid observations, but also some quite superficial and wrong impressions. To illustrate my meaning I will confine myself to the figure I know best, the Croatian president Franjo Tudjman. Zimmermann's description of the Croatian president is vivid and not far from the truth: "If Milošević recalls a slick con man, Tudjman resembles an inflexible schoolteacher. He is a former general and communist, expelled from the party under Tito, and twice jailed for nationalism. Prim steel eyeglasses hang on a square face whose natural expression is a scowl. His mouth occasionally creases into a nervous chuckle or mirthless laugh."[22]

An author interested in the facts and truth would not have accepted so easily the stereotype that Tudjman was "twice jailed for nationalism"; he would at least specify when, and what offense he had been convicted of. The Croatian president was convicted the first time because he publicized the results of his research on the number of World War II victims in Croatia (his figures were several times lower than the official statistics of the communist regime), and the second time because of an interview given to a foreign reporter. If he had specified these facts, Warren Zimmermann could have freely expressed his opinion that the research in question advocated, for instance, revisionist, nationalist, or any other values or political judgments.

To say merely that Tudjman had been "twice jailed for nationalism" is to accept the communist, totalitarian view of human rights, which banned the freedom of the press and all forms of expression guaranteed under the constitutions of democratic nations, including the First Amendment. A more ambitious writer would have taken yet another step and attempted to explain why Milošević recalled a "slick con man," while Tudjman's mouth "occasionally creased into a nervous chuckle or mirthless laugh." My intention is not to argue with the view of the Croatian president as an "inflexible schoolteacher" (in fact, a comparison with a "communist or Partisan commissar" would be more to the point), "former communist," or "general," or even the contention that Tudjman is a politician who does not understand or love democracy and often advocates mythomaniac, ethnocentric views. I myself will add two very important traits to the list of the president's negative characteristics: obsessive narcissism and nepotism (his elder son is one of the key figures in the Croatian intelligence service, while his other son and daughter, quite lacking in business sense, have been turned into rich capitalists).

When listing the numerous faults of the president of Croatia, an objective analyst would have mentioned at least some of his virtues: (1) he is the only active antifascist combatant among all postcommunist statesmen; (2) he is one of the few professional scientists or Ph.D.'s among postcommunist leaders (he has written about a dozen books, some of which are not at all bad); (3) he was a dissident during the communist regime, a political prisoner and outcast, a citizen who (along with his family) had been deprived of almost every human right for twenty years because of his theoretical and political convictions; and (4) he is the head of a state that was, and still is, a victim of pan-Serbian aggression, the leader of a nation that has been, with the consent of "the free world," disarmed and deprived of its right to self-defense.

As regards Tudjman's alleged "obsession" with nationalism and separatism: it is obviously not his original political conviction, but a result of his unusual experience and permanent "learning by trial and error." In his long political life, the Croatian president has been a communist and an anticommunist, an internationalist and a nationalist, an atheist and a believer, both a great admirer and an opponent of Belgrade, an elitist and a populist. During World War II, the Tudjman family was, like the majority of the Croatian people, tragically divided by ideology and party tenets. The only common family feature was antifascism. Everything else conspired to disunite the family. Tudjman's parents were members of the Croatian Farmers' Party, that is, peace-oriented, but also nationally and religiously conscious, with a more or less pronounced anticommunist bias (however, during the war his father joined the Communist Party). The three sons of the Tudjman family joined the antifascist Partisan movement, but they were also dyed-in-the-wool communists, atheists, and idealists, passionately believing in Yugoslavia and the revolution. The president's younger brother, Stjepan, was killed fighting against the Ustashe.

After the war, Tudjman's parents met their death under mysterious circumstances at their home in their native village, as victims of circumstances and/or repression. Tudjman believes that they were murdered by the Yugoslav secret police because of their democratic, nationalist, and religious views, while the official police investigation established that it was classic textbook suicide (modern psychoanalysts would call it suicide committed "under the influence of post-traumatic stress syndrome"). In any case, whatever really happened to his parents, taken in conjunction with his own political persecution and imprisonment, the tragedy of his parents should play an important part in a fair and tolerant analysis of Franjo Tudjman as a person and politician.

The divisions in the Tudjman family, the divided identity (and loyalty) between "Yugoslavhood" and "Croathood" are typical for the majority of Croatian people. In general terms, one can say that the Croatian and Serbian views of "Yugoslavhood" had been fundamentally different from the very beginning, that is, since the integration of the two states. For the Croatian people, who had lived in a subordinate position in complex, multicultural unions (the Hungarian and Austro-Hungarian empires) without the right to their own (national) state and national identity, "Yugoslavhood" was a symbol of freedom, equality, and their aspirations to a state of their own (all Croatian myths are dominated by the idea of powerful Croatian states and kingdoms during the early Middle Ages). Escaping from one developed complex state (the Austro-Hungarian Empire), which was, in its name and political order, a negation of Croatian national identity and statehood, the Croats did not want just any Yugoslavia, but had a definite idea of the kind of Yugoslavia they wanted. They wanted a federal state of the southern Slavs, which would recognize the national identities and statehoods of its federal states, and which would be based on the rule of law, democracy, pluralism, multiculturalism, and federalism. Such a federal and multicultural "Yugoslavhood," which contains some elements of American federalism, but also certain elements of the Swiss confederal model, is a home-grown Croatian intellectual and political ideal. All, or nearly all, political projects and programs as well as the mythologies and ideology of federal and democratic "Yugoslavhood" were created by Croats: Frano Supilo and Stjepan Radić created the political philosophy of southern Slav federalism (which was the reason Radić was treacherously and perfidiously assassinated in the "federal" parliament in Belgrade in 1928); Josip Juraj Strossmayer preached and practiced the ideas of southern Slav religious tolerance and ecumenism; the Croatian sculptor Ivan Meštrović transformed his "Yugoslavhood" into sculptures, statues, and mausoleums funded by the

Serbian king Aleksandar Karadjordjevic; Vladimir Dvorniković discussed the philosophical and psychological implications of the so-called character of Yugoslavhood; and Miroslav Krleža did the same work in the field of encyclopedias. Even communist "Yugoslavhood" was the work of Josip Broz Tito, a Croat. Even if this "Yugoslavhood" had many primitive and undemocratic traits, it retained some elements of (con)federalism, such as upholding the statehood of the republics that made up Yugoslavia.

While the Croatian idea of "Yugoslavhood" is based on the "right to difference," the Serbian concept is based on a negation of differences in language, culture, religion, classes, and interests. Cross-cultural differences in the understanding of the "brotherhood and unity" tenet can be seen most clearly in the ostracism of so-called nationalism in the periods of monarchical and communist Yugoslavia. Thousands of Croats were brought to trial for singing the Croatian national anthem or certain folk songs, hoisting the Croatian flag, saying the name of the Croatian viceroy (*ban*) Josip Jelačić, using certain Croatian words and phrases that were labeled "nationalist," or merely stating their Croatian national affiliation in a public place. The statistics of political criminal trials and verdicts in the period between 1970 and 1990 show that over 70 percent of the convicts were Croats.

That the symbolical expression of national identity was defined and prosecuted as a criminal offense is obvious from the structure of the new political elites: while in the new Serbian elite it is very hard to find an individual who was convicted of "counterrevolution" (that is, anticommunist views) or "nationalism," at least 30 percent of members of the Croatian parliament served prison sentences because of an interview, a song, or a different expression of their Croatian national feelings. For instance, Vladimir Seks served one year, Vlado Gotovac five, Marko Veselica eleven, and Duro Perica thirteen years in prison for such "offenses."

The Serbian idea and political model of "Yugoslavhood"—diametrically opposed to its Slovenian and Croatian counterparts—that the national socialist movement led by Slobodan Milošević wanted to restore and impose by force on all non-Serbs in 1986 is based on the principles of territorial expansion and the political domination of only one "chosen" nation, the Serbian nation. The right to be a "chosen nation" and dominate others is mainly based on the mythological consciousness of the greatness, heroism, and Piedmonte-style sense of mission of the Serb nation, which is surrounded by allegedly upstart, genocidal, and in every way inferior nations: Croats, Slovenes, Albanians, Macedonians, and Muslims. The Serbian idea of "Yugoslavhood" does not know or recognize any form of federalism and multiculturalism as a political value or constitutional principle.

For Serbs, who (unlike Croats and Slovenes) did not have the historical experience of living in complex state unions, "Yugoslavhood" always meant something else: the territorial expansion of Serbia, the negation of differences, the domination and negation of religious differences (that was the purpose of militant atheism) and cultural differences. In Serbian philosophy and realpolitik, federalism is not a recognized positive value. The key slogan of communist Yugoslavia, "brotherhood and unity," expressed this concept of "Yugoslavhood," which did not recognize very well the other two key slogans of the French Revolution: the freedom and equality of citizens and nations.

The conflicts in the former Yugoslavia after the 1980s were about the understanding of the fundamental political and constitutional principles on which the postcommunist "Yugoslavia" was to be based. While Slovenia and Croatia aimed for freedom, federalism, human rights, a multiparty system, and a market economy, the movement that simultaneously emerged in Serbia and the JNA leadership aimed for the negation of these ideas and principles. Nationalist and secessionist movements in Slovenia, Croatia, and Bosnia were therefore not the cause, as stated by Warren Zimmermann, but the inevitable consequence of the pan-Serbian national socialist and racist movement that openly threatened to undermine all the federal and democratic institutions (which were defective anyhow), forcibly prevented the emergence of a multiparty system and private ownership, and promoted the racist negation of all ethnic and cultural differences (racist rhetoric and practice were initially directed against Albanians in Kosovo, and were gradually expanded to include all non-Serbian peoples).

The actual roots, causes, and motives of the postcommunist wars in Slovenia, Croatia, and Bosnia are to be found in the Serbs, Serbia, and the JNA. The national socialist movement led by Slobodan Milošević since 1986 had not wanted to accept either a true federalization or a democratic transformation of the SFRJ. The goal of this movement was either total Serbian domination or aggression. Some of the causes and reasons for this aggression are also to be found in the JNA: all the elements of the new political movements in Croatia and Slovenia were absolutely unacceptable to the ideologically xenophobic communist army.

The demands for a multiparty system, market economy, and democratic federalism were, for the JNA, the immediate reason for a coup or war.

The causes and reasons for the wars in Slovenia, Croatia, and Bosnia-Herzegovina do not, as Warren Zimmermann believes and claims, lie in nationalism per se, but in the specific forms of nationalism (or national socialism) and totalitarianism that developed, both spontaneously and on an organized basis, in the leadership of the JNA and in Serbia in the mid-1980s. Finally, by the time the multiparty system and the first intimations of secessionist movements began to emerge in Slovenia and Croatia (between 1989 and 1990), the national socialist movement in Serbia had some four of five years of destructive and racist practice (Slobodan Milošević had come to power in 1986).

By the time the new political elites and their parties came to power in Slovenia and Croatia, the national socialist movement in Serbia had already completed all its preparations for overthrowing these elites, or waging wars of aggression in these countries. By the time people in Croatia and Slovenia began to seriously ponder multiparty elections and the overthrow of Communism in the fall of 1989, the various projects for the military overthrow and aggression in Croatia and Slovenia were already completed. As Slavenka Drakulic once put it, "The war is not difficult to understand at all: There existed a Serbian political elite determined to start a war; it controlled the army; it controlled the media, and it had four years of systematic nationalist propaganda behind it. This is all it takes to start a war."[23]

As a direct witness, and for a time, a participant in these events, I can state that the Croatian government was aware of the above-noted preparations for aggression on the part of the Yugoslav Federal Army and Serbia. Given that the mechanism of this aggressive and imperialistic Greater Serbian attitude could not be changed, the Croatian government tried to prevent aggression by limiting the potential of ethnic conflicts, then by proposing a "confederation" designed to peacefully transform the former Yugoslavia into a commonwealth of sovereign south Slavic states. The theoretical underpinnings of the confederation agreement were completed by August 1990 and were drafted along the lines of the European Community prior to the 1992 model, so that they retained a customs and monetary union, a confederate judiciary for human rights, and also an organization to defend the confederation, modeled after NATO. This proposal was offered for discussion and debate to all the republics of the former Yugoslavia, but for various reasons it did not obtain their support.

The proposal to peacefully transform the Yugoslav federation into a commonwealth was also submitted to representatives of the Bush administration (in mid-September 1991), but it did not receive their diplomatic support either; on the contrary, it was opposed in favor of the unity of the communist Yugoslavia and the reformist government of Ante Marković.

Last, there remains the need to answer a series of rhetorical questions as to whether the new Croatian government, through any concrete political decisions, rhetoric, symbolism, or gesture, incited the Serbian minority in Croatia to armed rebellion (which formally began in Knin on August 18, 1990).

In his memoir, Warren Zimmermann states that the new Croatian leadership and the president personally oppressed the Serbian minority: "He (Tudjman) presided over serious violations of the rights of Serbs, who made up 12 percent of the population of Croatia. They were dismissed from work, required to take loyalty oaths, and subjected to attacks on their homes and property."[24] In this statement Warren Zimmermann repeats a stereotype that the wars in Croatia and Bosnia-Herzegovina are ethnic conflict and civil wars caused by minority problems in these republics or states. Paradigmatic of this type of "analysis" is an opinion piece by Roger Cohen published in the *New York Times:*

> Many of the Serbs now living in Vukovar fled persecution elsewhere in Croatia, where Mr. Tudjman's Croatian Democratic Union adopted measures in 1991 aimed largely at undermining the republic's 600,000 Serbs. Among those steps were a ban on use of the Serbs' Cyrillic script, the abrupt dismissal of many Serbs from their jobs and reintroduction of symbols formerly used by the Ustashi, or Croatian fascists, who killed thousands of Serbs when a government installed by the Nazis ruled Croatia during World War II.[25]

The fundamental criticisms of Croatia voiced by Zimmermann, Cohen, and some others can be reduced to several "causes" of the rebellion:

1. constitutional changes, which allegedly discriminated against the Serbian minority and forbade the Cyrillic script that Serbs favored;

2. expulsion of Serbs from positions of employment and general discrimination against them;

3. use of symbolism of the Independent State of Croatia;

4. inadequate communication and political links with the Serbian minority in Croatia at the beginning of 1990.

In order to determine the legitimacy of these complaints, we will strive to make use of original texts and facts, as opposed to interpretations thereof.

We begin with the Croatian Constitution and its definition of sovereignty and statehood. The new constitution of the new Croatia, which was no longer to be considered part of a collective state of a "higher order" (communist Yugoslavia) so that it no longer could be said to have a divided sovereignty, adopted the conception of civil sovereignty according to the logic of the American Constitution. Sovereignty is decreed in the first article of the constitution:

> The Republic of Croatia is a united and indivisible democratic and social state. Power in the Republic of Croatia derives from the people and belongs to the people as a community of free and equal citizens.
>
> The people shall exercise this power through the election of representatives and through direct decision making.

The adoption in that article of the concept of a modern, civil sovereignty makes it clear that the constitution does not allow any ethnonational conceptions, be they Croat or Serb. Sovereignty at the very highest governmental level belongs to the "people" in the sense of the civil community of all citizens. In the preamble of the constitution, the first reference to the concept of nation-state uses the following definition:

> The Republic of Croatia is hereby established as the national state of the Croatian nation and a state of members of other nations and minorities who are its citizens: Serbs, Muslims, Slovenes, Czechs, Slovaks, Italians, Hungarians, Jews, and others, who are guaranteed equality with citizens of Croatian nationality and the realization of ethnic rights in accordance with the democratic norms of the United Nations and the free world countries.

Therefore, the Croatian Constitution can neither in its conception nor in its concrete formulation be said to "expel Serbs from the constitution," but rather, explicitly names Serbs and other nations and minorities living in Croatia in the very definition of Croatian statehood.

With regard to the constitutional status of the Cyrillic script, it is established on two levels: (1) as an explicit constitutional right in Article 12 and (2) as a fundamental human and civil right in Article 15. Article 12 states, "The Croatian language and the Latin script shall be in official use in the Republic of Croatia. In individual local units another language and the Cyrillic or some other script may, along with the Croatian language and the Latin script, be introduced into official use under conditions specified by law." Article 15, second paragraph, states, "Members of all nations and minorities shall be guaranteed freedom to express their nationality, freedom to use their language and script, and cultural autonomy." Considering Articles 12 and 15 together suggests not only that the Cyrillic script has in no way been "expelled from the constitution" but rather that its use as an official script is sanctioned at the regional level. By the very logic of the document, it would apply to all administrative units that are ethnically mixed and in which there exists a relative or absolute majority of ethnic communities that utilize the Cyrillic script, that is, Serbs.

Therefore, when we ex post facto analyze the phenomenology of the development of the ethnic conflicts in Croatia, what is surprising is not the fact that Greater Serbian propaganda falsified the content of the constitution, but the fact that the Croatian government did not provide an efficient counterargument to this propaganda.

Manipulation of the historic traumas of Serbs within Croatia—specifically, their tragic fate during the course of World War II (the Independent State of Croatia [NDH] adopted the racial legislation of Nazi Germany and practiced a policy of genocide: deportation, concentration camps, mass executions, etc.)—was furthered by way of the thesis alleging "the return of symbols of the NDH in the Croatian Constitution."[26] The constitution establishes the state "iconography"—the coat of arms, flag, anthem—in Article 11, which as can be plainly seen contains not a single symbol of the NDH. That is, the key symbol of the NDH, which was the letter *U* (the Croatian counterpart to the so-called hooked cross, or swastika, used by the Nazis), is completely absent from the constitution. On the contrary, the flag, coat of arms, and anthem "Lijepa nasa" (literally, "Beautiful, our homeland") are traditional expressions of Croatian statehood, which Croats and Serbs in Croatia displayed and sang with pride for centuries.

The final complaint, that the Croatian government did not adequately communicate with the leaders of the Serbian minority and the Serbs themselves, deserves the greatest attention. Facts point to an entire series of contacts, attempts to reach a compromise, repeated offers of choice political concessions (the president of the republic, by way of public announcements as well as private contacts, offered to place Serbs in various functions throughout the government, including the parliament and the collective presidency), the final responses to which were always negative. In the middle of 1990, representatives of the Serbian minority conclusively rejected further participation in the Croatian parliament, and afterwards urged their nation to collective civil disobedience and ultimately, armed insurrection.

The most simple and plausible explanation of this phenomenon of mistakes in communication regarding the government, the minority leadership, and the minority itself follows the form of the above-noted thesis that the manipulation of information and the severing of such communication links were two of the key elements of Slobodan Milošević's war strategy. Furthermore, tracking the chronology of the ethnic conflicts and the JNA's implementation of low-intensity conflict in Croatia serves to demonstrate how the destruction of communication links and communication technology, with the intent of isolating the Serbian minority, was one of the key strategic objectives before and during the war. Air attacks on television relays, the construction of special transmitters that served as instruments of Greater Serbian and military propaganda, as well as other attempts to sever communication lines within the Zagreb-Knin-Beli-Manastir nexus, were all a part of this strategy.

The moment, in May 1991, when an army of Serbian reservists under the label of the JNA came from Serbia into Croatia for the alleged purpose of "separating the warring parties" marked the end of all communication between the Croatian government, the leadership of the Serbian minority, and the Serb minority itself. The tanks and other weaponry of the Yugoslav National Army became thereby not only an occupying force but also a communications barrier. A similar role was in some ways taken over by UNPROFOR units, which continued the status quo of Serbian occupation of the Croatian territory into 1995.

Ultimately, with regard to the sources and mechanisms by which ethnic conflicts began within Croatia, one can conclude the following: the disappearance of the Yugoslavian and the appearance of the Croatian state created among Croatia's Serbs a kind of emotional vacuum and deep frustration. The formation of a new nation-state, in this case the Republic of Croatia, inevitably involves the formation of new feeling regarding affiliation toward that new political community and loyalty to that state. The government of Slobodan Milošević, which had four years of practical experience in manipulating the masses, succeeded to a greater extent than the government of Franjo Tudjman, as far as the Serbian minority in Croatia was concerned, in projecting ideas regarding affiliation to a political community (Greater Serbia) and loyalty to a state (whether toward "Yugoslavia" or the so-called Krajina, as opposed to the Republic of Croatia).

Whether and how such a situation could and/or can be changed is a crucial question. A similar scenario unfolded in Bosnia-Herzegovina, and is likely to emerge in Macedonia in the near future.

Appendix: A Memoir of the Visit to the White House, September 25, 1990

The visit to the United States in the fall of 1990 was the first international trip by President Tudjman. This is a very important fact, because the Croatian president made a deliberate decision to establish a democratic, postcommunist Croatia modeled not on Europe, or even Germany, but the country and administration that all regard as the undisputed leader of the free world.

Prior to the trip to Washington, D.C., the Croatian administration had a clear picture of its status in the former Yugoslavia. Some factors were especially important:

1. Croatia was the only former Yugoslav republic that had been completely disarmed by the Yugoslav Federal Army (JNA). Croatia literally did not have more than a thousand automatic rifles.

2. All attempts at high-level negotiations with representatives of the Serbian minority in Croatia, aimed at seeking compromise and preventing ethnic conflict in Croatia, were broken off at the instigation of Milošević's regime.

3. The JNA had very precise plans for military intervention in Slovenia and Croatia and for ruining the democratically elected governments in these nations.

4. Croatia had, by my personal assessment, from May to September 1990, finished the project of peaceful transformation from the communist Yugoslavia into Commonwealth of Independent Nations. The draft memorandum of understanding for this commonwealth and all related documents had been written.

In my thinking, this commonwealth of former Yugoslav republics had to have a defense plan modeled after NATO. The commonwealth had to be a mini-EC (EU), with a common market and monetary and tariff union. Serbia and the JNA rejected every attempt we made to put forth this Croatian-Slovene proposal.

Because we were without weapons and felt that military intervention or war was imminent, we concluded that diplomacy and pressure from the

American administration of George Bush on Serbia and the JNA were our only chance to escape catastrophe, of which we were fully conscious.

• • •

The text that follows is from my personal diary, which I wrote on September 25, 1990:

At exactly 4:22 P.M. we entered the West Wing of the White House. The delegation consisted of Franjo Tudjman, Hrvoje Šarinić (chief of staff), Ilija Letica (a Croatian American businessman), and myself. Prior to our entry a photographer took a picture of President Tudjman, which evoked pride and hope in him. Of course, the Yugoslav diplomats tried to thwart our success in this trip to the United States at every turn. Prime Minister Ante Marković even tried to bet with President Tudjman that he would not even be allowed to set foot on the White House lawn.

When we entered the West Wing we were unpleasantly surprised by a "translator," Mrs. K. G., whose services had been arranged against our wishes by the U.S. State Department. Because we concluded immediately that the role of this lady was not translation (since we all spoke English), we surmised that she was an agent for Slobodan Milošević and the JNA to let them know the contents of our meeting. We therefore asked Brent Scowcroft's secretary to not let Mrs. K. G. translate. Our request was granted.

We did not have any advance information of what would happen in the White House. We knew we would meet with General Scowcroft, but Mara Letica mentioned to me that there was a chance of meeting with George Bush. While we waited in the salon, the door opened suddenly and there entered into the room a number of bodyguards (Secret Service agents)—and George Bush. We were caught off guard. The American president gave us a warm greeting. This was to be a shaking hands meeting, arranged after pressure from Senator Bob Dole and, presumably, George J. Mitchell.

The entire diplomatic strength of the former Yugoslavia had been used to thwart the proposed meeting of Tudjman, Bush, and Scowcroft. Especially active in this campaign against the Croatian president were Budimir Loncar and Ante Marković. These saviors of the new type of socialism in the Socialist Federal Republic of Yugoslavia (SFRJ) tried in telephone conversations with James Baker and Lawrence Eagleburger to do all they could to obstruct our visit in Washington.

On the other hand, we believed that only the American administration had the real power to avert war, by establishing direct economic links with the new independent republics, by deligitimizing the SFRJ, and by putting pressure on Serbia and the JNA. Regarding the Tudjman-Scowcroft conversation, it lasted about forty-five minutes, and was correct by standards of protocol, but lacking in substance. That is, President Tudjman tried to explain that over 95 percent of the citizens of Croatia and Slovenia voted for political parties that had platforms representing confederalist or secessionist options, so that a commonwealth/confederation was the only peaceful option. Our host, General Scowcroft, repeated coldly that his administration supported the unity of Yugoslavia at any cost, as well as that of the Soviet Union. On the request to put pressure on Belgrade not to use force and weapons, Scowcroft answered that they supported the government of Ante Marković and the unity of Yugoslavia.

All in all, our hopes that George Bush's administration would support the new democracies and nations (in the former Yugoslavia) were completely buried. At the same time, we were conscious of the tragic consequences of Belgrade's preparations for war. Yet our meetings and conversations with members of Congress and the Senate indicated more tolerance toward the new democracies than the administration showed. This was especially true regarding our meetings with Senators Bob Dole and George J. Mitchell.

Bob Dole, especially, seemed extremely familiar with the technology of Serbian repression and terror in Kosovo, and had visited Croatia with a group of Congressmen. Because of his knowledge or political instinct he felt that war was imminent and was ready for the United States to do something serious to avert it. All our efforts to organize a meeting between President Tudjman and James Baker failed. Instead, a meeting with Lawrence Eagleburger was offered to our president. Because we knew that Eagleburger had material interests in the former Yugoslavia, namely, Serbia, our president wished to avoid meeting him, thinking it would not be useful. I thought differently and thought that such a meeting could be useful.

Regarding the rest of our meetings in Washington, two are worth noting: the meeting with the Anti-Defamation League and the meeting with Henry Kissinger.

The meeting with Henry Kissinger was a special wish of President Tudjman because he had heard him lecture at Harvard. The meeting was held October 1, 1990, at 4 P.M., Gina Mare, 350 Park Avenue. The gist of this meeting was that President Tudjman wanted to know Kissinger's thinking on the possible dissolution of the USSR and Yugoslavia, and to see whether he would agree with him on the idea of a Commonwealth. In addition, we wanted to invite Kissinger to Croatia, and to ask eventually for his expert advice. President Tudjman explained to him that Croatia had two political priorities: to create its own nationhood and to escape war. Much like Scowcroft, Kissinger did not show the slightest positive emotion or support for our ideas. He too concluded that American policy would be and should be support for democracy, free markets, federalism, and unity.

NOTES

1. October 24, 1993, 21.
2. Ibid.
3. "The Last Ambassador: A Memoir of the Collapse of Yugoslavia," *Foreign Affairs* 74, no. 2 (March-April 1995): 2–20.
4. R. N. Bellah et. al., *Habits of the Heart* (Berkeley: University of California Press, 1985).
5. R. N. Bellah, "Civil Religion in America," *Daedalus* 96 (1967): 1–21. The "resignation phenomenon"—observed among politicians who regain their reason, conscience, and sense of ethics after the fact—merits an analysis in its own right, including the cases of Marković, Zimmermann, and myself.
6. Zimmermann, op. cit., 2.
7. Ibid., 14.
8. Ibid., 7.
9. Ibid., 5; my emphasis.
10. Ibid.
11. Ibid., 8.
12. Ibid., 7.
13. Ibid., 8.
14. Ibid.
15. Ibid.
16. Ibid., 12.
17. Ibid., 18.
18. Ibid.
19. Ibid., 17.
20. Ibid., 2.
21. Ibid., 11.
22. Ibid., 7.
23. *Los Angeles Times*.

24. Zimmermann, op. cit., 7–8.

25. *New York Times,* April 18, 1993.

26. On this manipulation and its importance for the Serbian war effort, see Branka Magas, *The Destruction of Yugoslavia: Tracing the Break-Up, 1980–92* (London: Verso, 1993), 342–43.

Brad K. Blitz

Serbia's War Lobby: Diaspora Groups and Western Elites

The current war in Bosnia-Herzegovina has been characterized by two main conflicts: an ideological battle between forces advocating the creation of an ethnically pure Serbian state and those calling for the restoration of a multiethnic country; and a struggle over material resources, notably heavy weaponry and food.[1] The two conflicts are closely connected. The deliberate physical deprivation brought on by a three-year siege and the inequitable distribution of aid has done much to advance the goal of ethnic purity and the elimination of specific populations.[2] Yet there is an additional link that is most relevant to a discussion of the Western powers and their responses to the war in Bosnia. Agreement on the ideological dimension of the conflict has had a decisive influence on political outcomes, which in turn affect the delivery and distribution of critical resources. This is most clearly illustrated in the controversy over Bosnia's right to self-defense.

The issue of Bosnia's right to self-defense became a major source of debate in the U.S. Congress in 1994 and 1995. By the summer recess of 1995, the Senate had voted seven times on bills and amendments which called for an end to US participation in the UN-imposed arms embargo against the Bosnian government.[3] Following the Market Place Massacre in Sarajevo on February 5, 1994, this issue attracted increasing interest from the American public. Congressional debates in both the House and Senate were preceded by energetic grassroots lobbying campaigns throughout 1994 and 1995. Pro-Bosnian organizations argued that Bosnia's territorial integrity had been threatened since 1992 when Serbian forces under the command of the Yugoslav Federal Army (JNA) invaded Bosnia-Herzegovina and launched a war of genocide against its people.[4] Activists pleaded with their elected representatives to "lift the embargo" and restore Bosnia's right to self-defense. Their lobbying efforts were challenged by members of the Serbian American community, which denied their charges of genocide and resisted any change in official U.S. policy.

Pro-Bosnian groups maintained that the UN-imposed arms embargo of September 25, 1991, violated Bosnia's rights to territorial integrity, political independence, and self-defense granted under the UN Charter. They therefore insisted that the arms embargo was illegal. Central to their argument was the recognition that (1) the Serb-dominated government of Yugoslavia requested the imposition of an arms embargo on the whole of the fragile federation; (2) the arms embargo could not be legitimately applied to the independent state of Bosnia-Herzegovina since it was imposed on another legal and political entity; (3) the ineffective protection offered by the international community undermined Bosnia's rights to territorial integrity and self-defense, as laid out in Articles 2(4) and 51 of the UN Charter, and made the continuation of genocide possible.

In their defense, Serbian Americans argued that Serbs too were victims of the war and that their suffering was not being heard. According to Serbian American leaders, they were in fact twice victimized since they alleged that bias and a lack of access to the media prevented them from getting their message across effectively.[5] Counterclaims of genocide were made amid tortuous accusations that defied standard rules of logic. One of the most prominent Serbian American organizations, SerbNet, went so far as to suggest that U.S. policy was designed "to promote German/ Turkish influence in the Balkans thereby, extinguishing the Serbian people and the Serbian Orthodox Church."[6] But logic—or the lack of it—did not seem to matter. "In all fairness," they argued, Serbs also had a "point of view," which should be equally respected. The questions, "how did the war begin?" "who is most responsible?" and "should the arms embargo be lifted?" therefore led to an intensely political contest between revisionists who denied the occurrence of genocide and those who maintained that it was the defining characteristic of the Bosnian conflict.

This chapter analyzes the domestic contest between revisionists and their opponents outside the former Yugoslavia. I argue that the invasion of Bosnia-Herzegovina by the Yugoslav Federal Army in 1992 and the continuation of its war aims through the Bosnian Serb Army has been supported by an unknown source of political influence: the Serbian diaspora. Image merchants in the form of Serbian community groups, hired professionals, and public relations firms have helped political leaders protect their territorial gains by fostering a climate of appeasement and confusion abroad. This chapter explores the political strategies used by Serbian political leaders, in concert with the Serbian diaspora, to undermine serious intervention in support of the Sarajevo government.

The Serbian Context: Revisionism and the Politics of Strategic Deterrence

In his book *Genocide in Bosnia: The Policy of Ethnic Cleansing,* Norman Cigar argues that the genocide launched against the people of Bosnia-Herzegovina was a calculated program devised by former communist apparatchiks, the Serbian intelligentsia, and political elites. A number of institutions were involved—not least the Serbian Orthodox Church. Top-down leadership and official legitimation were crucial to the implementation of their plans for a Greater Serbia, which was to be carved out at the expense of the indigenous population of Bosnia. Cigar maintains that the creation of an explicitly ultranationalist ideology was secondary to the political goals of Serbian leaders. Rather, they found it necessary "to engage in a systematic and intensive propaganda campaign in order to create a nationalist movement and exacerbate intercommunal relations to the extent that genocide could be made plausible."[7]

Yet if genocide was to be made plausible and later realized, it also had to be justified. It was here that official propaganda came into full effect as state-run television and governmental news agencies in Serbia executed Slobodan Milošević's disinformation campaign. In order to make the case that the conflict in Bosnia was a "civil war" in which all sides were guilty, propaganda alleging comparable acts of brutality against Serbs was quickly produced. Just as the first rumors of Serb-run concentration camps were being heard in Bosnia, Serbian political leaders in Pale and Belgrade tried to impress on the international community that Serbs too were victims. Although their efforts were at first unconvincing,[8] they paved the way for a longer struggle in which historical memory would be manipulated in an effort to destroy the sovereignty of Bosnia-Herzegovina. The aim of this campaign was twofold: first, to deter unilateral criticism that might bring outside intervention and interfere with the pursuit of Serbia's war aims; second, to reiterate a theme of historical struggles that would, in the long term, undermine the idea and acceptance of a multiethnic Bosnia. To these ends, Serbian political leaders sought to appropriate the suffering of the people of Bosnia-Herzegovina through an elaborate propaganda campaign based on revisionism—both historical and contemporary—and moral relativism.[9]

A list of major concentration camps, prisons, and detention sites set up by the "Muslims" and dated June 22, 1992, was issued by Velibor Ostojić, secretary for information of the self-proclaimed "Serbian Republic of Bosnia." A similar document was brought to London on July 15, 1992, by Radovan Karadžić, the self-appointed leader of the Bosnian Serbs. According to Serbian sources, Karadžić's list was to be issued at a House of Commons press conference hosted by Conservative M.P. Henry Bellingham and the Serbian-born lobbyist John Kennedy.[10] The press conference, entitled "Concentration Camps in the New Europe 1992: An Appeal to the Civilized World," was scheduled for the very same day that Karadžić was received by Lord Carrington, chair of the EC-sponsored peace process.[11]

The substance of this official propaganda was immediately questionable. The various entries were written in poor English and relied on vague descriptions that were blended with fantastic accounts. Ostojić's list claimed that at the hot water plant in "Ali-Pashino Polje (A. P. Field)" over six thousand inmates were the victims of a "mass liquidation." In Bradina, over four hundred inmates, "predominantly children—left orphans—fathers killed by Muslims and women" were allegedly herded into a railway tunnel. The story of the "railway children" could not be substantiated independently by human rights authorities. Karadžić later added his own revisionist twist by suggesting that Bosnian forces were the ones besieging Sarajevo. In the course of this alleged aggression, the number of Serbian inmates held in Sarajevo—which was reported as two thousand plus "unknown" in Ostojić's list—was multiplied three-fold in Karadžić's document.

6,000 Bosnian-Serbs are detained in a variety of location including: "Kosevo" football Stadium, Zetra railway station, the women's prison, the Mladen Stojanović student hostel, the Viktor Bubanj barracks, the 25 May children's home in Svrakino Selo, the Šipad storehouse and the central prison which comes under the command of the notorious criminal nicknamed "Celo."

John F. Burns points out the irony of the situation in his *New York Times* article of June 23, 1992, "Sarajevo Tries a Normal Life; Bombs Forbid It," showing that, just as Karadžić accused Bosnian forces of besieging the city, he was seen on Serbian television peering at Sarajevo through field glasses and congratulating Serb gunners on their acts of terrorism and murder. In spite of its inconsistencies and dubious content, the disinformation circulated by the Bosnian Serb leadership reached wide audiences within hours of its publication. Ostojić's account of the "railway children" and claim that Bosnian Serb villagers from Konjić were being detained in grain silos near the city of Tarčin were received by the *Chicago Tribune* the same day. The minister's stories were revised and reported in the final edition of the Midwest newspaper on June 22, 1992.[12] One additional piece of information included was the new number of detainees supposedly held in the Bradina railway tunnel; the number had grown from four hundred to three thousand. The revised count was to become the official figure used by Karadžić in July. The *Chicago Tribune* article was syndicated and reappeared with a slightly different title in the *Toronto Star* and the *Calgary Herald* two days later.[13]

In order to substantiate the allegations of Serbian victimization, Karadžić offered to expose "some typical examples of massacres of Bosnian-Serbs by units of the Croatian Army in Bosnia and Herzegovina and the Bosnian Territorial Defense." The Bosnian Serb leadership tried to present the case for well-armed Muslim-directed aggression against Serb civilians and even charged the Bosnian forces with "genocide." These accusations were repeated later that summer when a Bosnian Serb representative, Misha Milošević, appeared before an extraordinary meeting of the UN Human Rights Commission in Geneva. Milošević claimed that forty-two thousand Bosnian Serbs were being detained in twenty one concentration camps run by Croat and Muslim forces. Over six thousand detainees had been killed while three hundred thousand Bosnian Serbs had fled their homes, he asserted.[14]

The accusations contained in official lists and public declarations were unconvincing. There were of course documented cases of "Muslim" and Croatian-run prison camps. In 1992, human rights groups, such as Helsinki Watch, collected and published detailed evidence on abuses conducted by Bosnian and Croatian soldiers against detained civilians (see *War Crimes in Bosnia-Hercegovina,* vols. 1 and 2, Human Rights Watch, 1992–1993). However, there was nothing comparable in the reports issued by the Bosnian Serbs which relied on anecdotal evidence and exaggerated statistics. Karadžić's reports were based on fantastic stories and suggested a most unusual practice of collecting human rights data. They even gave the impression that the Bosnian Serb command was in the practice of making "video-nasties" while alleged abuses were being committed.

> In the town of Kupres, by the beginning of April, 52 Bosnian-Serbs had been murdered. The principle [*sic*] methods of execution and mutilation were the severing of heads or the extraction of the brains of living victims. In addition mallets were often used to smash skulls. Prior to death it was common practice to gouge out eyes, cut off ears and break both arms and legs of victims. An unidentified number of Bosnian-Serbs were murdered around the village of Gornji Malovan near Kupres. The corpses were buried in a mass grave on Borova Glava. We are now in possession of proof, in the form of photographs, video tapes and tape recordings which can be produced.

In some cases, these "depositions" invited greater poetic license and read as if they had been dictated by the doctor-poet-war criminal leader himself. In Srebrenica, it was claimed that one young woman escaped being burned alive but "needed to be detained in hospital for 20 days and has subsequently had a complete nervous breakdown."

As more evidence of Serb-run concentration camps was discovered by journalists and human rights workers in August 1992, the earlier charges made by the Bosnian Serb leadership became increasingly inconsistent with the course of official propaganda. Statements made by Bosnian Serb representatives in July and early August 1992 were soon contradicted by subsequent declarations. On August 13–14, Misha Milošević tried to impress upon the UN Human Rights Commission that the idea of Serb-run concentration camps in Bosnia was pure fiction. Milošević told the Commission that, (1) no concentration camps existed in Serbian territory in Bosnia-Herzegovina; (2) no hidden camp had been created; (3) the self-proclaimed Serbian government of Bosnia-Herzegovina had never carried out operations of "ethnic cleansing" on its territory; and (4) that the same government had never refused international control over prison camps in its territory.[15] Less than two weeks later, Karadžić corrected some of Milošević's claims. The self-appointed president delivered a cautious admission that there were camps in Bosnia that were under the control of Bosnian Serb forces. Before representatives of some twenty countries, Karadžić told delegates at the 1992 London Conference that the Serb-run "prisoner-of-war" camps would be closed down.

If the practice of circulating revisionist propaganda to the international community was publicized by Bosnian Serb leaders, the program of denial could ultimately trace its way back to Belgrade and to forces under the command of the Serbian president, Slobodan Milošević. As the fighting intensified, official denials from Belgrade became commonplace. In April 1992, as soon as the Serbs' aerial bombardment began in western Bosnia, the military command of the JNA and political leaders in the Serbian capital denied any direct involvement in this offensive. On June 6, two days after its declared withdrawal from Bosnia, the Milošević government again tried to distance itself formally from the aggression and, in a cosmetic effort to deceive the international community, called on the Bosnian Serbs to stop the fighting. As press reports of Serbian military involvement in Bosnia were to reveal three years later, there was no change in policy from Belgrade. Milošević's state apparatus continued to direct both the course of the war and the self-justifying campaign of propaganda that he and Karadžić had perfected.[16]

Milošević's direction of the propaganda campaign required total control of the system of communications in Serbian-held territories. To this end, the official Yugoslav news agency Tanjug placed correspondents in a number of Bosnian cities throughout 1992 and 1993, where they worked in tandem with Karadžić's Serbian Democratic Party and his news agency, SRNA. Reports from Bosnia of Serbian attacks in Sarajevo were routinely censored and corrected by the Belgrade bureau until the practice of self-censorship and vague commentary was institutionalized.[17] News agencies executed both a local and international disinformation campaign. Not only did they target the Serbian populations of the former Yugoslavia but, since information was not covered in the UN-imposed sanctions against Serbia-Montenegro, these agencies also served to represent the Milošević government abroad. Three years later, state-run news agencies would do the same for Karadžić.[18]

War crimes reports similar to those produced by Ostojić and Karadžić were released by the highest-ranking official of the Yugoslav mission to the United Nations, Dragomir Djokić. Serbian American propaganda organizations, with direct links to Belgrade, claimed to have sponsored the findings that were ultimately received by Djokić's office.[19] A letter sent by Djokić to the UN secretary-general on November 24, 1993, offered the text of "a memorandum on war crimes and crimes of genocide in eastern Bosnia (communes of Bratunac, Skelani and Srebrenica) committed against the Serbian population from April 1992 to April 1993." The reports repeated the accusations of "ethnic cleansing" previously made in Karadžić's list:

> The aim of the terror the Serbs are now exposed to is the same as during the previous wars. It is to expel now and for all the Serbs from these regions. That is why every attack on Serbian villages leaves in its wake only desolation, burned buildings, looted and destroyed property, destroyed monuments, cemeteries and churches.

The letterhead indicated that the State Commission for War Crimes had produced the report, but other sources would try to persuade the Serbian faithful that the information was collected independently. According to the British journalist and Serb publicist Nora Beloff,[20] a certain Milivoje Ivanišević was responsible for preparing the documentation. Her attempts to convince the readers of the Serbian Unity Congress's *Unity Herald* were hardly persuasive. The sources that Beloff claimed were central to Ivanišević's investigation immediately challenged the veracity of his dossier. Beloff even acknowledged that among Ivanišević's primary sources were the Serbian militia, police, and local authorities—the apparatus of the Serbian state.[21]

Official propaganda on war crimes continued to be produced in a number of disguises. The Serbian Council Information Center (SCIC), which described itself as a "non-governmental and non-political association of independent experts, writers and other intellectuals from Belgrade," offered another vehicle for Milošević's propagandists. Reports issued from this research body circulated on electronic newsgroups that linked Serb-nationalist communities in the diaspora. A dossier published by the supposedly independent information agency reviewed alleged abuses that had occurred prior to April 1993. Ostojić's hand could again be found in these infected sources of documentation. This was evident in the findings presented by the SCIC "regarding the violation of human rights, ethnic cleansing, crimes and violence by Croatian and Moslem armed formations against the Serbian civilian population in Bosnia-Herzegovina."[22] Common motifs resurfaced, as Ostojić's story of the railway children of Bradina was repackaged, this time with a Koranic emphasis. One testimonial from an alleged detainee recorded the entry of Islamic texts into the story.

During my stay in the camp I watched the Serbs who were tortured by the Muslims. I watched the "No 9" tunnel at Bradina, I watched the Muslims take the Serbs out, line them against the wall where they had to stand for hours with their hands up, they sat for hours in cold rain, soaking wet, and they were forced to sing and learn the Koran. Those who didn't know the Koran were beaten.[23]

In spite of the odd editorial change as different institutions and agencies selectively transmitted official lies, the Serbian revisionist program was essentially circular. The same source material appeared again and again in both the Serbian and the Serbian American press.

While Serbian political leaders attracted little sympathy from the international community in 1992, their propaganda had other uses back home. Government-sponsored disinformation proved to be an effective means of mobilizing the Serbian public behind an exclusive nationalist ideology. For Milošević and Karadžić, the Serbian populations under their control became an essential tool in the continuation and conduct of their war aims.[24] Having planted the idea that comparable tragedies had befallen the Serbian people in the former Yugoslavia, leaders in Pale and Belgrade were able to undermine any serious resistance to their political goals: the creation of a Greater Serbia at the expense of the local population of Bosnia-Herzegovina. Nevertheless, securing their ethnically pure lands required constant legitimation and inventive propaganda.

As the level of violence escalated and as hundreds of journalists arrived in Sarajevo, the revisionist campaign took a new turn. Serbian leaders in Belgrade and Pale could no longer concentrate on creating the illusion that Serbs were simply the victims of the genocidal crimes that they had been accused of by the international press. There was still no acceptable explanation for the savagery carried out against the Bosnian people, who were now the subject of international attention. Serbian political leaders therefore introduced a new component into their disinformation campaign. In order to rationalize their denials of complicity in crimes committed against Bosnian civilians, Serbian leaders created an unlikely scapegoat, the Sarajevo government and its embryonic army. News agencies under the control of Milošević and Karadžić charged the Bosnians with self-inflicted massacres on the pretext that the Bosnian government needed to attract sympathy from the international community. Serbian allegations of choreographed and "self-inflicted" attacks required a certain fidelity among official propagandists, as one source of disinformation fed off the other. The most popular Serbian daily, *Politika,* repeated claims made by Karadžić's news agency, SRNA, and accused Bosnian forces of stage-managing the massacre of May 27, 1992, when seventeen people were killed.[25] This incident, later to be known as the Bread Line Massacre, set the tone for Serbia's domestic and international propaganda program based on denial and cynical conspiracy theories that served to redistribute blame.[26]

Yet what stands out from the history of the genocide in Bosnia is not that Serbian leaders were able to mobilize local populations in pursuit of ethnic purity, but that they were also able to export their political objectives so effectively to the Serbian diaspora in the Western world. The crude tactics of revisionism and outright denial used by ultranationalists in the former Yugoslavia found an accommodating niche of willing sponsors in the United States and Canada. What was most astonishing was the absence of dissent from members of the Serbian American community. Those who openly recognized Serbia's genocidal policies remained faceless individuals and their voices were inaudible. Although many of its members were educated in Western democracies, one could reasonably say that the Serbian American community championed the claims of authoritarian politicians and advocated the official line from Serbian political leaders. However independent they pretended to be, their ideological manifestos were virtually indistinguishable from those drafted in Belgrade and Pale. Serbian American groups adopted the same policies: an end to sanctions against Serbia-Montenegro, full recognition of the "Bosnian Serb Republic," and "fair" treatment for all the parties concerned. Above all, these Serbian American organizations insisted that, in the name of "evenhandedness," the arms embargo against the Sarajevo government should remain in place. As a result of the Serbian diaspora's sponsorship of Karadžić's policies, the Serbian disinformation campaign was brought to a new political arena where causal uncertainty and moral relativism would eventually take root. As the Serbian American community transmitted official propaganda issued from Belgrade and Pale, it soon became the executor of Serbia's war lobby overseas.

The Genesis of a Lobby

Prior to the war in the former Yugoslavia, the Serbian American community had little tradition of political organization. Scores of community groups like the Serbian Benevolent Society, the Serb National Federation, and the Serbian Singing Federation had established chapters in industrial centers such as Pittsburgh, Chicago, Cleveland, Los Angeles, and the San Francisco Bay area, but their focus was predominantly religious or cultural. Within this community, there was no record of elaborate political organization. It was only in 1990 that returns from the Federal Election Commission began to record specific Serbian political action committees (PACs) that were set up to lobby on behalf of Serbian interests.[27] As former congresswoman and Serbian American leader Helen Delich Bentley noted, the creation of a Serbian lobby in the United States was by all accounts a new phenomenon: "This is something which has never been done before, and let me assure you we are making a difference. We are building a Serbian-American grassroots political lobby and network in this country from the ground up."[28] Five years later, Bentley was to be proved correct. Today, the Serbian lobby consists of hundreds of groups and individuals united behind a set of shared values and political goals. The belief system of this lobby is best characterized by its members' unequivocal support for the concept of ethnic purity, defended as the exclusive right to territorial unification and self-determination for the Serbian people. Two other points are central to the lobby's doctrinal foundation. These are self-identification as a persecuted group—the belief that Serbs are the principal victims in the former Yugoslavia—and a denial that genocide has been committed against the people of Bosnia-Herzegovina.

The ultranationalist and xenophobic sentiments of Serbian leaders in Pale and Belgrade were exported to the United States through two principal carriers. The first was politicians and emissaries who traveled between North America and the former Yugoslavia. The second was the Serbian Orthodox Church. In effect, the Serbian diaspora was mobilized through similar community and institutional structures that had so successfully marshaled the Serbian public behind the nationalist agenda in Milošević's Yugoslavia. Indeed, the red-brown-black order that Norman Cigar describes[29] could also find its expression among the Serbian community overseas.[30]

In the United States, it was the then Congresswoman Helen Delich Bentley who took charge of broadcasting Milošević's political agenda to Serbian émigré groups. In 1989, Bentley traveled to Yugoslavia and was present at a crucial juncture in the history of the Balkans. Bentley had been invited to commemorate the six hundredth anniversary of the defeat of Serbian forces at the hands of the Turkish armies in 1389 and joined Milošević at a nationalist rally on the sacred battlefield in Gazimestan,

Kosovo. Having celebrated the fervent nationalist spirit that gripped the hundreds of thousands of faithful as Milošević held out the promise of Serbian grandeur, Bentley returned to the United States as his main crusader. From her congressional office in Washington, D.C.—and at the taxpayers' expense—she approached Serbian Americans directly and tried to forge a community lobbying effort.[31] Letters and invitations sent out recorded her allegiance to Milošević's Serbia and the repressive policies it stood for. Her support for Milošević's brutal program of underdevelopment and impoverishment for the indigenous Albanian population in Kosovo was evidenced by her campaigning efforts back home.

Bentley's first action was recorded in a controversial appeal released on personal letterhead. On August 4, 1990, Bentley approached the Serbian American community and asked members to pressure their elected representatives in opposition to a House resolution that she described as HR 352, the "Broomfield bill on Kosovo and Yugoslavia."[32] She also urged members to resist the active petitioning of Congressmen Tom Lantos and Benjamin Gilman to suspend Yugoslavia's most-favored-nation status. In response to these challenges, Bentley provided the Serbian American community with a comprehensive lobbying guide:

> For your information, most members of Congress will be in their home districts for the entire month of August. So first, right away, send a letter to their Washington Office so that it will be on their desk when they return to Washington. Second, during August, organize large delegations of Serbian Americans from your churches and groups, and make appointments to see your Senators and Congressmen during the month of August while they are in their home states.

Together with this letter, Bentley included a position paper on why the "Broomfield bill" was to be opposed, as well as lists of congressional representatives. She had well-rehearsed justifications for rejecting criticism of Serbian actions, as well as ideological arguments to counter the demand for local autonomy for the Albanian population. Two days earlier, in a sixty-minute speech before the House, Bentley tried to make the case that Serbs had been long-standing victims in Tito's Yugoslavia. The 1974 Federal Constitution of Yugoslavia had been imposed on Serbs by a ruthless communist dictator who wanted to "split the vast majority of the Serbian people from Kosovo, their ancestral homeland, for hundreds of years." In light of the unjust introduction of the constitution, the powers of autonomy it granted to the local Albanian population of Kosovo should be reevaluated, Bentley argued.

The manner in which she reviewed the situation was open to question. In spite of the establishment of a de facto police state in Kosovo by the Serbian parliament on June 29, 1990, Bentley justified these policies by blaming the victims. Recorded incidents of arbitrary arrest, detention, and dismissal of thousands of local Albanians as well as the creation of segregationist policies were brought on by local community leaders in Pristina, Bentley insisted. The indigenous Albanian population of Kosovo was condemned as "criminal" and its parliament, secessionist. Kosovo itself was also declared a bastion of Islamic activity.[33] Following these accusations, and in an effort to minimize the significance of Belgrade's repressive policies, Bentley then asserted that Serbs were worse off than the Albanians of Kosovo: "I can say with no hesitation that the Albanians of Kosovo have more freedom and autonomy than Serbs and Jews living in the so-called liberal northern Yugoslav republics of Croatia and Slovenia."[34] What Bentley was doing was no different from the standard relativist tactic used by authorities under the command of Milošević and later Karadžić: she was redistributing blame so as to distract attention from genuine human rights abuses committed by Milošević's brutal regime.

Bentley's own battles continued well after this particular episode. Until her departure from the House of Representatives in 1994, she repeatedly fought against the imposition of sanctions on Serbia-Montenegro and the creation of resolute policies aimed to ensure the delivery of humanitarian aid to those most in need in Bosnia. Almost exactly two years after her first real fight in the Congress, Bentley could be found receiving Serbian representatives[35] and offering official apologies for the ineffective distribution of humanitarian aid to the besieged people of Bosnia-Herzegovina.[36] Resisting calls by Senator DeConcini and Representative Hoyer for the United Nations to use force to ensure the delivery of aid, Bentley cited UN General Lewis MacKenzie,[37] and insisted that any attempt to strengthen the ineffective aid effort with military force would lead to a major escalation of the "ancient blood feud" and to the loss of American lives. She therefore advocated that the U.S. policy should be to secure a negotiated settlement based on "fair treatment" of the "three sides." In effect, Bentley was simply trying to protect Serbian war gains with the same language of self-victimization used by her ideological mentors in Belgrade.

In an attempt to promote "fairness," Bentley had founded a major propaganda campaign of her own. While she complained to the Congress that "the United States has been inundated with a professionally run public relations campaign on behalf of Croatia which makes the treatment and fairness of information of the Balkans highly suspect,"[38] few Balkan advocacy efforts could match those sponsored by the congresswoman. Her aim was to diminish Belgrade's responsibility for starting the war by shifting the blame—first on the Albanians of Kosovo, then on the Croatians, then on the Bosnians.

In October 1991, Bentley invited prominent Serbian Americans to join her in Chicago, where she tried to unite the Serbian community under a single banner. On that occasion she claimed that "the idea grew of forming an umbrella organization of members representing all existing Serbian American groups which would articulate the Serbian position and speak with one voice on behalf of all Serbs."[39] In spite of the noticeable opposition against the Milošević government in 1991, there was only one Serbian position for Bentley, the one defined by the Serbian president. By exploiting common fears and nationalist stereotypes, Bentley was largely successful in creating a base of support for Milošević.[40] Persistence and ideological commitment seemed to pay off. By 1992, Bentley had made scores of visits to the Serb diaspora communities in the United States[41] and was recognized as their protector. SerbNet, the propaganda organization that had been set up by Bentley at the end of 1991, was positively identifiable with its founder.

SerbNet's strength lay in its preparation of promotional materials and later, in its patronage of Serb-biased personalities. In an article in the Belgrade tabloid *Intervju,* "The Unifiers of the Serbian Diaspora," SerbNet was credited with having secured financial support from the Serbian Orthodox Church to lead a delegation including four congressmen and senators to "the Fatherland."[42] However, in its first few years, much of SerbNet's resources were devoted to its domestic audience.

In 1993, SerbNet concentrated on preparing a video to be distributed through the Serbian American community to influential politicians, journalists, and other ethnic groups. The title of the twenty-six-minute video, "Truth Is the Victim in Bosnia," immediately set the tone for a revisionist intrigue. It was narrated by a woman with a BBC accent; the Serb propagandists tried to copy serious documentary format. Official myths were fused with partial citations from the former British ambassador to the United Nations, Sir David Hannay, which were added to excerpted statements from respectable authorities. Jeri Laber, director of Human Rights Watch, was just one of the experts quoted out of context. Yet if the filmmakers had been involved in manipulative editing practices, they were also able to purchase actors and extras. Guest appearances were also arranged with the former UN general Lewis MacKenzie. Three interviews with MacKenzie were followed by extracts from an academically obscure journal, *Strategic Policy,* which were used to reinforce the myth of equal guilt.[43] Arguing that the media were biased and favored the Croatians, the video repeated the SRNA-inspired myth that the Bread Line Massacre in Sarajevo was staged by the Bosnians to gain sympathy from the West. The producers let MacKenzie do the talking.

The incestuous manner in which this video was produced was truly staggering. MacKenzie had been sponsored by SerbNet to give a dozen speeches in the United States. Since he was one of the first to publicize Karadžić's claim that Bosnians had bombed themselves, his own objectivity was cast in doubt as he seemed to take on the role of Serbian publicist. MacKenzie's appearance at U.S. congressional hearings was later questioned by journalists who sought an explanation for his visits and new role.[44] When asked about his appearance in the SerbNet video, he later claimed that he had simply been filmed by accident at a rally to commemorate the UN peacekeeping monument in Ottawa. He failed to mention that his speaking engagements had been organized by SerbNet, and he denied any formal relationship with the organization.[45] MacKenzie even argued that it was not until afterwards that he learned where the money for his speaking tour was coming from. However, MacKenzie's subsequent declarations were to reveal the extent to which the Serbian propaganda front organized by Helen Delich Bentley had opened up access to Congress. Inadvertently, MacKenzie later admitted that the testimonies he gave before the U.S. Congress were organized and suggested that SerbNet was behind his lobbying efforts. Writing in the *Calgary Sun* two months later, MacKenzie insisted that both of his appearances in Washington were "arranged by an elected member of the U.S. Congress through a U.S. speaking agent and my own Toronto based agent. There was absolutely no indication of SerbNet sponsorship until after the events were history."[46] In spite of MacKenzie's denials,[47] SerbNet did not conceal its sponsorship. In its newsletter that very same month, the MacKenzie speaker tour was well documented. There was little doubt which elected member of Congress had arranged his speaker tour. Certainly, Helen Delich Bentley knew how MacKenzie was brought to Washington. The then honorary president of SerbNet could not plead ignorance.

As SerbNet sought to communicate official propaganda from Belgrade and Pale, Bentley tried to attract funds and patrons for her project.[48] The congresswoman's efforts were acknowledged in the Serbian press and by the Milošević government, which described her as a "fighter for Serbian rights in the USA." Yet, if she was a fighter for Serbian rights, she was above all a fighter for Milošević and the policies of a Greater Serbia.[49]

Helen Delich Bentley's success at introducing Milošević's goals of ethnic purity to the heart of the Serbian American community through SerbNet and her own congressional campaigns could not have been sustained without the assistance of preexisting Serbian institutions. In addition to well-established newspapers like the Pittsburgh-based *American Srbobran*,[50] which published advertisements for SerbNet, the Serbian Orthodox Church was of paramount importance to the realization of Bentley's vision—a Serbian American lobby. SerbNet's work was reportedly blessed by clerical leaders[51] while Serbian churches throughout the United States and Canada served as meeting points for foreign representatives, political figures, and the diaspora community as a whole. Not only the standard ideas of Serbian grandeur and victimization but also considerable sums of money were exchanged during these gatherings. Much of this was used to support declared humanitarian aid efforts through bodies like the International Organization of Christian Charities.[52] However, there was a significant element that could not be classified as "humanitarian." SerbNet frequently held propaganda functions in local Serbian churches where political statements from Patriarch Pavle in Belgrade were distributed. Official documents from the U.S. Department of Justice also recorded instances in which clerical leaders lent their charitable offices to organize political protests[53] and fund-raisers aimed at financing Serbian emissaries. Zoran Djordjevic, who was registered with the Foreign Agents Unit as a representative for the "Government of Serbian Krajina," recorded that he gave eight lectures to the Serbian American community in Serbian churches in Chicago, Cleveland, and Milwaukee and in the California cities of Saratoga, Acadia, and San Marcos. During these visits, Djordjevic admitted to raising $15,645, which was used to finance his public relations campaign. Four churches in particular seemed unconcerned that their political sponsorship was being reported to the Justice Department and instead facilitated the disinformation effort.[54] The Orthodox Church and the Serbian polity, both in the former Yugoslavia and in the diaspora, were firmly united.[55] In some cases, religious leaders even joined their congregations and contributed directly to the accounts of foreign agents working on behalf of renegade regimes.[56]

While the Serbian Orthodox Church served to assemble the local community, a handful of Serbian American political leaders emerged from newly created citizens' organizations. In 1990, two propaganda agencies, SerbNet and the Serbian American Voters Alliance PAC, were created. A year later, the Serbian Unity Congress (SUC) was formed. While the Serbian American Voters Alliance issued satirical cartoons and offensive press releases, SerbNet and the SUC appeared remarkably professional. They produced and distributed videos, organized lectures, and promoted Serbophilic journalists. These two groups signaled a shift away from the haphazard protests during the first few months of the war in Croatia. Rather, these new organizations were modeled on American civic associations and gave the semblance of having a democratic structure, a clear mission, and professional leadership.[57]

The presence of member organizations such as the Serbian Unity Congress at first disguised the birth of a Serb-nationalist lobby on American soil. It was simply a matter of spin. Instead of introducing themselves as the crusaders for an ethnically pure Serbian state carved out of a destroyed Bosnia-Herzegovina, Serbian American groups argued that their demands for fairness and equality should be heard as a matter of principle. By framing its arguments as a matter of "opinion," to be tolerated according to its basic civil "rights," the Serbian American community skirted around any injurious decision that might exclude its voice. This tactic opened the debate up to deceptively rational notions, like "Serbs have the same right to self-determination as any other people." The argument was a simplistic one that ignored the manner in which self-determination was to be achieved. However simplistic, the Serbian proponents' line of reasoning was barely challenged and, often in the name of multiculturalism and fairness, it was agreed that Serbian "rights" should also be respected.

Where Milošević, Karadžić, and Helen Delich Bentley had succeeded was in convincing the Serbian and Serbian American public that they were part of a great nation. Serbian American supporters sincerely believed in the morality of their claims to create an ethnically homogeneous state inside Bosnia. Nationalist pride overcame any real inquiry into the genocidal policies through which this ethnically pure Serbian homeland would be achieved. In practice, affiliates of these Serbian American groups boldly defended their actions as expressions of their constitutional rights to association and free speech. Demonstrations held in front of UN offices, foreign embassies, and the press were considered legitimate acts of political participation.[58] Advertisements that defied the Clinton administration were placed in newspapers and were also justified on the basis of free speech.[59] To the discerning observer, however, it was clear that what these groups exhibited was a far cry from the American traditions of voluntarism and civic protest.

In the name of defending Serbs against defamation, these Serbian American groups promoted a well designed political campaign of appeasement that was coordinated with the Serbian leadership in the former Yugoslavia. In many respects, the Serbian American leaders duplicated the practices of historical revisionism and Holocaust denial designed by right-wing extremists. If they made their own arguments seem more respectable than those of Holocaust deniers, there was little virtue in the distinction. The Serbian American lobby was simply engaged in a more popular campaign of denial, but the rationale behind its program was strikingly similar: it too needed to justify a political agenda based on ethnic purity, territorial conquest, and genocide. Although Serbian American groups maintained the appearance of independent civic organizations, their resolutions advocated official policies from Belgrade and Pale, namely, the creation of ethnically pure states as well as the transfer of indigenous populations. The most deceptive of these organizations was the Serbian Unity Congress.

The Serbian Unity Congress and Karadžić's War Lobby

The Serbian Unity Congress is the most extensive Serb-nationalist organization in North America. Based in Napa, California, and Washington, DC, it was created as a membership organization devoted to political lobbying on behalf of the regimes in Belgrade and Pale. It represents the interests of Serbian political leaders by (1) financing an official representative for the Bosnian Serb regime in Washington, DC; (2) sponsoring a deliberate disinformation campaign that targets the U.S. Congress, media, university campuses, and research centers; (3) engaging public relations firms to lobby on behalf of the Serbian leadership in Pale and ensure representation during congressional committee hearings; (4) purchasing the support of speakers and journalists.

Formed in December 1990, the SUC was later incorporated in the state of Nebraska as a tax-exempt organization on February 14, 1991. Under Article 2, its declared mission was recorded: "The Corporation is a not-for-profit corporation organized and to be operated under the Nebraska Nonprofit Corporation Act exclusively for religious, scientific, literary and educational purposes within the meaning of section 501(c)(3) of the Internal revenue Code of 1986 (26 U.S.C.) as now enacted or as may be amended or succeeded by a new provision." Since its inception the Serbian Unity Congress has operated from northern California. Its provisional base in Berkeley was transferred to Napa in 1993. From there, the director of the central office, Jelena Kolarovich, managed the accounts and administered the day-to-day running of the organization, in concert with Mirjana Samardzija, the former executive director in San Francisco. The director of the Serbian American Affairs Office in Washington, DC, Danielle Sremac, is also a key figure in the SUC. These offices are small, one-person outfits, and the SUC therefore remains highly dependent on the activism of its reported six thousand members.

The creation of a tax-exempt and charitable organization of Serbian Americans was immediately questionable. While the directors of the Serbian Unity Congress tried to impress on the secretary of state for Nebraska that the SUC fell within the meaning of the Internal Revenue Code,[60] newsletters circulated by the organization revealed an active pan-Serbian political agenda. According to the introductory letter of its former president, Nick Petrovich, the goals of the Serbian Unity Congress could be easily summarized: "the SUC's short term goal as adopted is to contribute to the reconstruction of the territories on which the Serbian people find themselves." If the aim of unifying Serbs was understood in Petrovich's concern to help "reconstruct" Serb-held lands, the goal of ethnic purity based on the transfer of populations underlined the SUC's real agenda. Former SUC president Michael Djordjevich made this point clearly during an interview with the Serbian newspaper *Intervju*. Ignoring the contradictions the creation of an ethnically pure state poses to the establishment of a democratic order, Djordjevich told the Belgrade tabloid, "Our main efforts are directed toward ending the war in Bosnia and to have Serbia gather all the Serbs into a democratic, constitutional and traditional Serbian state."[61] To its members, the SUC's political program was clearly expressed in the resolutions recorded at annual conferences in 1991, 1992, 1993, and 1994. These resolutions urged

1. the U.S. Congress and the international community to lift the economic sanctions against Serbia and Montenegro;

2. the United States and the international community to recognize the rights of Serbian people in Serbian-occupied territories of Bosnia and Croatia to self-determination;

3. all authorized groups and responsible institutions to identify "illegal" immigrants from Albania who "migrated" to the territory of Kosovo from April 6, 1941, to the present and transfer them to the United Nations for resettlement.

It went without saying that the arms embargo against the Sarajevo government was to remain in place. Fairness and evenhandedness—Bentley's favorite terms—were two of the slogans used by the Serbian Unity Congress to appease the American conscience.

To its own members, the Serbian Unity Congress boasted of its unique status within the Serbian diaspora. Claiming to be the foremost Serbian organization, it reported that it combated misinformation by maintaining a full-time Washington, DC, office for public relations and provided grant support to "objective publications by internationally renowned non-Serb sources." With much bravado, the SUC advertised its declared accomplishments. The list sounded impressive:

- Our representatives testify in Congress.
- [The] media considers Serbian Unity Congress as #1 information source on Serbian point of view.
- Our Washington office representative achieved many media appearances.
- We sponsored a rape report with international recognition, used by War Crimes Commission, the Yugoslav Mission to the UN, authors, etc.
- We are a major source of research and financial support to authors, journalists and academics.
- We initiated an Alliance of Orthodox Peoples with plans for internationalization.
- We developed a media watch group (engaged in anti-defamation of Serbs) with a global network.
- We initiated efforts to get sanctions lifted.

While its achievements were largely exaggerated in its own publicity, there was some truth to its claims. The founder of the SUC did testify before Congress, but his was the only appearance made by a Serbian American leader. Money was paid to journalists, to promote the SUC's agenda, as was later revealed in the SUC's information returns filed with the Internal Revenue Service in 1994.[62] In 1993, a report that questioned the practice of mass rape against non-Serbian women was drafted and disseminated by the SUC's executive director, Mirjana Samardzija, through her front, the "North American News Analysis Network." Elements of this report, *Rapes in Yugoslavia: Separating Fact from Fiction*, would later be found in a notorious piece of revisionism entitled "Dateline Yugoslavia: The Partisan Press," published by Peter Brock in *Foreign Policy* in January 1994. With Samardzija's assistance, Brock was able to introduce official disinformation from Belgrade into one of the most respected journals on foreign affairs.[63] Above all, the SUC did create an active Serbian American lobby with both a grassroots and a congressional dimension. By 1994, the SUC had indeed started to penetrate the media and Congress, as it advertised. It did so by launching an energetic pressure campaign and by employing hired professionals to direct its public relations effort in cooperation with its Belgrade office.

Grassroots Lobbying

At the grassroots level, the Serbian Unity Congress organized a major letter-writing and protest campaign. Lists of elected representatives, media offices, and prewritten scripts were sent to members of the six-thousand-strong Serbian Unity Congress. Under the heading "Serbs, Write and Call!" the leadership of the SUC New York chapter prepared ready-made campaign materials that were published in the quarterly *Unity Herald*. Using the same scare tactics Helen Delich Bentley had initiated, the Serbian Unity Congress impressed on its members that they were engaged in a moral struggle for truth and justice in the United States where there was a "malevolent, aggressive and persistent propaganda campaign against the Serbian people."[64] The Serbian American community just needed to be better organized and funded if it was to have a chance, they argued, following the medieval slogan, "Only unity can save the Serb." Self-victimization was essential to the SUC's motivation tactics. Like Milošević's new "Yugoslavia," which had been unfairly denied membership to the United Nations, Serbs in the diaspora were no different from their brethren overseas, and they argued that the American government and media were perpetuating their suffering.

In order to convince its membership, the Serbian Unity Congress repeated the charge that its opponents had hired the services of public relations firms and had considerable financial backing. The message from the Serbian American leadership was that Serbs were the underdog. In the course of this propaganda effort, the public relations firm of Ruder-Finn and, in particular, its vice president James Harff were defamed, as perjured interviews were circulated to substantiate revisionist claims.[65] At one point, Serbian American leaders maintained that the Croatian community had launched a major lobbying effort and was seeking a $550 million financial aid package for Croatia. This was a frequent rallying cry that served an additional goal: to the non-Serbian community, talk of public relations firms and foreign sponsorship helped foster the myth that press reporting reflected an anti-Serbian bias. By presenting the conflict as a struggle over truth, the Serbian propaganda campaign sought to create an epistemological debate that would be used to confuse the American public over the nature of the war and undermine meaningful criticism of Serb-directed atrocities in the former Yugoslavia.

The first published script for calling the "President and other politicians" appeared in the *Unity Herald* in November 1992. In disgust at perceived anti-Serbian policies, the Serbian Unity Congress directed its members to repeat five main points: (1) the sanctions against the Serbian people were to be lifted; (2) the United States was to refrain from military intervention in the Balkans; (3) Yugoslavia's membership in the United Nations was to be reinstated; (4) the arms embargo was to be reinforced equally on the "Croatian and Muslim" sides; (5) pressure was to be applied to the Croats and Muslims to negotiate a peaceful territorial settlement and redraw the communist-drawn borders of the former Yugoslavia. The November 1992 script then concluded with a request to meet representatives of the Serbian Unity Congress.

Subsequent campaigning materials distributed to the SUC membership repeated the abovementioned policies and the themes of "evenhandedness" and "nonintervention." In November 1992, a letter inviting change in U.S. policy in the former Yugoslavia addressed to President-Elect Clinton was circulated among the delegates at the SUC's annual conference in San Diego.[66] The following year, when it appeared that the Clinton administration might issue air strikes against Serbian forces, the SUC sent letters and information packs to the president, U.S. senators, congressional representatives, the State Department, Jewish organizations, and the American media.[67] However, the SUC's pressure tactics and use of emotional blackmail did not originate only from Serbian Americans. An SUC newsletter of December 26, 1993, advertised the SUC-cosponsored campaign to direct children in Belgrade to write letters protesting against "the unjust sanctions imposed on innocent civilians."

By 1995, the SUC's letter-writing campaign reflected a genuine sense of panic. Letters faxed from the SUC central office suggested that the Serbian lobby effort was often reactive, however systematic. In anticipation of a proposed cease-fire, which would freeze Serbian gains in Bosnia, Michael Djordjevich sent an urgent letter appealing to SUC members, friends, and family members to write and visit their representatives in support of Jimmy Carter's initiative.[68] The same day, Djordjevich wrote to Senator Phil Gramm advocating an amendment to the "Contact Group" proposal. The SUC's demands for appeasement were actively circulated in the form of model letters throughout January 1995. Members of the lobby were simply told what to write and say. The newly elected SUC President, John Delich, drafted three model letters on January 10, following Djordjevich's example. He first approached chapter presidents, urging them to write to certain congressmen, asking them to "use their efforts and influence to help end the carnage in Bosnia now."[69] Attached to this were two additions letters, one to Senator Jesse Helms, the other to Representative Charles Wilson. This grassroots campaign was later to be supplemented by a three-day lobbying effort on Capitol Hill.

The SUC's internal publications publicized scores of its own protests. The *Unity Herald* recorded multiple examples of demonstrations across the United States from 1991 onward. According to this source, demonstrations were held in front of the German consulate in San Francisco (January 11, 1992) and in Chicago, where the SUC later boasted of ten thousand participants at its Serbian parade (June 20, 1992). The *Unity Herald* also mentioned a gathering of five thousand Serbian Americans in front of the UN headquarters in New York, where SUC members demanded "the right to self-determination for all Serbs in all Serbian lands, and the lifting of sanctions against the Serbian people." On the West Coast, Serbian activists were again mobilized to protest in front of the *San Diego Union Tribune* offices for a second time (August 29, 1992). Two months later, SUC members returned to stand outside the UN headquarters in New York, where they complained against "threats of the United States military intervention against Serbs in Bosnia and Herzegovina."

In spite of its charges that an anti-Serbian bias in the media prevented the Serbian community from being heard, the SUC's pressure tactics were well documented by the press. In November 1991, *USA Today* (November 5) and the *Chicago Tribune* (November 4) announced the creation of the Serbian Unity Congress and publicized its goal of securing "balanced coverage" of the conflicts in the former Yugoslavia. Michael Djordjevich, founder and first president of the Serbian Unity Congress, saw three letters published in the *San Francisco Chronicle* and *Washington Post* in 1991 and 1992.[70] Djordjevich's associate in Calgary, Nesa Ilić, was even more successful in promoting their cause. Between June 1992 and mid-January 1993, the *Calgary Herald* recognized the activities of the Serbian Unity Congress in an article and included three letters signed on behalf of SUC representatives and local chapters.[71] Ilić even thanked the newspaper for its "fair" coverage. "It sure is nice to see the words of Bosnian Serbs for a change and read what they have to say," he wrote on December 10, 1992.

Protests staged by the SUC were also reported. The *Los Angeles Times* journalist Irene Chang quoted the head of the SUC chapter in Los Angeles, and noted that activists were "writing letters and making telephone calls to their elected officials and the media to increase their profile."[72] The *San Diego Union Tribune* covered a demonstration organized against its editorial management in August 1992. Rex Dalton, writing for the *San Diego Union Tribune,* quoted one of the SUC's directors, Zika Djokovich, and commented on a similar SUC demonstration in Los Angeles the week before. In the fall of 1992, the SUC held a rally in Phoenix, Arizona, where Channel 10 TV was condemned as biased. A few months later, the Serbian Unity Congress achieved a public relations hat trick. In February 1993, the Associated Press (February 23), the *Los Angeles Times* (February 20), and the *Atlanta Journal and Constitution* (February 9) remarked on the SUC's grassroots lobbying effort and claims of media bias and exaggeration. Allegations that the "Muslims" were stage-managing atrocities in order to attract sympathy again resurfaced in some of these articles. Uncritical reporting of the SUC's true intentions was to continue. On March 5, 1995, Almar Latour, writing in the *Washington Times,* commented on the Serbian American lobbying effort and presented the SUC's case for an ethnically pure state as if it were a legitimate one. In the course of his reporting, Latour repeated Karadžić's declared "willingness" to trade land for peace, although there was never any suggestion that the Bosnian Serb leader would give up his claim to the territories around Sarajevo.

The group has lobbied for the Bosnian Serbs since the start of the conflict in 1990, and claims the Serbian viewpoint has been ignored by Western governments and the media. The Serbian Congress argues the contact group plan truncates the Bosnian Serb part of the former Yugoslavia into three areas that would make it more difficult for Serbs of each region to move freely, without having to cross a Muslim area. Radovan Karadžić, leader of the Bosnian Serbs, has suggested trading several traditionally Muslim areas separating the Serbian zones for Serbian areas surrounding Sarajevo.[73]

In spite of the SUC's claims of Serbian victimization and hostile press reporting, there was indeed a Serbian voice in the United States, a voice that was amplified through public relations firms and paid propagandists.

The Serbian Public Relations Drive: Entry to Congress

From 1992, four main public relations firms were sponsored by the Serbian American community to further Serbian interests. David Keene and Associates and McDermott O'Neill were engaged through SerbNet, while the SUC employed the Washington-based Manatos and Manatos. Another firm, Craig Shirley and Associates, was also hired to support the Serbian campaign.[74]

The SUC's establishment of a public relations team with Manatos and Manatos was central to the Serbian American outreach effort. The Serbian Unity Congress had had a difficult time attracting interested firms, in spite of the $400,000 account that was advertised in the *Legal Times*.[75] Only the Hellenic American firm of Manatos and Manatos accepted the SUC's offer; it was hired on September 15, 1992.

Manatos and Manatos was recruited to foster better relations between the Greek and Serbian public, and, above all, to secure political support from the established Hellenic American community. The firm was especially well placed to organize this public relations exercise since it already represented a number of Hellenic institutions as well as the city of San Francisco, near the SUC's headquarters. Andrew Manatos's clients included the embassy of Greece, the United Hellenic American Congress, and the Pan-Cyprian Association of America. By 1994, the Serbian Unity Congress seemed to have succeeded in drawing in the leaders of the Hellenic American community and forging a joint political lobby.

In 1993 and 1994, a concerted lobbying effort to further the SUC's interests was largely financed by Greek American money. Although these monetary contributions did not stand out immediately from the Federal

Election Commission reports, there was considerable evidence of a campaign led by Andrew Manatos to support a select number of members of Congress who might have pro-Serbian sympathies. According to Morton Kondracke, current editor in chief of *Roll Call,* by the late 1980s Manatos had developed an extremely successful fund raising and lobbying effort with a small group of wealthy Greek American businessmen. In a 1988 article for the *New Republic,* Kondracke noted that the network set up between Manatos and Senator Paul Sarbanes had been exploited for raising vast sums of money from small numbers of sponsors to support Dukakis's presidential ambitions.[76] Kondracke described how Manatos's network had also managed to attract potential non-Greek American contributors to the Greek lobby.

Kondracke alluded to Manatos's employment of "bundling" practices—the grouping of individual contributions made simultaneously to elected representatives, as if they had been made by a political action committee—which was the standard technique used to direct the Serbian American lobbying campaign. Prior to the engagement of Manatos and Manatos, the Serbian Unity Congress had led a haphazard effort to influence congressional representatives through its own political action committee. Contributions were made to elected officials as indicated in table 1.

Apart from the donations to Helen Delich Bentley, there was little

TABLE 1.
Campaign Contributions by Serbian Unity Congress PAC

Date	Amount	Recipient
September 7, 1991	$ 700	Dan Burton for Congress
December 3, 1991	$1,000	Helen Delich Bentley for Congress
December 6, 1991	$3,000	Dan Burton for Congress
July 16, 1992	$1,000	Randy Cunningham for Congress
June 21, 1992	$1,000	Bill Baker for Congress
July 8, 1992	$1,000	Nancy Pelosi for Congress
July 20, 1992	$1,000	Doug Weed for Congress
September 3, 1992	$3,000	Dan Burton for Congress
October 27, 1992	$1,000	Joe Knollenberg for Congress
October 27, 1992	$1,000	Sam Gejedenson for Congress
October 31, 1992	$ 500	Anna Eshoo for Congress[77]
March 9, 1993	$1,500	Dan Burton for Congress
May 17, 1993	$1,000	Kay Bailey Hutchinson for Senate[78]
July 12, 1994	$ 500	Ronna Romney for Congress
July 25, 1994	$ 500	Joe Knollenberg for Congress
July 25, 1994	$ 500	Dick Chrysler for Congress

SOURCE: Federal Election Commission

indication that the Serbian Unity Congress PAC had developed a coherent strategy for targeting members of Congress by offering monetary contributions. Congressional candidates Kay Bailey Hutchinson and Sam Gejedenson returned their contributions almost immediately.[79] Others, such as Representative Anna Eshoo, claimed that they were unaware that they had even been the beneficiaries of SUC contributions and denied having had any contact with Serbian American groups.[80] The FEC returns also threw light on the disorganized accounting and reporting practices of the SUC. On several occasions, the Federal Election Commission staff wrote to the Serbian Unity Congress asking for reports to be submitted, reminding the organization of past deadlines. In addition, the FEC pointed out that the accounts reported by the SUC did not correspond with declared donations and receipts, raising questions about the SUC's internal administration and use of funds.

The hiring of Manatos and Manatos signaled a complete change from the amateur lobbying practices associated with the Serbian Unity Congress PAC. Manatos's approach was not only more subtle and calculated than the SUC's own homemade initiative, but was based on tested practices taken from the Greek American experience.

From 1993 onward, Manatos led a focused campaign that aimed to open congressional doors to the Serbian American community. This was done in two ways. First, his clients, prominent figures and sponsors of the SUC together with leaders of the Hellenic American community, were to be found making simultaneous group contributions to select members of Congress. Second, the practice of "bundling" was central to the joint lobbying effort.[81] Those participating included Michael Djordjevich, former president of the SUC; George Bogdanich, director of SerbNet; and both the director and chairman of the Serbian American Media Center, Peter Samardzija and Nicholas Trkla, respectively. Milan Panić, the former political challenger to Milošević was also among the Serbian contributors who made repeated donations. The aim of this campaign was twofold: first, to lend support to potentially sympathetic representatives by bolstering their campaign funds; second, to create an image of a powerful lobby. While the Serbian contributions on their own do not amount to large sums of money, combined with Greek American sponsorship, the Serbian lobby appeared to carry greater influence. The impression given was that of a community of individuals who could unite quickly to raise large sums of money when necessary. The most popular recipient of Serbian American and Greek American contributions was the former chairman of the House Foreign Affairs Committee, Representative Lee Hamilton. In addition, Manatos led a personal lobbying effort to introduce Serbian Americans to members of Congress, State Department officials, and presidential advisors.

Lee Hamilton: Balkan Profiteer

In twenty months, Congressman Lee Hamilton accumulated significant campaign contributions from Balkan lobbyists and political leaders associated with Manatos and Manatos. The 1993, 1994, and 1995 reports from the Federal Election Commission record that Hamilton received $47,141 in itemized contributions from leaders of the Serbian American and Greek American communities. A number of those donating to Hamilton's campaign account could be easily identified with Andrew Manatos—in fact, many of the contributors were Manatos's clients and ethnic leaders who had specific political agendas to promote.

The amount of money credited to Hamilton's account in this manner is significant. Commenting on the 1992 election, Larry Makinson and Joshua Goldstein of the Center for Responsive Politics noted that the largest bundle of cash given to a House member was $61,300. The Serbian American and Greek American contributions made to Hamilton during the twenty-month period in question even challenged the thousands of dollars collected from Emily's List, the well-coordinated political action committee that had done so much to promote specific women candidates in the 1992 elections.[82]

The nature of Hamilton's involvement with the Serbian American and Greek American communities and their political lobbies raises a number of questions concerning the representative's ideological leanings. Hamilton's record on the Balkans is mixed. He has been particularly critical of Macedonia and has clearly demonstrated Hellenic-friendly tendencies. In spite of this bias, Hamilton has not always been such a vocal opponent of the "lift and strike" policy that was first advocated by his fellow Indiana Democrat, Representative Frank McCloskey. An article in the *National Journal* noted Hamilton's ambiguous position on the war in Bosnia from the fall of 1993 onward. Since 1994, however, Hamilton has consistently resisted lifting the arms embargo against the Sarajevo government and had lobbied his fellow members of Congress to vote down legislation initiated by his colleagues to end U.S. participation in the embargo.

The motivation behind Hamilton's opposition to the restoration of

Bosnia's right to self-defense requires careful examination. Even though there is evidence of close cooperation between the Serbian and Hellenic communities, there is more than one Balkan agenda at play here. Whether the congressman sincerely believed that maintaining the arms embargo was the preferable option or was in any way influenced by monetary contributions is not certain. What is beyond dispute, however, is Hamilton's recorded contact with leaders of the Serbian American and Greek American lobbies and his reliance on their campaign contributions.

Until 1991, the only noticeable special interest groups that had made sizable donations to Hamilton's campaign account were pro-Israel groups. The Center for Responsive Politics noted that in 1991, Hamilton received $21,800 from pro-Israel PACs.[83] According to the FEC reports, from 1992 onward, there was a steady decline in Hamilton's receipt of contributions from ideological groups. In effect, there was considerably less money reaching his account as fewer PACs supported the congressman in subsequent elections. As pro-Israeli groups reduced their sponsorship of Hamilton's biennial campaigns, the only special interest groups and individuals that stood out from Hamilton's FEC returns were Serbian American and Greek American patrons. In both cases, contributions sent by these Balkan communities exceeded those made by pro-Israeli groups.

On September 29, 1993, Hamilton received $24,000 from an assembly of over forty-five prominent Americans. The amount of money credited to Hamilton's campaign account on this one day was disproportionately important. This series of donations represented over 35 percent of contributions he received in the preceding six-month period from January to July 1993 and over 10 percent of his receipts for the whole fifteen-month FEC cycle.[84] Over 90 percent of these contributors resided in the Chicago area and fell almost exclusively into one of three ethnic groups: Serbian, Greek, or Jewish. Most of the contributors to Hamilton's account, like Lester Crown, a distinguished member of the Chicago community, occupied senior management positions. According to his own FEC returns, Hamilton's staff traveled to Chicago on September 23, 1993, just a few days before his account was credited. The question remains, what were they doing there and did they engage in a private fund-raiser for the congressman?

On April 25, 1994, Hamilton received a further $9,525 through multiple contributions from twenty-five members of the Greek and Serbian communities. This included $2,000 from two PACs, notably the pan-Hellenic Dynamis Federal. The majority of the contributors were from

TABLE 2.
Campaign Contributions to Lee Hamilton, September 29, 1993

Contributor	Amount
Robert Adler	$ 500
John Alexander	$ 250
Bob Asher	$1,000
Daniel Asher	$1,000
Helen Asher	$ 500
Nathan Asher	$1,000
Andrew Athens	$1,000
Paul Athens	$1,000
Michael Bakalis	$1,000
Gilbert Blechman	$ 500
George Bogdanich	$ 250
Thomas Cappas	$ 500
Lester Crown	$1,000
Ilija Djurisic	$ 250
Marko Duric	$ 500
Sidney Epstein	$ 500
Sid Feiger	$1,000
Richard Fleisher (Karlin and Fleisher)	$ 250
Martin Gecht	$ 400
Manny Giannakakos	$ 250
Julius Hemmelstein	$ 250
Andrew Hochberg	$ 250
Bernard Jaffee	$1,000
David Kahn	$ 250
Charles Kanakis	$ 250
Andrew Lappin	$ 250
Stuart Levine	$1,000
Lorry Lichtenstein	$1,000
Milos Ljuboja	$ 250
John Marks	$ 250
Robert Mazer	$1,000
Clara Moranis	$ 500
Arnold Newberger	$ 250
John Ostojić	$ 250
Kenneth Pontikes	$1,000
Milo Popovic	$1,000
Milan Rakic	$ 250
Sol Rosen	$ 300
Peter Samardzija	$ 500
Roger Schoenfeld	$ 250
Eli Sreckovic	$ 500
Thomas Stacy	$ 500
Chris Tomaras	$ 250
Nicholas Trkla	$ 250
Branko Tupanjac	$ 500
Irving Wein	$ 250
Richard Weinberg	$ 500

SOURCE: Federal Election Commission

216

Maryland and Virginia, and almost every contribution was of the order of $300. Contributors again included Michael Djordjevich of the SUC; his vice president, Ronald Radakovich, and both leaders of the Greek and Cypriot communities, Andrew Athens and Philip Christopher, respectively. What was interesting about this second series of contributions was that it coincided with Manatos's testimony before Congress on behalf of leaders of the Greek and Serbian communities. Those making payments to Hamilton's campaign account on April 25, 1994, were Manatos's clients whose interests he was representing in Congress that very same day. At that time, Manatos appealed to the Appropriations and Foreign Operations Committee not to renew U.S. aid to Turkey. He also called for a halt to U.S. recognition of the former Yugoslav Republic of Macedonia. Three weeks after this series of contributions, the former president of the Serbian Unity Congress, Michael Djordjevich, was invited to speak before a hearing of the House Committee on Foreign Affairs chaired by Hamilton. As the series of donations made on April 25, 1994, demonstrated, Hamilton's receipt of Serbian and Greek contributions was a strategic program coordinated by Andrew Manatos. Hamilton himself knew some of the contributors and was familiar with the agendas they were promoting. Evidence of Hamilton's relationship with the Serbian community could be found in an exchange of personal correspondence published in the *Unity Herald* in 1992 and 1993.[85] Although these letters signaled the first recorded contact between Hamilton and the Serb-nationalist lobby, Michael Djordjevich later boasted in the Serbian press that the Serbian Unity Congress had established good relations with a number of key politicians, including the chairman of the House Foreign Affairs Committee.[86]

Hamilton's acquaintance with his sponsors was further suggested by the repeated appearances made by Manatos's clients before Hamilton's committee. The leader of the Cypriot community, Philip Christopher, and the former SUC president Michael Djordjevich had both testified before Hamilton's committee. In the case of Djordjevich, it was shortly after payments had been made into Hamilton's campaign account. Manatos too, for that matter, contributed directly to Hamilton's account in June 1995, five months after he was seen leading a delegation of Serbian Americans to Capital Hill.

As Hamilton's returns from special interest groups and PACs declined, the amount of money originating from Serbian American and Greek

TABLE 3.

Campaign Contributions to Lee Hamilton, April 25, 1994

Contributor	State of Origin	Amount
Individuals		
Michael and Vasiliki Angelakis	MD	$ 300
Andrew Athens	IL	$ 300
Panayiotis Baltatzis	MD	$ 300
John Billinis	MD	$ 300
Demetri Boosalis	VA	$ 300
Philip and Christina Christopher	NY	$1,000
Michael Djordjevich	CA	$ 150
Michael Djordjevich	CA	$1,000
William Karas	MD	$ 300
George Kartsioukas	CA	$ 250
E. N. Koulizakis	VA	$ 300
Panos Koutrouvalis	VA	$ 300
Charis Lapas	VA	$ 300
Ana Maria Laveglia	MA	$ 300
Efstratios Likakis	MD	$ 300
Charlie Marangoudakis	NY	$ 300
Constantine Marinakos	VA	$ 300
Alekos Maroudas	DC	$ 300
Chris and Tula Mouroufas	CA	$ 250
Konstantinos & Susan Papadopoulos	MD	$ 300
Ronald Radakovich	CA	$ 225
Panagiotis Silis	VA	$ 300
George Siskos	CA	$ 250
Despina Skenderis	MD	$ 300
Paul Vangellow	VA	$ 300
PACS		
Allied		$1,000
Dynamis		$1,000

NOTE: These contributions were made to Lee Hamilton on the same day Andrew Manatos testified on behalf of United Hellenic American Congress before the House Appropriations and Foreign Operations Committee.

SOURCE: Federal Election Commission

American sponsors became increasingly significant. In the first six months of 1995, Balkan donations made up just under 40 percent of Hamilton's itemized contributions. Again, the names of the leaders of the Hellenic American community could be found next to those of Manatos and Milan Panić.

Hamilton's receipt of Serbian American and Hellenic American contributions stands out as a highly irregular practice. None of Hamilton's colleagues on the House Foreign Affairs Committee could claim a similar source of sponsorship. The pattern in which contributions were made to Hamilton's account suggests that the congressman has in fact profited

TABLE 4.
Balkan Campaign Contributions to Lee Hamilton,
January 1–June 30, 1995

Contributor	Amount
June 26, 1995	
Michael and Vasiliki Angelakis	$ 250
Andrew Athens	$ 500
John Charalambous	$1,000
Hunter Johnson (Jones and Walker)	$1,000
Stelios Kimilis	$ 250
Margery Kraus	$ 500
Charles Lapas	$ 250
Andrew Manatos	$ 250
Lloyd Meeds	$ 871 (in kind)
Constantine Papavizaz	$ 250
James and Wanda Pedas	$ 250
George Tsentas	$ 250
Total	$5,621
June 30, 1995	
Robert Keefe	$ 500
Gregory Keever	$ 250
Peter Krist	$1,000
Peter Krist	$1,000
Elias Kulukundis	$1,000
Yannis Kulukundis	$1,000
Roger Loomis	$ 250
Milan Panić	$1,000
William Tavoulareas	$1,000
William Tavoulareas	$1,000
Total	$8,000

SOURCE: Federal Election Commission

from the recent wars in the Balkans. While it would be wrong to conclude there was a definite cause and effect between the donations made to Hamilton and his voting record, it would be fair to underscore that his acceptance of this money raises a number of ethical questions. The systematic nature of Manatos's lobbying effort and the deposit of money into Hamilton's campaign account could be partially understood against the background of the war in the Balkans and the external situation that prompted a Serbian-Greek attempt to influence the congressman.

With Manatos's assistance, leaders of the Serbian American and Greek American communities joined to make sizable donations to Lee Hamilton at critical points in the conflict in the former Yugoslavia. The first series of contributions received by Hamilton followed an active publicity drive in July and August 1993, when SerbNet placed advertisements in the *New*

York Times and the *Washington Post*. They also coincided with an energetic campaign led by Bosnian president Alija Izetbegović, who aimed to rally support for the use of force against Serbian positions as well as the lifting of the arms embargo against his government. Izetbegović's efforts were being challenged by attempts made by the EU and UN mediators, Owen and Stoltenberg, to carry out a three-way partition of Bosnia. As Izetbegović traveled to Turkey (September 2–5), the United States (September 5–9), Saudi Arabia (September 12), Iran, and Kuwait (September 13) in the hope of securing political support and financial assistance, increasing pressure was applied to the Clinton administration. The Organization of the Islamic Conference met in Istanbul to discuss Bosnia; immediately after that, the UN Security Council met on September 7, 1993. During this time, the Bosnian president appealed directly to the Clinton administration. The response from the former U.S. defense secretary, Les Aspin, was the first suggestion that the United States might be prepared to send troops to enforce a peace agreement (September 12).

The second series of donations, made on April 25, 1994, to Hamilton's account also coincided with two foreign policy debates: one diplomatic, the other strategic. The principal issue, the establishment of full diplomatic relations with Macedonia and the release of funds to Turkey, led to a major contest between Andrew Manatos and the Clinton administration. *Washington Post* columnist Jim Hoagland noted that the "influential Greek-American political lobby has rolled President Clinton back from his declared intention to establish full diplomatic relations with Macedonia, despite urgent pleas to Clinton from Macedonia's president for visible support for his tottering government."[87] Arguing that the effort to postpone full diplomatic relations with Macedonia would undermine Clinton's decision to send three hundred American peacekeepers to the region, Hoagland reported on an influential meeting at the White House on March 9 led by Andrew Manatos, whom he quoted. "The policy he [Clinton] outlined there is very consistent with what Greece would like it to be," claimed Manatos. As Clinton appeased the Greek lobby, Manatos's clients credited Hamilton's campaign account with new Balkan dollars.

At the international level, it was not only the issue of Macedonia that was of interest to Greek Americans and Serbian Americans. In April 1994 considerable pressure was placed on the Clinton administration to launch air strikes against Serbian forces as they assaulted the UN "safe area" of Gorazde. There was genuine reason for Serbian anxiety. It was not until later on in the day contributions appeared in Hamilton's campaign account that the UN special envoy Yasushi Akashi ruled out the use of air strikes. The donations therefore reached Hamilton's account when the use of NATO air power was becoming increasingly realistic. It was only afterwards that it was established that air strikes would not be launched and that Serbian forces would not take the UN safe area at that time.

Again the pattern continued. The contributions in June 1995 were also made during a period of political uncertainty, when Hamilton was emerging as the most prominent voice of opposition in the House on the issue of lifting the arms embargo. During this month, Hamilton had a real fight on his hands. On June 8, 1995, the House voted 319–99 in favor of lifting the arms embargo. This successful vote encouraged pro-Bosnian forces to move ahead in the Senate, and Hamilton, in turn was occupied with another major lobbying effort to undermine the plans of Dole and Lieberman to lift the arms embargo. Throughout June and early July, Hamilton appeared on numerous television programs where he repeatedly advocated maintaining the embargo and seeking a diplomatic end to the conflict.

The net decline in Hamilton's campaign contributions from 1991 onward might explain the reason the congressman so willingly accepted this Balkan money. Nonetheless, the central question remains: what political objectives did his sponsors seek to achieve? While the Serbian and Greek lobbies have individual agendas, there were several points that united the two communities, especially regarding the issues of Bosnia and Macedonia. A central concern for these two Orthodox lobbies is a shared anti-Islamic and anti-Turkish sentiment. Such bias could be found recorded in Manatos's testimonies before Congress; in the advertisements placed by the Serbian Unity Congress in major newspapers; in the propaganda disseminated by Helen Delich Bentley; and, most frequently, on electronic systems such as the Serbian Information Initiative. Hamilton's acceptance of Serbian American and Greek American contributions therefore raises the question, has the congressman been capitalizing on this particular bias? And to what extent have Serbian American and Greek American contributions influenced the congressman's own policy of appeasement of Serbian aggression in Bosnia? An answer to these questions is important. For the past two years, an elected official and one of the most prominent members of Congress is on record as having received significant donations from proponents of Radovan Karadžić's policies in the United States.

The Serbian Lobby Approaches Political Leaders

The first significant record of group lobbying organized by the Serbian Unity Congress was on April 25, 1993, when SUC leaders met with members of the Senate Foreign Relations Committee and the National Security Council.[88] Four months later, the *Unity Herald* again noted a lobbying effort with H.R.H. Crown Prince Alexander when it was claimed that the SUC met with "some of the most important leaders in the U.S. foreign policy circles."[89] However, it was not until May 1994 that the SUC secured a real coup when it was invited to testify before the House Committee on Foreign Affairs, chaired by Lee Hamilton.

On May 11, 1994, with Manatos's assistance, the former president of the SUC, Michael Djordjevich, appeared before Congress. He addressed the House on the situation in the former Yugoslavia. In his conclusion, Djordjevich advocated that the United States suspend the sanctions against Serbia and take the following three steps: (1) enforce a total cease-fire in Bosnia; (2) impose on all belligerents the condition that they settle their territorial claims by binding arbitration; (3) establish an arbitration panel consisting of two experts appointed by Croats and Muslims and two appointed by Serbs. What was most interesting about Djordjevich's testimony was the extent to which he went to justify the creation of an ethnically pure Serbian state. Djordjevich employed classic apologetic arguments to make his case for "self-determination." While he acknowledged that the conflict was tragic and unfortunate, the causes of the war lay with the "premature" recognition of Slovenia, Croatia, and Bosnia and with nationalist and secessionist parties outside Serbia, he claimed. It was unfair to let Germany unify and not the Serbs, he maintained. In reply to questions asked by House members, he insisted that the war in the Balkans was analogous to the American Civil War. The SUC would later use the fact that Djordjevich appeared before Congress to gain legitimacy in Belgrade, as his testimony was advertised to ultranationalist opposition parties[90] and to the SUC membership in general.

In February 1995, the SUC launched its most extensive lobbying campaign on Capitol Hill, where delegates advocated Karadžić's policies and distributed the SUC's official memorandum. The Serbian presence in Washington was reported by Almar Latour in the *Washington Times* on March 5. The newsletter of the Serbian Unity Congress, published ten days later, gave more information on the SUC's visit of February 21–23, 1995.[91] According to this source, the delegation met with four senators, twenty-one House representatives, and twenty-four congressional staff officials. The Serbian lobby had two objectives: "to ascertain the current opinion of the key congressional and governmental officials about the crisis, and to provide them with up to date information on the situation in former Yugoslavia."

By early 1995, the Serbian Unity Congress was presenting itself as the face of the Serbian lobby in the United States. However, this lobby was still highly dependent on the expertise of professionals like Manatos and Manatos. It would be fair to say that the SUC's success depended less on its lobbying power and more on the predisposition and willingness of influential actors to tolerate seemingly "balanced" and nonviolent solutions to the conflict in Bosnia. The role of former president Jimmy Carter in the Serbs' international campaign of appeasement is one episode that requires further investigation. In December 1994, the SUC hinted that it had initiated Carter's visit to Pale[92] when a cease-fire was negotiated that froze Serbian gains and enabled forces under the control of General Ratko Mladić to regroup in preparation for a subsequent genocidal campaign in eastern Bosnia. The involvement of the SUC in this victory was later recorded in the Serbian press by Michael Djordjevich, although sources from Belgrade also took credit for this coup.[93]

In spite of its tendency to exaggerate, the Serbian Unity Congress had made itself known on Capitol Hill and, with a constant presence in Washington, was chipping away at the official position of the Clinton administration: that Bosnia should remain an undivided, sovereign state.

The SUC and Karadžić's Representative Office in Washington

From the beginning, the SUC knew that it required a permanent office in the nation's capital to carry out a significant public relations campaign. In November 1992, the Serbian Unity Congress opened the Serbian American Affairs Office in Washington, DC. This bureau was directed by Danielle Sremac, an articulate twenty-six year old who had recently graduated from American University. The Belgrade-born Sremac was to work as a liaison between the Serbian Unity Congress and the newly hired lobbying firm of Manatos and Manatos. Her duties were to distribute newsletters and invitations to conferences to think tanks, newspapers, UN dignitaries, and other offices; monitor print and broadcast media; create a media contact list; draft memorandums for congressional members; and instruct the Serbian community on which members of Congress should be targeted.[94]

As a result of the war in Bosnia, Danielle Sremac's career accelerated. By 1994, the Serbian Unity Congress was functioning as a front for Radovan Karadžić through the appointment of Sremac. Less than two years after her engagement by the SUC, Danielle Sremac was traveling back and forth to Pale and acting as the official representative for the Bosnian Serb leader in Washington. For this purpose, the SUC's Serbian American Affairs Office was converted into the Serbian American Affairs Council. Sremac's letterhead was amended and under the new name an additional title, the "Representational Council of Republika Srpska", was included in both English and Serbian. Just as the Serbian Unity Congress sought to legitimate the Bosnian Serb leadership, Sremac too tried to present herself publicly as an official representative. Letters signed by Danielle Sremac, "Emissary of the Republika Srpska to the United States and Canada," were stamped with an impressive seal that added no more legitimacy to her office, but simply recorded "Serbian-American Affairs Council" in Cyrillic.

On July 15, 1994, Sremac filed documents with the U.S. Department of Justice Foreign Agents Registration Unit and claimed that she had an oral understanding to act as a spokesperson for the Bosnian Serb leadership. She would deal with Aleksa Buha, minister for foreign affairs of the declared "Bosnian Serb Republic." The only conditions of Sremac's engagement were that she would not receive fees or compensation for expenses from Pale. She was to work for the Bosnian Serb leadership on a voluntary basis. Sremac therefore reported that her fees were to be covered by American contributors. In practice, Sremac was to remain an employee of the Serbian Unity Congress and would represent the Bosnian Serb regime as part of her daily duties. There was no change in her official responsibilities and she continued to receive a salary collected, in large part, through tax-exempt contributions.

The Serbian Unity Congress's sponsorship of the Representational Council of the Republika Srpska raised a number of questions. Since the SUC had received tax-exempt status as a 501(c)(3) organization, it was supposed to meet a number of tests. The restrictions on lobbying laid out by the Internal Revenue Code were explicit: lobbying, as defined as "attempts to influence legislation" was not to be a substantial part of the organization's activities.[95] Since its inception, however, the Serbian Unity

Congress engaged in both grassroots and direct lobbying, and Sremac's direction of these campaigns was beyond dispute.[96] By 1994, it was clear that the Serbian Unity Congress and the Serbian American Affairs Council were conduits for tax-exempt dollars used to promote the Bosnian Serb leadership in the United States.[97]

It was Sremac herself who tipped her hand and admitted that she was to serve as Karadžić's propaganda agent through the sponsorship of the Serbian American community. On July 20, 1994, Sremac mistakenly swore that she would be conducting activities that challenged the regulations of the Internal Revenue Code. Under section 5 of her registration statement, she declared that she would be engaged in the dissemination of "political propaganda," which was clearly defined at the top of the official form.[98] Sremac acknowledged that she would be using radio, television broadcasts, press releases, letters, and telegrams, as well as lectures and speeches, to prepare and distribute "political propaganda." Her target groups were government agencies, civic associations, nationality groups, and the media. Her activities on behalf on the Bosnian Serb leadership were identical to those as director of the Serbian Unity Congress in Washington. In both cases, Sremac was instructed to provide press releases and articulate the positions and policies of the Bosnian Serb republic, including "the right to self-determination for the Serbian people in territories of Bosnia-Herzegovina, and promotion of equal treatment of all conflicting parties in the region."[99]

The statements filled out by Sremac proved to be remarkably revealing. A close reading of these documents unmasked the Serbian propaganda campaign that was camouflaged under the slogan of evenhandedness.[100] Appeasement in the name of "equal treatment" was an official policy of the Bosnian Serb Republic. Sremac was indeed advocating a political policy rather than opening up the debate to the Serbian viewpoint, as she would argue.

Six months later, when Sremac was again required to report her activities to the Justice Department, she declared a number of her activities undertaken on behalf of the Bosnian Serb regime, including lectures and television and radio interviews, but denied that she had conducted *political* activities on behalf of the "Republika Srpska." Checking "None" next to every question that inquired about her possible preparation and dissemination of political propaganda, Sremac deliberately submitted an incomplete form to the Foreign Agents Registration Unit under oath.

Following the example of her political leaders in Pale, Danielle Sremac had repeatedly lied in the course of her work for the Serbian American lobby.

From 1994 through 1995, Sremac was regularly seen and heard on CNN, CSPAN, National Public Radio, and even on Sky and BBC *Newsnight* in the United Kingdom. According to the documents filed with the Justice Department, Sremac admitted to participating in an impressive range of television and radio interviews.[101] During these broadcasts, Sremac repeated the official line passed down from the Bosnian Serb leadership and frequently tried to inject a "historical" analysis into her discussion of the conflict. In essence, she repeated the traditional charge that Serbs were facing a real threat from "fundamentalist Islamic" and "Nazi" forces in the form of the Bosnian and Croatian armies. Danielle Sremac was indeed a paid propagandist for the Bosnian Scrb leadership. Her role was to confuse American viewers over the nature of the war and make the route of appeasement, disguised as a diplomatic solution that treated all the combatants equally, the most favorable political option.

The Serbian Lobby: An Evaluation

In five years, the Serbian American community did manage to create an active political lobby. However, its overall success depended less on its own abilities, and more on the powers of other agencies to take on or at least listen to its cause. As the reports from the Federal Election Commission for the Serbian Unity Congress PAC illustrated, on its own, the Serbian American effort was often quite amateur. Without the help of public relations firms such as Manatos and Manatos, the Serbian American community would not have had access to elected officials other than Helen Delich Bentley. With her departure in 1994, no member of Congress was prepared to champion the Serbian cause to such a great degree. The Serbian American lobby was therefore highly dependent on its grassroots base.

It was the grassroots element of the Serbian propaganda campaign, however, that earned the Serbian Unity Congress its reputation as a recognizable pressure group. Members were truly motivated to write and call, as the SUC directors requested. The bullying tactics behind the SUC's phone and letter-writing campaign did in fact have much to do with the persistence of Serbian Americans who sincerely believed in their crusade. When the Serbian lobby did express its voice, it was usually in the semi-friendly company of journalists who were opposed to the prospect of foreign intervention or those who simply wanted to capitalize on a topical debate and who accepted the apologetic claims of Danielle Sremac, Peter Brock, and the SUC's directors.[102]

The successful tactics used by the Serbian lobby demand further discussion. Elsewhere, others have commented extensively on the growth of popular relativist and deconstructionist philosophies that appear uncritically tolerant.[103] The reception given to the Serbian lobby introduces a greater issue than just the presence of ultranationalist sentiments conveyed from Belgrade. The real issue is the way ethnic groups could exploit the contemporary cultural climate under the guise of multiculturalism to push forward exclusive and antagonistic political agendas. As the Serbian propaganda effort illustrated, under the banner of tolerance, intolerant ideologies could be admitted to the mainstream media, often indiscriminately.

The relative success of the Serbian pressure campaign should not, however, be exaggerated. As Serbian Americans insisted that they were simply offering their own "side of the story," they needed to create a story. In spite of the odd article such as Peter Brock's piece in *Foreign Policy,* the Serbian side was hardly credible. Moreover, it was patently obvious that the Serbian publicists relied on contradictory argumentation to sell their fabrications. Like the Serbian leaders in Belgrade and Pale, the Serbian American community attempted to reduce the actual conflict in the former Yugoslavia to competing accounts whose validity rested on interpretation. While propagandists could look to divisive college campuses to understand how the notion of interpretation could be used to grant them a hearing in the highly charged "multicultural" atmosphere of the 1990s, few outside the Serbian community took their claims seriously. While SerbNet and the Serbian Unity Congress issued releases and materials that revealed their true motives, their real achievement was not in conveying a persuasive argument but in mobilizing their members. The deconstructionist approach was not only unconvincing, but also internally inconsistent. On the one hand, the propagandists contested the idea that there was "objective knowledge" of atrocities committed in the former Yugoslavia and argued that press reporting was highly politicized. On the other hand, they insisted that journalists and politicians should be both "objective" and "balanced" in their assessment of the war. The deliberate assimilation of objectivity to balance and the assumption that an "even-handed" approach was required when the fighting was obviously uneven forced a false epistemological debate which the propagandists believed would not only disguise but also justify Serbia's war aims. If the intention was to dispel the notion of truth and accurate reporting, in order to discredit personal testimonies and serious journalism, SerbNet and the SUC really only managed to advance their own politically motivated agendas within their community. The party faithful remained the local Serbian community—it seems as though there were few converts, although their claims may have contributed to confusion about the Balkan situation in the minds of the American public.

In order to sustain the charges of bias and unite its membership behind these myths, the Serbian American community had to enlist the help of publicists. With the exception of A. M. Rosenthal of the *New York Times,* the Serbian lobby did not attract big names, and there was little indication in a change of public opinion in the United States.[104] Reports issued by fact-finding missions, the CIA, and human rights agencies, as well as journalistic exposes all recorded that the overwhelming majority of abuses carried out in Bosnia were the result of Serbian forces. The argument of media bias that ignored Serbian claims of victimization had not managed to shift the jury.[105]

Conclusion

Overall, the Serbian propaganda effort succeeded in activating hundreds of Serbian Americans. It was their constant pressure and vocal outbursts that made their lobby more visible. Whether the Serbian American community really influenced politicians like Lee Hamilton and effected changes in policies remains a matter of speculation. Certainly their efforts did not hurt their cause. There were, however, other reasons why the revisionist arguments made by Serbian leaders in Pale and Belgrade had such appeal in the United States. As the siege in Bosnia dragged on into its third year, it was evident that the international powers had adopted a policy of expediency that would ensure that significant Serbian war gains should be protected. Croatia too would gain considerably as a result of the Bosnian partition plan that U.S. envoy Richard Holbrooke actively tried to sell to the governments in Sarajevo, Belgrade, and Zagreb. President Franjo Tudjman would inch closer to his dream of establishing a secure Croatian foothold in Bosnia-Herzegovina.

The argument for appeasement was by no means the exclusive property of the Serbian lobby. Although their motivation was different, in the end, there was considerable ideological accommodation between a reluctant Clinton administration and Serbian proponents of ethnic purity. The fight to maintain an integral Bosnia-Herzegovina was all but abandoned by the American leadership. Retaining the territorial integrity of the Bosnian state and dividing it on a near-equal basis between Serbs and the Croat-Muslim Federation were mutually exclusive options. Bosnia was to be partitioned, to the benefit of Radovan Karadžić and his illegitimate regime. To that extent, Serbia's ethnic purists and their American lobby won by default.

NOTES

The author would like to thank the staff at the U.S. Department of Justice Foreign Agents Registration Unit; the Public Records Office at the Federal Election Commission; the Internal Revenue Service public relations office in Los Angeles; and the reference staff at Stanford University Libraries, the Hoover Library, the British Library of Politics and Economic Science, and the library at the School of Slavonic and East European Studies, University of London. I am also extremely grateful to a number of individuals from the former Yugoslavia and beyond who collected documents and information on my behalf. Their assistance has been invaluable to the development of this research.

1. There have of course been other wars in Bosnia-Herzegovina since its declaration of independence in 1992. This chapter does not concern itself with the brutal Croat-Muslim war in Herzegovina and central Bosnia. The role of the Herzegovinian lobby overseas and its influence on the conduct of the HVO's (Croatian Council of Defense) and HDZ's (Croatian Democratic Union) war aims is nonetheless an important subject for investigation.

2. For a devastating analysis of how the United Nations humanitarian effort in eastern Bosnia has assisted the Serbian goal of ethnic purity through the uneven distribution of aid, see Carole Hodge, "Slimy Limeys," *New Republic*, January 9 and 16, 1995.

3. Congressional activity accelerated after January 27, 1994, when the Senate, led by Dole and Lieberman, voted eighty-seven to nine to support a nonbinding amendment that requested an end of the arms embargo. Five months later, on May 12, the Senate voted on two amendments. The first one was drafted by Senator George Mitchell and sought a multilateral lifting, through the UN Security Council. The second one, again sponsored by Dole and Lieberman, sought a

unilateral termination of the embargo. Both received equal numbers of votes: fifty to forty-nine in favor of their respective demands. On July 1, 1994, Dole and Lieberman again attempted to terminate U.S. participation in the embargo, but the vote was split fifty-fifty. Five weeks later, on August 11, the Senate voted again. The amendment, presented by the chairman of the Senate Armed Services Committee, Sam Nunn, was designed to end U.S. enforcement of the embargo, but it did not seek to terminate it altogether. Nunn's amendment was adopted fifty-six to forty-four and was countered by Dole and Lieberman, who secured fifty-eight votes in favor of a unilateral lifting (there were forty-two votes opposed). On July 26, 1995, the Senate voted in favor of bill S21 presented by Dole and Lieberman by sixty-nine to twenty-nine.

4. Genocide is defined under Article 2 of the Geneva Convention on the Prevention and Punishment of the Crime of Genocide (U.N. GOAR Res. 260A (III) of December 9, 1948) as acts "committed with intent to destroy, in whole or in part, a national, ethnical, racial, or religious group, as such: (a) Killing members of the group; (b) Causing serious bodily or mental harm to members of the group; (c) Deliberately inflicting on the group conditions of life calculated to bring about its physical destruction in whole or in part; (d) Imposing measures intended to prevent births within the group; (e) Forcibly transferring children of the group to another group."

5. See Carroll J. Doherty, "Bosnia's Weapon in the U.S.," *Congressional Weekly Report,* July 29, 1995.

6. *Demonstration in DC on September 9, 1995,* SerbNet press release, dated August 26, 1995, and broadcast on the Serbian Information Initiative.

7. Norman Cigar, *Genocide in Bosnia: The Policy of Ethnic Cleansing* (College Station: Texas A&M University Press, 1995), 5–6. This is an important conclusion that introduces a critical issue: the role of national ideologies in the planned destruction of Bosnia-Herzegovina. Within the canon of writings on nationalism there has been an ongoing debate that has greatly influenced political commentary on the war in Bosnia. In essence, it is a debate over cause and effect. Do national ideologies have a degree of autonomy that precedes and shapes political outcomes? Or rather, as Ernest Gellner argues, is nationalism a theory of political legitimacy that evolves in order to justify the emergent political reality? Those who refute Gellner's thesis and suggest that "nationalism" is the initial source of provocation for the conflict in Bosnia-Herzegovina often wade into the troubled waters where historiography meets mythic interpretation. In order to make the claim that the war was "historically inevitable," many petitioners have resorted to a mélange of folkloric tales and politicized accounts of earlier atrocities in the name of "historical analysis." The most commonly heard justification for the war is that the conflict is the result of "age-old ethnic hatreds" where history is the primary battleground.

8. During the London Conference of August 1992, Serbia and the Bosnian Serb command were clearly identified as the aggressors. There was no recognition of a separate Serbian state within Bosnia. Rather, the international community recognized the territorial integrity of Bosnia-Herzegovina.

9. The concept of revisionism should be carefully defined. In this context, I use the term without specific reference to the traditional ideological spectrum with its right and left axes. Rather, in this account, the term "revisionism" denotes the attempt to recast history and current affairs in order to justify a particular agenda.

By "moral relativism" I mean the attempt to sweep away any absolutes of conduct. I include the notion of moral equivalence, which in the context of the Serbian propaganda campaign presupposes a relativist climate, although the two terms are distinct.

10. The story of John Kennedy was revealed by Robert Hardman, "Lobbyist Has Clutch of Royal Contacts," *Daily Telegraph,* January 28, 1995; and by David Leppard and Adrian Levy, *Sunday Times,* January 29, 1995. Kennedy had stood for Parliament as a Conservative candidate, worked for a number of lobbyists and Prince Michael of Kent. He was also a researcher for Henry Bellingham, the private secretary of the then defense secretary, Malcolm Rifkind. The *Sunday Times* article described Kennedy as a "Serbian hardliner" and reported on an intelligence dossier assembled on him which "claimed to show that the 29–year old Yugoslavian born aristocrat is the figurehead of a network of Serbian militants who have gained a foothold in Britain." The *Daily Telegraph* article stated that Kennedy had promoted the "interests of a group of Serbian industrialists in London" and reported that "In the last few years, he has had many meetings with the Bosnian Serb leader, Dr. Radovan Karadžić, and the Serbian President, Mr. Slobodan Milošević. Referred to as 'Senator Kennedy' by elements of the media in Belgrade, he has arranged trips to the former Yugoslavia for British MPs."

11. The press conference was scheduled for noon on July 15, 1992. Later that day, Karadžić again promised a cease-fire. For a discussion of Karadžić's visit to London and meeting with Lord Carrington, see Mark Almond, *Europe's Backyard War* (London: Mandarin, 1994), 251.

12. Storer Rowley's reliance on Ostojić's information was immediately evident from his description of the tunnel. Rowley wrote, "South of Sarajevo, Serbs said, Bosnian forces routed Serbs living in towns like Bradina, killing and executing some Serb prisoners and keeping up to 3,000 Serb civilians in a dark railroad tunnel for several days. Other Serbs were said to have been held inhumanely in grain silos in the nearby town of Tarcin and in a 'concentration camp' at Konjic." See "Atrocities Mount in Bosnian War," *Chicago Tribune,* June 22, 1992.

13. Rowley's article first appeared in the *Chicago Tribune* on June 22, 1992,

as "Atrocities Mount in Bosnian War." On June 24, it was published in the *Toronto Star* with the title "The Brutal Killing Fields of Bosnia." The same day, the *Calgary Herald* offered a more extensive history and charged that in the "Battle for Bosnia: Atrocities Bring Back Memories of War."

14. *Keesing's Record of World Events,* News Digest for August 1992, 39035.

15. Ibid. 39035.

16. There was no question of Serbia remaining in isolation, as its leaders maintained. Further evidence of direct assistance to the regimes in Pale and Knin was revealed in the first few months of 1995. See, for example, Roy Gutman, "Crossing the Border: Russia Helps Yugoslavia Send Weapons," *Newsday,* March 30, 1995.

17. See Mark Thompson, *Forging War: The Media in Serbia, Croatia and Bosnia Herzegovina* (London: Article XIX, 1994) 22–31.

18. By 1995, with the help of electronic technology, Karadžić too was represented abroad as his news service, SRNA, found correspondents in New York, Cleveland, London, and Moscow and started broadcasting on electronic newsgroups like the Serbian Information Initiative.

19. Brochure issued by the Serbian Unity Congress in 1994.

20. Nora Beloff, *Tito's Flawed Legacy: Yugoslavia and the West, 1939–84* (London: V. Gollancz, 1985) is one of the most prominent pro-Serbian voices in the United Kingdom. In numerous letters published in the *Daily Telegraph,* Beloff has questioned the reports of mass rape and genocide conducted by Serbian forces and instead accused official German sources of disseminating anti-Serbian propaganda. Her letters mirror the official line put out by the Milošević and Karadžić regimes. See, for example, "Doubts about Serbian Rapes," *Daily Telegraph,* January 19, 1993, where Beloff argues, "the most likely explanation for German behavior is that they need to 'satanise' the Serbs in order to cover their own responsibility for pitching Yugoslavia into civil war. In the interests of EC consensus at the time of signing the Maastricht Treaty, the British government endorsed the break-up of Yugoslavia without consulting the Yugoslav electorate." More recently, Beloff has been lobbying the highest representation of the Jewish community in the United Kingdom, the Board of Deputies, arguing that genocide did not take place in Bosnia. See "Beloff in 'Stimulating' War Report to Deputies," *Jewish Chronicle,* September 29, 1995.

21. Nora Beloff, "The Dossier of Milivoje Ivanišević: Evidence of Crimes against Serbs in the Srebrenica-Bratunac-Skelani District from April 1992 to March 1993," *Unity Herald,* May 1993.

22. This dossier, "Moslem Camps in Konjić Municipality: Celebici, Sport Hall-Musala in Konjic and Donje Selo," was published by the Serbian Council Information Center and reportedly prepared by Vojin S. Dabić, Ema Miljković, Ksenija Lukić, Sreten Jakovljević, Mila Djordjić, and Marko Marcetić.

23. Ibid.

24. As Mark Thompson, op. cit., notes, "the propagandists of nationalism in Serbia . . . had won once the fighting began. The logic of the war then ensured the maximum mutual alienation of the peoples represented by the warring sides, confirming the imperative for national territory, justifying the conflict and even legitimating, retrospectively, the politics which had produced the war" (52).

25. From 1991 onward, *Politika* became increasingly blatant in its support for Karadžić and his party, the Serbian Democratic Party in Bosnia. The shift in editorial bias was noted in the gradual character assassination of Alija Izetbegović. In February 1991, Izetbegović's authority to represent Bosnia in the Presidency of the Socialist Federal Republic of Yugoslavia was challenged. By July 1991 *Politika* was parroting the SDS's demand that the "principle of self-determination up to secession should apply to all peoples" but not to the exclusion of others. It had become the organ of the SDS.

26. For a detailed discussion, see Thompson, op. cit., 67–83.

27. The Serbian American Voters Alliance based in Los Angeles is the first entry for Serbian PACs.

28. Letter from Helen Delich Bentley to "all Serbian Americans," August 4, 1990.

29. See Cigar, op. cit., 32–34.

30. In the pluralist democracies of the United States, Canada, and Britain, ultra-left-wing groups and journalists were joined with right-wing xenophobes, representatives from Belgrade and Pale, and the leadership of the Serbian Orthodox Church in a program of political action For example, a parliamentary group calling itself the Committee for Peace in the Balkans was established in the United Kingdom in 1995. Among its founding members were the Socialist champion of the Labour Party, Tony Benn M.P., and Sir Alfred Sherman, a former Thatcherite notorious for his racist and anti-immigrationist writings in the 1970s. The union of the extreme left and extreme right was regularly recorded in the journals and newsletters of Serbian American organizations as well as on popular electronic newsgroups. Sherman was remembered for introducing Jean-Marie Le Pen, neo-Nazi and leader of the French National Front, to the United Kingdom in 1987. Sherman's own racist polemics are an interesting read. See Alfred Sherman, "Britain Is Not Asia's Fiancée" *Daily Telegraph,* September 11, 1979; idem, "Spain Had Heroes; Bosnia Only Laptop Bombardiers," *Daily Telegraph,* May 3, 1994; idem, "The Coming of the Sword," *Jerusalem Post,* March 23, 1994; idem, letters, *Spectator,* May 8, 1993. *Living Marxism,* the journal of the Revolutionary Communist Party and its front, the Campaign against Militarism, were two of the main revisionist standard-bearers under the guidance of journalist Joan Phillips. A few papers, like the *Workers Revolutionary Party's Workers Press Weekly,* could point to the infiltration of right-wing extremists among Serbian propagandists. See David Dorfman, "C18 Sides with Serb Chetniks," *Workers Press,* June 24, 1995.

31. For a more detailed discussion, see Tom Bowman, "Bentley Support for Serbs Raises Question of Conflict: Republican Used Office for PR effort," *Baltimore Sun,* June 8, 1992. See also Philip J. Cohen, *Serbia' Secret War: Propaganda and the Deceit of History* (College Station: Texas A&M University Press, forthcoming).

32. There was something most peculiar about Bentley's lobbying efforts. According to a letter dated August 4, 1990, the representative from Maryland was concerned about HR 352, which she described as the "Broomfield Bill on Kosovo and Yugoslavia." At the time, there was a "Broomfield Bill," but it aimed to scrap all navy ships built before January 1, 1946 and could not be confused with Serbian American interests. It made no mention of Kosovo and Yugoslavia. See Daniel Machalaber, "Does This Old Fleet Never Go to Sea? Well Hardly Ever," *Wall Street Journal,* November 12, 1990. The author could find no record of a Broomfield bill on Kosovo reported in official congressional journals. Was Helen Delich Bentley, a concerned representative for the Seafarers Union and other maritime bodies, encouraging the Serbian American community to support another political agenda?

33. *Congressional Record,* August 2, 1990, H6821.

34. Ibid.

35. The former representative for the "Serbian Republic of Krajina" recorded a private meeting on January 22, 1992, when she was provided with information on "the attitude of the people of Krajina towards current crisis." U.S. Department of Justice, Foreign Agents Registration statement for Zoran B. Djordjevich, filed August 31, 1992.

36. *Congressional Record,* August 11, 1992, H8009.

37. For a full account of MacKenzie's relations with Serbian public relations firms, see the Roy Gutman, "Serbs Bankroll Speeches by Ex-UN Commander," *Newsday,* June 22, 1992, reproduced in idem, *A Witness to Genocide* (New York: Macmillan), 168–73.

38. *Congressional Record,* August 11, 1992, H8010.

39. Letter sent by SerbNet, May 5, 1992.

40. Her letters and requests to the Serbian American community always ended with a postscript that reinforced the idea of victimization—Serbs struggling against greater forces. Emotional blackmail was her preferred tactic. On August 4, 1990, Bentley wrote, "PS. Several anti-Serbian Members of the House took to the floor last week to attack the Serbs in Kosovo and call for ethnic-Albanian control of the Province. I immediately took to the floor myself and was joined by Congressmen Jim Moody and John Murtha, in presenting our side of the story. *The American Srbobran* will soon include a copy of this entire debate on the floor of Congress, so you can see for yourselves what I am up against, and how the battle never lets up." She later would use a more direct technique to persuade her

followers of their common struggle. On May 5, 1992, Bentley wrote, "You need to know that the Croatians have spent about $17 million on the public relations program which has successfully portrayed Croatia as the 'innocent victim.' We have nothing to offset this."

41. See Cohen, op. cit.

42. See Vladimir Grečić and Marko Lopusina, "Ujidenitelji srpske emigracije" (Chronicles of Serbian Emigration), *Intervju,* September 2, 1994.

43. This journal, which was published in London and New Delhi, repeatedly included articles that apologized for the Serbian leadership's role in the Balkan conflict. Its most prominent writer was one of its editors, Yossef Bodansky, an Israeli who is also director of the House Republican Task Force on Terrorism. Bodansky is an enigmatic figure whose articles reflect a strong anti-Islamic bias in their discussion of the Balkans.

44. Gutman, *Witness to Genocide,* 168–73.

45. See *The Big Story,* "Sold Out," Carlton Television, December 1994.

46. Letter of the Day, *Calgary Sun,* August 19, 1993.

47. The MacKenzie episode was just one illustration of the circularity behind the Serbian public relations campaign. MacKenzie continued to be a common source of authority behind Serbian American claims of media bias. Other paid propagandists were routinely cited, along with MacKenzie, including the notorious Sir Alfred Sherman. The 1993 Internal Revenue Service tax returns from the Serbian Unity Congress recorded that Sherman had in fact been paid for his writings. In the House of Commons on June 26, 1995, Sherman revealed that he was, as others had reported, one of Karadžić's key publicists offering advice to the Bosnian Serb leader. Sherman's appeals for ethnic purity and the expulsion of the indigenous population from Serb-held territories in Bosnia were reminiscent of his earlier racist campaigns and suggested that he was indeed a sincere sponsor of Karadžić's program of ethnic purity.

48. The actor Karl Malden was even asked to join SerbNet's finance committee, according to Bentley's letter of May 5, 1992.

49. On September 18, 1992, Bentley spoke before the Congressional Human Rights Caucus and tried to persuade members that she had privileged information. Milošević would not run in the elections, "according to her intelligence." Such intelligence was questionable. The liaison between Bentley and Milošević seemed to be directed more from her end. Even after the JNA assault in Bosnia, Bentley extended an invitation to Milošević to visit the United States, according to an interview published in *Serbia: News, Comments, Documents, Facts, Analysis* (Serbian Ministry of Information), no. 12 (May 18, 1992).

50. For example, on June 9, 1993, the *American Srbobran* published an advertisement on behalf of SerbNet entitled "Send Your Donations to SerbNet and Publicity Will Continue to Be—Better."

51. According to Grečić and Lopusina, op. cit., "SerbNet received for its work the blessing of Bishop Christopher from Los Angeles and Bishop Irinej from Libertyville."

52. A release about the IOCC broadcast on the Serbian Information Initiative raised some questions about the IOCC's practices of delivering aid. In a statement issued by Mirjana Petrović, on June 5, 1995, it appeared that the IOCC was handing over humanitarian aid to the Bosnian Serb Army for shipment to Banja Luka. She wrote, "On Friday, May 12, IOCC staff members left Belgrade destined for Banja Luka with two trucks carrying 2,174 family food parcels. The trucks were allowed passage through the corridor about 3:30 am shortly before it was closed to all traffic at 4:00 am. Military police controlling the traffic at the check point advised IOCC staff that there was absolutely no way any non-military vehicles would be allowed through Brčko as it was being shelled heavily. IOCC staff returned to Belgrade and were then able to confirm that the trucks had safely reached Banja Luka, had been unloaded, and were waiting in Modrica to pass back through the corridor. The corridor opened late Saturday evening and the trucks were back in Belgrade by Sunday morning. The challenge to provide assistance to these refugees has been accepted, the task has begun."

53. A recent example is the press release issued by St. Sava Orthodox Church of Milwaukee on August 18, 1995. Addressed to President Clinton, U.S. senators, and members of Congress, it read,

> Mrs. Sadako Ogata, Director of UNHCR stated on Monday, August 7th that the most recent act of aggression against the Serbian civilians of Krajina constitutes "the greatest humanitarian disaster in this war." On August 7th, 1995, at least 150,000 refugees are on the road fleeing bullets from the ground and the air from the Croatian forces. A similar number were trapped in Croatia and at the mercy of the brutal Croatian forces intent on a pure Croatia. Some 700 civilians were in hiding in Knin alone in a UN camp abandoned by the UN and by some accounts have since been slaughtered. This follows on the heels of another major aggression and ethnic cleansing of the Serbian civilians which occurred in Slavonija last May where the Croatian forces drove out between 15,000 and 20,000 Serbian civilians. Our United States Government representatives, White House and the Congress, have not uttered a single public objection to this disaster. Does our Government support the Croatian killing and ethnic cleansing of 300,000 innocent Serbian civilians just because they are Serb? If they do not, why do they watch and approve by words and deeds this greatest human disaster in the Yugoslav war. We respectfully request of our representatives that in the name of justice and human decency they assist in the following ways: 1. Public condemnation by the Executive and the Congress of Croatian aggression against Serbian civilians. 2. Demand of

Croatia that the UN be given full and free access to the occupied Serbian territories in the Krajina and that a full report be given to Congress within a reasonable period. 3. Full fledged hearings in Congress with Serbian representatives from Krajina, Bosnia and the republics of Yugoslavia. 4. A full explanation by the White House of the US role in the Croatian offensive and slaughter of Serbian civilians: state of the art American tanks used by Croatian forces, NATO and perhaps US planes involved in the bombing out of Serbian military communication posts, making Serbs defenseless in protecting civilian population against known massive military Croatian onslaught; Croatian officials publicly admitted US Government assistance and "tacit approval"; US military advisors have been working with the Croatian military since 1994. Are these actions in violation of the UN "arms embargo?" 5. That US AID fund humanitarian programs to help the Serbian refugee population: USAID has a specific policy, in place since the imposition of sanctions, which denies financing of humanitarian aid to Serbian civilians in need and which is in violation of UN resolutions that explicitly exempt humanitarian aid from the sanctions. The dangers of diseases spreading through Serbia and Montenegro which are under sanctions and without adequate medical supplies, and outside their borders is very real and will be a tragedy to which US policy has contributed. 6. If the US Government will not take a position for imposing sanctions against Croatia, they should lift sanctions against Yugoslavia. 7. Support for a veto of US violation of the UN arms embargo.

54. Over one fifth of Djordjevic's contributions were marked with church address: St. Sava Cathedral in Milwaukee, St. Petka Serbian Orthodox Church in San Marcos, St. Archangel Michael Serbian Orthodox Church in Saratoga, St. Elijahu Serbian Orthodox Church in Saratoga.

55. In 1995, the Serbian American community sponsored a number of demonstrations under an umbrella organization called the Serbian American Coalition for Peace in the Balkans, which was supported by the Serbian American Orthodox Church.

56. Father Rade Stokic of the Serbian American Society in Saratoga, California, and Reverend Krosnjar Djuro of Libertyville, Illinois, both made recognizable donations to Djordjevic in April and June 1992, respectively.

57. The deliberate Americanization and democratization of these Serbian groups was particularly important. The fact that their directors were elected and that representatives could be found in other North American cities gave them an appearance of legitimacy that served to polish the tarnished image of Serbs in the United States. To the outside examiner, they resembled civic organizations, little different from those found in other ethnic and minority communities. The structured and democratic appearance of associations such as the Serbian Unity

Congress was critical, since many relied almost exclusively on public contributions for their survival.

58. This point was stressed in a news release issued on August 26, 1995, calling Serbian Americans to Washington: "And it is our right as American citizens to protest these discriminatory actions."

59. The most notable advertisement placed by the Serbian Unity Congress, signed by eight of its directors, appeared in the *Washington Times* on September 8, 1995. The advertisement read:

> Dear Mr. President: You are now committing a war crime, violating our constitution and offending American moral standards by continuing to bomb Christian Serbs in Bosnia, who only serve their God-given right of freedom and self-determination in their ancestral lands.
>
> Your authority to permit the U.S. military under NATO's command to wage war against people who never threatened us is unconstitutional. Your authority to spend billions of our hard earned money in an undeclared war is downright irrational.
>
> Your moral authority to involve our country in a civil-religious war which we helped start and have sustained by lies, double-standards and covert military assistance to the fundamentalist Islamic regime in Sarajevo and neo-fascist regime in Croatia is non-existent.
>
> Mr. President, you and your advisers know full well that the Christian Serbs accepted our new peace proposal in principle three days before this terrorist bombing was ordered.
>
> Therefore, Mr. President, we urge you to stop these punitive, grotesque and shameful aerial acts of terrorism and murder of civilians and give peace a real chance.

60. The fourteen directors who set up the Serbian Unity Congress were Miroslav Djordjevich of San Rafael, CA; Momcilo Tasich of Oakland, CA; Milovan Popovich of Prospect Heights, IL; Jasmina Wellinghoff of San Antonio, TX; Milosh Milenkovich of Elk Grove Village, IL; Milosh Kostic of Falls Church, VA; ; yet another Milosh Milenkovich of Parma Heights, OH; Peter Chelevich of Bloomfield Hills, MI; Milan Nedic of Van Nuys, CA; Danica Majostorovic of Chicago; Branimir Simic-Glavaski of Cleveland Heights, OH; Peter Djovich of Santa Ana, CA; as well as two Canadian-based officers, Marko Sandalj of Kitchener, Ontario, and Ljubomir Velickovich of Hamilton, Ontario.

61. Michael Djordjevich, "Amerikanci više ne napadaju srpsko varvarstvo" (The Americans are no longer attacking Serbian barbarism)," interview, *Intervju* (Belgrade) March 2, 1995, 39

62. According to the SUC's IRS returns for 1993, filed on November 17,

1994, the British commentator Alfred Sherman received $1,500 from the SUC on June 28, 1993, to prepare a "research study" for the organization.

63. Charles Lane has already exposed Brock's misinformation and connections with the Serbian lobby. See "Brock Crock," *New Republic,* September 5, 1994. David Erne, a non-Serbian activist, approached the public relations campaign from a different angle and interfered with the investigation of war crimes. In March 1994, the Milwaukee lawyer and director of the SUC's information program deliberately abused his relationship with Professor Cherif Bassiouni to upset the work of the UN Commission of Experts. It was Bassiouni, the director of the International Human Rights Law Institute of DePaul University and chair of the UN commission, who was Erne's target. Claiming that he held the position of rapporteur on the UN commission, Erne produced a document entitled *The Historical Background of the Civil War in the Former Yugoslavia,* which was printed on UN letterhead with Bassiouni's name on the cover. The inclusion of Bassiouni's name and the UN emblem suggested that Bassiouni himself had authored the report, which argued that Bosnia had suffered from ancient hatreds and legitimated Karadžić as an "elected leader." According to the Commission of Experts, Erne had simply volunteered his services to Bassiouni's International Human Rights Law Institute based at DePaul University. This was spelled out by Carolyn M. Durnik, assistant project director, in a letter to Tomislav Z. Kuzmanović on January 30, 1994. Although Erne had no relationship to the UN commission, his aim was to influence Bassiouni's staff members and misrepresent Bassiouni's research to the international media and foreign governments. "In connection with this document, Professor Bassiouni has confirmed that you were not asked to write anything for the Commission of experts, but that you were requested by him to write background material for the DePaul University International Human Rights Law Institute, without any commitment or understanding that your contribution would be used in any way," wrote the UN under secretary-general for legal affairs, Hans Corell, who later accused Erne of violating the UN General Assembly rules regarding the use of the UN emblem. The breech of Erne's confidentiality agreement and the "distribution and misrepresentation of the report" was a "very serious matter," stated Bassiouni. However serious the matter, no charges were brought against the long term member of the Wisconsin bar, who escaped with an apology.

64. *Unity Herald,* November 1992, 27.

65. In a book by the French journalist Jacques Merlino, *Les vérités yugoslaves ne sont pas toutes bonnes à dire,* it was reported that Harff and Ruder-Finn had succeeded in "outwitting" Jewish opinion on the issue of Croatia. Merlino's charge later reappeared in the Serbian press and elsewhere. SerbNet assisted in the distribution of this perjured interview.

66. *Unity Herald,* February 1993.

67. *Unity Herald,* May 1993.

68. Fax dated January 4, 1995.

69. Letter faxed from Jelena Kolarovich, director of SUC central office, January 10, 1995.

70. See "Serbian Rights," *San Francisco Chronicle,* December 10, 1991; "Balkan Rights," *San Francisco Chronicle,* May 28, 1992; "The Serbian Perspective," *Washington Post,* March 11, 1992.

71. Alan Boras quoted Nesa Ilić as SUC spokesperson in the *Calgary Herald* on June 21, 1992. Slobodan Rascanin and Slavko Grujicuc sent a letter on behalf of the SUC entitled "Media Politicians Unfair in Casting Serbs as Villains," published on July 18, 1992. The SUC secretary, Momcilo Tasich, published an article, "Yugoslavia: Serbians Warn of New Horrors at the Hand of Old Enemies," which advocated diplomatic negotiations and population transfer. On January 15, 1993, Nesa Ilić sent a letter signed on behalf of the SUC defending Milošević as "the best choice for Serbians."

72. *Los Angeles Times,* March 15, 1992.

73. *Washington Times,* March 5, 1995.

74. For a brief account of Balkan lobbyists, see "So Far, K Street's Doing OK," *National Journal,* March 19, 1994.

75. *Jack O'Dwyer's Newsletter* suggested that the Serbian Unity Congress was actually offering more, and noted that the account was reportedly $25,000 per month on top of a $150,000 start-up fee for three months. See *Jack O'Dwyer's Newsletter,* September 9, 1992. In a matter-of-fact fashion, the *Legal Times* described the SUC's bid and recognized the efforts of SUC vice president and Milwaukee lawyer David Erne to secure the funds necessary to publicize the Serbs' message. See Judy Savasohn's report in the *Legal Times,* September 14, 1992.

76. Morton M. Kondracke, "Grecian Formula: The Arrival of an American Ethnic Group," *New Republic,* June 6, 1998.

77. In a personal letter to the author dated September 24, 1994, Rep. Anna Eshoo declared that "Having researched the Serbian Unity Congress PAC's Federal Elections Commission report for 1992, we discovered that they reported to the FEC a $500 contribution to my campaign. However, I never received this contribution. My treasurer has no record of it, nor does any FEC report from the period reflect such a contribution."

78. Bennett Roth of the *Houston Chronicle* reports (August 19, 1993) that a donation was made on May 24, 1993, and returned two days later.

79. On May 17, 1993, and December 10, 1992, the SUC PAC made donations of $1,000 to Hutchinson and Gejedenson, respectively. In less than one month both had returned their contributions.

80. Anna Eshoo, in private meeting at her office in Palo Alto, California, July 16, 1994.

81. Only one PAC stands out in the Federal Election Reports as explicitly pan-Hellenic. This is Dynamis Federal PAC, registered in Sacramento and based in Palo Alto, California. The number of donations made on behalf of this PAC to congressional representatives is quite small.

82. See Larry Makinson and Joshua Goldstein, *Open Secrets: The Encyclopedia of Congressional Money and Politics* (Washington, DC: Center for Responsive Politics, Congressional Quarterly, 1994), 26–29.

83. Two other PACs stand out from the 1992 records, the Hellenic American Council and the National Albanian American PAC. See Makinson and Goldstein, op. cit., 701.

84. According to the report *FEC Releases 15 Month Congressional Election Figures,* May 9, 1994, Hamilton received $193,441 from individual contributions.

85. On September 3, 1992, Michael Djordjevich sent a letter to Representative Hamilton that praised him for being a fair and reasonable politician and invited him to attend the forthcoming SUC convention in San Diego. Hamilton's reply came on November 20, when the representative apologized for his intended absence. The letter was personal in tone and was sufficiently moderated to give the impression that the congressman believed that Serbs too were being unjustly punished. See *Unity Herald,* February 1993.

86. Djordjevich, op. cit.

87. See Jim Hoagland, "Caving in to Greek Lobby," *Washington Post,* March 30, 1994.

88. *Unity Herald,* May 1993.

89. *Unity Herald,* winter 1993.

90. On June 3, 1994, leaders of the Serbian Unity Congress met with the Serbian Renewal Party. Michael Djordjevich was listed on the visitors' agenda not only according to his professional function but also as someone who has "testified before the U.S. Congress." Conversation with Dick Christiansen of Meridian International.

91. *SUC Newsletter,* March 15, 1995.

92. See *SUC Newsletter,* December 1994.

93. Djordjevich, op. cit.

94. "Opening of the Serbian-American Affairs Office in Washington DC: Goals and Expectations," *Unity Herald,* November 1992, 21.

95. The clause of limitations was defined as "any effort to affect the opinions of the general public and direct lobbying, understood as attempts to influence legislation through communication with members or employees of legislative or any other governmental committees."

96. In one of her first public duties as director of the SUC's Washington office, Sremac was scheduled to hold a workshop on "lobbying, organization and activities" at the annual convention in San Diego. *Unity Herald,* November 1992.

97. The attempt to present the SUC as a non-political organization was critical

to the survival of the Serbian American lobby. From 1991 to 1994, the SUC's membership base expanded but dues paid amounted to only about 13 percent of its annual revenue for this four-year period. The overwhelming source of the SUC's income came from tax-deductible donations made as "public contributions." In later years, over 80 percent of the SUC's income was collected as tax-exempt donations.

98. According to the Foreign Agents Registration Act of 1938 Section 1(j), political propaganda was defined as including

> oral, visual, graphic, written, pictorial, or other communications or expression by any person (i) which is reasonably adapted to, or which the person disseminating the same believes will, or which he [*sic*] intends to, prevail upon, indoctrinate, convert, induce, or in any other way influence a recipient or any section of the public within the United States with reference to political or public interests, policies, or relations of a government of a foreign country or a foreign political party or with reference to the foreign policies of the United States or promote in the United States racial, religious, or social dissensions, or (ii) which advocates, advises, instigates, or promotes any racial, social, political, or religious disorder, civil riot, or other conflict involving the use of force or violence in any other American republic or the overthrow of any government or political subdivision of any other American republic by any means involving the use of force or violence.

99. Foreign Agents Registration Statement, Schedule B, dated July 15, 1994.

100. This was a standard tactic used by revisionists and deniers in other communities. Deborah Lipstadt, *Denying the Holocaust: the Growing Assault on Truth and Memory,* (New York: Maxwell Macmillan International, 1993), argued that under the banner of constitutional freedoms, Holocaust deniers had used their appeal to respect their rights to free speech, not as a shield, as was intended by the Constitution, but as a sword. In the process, they would confuse thousands of Americans.

101. CNBC *America Talking* (November 21, 1994); *CNN International* (November 22, 1994); CSPAN (November 25, 1994); Pat Buchanan Radio (November 28, 1994); CBS *Up to the Minute News* (November 28, 1994); Jim Bohanan Radio (December 5, 1994); Voice of America (January 27, 1995).

102. In the Serbian press, Michael Djordjevich acknowledged some "honest journalists . . . [who] were of great help." He listed Peter Brock, David Binder, and Abe Rosenthal. See Djordjevich, op. cit.

103. See, for example, Allan Bloom, *The Closing of the American Mind* (New York: Simon and Schuster, 1987): and Charles Taylor, *The Ethics of Authenticity* (Cambridge: Harvard University Press, 1991).

104. While leaders of the Serbian American community have shown their

appreciation in the Serbian press for Rosenthal's writings, the *New York Times* columnist has not concealed his proximity to the Serb-nationalist cause. See Djordjevich, op. cit. In "Arrest Warrants Raise the Stakes," *New York Times,* July 28, 1995, Rosenthal admitted to having direct communication with Karadžić and the Serbian lobby in the United States.

105. It was only after Croatia's recapturing of the Krajina in the summer of 1995, when human rights abuses were conducted by Croatian troops against local Serbs, that the international press paid greater attention to Serbian victims. The difference here was that after "Operation Storm" there were genuine grievances and atrocities that one could identify. Serbian victims were documented as a result of factual reporting rather than fabricated propaganda, as the lobbyists intended.

NINE

Daniele Conversi

Moral Relativism and Equidistance in British Attitudes to the War in the Former Yugoslavia

The causes of the war in the former Yugoslavia are multifarious, and have been discussed in detail by several authors. Most of these causes are internal and relate to the shape taken by postcommunist politics in Belgrade.[1] However, international factors that are not always encountered in other ethnonational conflicts have also played an important role in the breakup of Yugoslavia and subsequent developments in the region.

Few countries, if any, had an interest in the fragmentation of Yugoslavia, and since the beginning international efforts were concerted in preserving its unity. Even Germany began pressing for recognition at a relatively late stage. For many, this resolve to preserve the status quo constituted a form of direct interference in Yugoslav politics, to the point that it heavily influenced political decisions in Belgrade. In a nutshell, the Serbian leadership felt secure and protected enough by the international "community" to press first for its idea of a recentralized Yugoslavia, and then, failing this, an enlarged and ethnically pure state to reunite all the Serbs.

Within the European Community, Greece, France, and Britain were the most fervent supporters of a Serbian-dominated Yugoslavia. In Greece, the memory of a common tradition of struggle against the Turk was revived. France had traditionally maintained an alliance with the Yugoslav government. The focus of this chapter will be limited to the British case. The choice of Britain is significant for three reasons: first, a crucial role has been played by British academics and governmental institutions in legitimizing the impasse. Second, Britain held the EC presidency through the most critical period of the war (July to December 1992, participating in the "troika" from January 1992 to June 1993) and tried to secure the maximum advantage offered by this role. Finally, Britain was—and is— in a privileged position as one of the five permanent members of the UN Security Council. Any study trying to fathom why the West has been so reluctant to intervene in Bosnia at a time when its help has been most urgently needed must focus on British attitudes and rationalizations.

I would like to argue that, overall, British attitudes toward Yugoslavia in general and toward events that have occurred since the breakup have been characterized by a certain degree of Serbophilia. In analyzing the reasons for this Serbophilia, I will lay emphasis on two main sets of factors: historical and contingent. Obviously the two overlap, and, in the absence of any credible interpretive and decision-making competence, Britain's Foreign Office has often fallen back on historical determinism. Historicism provided an easy track on which to funnel and subdue confusion, as a vacuum of ideas became evident. As we shall see, pseudo-academic rationalizations helped inform British foreign policy throughout the war.

At least two forces have contributed to a Serbophilic tendency in Britain: one, a small elite of pro-Serbian activists, the other an amorphous mass of minor scholars and key politicians ready to be lured by the propaganda of this minority and hence swept by the tide of revisionism. After weighing the historical roots of Serbophilia, I will analyze the main tool of legitimation of noninterventionist choices.

The main characteristic of British official—and elite—discourse on Bosnia will be identified as *moral relativism*. Moral relativism, as it emerged in Western reactions to the Bosnian War, can be best identified as an underlying current of public opinion that, even at the peak of Serbian atrocities and ethnic cleansing, was determined to view all parties in the conflict as "warring factions" engaged in a "civil war." The basic attitude was one of "equidistance," which assured us that all the parties in the conflict were "equally to blame." Hence this became a war without victims and aggressors, as if the hundreds of thousands of Bosnians who were massacred as a consequence of the Serbian invasion were themselves to blame.

The concept of relativism is often opposed to that of universalism. For the sake of precision, we should also distinguish moral relativism from cultural relativism.[2] Moral relativism reflects a belief in the non-universality of human values, including human rights. Cultural relativism does not necessarily result in moral relativism. Moral relativism is the claim that there is no superior moral judgment and human beings should not adhere to the same values; cultural relativism is the claim that there is no superior culture and all cultures should be treated equally. One may espouse universal values (normally a selection of them) while at the same time propounding that each culture has the right to survive and none is intrinsically superior to any other.

Opposing relativism to objectivism, Ernest Gellner provides a good recapitulation of my argument:

> Scepticism or the inversion of truisms by now has an inverse or boomerang effect: by undermining the criteria of all rational criticism, it confers carte blanche on any arbitrary self-indulgence. Total relativism ends by underwriting cheap dogmatism. If anything goes, then you are also allowed to be as utterly dogmatic as you wish: the critical standards, which might once have inhibited you, have themselves been abrogated. What could there be to check you? He who tries to restrain you, in the name of fact or logic, will be castigated as positivist, or imperialist, or both: after all, objectivism was at the service of domination. Total permissiveness ends in arbitrary dogmatism.[3]

Gellner does not distinguish between moral and cultural relativism, yet his refutation can be applied congruously to my conception of moral relativism. The latter is not necessarily about cultural traits as much as it is about values. But the overall opposition remains between relativism and universalism (or universal objectivity).

In general the kind of moral relativism I am talking about is not a constant in Western politics and thought, but rather an ad hoc attitude that is conveniently espoused when it best suits the interests of a particular elite. I will argue that moral relativism has prevailed in British intellectual and governmental elites' reactions to unfolding events in the former Yugoslavia. I will consider the effects, the consequences, and in particular the aims of such a politics of moral relativism as practiced by the British government.

The Curse of Cultural and Historical Determinisms

The first part of this chapter will focus on the historical dimensions of pro-Serbianism in the United Kingdom. Yet history offers only part of the explanation. It would be against my general argument to assert, as historical determinists do, that there are unshakable alliances that endure over the centuries. Historical determinism has plagued academic endeavors, governmental rhetoric, and popular discourse on the Balkan conflict. There have been repeated references to a supposed tradition of relentless bloodletting and endemic warfare in the Balkans. This has served to create an aura of historical inevitability that has in turn been used to justify current events. The resurgence of historical determinism is an indication that many scholars and politicians, as well as ordinary people, are moving in an interpretive vacuum. Lacking more rational and convincing explications, they fall back onto primordialist accounts of the war.

Yet there is also a difference between cultural and historical determinism. Cultural determinists argue that national conflicts are cultural in origin and substance, then focus on supposedly unbridgeable "fault lines." Their main soothsayer is Samuel Huntington who has formulated a theory of the "clash of civilizations."[4] Accordingly, the new post-Cold War world order is reshaping itself no longer along ideological cleavages, but along cultural fault lines. In other words, now that the two blocs have dissolved, we are entering an era in which being Muslim, Catholic, Orthodox, Confucian, or Shinto matters more than ever before. This is occurring despite increasing secularism and modernization—perhaps precisely as a result of that: religions are not to be taken as they were in the past, that is, as belief systems, but rather as civilizational aggregates. Huntington has applied this approach to, and was probably inspired by, the Yugoslav War. All the "warring" parties of the Yugoslav drama are merely reenacting ancient civilizational alliances and obeying the edicts of primordial loyalties. Thus, for instance, Greece is viewed as unshakably tied to, say, Serbia and Russia by virtue of its Christian Orthodox heritage. An avalanche of criticism has already submerged this thesis, and I do not wish to add my dissenting voice.[5] Cultural determinists often overlook many exceptions. For instance, Serb nationalists have not always been pro-Greek, and different versions of pan-Serbianism claim the region of Greek Macedonia, including Thessalonika, as part of southern Serbia.[6]

The myth of innate antagonisms and perennial hatred rests on the idea that people of different religious convictions decimated each other for thousands of years. However, most historical research demonstrates rather the contrary. In Bosnia, for instance, there was a heritage of tolerance, and this heritage has been shattered only during the last few years. Robert Donia and John Fine have argued that in Bosnia a rich tradition of diversity, pluralism, and toleration evolved over many centuries and flourished until very recently. This tradition in everyday life was echoed in politics by coalition building and a habit of pragmatic compromise.[7] Similarly, thought-provoking research by Christopher Bennett shatters the idea that Yugoslavia's collapse was the result of atavistic ethnic tensions.[8] Cultural determinism is a kind of "big lie" that was both a cause and an effect of Western inaction: it served the interests of noninterventionists by strengthening governments and politicians who opposed intervention, and it was also an effective strategy aimed at pulverizing the multiethnic fabric of Bosnian society. Its greatest "success" was to turn neighbors and friends into mortal enemies, almost overnight.

Historical determinists differ from cultural determinists in that they rely on historical memories rather than culture or religion as causal factors. Thus, people sharing the same religion and "grand civilization" may collide simply because they have already collided in the past. The conflict is explained as a recurring pattern of historical alliances or enmities: for instance, Bulgaria clashing with Serbia and Greece, or Germany allied with Croatia. Historical determinists are often nationalists themselves, and pretend to explain the current conflict as a *longue durée* epic battle, rooted in age-old hatreds. Thus, Greece has "always" been an ally of Serbia and Russia, but has also been an antagonist of Bulgaria, despite sharing a common Orthodox faith. Accordingly, the mildly anti-Serbian attitude in Bulgaria today merely revives old-time alliances dating back at least to the Second Balkan War.

But alliances in the Balkans have shifted over the centuries in unpredictable ways. Some more enduring coalitions may be discernible, but there is scarcely an unchanging relationship that has been able to withstand the vicissitudes of history. For instance, the traditional alliance between France and Serbia may have been radically altered by recent developments.[9] There is much to dispute even about the most discussed one, the nearly mystical bond between Russia and Serbia, originally conceived in the framework of Pan-Slavism. As for pro-Russian sentiments in Serbia, Stephen Clissold defined it as *ignorant admiration*. He recalled that during World War II "Moscow did not . . . lift a finger to help her new ally [Serbia] during the latter's ensuing ordeal [the German invasion], and withdrew recognition from the government of the dismembered state with cynical promptness. Yet when, on June 22, 1941, the Soviet Union was invaded, these things were forgotten in Serbia in an upsurge of popular emotion."[10]

The West's historical determinism recapitulates the dominant discourse in the Balkans. In the Serbian case, the crucial date was 1389, when the Serbs were defeated at the hands of the Turks in Kosovo Polje. Contemporary massacres against Bosnians, Sandjak Muslims, and Kosovo Albanians were invariably referred to as the latest chapter of an epic struggle against the Turk. David Rieff recounts, "When one went into a village where fighting had taken place, it was often easier to get a history lesson than a reliable account of what had occurred earlier the same day."[11] As casualties mounted, history came to the fore and gave major impetus and justification to an endless chain of revenge and counter-revenge. This discourse has been reproduced abroad and has percolated into Western public opinion. It is the clearest evidence of what Stjepan Meštrović calls the "Balkanization of the West."[12]

Not only has public opinion been swayed by this vision of enduring hatred, but the leaders of the main Western powers have tended to reproduce the same pattern among themselves whenever they have dealt with Yugoslavia. Thus, the only "contagion" that could be discerned was not the purported domino effect of expanding separatism, but a far more ominous one: the fragmentation of Western political elites within all the main international organizations—the EC, the UN, NATO. This division in blocs and counterblocs, this desire to carve up spheres of influence out of Bosnian flesh, paralyzed all possible solutions to the war.

The Balkanization of the Balkans, then, has resulted in the Balkanization of all forms of Western politics. The left-right divide can no longer help predict positions in relation to the war. Advocates of Western intervention and Serbian expansionism loom everywhere along the political spectrum, from neo-Nazis to unrepentant Marxists. Pro-Serbian propaganda has affected all political parties and ideologies, cutting across all sort of alliances in virtually every Western country, from Canada to Israel. We will examine how this has occurred in Britain. The following sections will chart the historical antecedents of British Serbophilia and analyze its consistency over the years. Subsequent sections will describe how this attitude manifested itself in the form of both legitimating discourse and political practice.

An Archaeology of British Serbophilism

British Serbophilia commenced well before World War II. In most of Europe, a certain sympathy for the Serbs emerged after their uprising against Ottoman rule at the beginning of the nineteenth century. However, a specifically British Serbophile trend can be traced back at least to the 1870s, when the liberal William Ewart Gladstone (1809–1898) openly declared his admiration for the nationalist rebellions shaking the Ottoman empire. Gladstone, a critic of imperialism, fought against the pro-Turkish policies of the Crown, which, according to him, were indifferent to the flagrant excesses perpetrated by the Turks in the Balkans.[13]

It may be difficult to identify a British uniqueness in these attitudes, which were quite widespread among "progressive" intellectuals of various Western countries. Throughout the entire European continent, the Greek struggle for independence evoked a wave of enthusiastic support. It struck a chord not only in Britain, but also in Germany, as can be seen in the Philohellenic passages of Goethe's *Faust* and in virtually all Classical and Romantic authors. A Romantic current of sympathy for the Serbs also developed in Germany, where the foremost historian, Leopold von Ranke (1795–1886), wrote a well-known *History of Servia,* in which he recommended "the necessity to separate the Christians from the Turks."[14] Significantly, Ranke's book was promptly translated into English and became influential in British academia. The English translator outdid Ranke in her pro-Serbian fervor as she called for "foreign intervention":

> in these days of enlightenment, when missionaries are diffusing the doctrines of Christianity among the heathen in the remotest parts of the world, . . . it is surely not unreasonable to hope that the condition of a Christian people so near to us as Servia, will excite the sympathy of their brethren in faith in this free country. . . . It is only by foreign intervention—not the less effectual for being of a peaceful nature—that the means and opportunities so earnestly desired by the Christian population of these countries can be afforded them. The Turks have been intruders in Europe from the first; . . . we should all unite in hoping that the Mahomedian religion and the obstructive despotism of the "Sublime Porte" should yield to the now swiftly-advancing tide of Christian civilization.[15]

Another crucial angle, which deserves fuller appreciation, is the Protestant-Orthodox connection. Since at least the nineteenth century, prominent Anglican clerics spoke out in defense of a chimerical, fictive image of Christian Orthodoxy conceived as being in opposition to Rome. Despite an evident lack of deep knowledge of Orthodox religion, these theologians and clerical writers put a great deal of effort into promoting a notion of affinity between the two religious traditions. The basic idea was that Eastern Christendom, by virtue of being called "Orthodox" and being apart from Rome, had kept intact the original spirit of Christianity, which the papacy had corrupted. Post-Reformation Anglicans were exhorted to restore this purity on a worldwide scale with the help of, and in alliance with, Eastern Orthodoxy. Several nineteenth-century clergymen underscored such imagined affinities. The priest John Mason Neale (1818–1866) translated several works from Balkan theologians and intellectuals, and published a book on the Orthodox Church in Serbia and other Balkan countries.[16] A generation later, Harold William Temperley (1879–1939) still posited a similarity between Protestantism and Christian Orthodoxy that bore scarce resemblance to any existing reality.[17]

Nationalists all over Europe heralded the heroic feats of the Serbs fighting against the Ottomans. As in the case of Greek nationalism, Serbian nationalism was touted as an epic deed in defense of Western civilization. The title of a book by Robert George Dalrymple Laffan, *The Guardians of the Gate,* suggests that the Serbs represented an outpost of white civilization in perpetual opposition to the loathed and feared non-Western world.[18] The "gate" was conceived as an imaginary cordon sanitaire against Islamic, Eastern, and other barbarian threats. In conjunction with this role, the Serbs assumed a military function of defense of the West—even though they also bedeviled Austria.

A more robust and less Romantic strain of sympathy for the Serbs developed in the wake of World War I. The Serbian struggle was so popular in England that several English nurses went to assist the Serbs in their fight against the Austro-Hungarians. Some of these idealists even enlisted in the Serbian army's ranks and went on to fight in the war.[19]

Not all Balkan specialists supported Serbia, but the few who did not were disliked by the British government. The case of Mary Edith Durham (1863–1944) was quite remarkable: although she was initially anti-Austrian and favored the creation of Yugoslavia, Durham turned increasingly anti-Serbian in the wake of the Sarajevo assassination. In particular, she became a fierce critic of Aleksandar Karadjordjević's dictatorship (1880–1934). An eccentric personality, she wrote letters to newspapers, magazines, and M.P.'s in which she routinely attacked Belgrade. Her lobbying activity was eventually unsuccessful, as she was abhorred by the Foreign Office.[20]

The Foreign Office preferred to consult other experts on the Balkans. The most sought after was R. W. Seton-Watson (1879–1951), who participated actively in the ongoing debate on the new shape of the Balkans during the first decade of the century.[21] Before and during World War I, Seton-Watson firmly believed in the principle of a South Slav confederation.[22] Only after the war did he begin to criticize Belgrade and show any disillusion with its antidemocratic turn.[23]

But best-known and most influential British Serbophile was certainly Dame Rebecca West (1892–1983). In the 1930s, she traveled throughout Yugoslavia accompanied by government officials. In her travels, she picked up a great deal of pro-Serbian sentiment. Her travelogue *Black Lamb and Grey Falcon* became a best-seller in Britain and was one of the first works to acquaint the British public with this area of the Balkans.[24] The dedication to the 1941 edition reads, "To my friends in Yugoslavia who are now all dead or enslaved." As it molded a first image of the country, it may be viewed as a key source for British and American attitudes to Yugoslavia.

In her dialogues, which are permeated with anti-German sentiment, West treats non-Serb subjects with a blend of condescension and superciliousness. All sorts of rationalizations are put forward to press the Serbian viewpoint. The same concoction about the dangers of Islam we encounter in contemporary media is discernible in West's work: praising her mentors, she points out that without people like them—that is, Serbian ultranationalists—"the Eastern half of Europe (and perhaps the other half as well) would have been Islamized, the tradition of liberty would have died for ever under the Hapsburgs, the Romanoffs and the Ottoman Empire, and Bolshevism would have become anarchy."[25] Moreover, West was viscerally anti-Catholic, as well as anti-Italian. The Roman Catholic Church was described as "the greatest stimulus to anti-Serb feelings lain outside Croatia."[26] And, after demonizing Croats and Slovenes time and again, she unwittingly reproached the Italian government for its treatment of the Slovenes in Istria.[27]

The book became very popular in English-speaking countries, particularly in America, where it scored three reissues in only two months. In short, the first great public introduction to Yugoslavia was provided by Rebecca West's best-seller, which remains perhaps the best-written of pro-Serbian accounts of Yugoslav history, politics, and lifestyles. Even a recent eulogistic biography of West concedes that "she had become a stooge for the government press bureau in Belgrade and had naively transmitted its propaganda for a unified and centralized Yugoslav state."[28]

The Legacy of World War II

In their search for allies against the Axis, the British were divided between the advocates of an alliance with the Yugoslav communists and those contemplating a partnership with Serbian nationalists.[29] The former were led by Marshal Josip Broz Tito (1892–1980). The latter were guided by Draža Mihailović (1893–1946) and his Chetnik movement. Although the Serbian Chetniks were nearly as nationalist as the Croatian Ustashe, they were also potential allies against the Germans. Yet there had been Serbian-Nazi collaboration, the extent of which only recently has been investigated in depth.[30]

In brief, my argument is that there have been two main pro-Serbian traditions in Britain: one was monarchical, pro-Chetnik, and anti-Titoist and was highlighted during the short period (September 1941–May 1943)[31] in which British intelligence tried to underscore the extent of anti-Nazi resistance among the Serbs; the other was pro-Partisan and pro-Titoist, and emerged after British liaison officers were parachuted into Partisan-controlled areas to fight the Axis powers. In its Balkan campaign, London was faced with three options: support for the Chetniks, support for the Partisans, and the possibility of forging an unlikely alliance between the two against the Nazis. There were also proposals to divide the country into political areas.[32] Thus "Mihailović should be supported in Serbia where he was thought to be strong, and the Partisans would be supported over the rest of the area. This remained SOE's idea . . . until the end of 1943."[33] The Special Operation Executive (SOE) was an agency instituted in July 1940 with the aim of exploring all possible resistance against the Nazis in the Balkans and the Middle East, including support for guerrilla movements there. The SOE's first mission in Yugoslavia was headed by Captain Duane Bill Hudson in September 1941. When the SOE was still attempting to co-opt the Serbs, the BBC was already campaigning for the Partisans, a fact that revealed deep divisions within Britain's higher echelons. Before taking any decisions over which side to support in the war, Winston Churchill (1874–1965) appointed Brigadier Fitzroy Maclean (b. 1911) for a special surveillance mission in Yugoslavia "to go in and find out who was killing most Germans and how we could best help them to kill more. Politics were to be a secondary consideration."[34]

As we can see, British policy in the Balkans was plagued by hesitancy and irresolution from the beginning, not the least for the contradiction between Britain's strategic interests and pro-Serbian lobbying. This internal mischief led the Foreign Office to be particularly susceptible to manipulations by each side. The pro-Chetnik side, represented by the monarchy-in-exile, was more established and had a better foothold in British society.[35] As the pre-war king of Yugoslavia was exiled in London, a strong pro-Chetnik diaspora congregated around his person and from there exerted a certain influence. When London's decision to support Tito became irrevocable, this nationalist diaspora became a permanent critic of British foreign policy.[36] Far from being isolated, its propaganda effort was directed to the left as well, the "natural" ally of Tito. The anti-Stalinist left was particularly vulnerable to the nationalist appeals. Thus, George Orwell expressed some superficial sympathy for the Chetniks and against the Titoists, whom he perceived as blatant Stalinists.[37]

Tito and his Partisans captivated both Marxist scholars and Cold War strategists. In the immediate postwar period, the reconstruction of Yugoslavia magnetized communist volunteers from all over the world, including 450 British, for the building of the Samac-Sarajevo "youth" railway.[38] During the 1950s and 1960s, interest in Yugoslavia increased among left-wing economists and Marxist political scientists concerned with the labor unions or genuinely intrigued by the Yugoslav experience of workers' self-management.[39] Their sympathies went exclusively to Belgrade, rather than to the opposition. In the late 1970s and early 1980s the quarterly journal *Praxis* became the main conveyor of this neo-Marxist thought, publishing Yugoslav and international theorists, pro-Titoists, and critics of the regime.[40] Yugoslavia's neo-Marxists claimed to be, and some probably were, antinationalist and thus enjoyed a formidable aura of respect in the West, where they were hailed for their attempt to create a new and more "liberal" form of Marxism.[41] One of the founders and leading figures of *Praxis* was Mihailo Marković (b. 1923), a future proponent of Greater Serbia.[42]

Moreover, during the Cold War, Yugoslavia was perceived as a potential ally in the West. Tito's regime received enormous benefits by playing the role of bridge between East and West. With its enlightened politics of nonalignment, Belgrade provided no serious reason for concern for the Western bloc, and we already noted that postwar British politics was staunchly pro-Titoist beyond ideological cleavages. Like Enver Hoxa's Albania, Yugoslavia remained at the margins of the strategic interests of NATO and the West. The roots of Western indulgence toward Serbian crimes is to be found in the Cold War assumption that Tito had to be wooed as a bulwark against Soviet expansionism. "Yugoslav authorities counted much on the tolerance of Western official circles, which, for fear of weakening Tito in front of the USSR, preferred to close both eyes before human rights violations perpetrated by his regime."[43]

Post-Yugoslav Serbophilia

After the collapse of Titoism and especially since the rise of Slobodan Milošević, the two strands we have so far described, the pro-Titoists and the pro-Chetniks, have slowly merged. In the beginning it was relatively easy to mold such an alliance through the expediency of anti-Croatianism, which ended up becoming a British obsession. Indeed, thanks to the works of Rebecca West and many others, Serbophilia was conveniently "balanced" by equivalent doses of Croato-phobia. Memories of Ustashe atrocities played a crucial role in this perception. As is known, Milošević and his nationalists rose to power by reviving a series of imaginary threats to the Serbian nation, but the most effective tactic in mobilizing support was the "fear" of a revived Ustashe movement in Zagreb. Franjo Tudjman was depicted, quite effectively, as an unlikely reincarnation of the Ustashe dictator Ante Pavelić (1889–1959). This paranoid speculation achieved some instant popularity among senior commentators in the British media,[44] where Serbian accusations of a new "Zagreb-Berlin axis" were reinforced by Germany's increasing sympathy for the Croats and the Slovenes at a time when the latter were being bombed by the Yugoslav Federal Army.

For a while, accusations of neofascism directed toward Croatian nationalists became common currency in Britain, even after the atrocities of the Serbian-led JNA became evident. Anti-Croats swallowed Belgrade's battle cry that all Croats were Ustashe.[45] Croatian protestations that Franjo Tudjman had been a Partisan fighting the fascists and that the ruling Hrvatska demokratska zajednica (HDZ), the Croatian Democratic Union, was simply a center-right coalition were ignored. This is astonishing in view of the relative silence surrounding British reactions to the ascent of right-wing movements in other countries, notably in Italy, where a center-right coalition dominated by the far right—in several respects more to the right than Tudjman's—achieved power in Rome. Curiously, eminent figures in this Italian rightist coalition also included staunch anti-Croats in the guise of ultranationalist irredentists.[46]

As we mentioned, the Yugoslav War does not respect traditional right-left divisions. Indeed, there are signs that an ideological alliance between the far right and the far left is taking shape under the auspices of moral relativism, if not outward sympathy for "ethnic cleansing." In the conclusion of his film *Bosna!* Bernard-Henri Levy has pointed to that chilling prospect. In Britain, this right-left entente has already been capitalized on and trumpeted by extremists.[47] As a recent Students against Genocide (SAGE) report and other research have disclosed, one group distinguished itself for its all-pervasive and well-funded propaganda combining Marxist dogmatism and the defense of exclusivist ideologies under a veil of trendy liberalism.[48] This group, the Revolutionary Communist Party (RCP), is organized in several fronts and subsidiary groups, but its discourse can be best analyzed in the monthly review *Living Marxism*.[49] Data from this magazine appeared in an article in the influential journal *Foreign Policy* by El Paso journalist Peter Brock.[50] According to Roy Gutman, "members of the Serb delegation were seen passing out copies of [the] article to mediators David Owen and Thorvald Stoltenberg."[51] The group consistently tried to deny that genocide was occurring, defined the siege of Sarajevo as a media "invention," and disseminated in strategic places images of alleged "Muslim atrocities" against the Serbs, kindly provided by the Belgrade official news agency Tanjug.[52] These few but well-organized militants may have been easily forgotten had their programs and slogans not resonated so well with the Foreign Office's interests. Interestingly, *Living Marxism's* former assistant editor Joan Phillips has been working since 1995 for the Economic Intelligence Unit (EIU) under the name of Joan Hoey.[53]

The more the pressures for Western intervention grew, the more the voice of Serbophiles was insinuated into mainstream political discourse. On May 31, 1995, emergency debates on the situation in Bosnia took place in the House of Commons and the House of Lords. While discussions in the latter were characterized by their usual composure, the debate raged in the Commons. There, it was possible to hear from Ulster Unionists, Conservatives, and the Labour's left the same arguments popularized by Serbian nationalists in their propaganda. All analytical attempts were diverted as Germany was blamed for its "hasty" recognition of Slovenia and Croatia, a leitmotif of anti-European isolationism. This was also a tremendous way of sheltering English national pride and marshalling nationalist sentiments at the very moment when London was at the center of international attacks for its failures in Bosnia. Following are some quotes from the May 1995 emergency debates: [54]

It is now absolutely impossible to judge and say, "These are the people who ought to be supported for a particular reason." (Former Conservative prime minister Edward Heath [col. 1018])

The Germans established a fascist Croatia during the war. Later, the German government recognised Croatia. The British Government went along with that decision, it is said because of a concession over the social chapter. [Hon. Members: "Rubbish."] Whatever the truth is, there was some negotiation that took a reluctant British Government into recognition of Croatia. (Former Labour energy secretary Tony Benn [col. 1019])

I condemn without hesitation the bombing of the Serbs. I know that it was American inspired and I think that it was politically, militarily and diplomatically a disaster. . . . If the recognition of Croatia, Bosnia and the other states of the former Yugoslavia was wrong—if we were bounced into it—why is that now the basis on which we foresee a settlement being made? Recognition was wrong then and it is still wrong today. (Ulster Unionist M.P. John D. Taylor [col. 1043])

Political friends of many years have asked me, "How can you do anything that seems to endorse ethnic cleansing?" But is it ethnic cleansing? Are we quite sure about that, because the history of those particular Muslims is not ethnic? (Senior Labour M.P. Tam Dalyell [col. 1049])

It is no wonder that the American President—far more interested in New Hampshire than in old Sarajevo—advocates a Balkan policy of bombing Serbia back into the stone age from a very safe height. (Senior Conservative M.P. Sir Peter Tapsell [col. 1053])

If one third of the Bosnian population in the Bosnia-Herzegovina conflict—the Serbs—are not interested in living with the other two thirds, how can we make them? (Senior Conservative M.P. Sir Geoffrey Johnson Smith [col. 1058])

The Bosnian Government and the Bosnian Serbs have attacked and counter-attacked each other. In doing so, both sides have violated the Sarajevo exclusion zone. (Leader of the House of Lords, Conservative Peer Viscount Cranborne [col. 1119])

As one can see, the same arguments appear across the political spectrum from the far left to the far right. But what is more tragic is that all these relativist statements and instances of German-bashing were used as rhetorical devices to stave off any idea of firmer British commitment in Bosnia. In particular, moral relativism was the dominant discourse used by those opposing the lifting of the arms embargo that, at that stage, would have saved thousands of Bosnian lives.

Where did the British politicians take their wisdom from? Where did they obtain their briefings? At this stage, all possible answers are still at a speculative level, but there are several clues. Until at least February 1995, the Foreign Office was staffed by "experts" who indeed lacked any overall expertise on the Balkans. On the other hand, Noel Malcolm suggests a connection between people like Conservative defense secretary Malcolm Rifkind and Serbian lobbyists.[55] In both cases, an important repository of information was precisely the pro-Serbian tradition we have previously described.

The journalist and part-time historian Nora Beloff deserves special mention here. A militant anticommunist and implacable critic of Tito,[56] she relied on the Serbian émigré community in London for her information. As expected, Beloff's interpretations are routinely filtered through the prism of Serbian nationalism. In one article, published well after Croatia and Slovenia started to mobilize for independence, she stated, "Reports on the death of Yugoslavia are . . . exaggerated."[57] This was in line with the upholding of Milošević's diplomatic pretense that Yugoslavia should be preserved as a single state, while stressing that "the concept of Yugoslavia was conceived in the 19th century by romantic Croats."[58] Echoing Belgrade's views, Beloff upheld the popular Tanjug picture of newly independent Croatia as a fascist laboratory: "Laws of citizenship favour patrial [*sic*] Croats, extortionate taxes are levied against Serb-owned properties, and no Serb can hope for redress in a Croat court against arson and assault. In these circumstances, constitutional guarantees of minority rights should not be taken more seriously than the whole array of human rights promised in Stalin's 1935 constitution, at the height of terror."[59] These arguments, mixing facts with fiction, are mirror images of Serbian propaganda that emanated from Belgrade since the late 1980s and prepared the ground for the war. Although Beloff's true allegiances were evident, she was still apparently consulted by British politicians and her views reported in the media. In her lobbying activities, Beloff mentions a correspondence with foreign secretary Douglas Hurd in which she argued against the recognition of Croatia and Slovenia. According to

Beloff, Hurd agreed with her, while contending that "he needed to placate Helmut Kohl."[60]

The same rationale and justification for Serbian propaganda are included in a monograph written by John Zametica and published in the London International Institute for Strategic Studies (IISS) Adelphi Papers series.[61] In this pamphlet, which in the British political environment was then accorded the status of an "objective" report, Zametica identified the causes of the war in the "incompatible national aspirations" of the peoples of Yugoslavia.[62] He also blamed the current war on Titoist politics and especially the "deeply divisive" 1974 Federal Constitution, which decentralized—or attempted to decentralize—the country to an unprecedented extent. But the main blame for the current tragedy was put on the Albanians as a people. It was their revolt that "provided the catalyst for the subsequent rise of Serbian nationalism"—that is, "Kosovo made Milošević."[63] He repeated the popular cliché that Serbs risked oblivion as a result of Albanians'—and other Muslims'—demographic increase.[64] As is well known, the author, who holds an M.A. from the London School of Economics and a Ph.D. from Corpus Christi College, Cambridge, became the mouthpiece of Bosnian Serb war criminals Radovan Karadžić and General Ratko Mladić (after Serbianizing his name into Jovan Zametica).[65]

Zametica's work provides us with the rare opportunity to see an important piece of moral relativism at work: his ideas were used directly to justify both the politics of ethnic cleansing and Britain's pro-Serbian line. We can also see how deep the influence of such inferences was on British academic and political circles. What is more revealing is that Zametica's public pronouncements had been readily and seriously taken by both politicians and academics.[66] Noel Malcolm advances the hypothesis that Zametica's public pronouncements condoning British politics in the Balkans had a convenient impact, since he "was still giving lectures to British military training courses as an 'independent' expert long after the start of the Yugoslav war."[67] British politics had been moving in a vacuum that was filled by Serbs, who controlled the most sophisticated propaganda machine in the Balkans, which they had inherited from the Yugoslav state (Croatian propaganda has been much more ineffective, due to internal divisions and lack of expertise; Bosnian propaganda was virtually nonexistent during the whole initial phase of the war).

Noel Malcolm also recalls the role of Belgrade-born Jovan Gvozedenović, whose used the name John Kennedy and is associated, through the Conservative Council on Eastern Europe, with Conservative M.P. Henry Bellingham. The latter was then parliamentary secretary to Malcolm Rifkind, a particularly staunch opponent to the lifting of the arms embargo. Another pro-Serbian advisor to Rifkind was the right-wing activist David Hart.[68]

I have mentioned here only a few examples of pro-Serbian activists, in both the Government and academia. The list is much longer, and there are works dealing with the subject in more detail.[69] With such a distinguished lineage of London-based authors ready to condone the Serbs' worst atrocities, the Belgrade government and its allies in Bosnia have felt immensely protected in carrying out their monumental onslaught in the 1990s.

A more tacit form of support for Serbian policies came not only from "intellectuals," but also from the highest echelons of the British government. Indeed, the appointment of Lord (Peter) Carrington as chairman of the European Union's Conference on the Former Yugoslavia, chairman at the peace conference in the Hague (September 7–December 12, 1991), and, finally, chief negotiator at the London Conference (August 26–27, 1992) may be conceived of as relating to this pro-Serbian tradition.[70] After the failure of his plan, Carrington had been strongly opposed to any German initiative in the Balkans. His pro-Serbian bent was probably due to the influence of Fitzroy Maclean, the same leading advocate of German-bashing who had been Churchill's envoy in the Balkans.[71] Lord Carrington was eventually replaced by Lord (David) Owen as a representative of the European Union in the August 1993 International Peace Conference on the Former Yugoslavia (ICFY), which took over from the London Conference.[72]

Prime Minister John Major, foreign secretary Douglas Hurd, and defense secretary Malcolm Rifkind (Hurd's protégé and his successor in the Foreign Office job) are among those most commonly singled out for their mismanagement of the Bosnian crisis.[73] This verdict is realistic in view of the fact that, as Adrian Hastings from Leeds University stresses, "Britain also effectively seized the control of the issue even before it began its Presidency [of the WEU] by getting Lord Carrington appointed as chief negotiator and ensuring that he represented the viewpoint of the Foreign Office."[74] This role was reinforced by the fact that Britain is also one of the five members of the UN Security Council. The French historian Jacques Julliard offers a similar assessment: "In the image of Carrington's European plan, which consecrated the victory of Serbian ethnic cleansing in Croatia, the Vance-Owen plan, which carries the double stamp of the European Community and the UN, has officialized and legitimized ethnic cleansing in Bosnia-Herzegovina."[75]

As critics of the Foreign and Commonwealth Office have disclosed, the latter listens carefully to its own officials. Yet, "while several have had long experience in the embassy in Belgrade, none has any experience of Bosnia where Britain did not even have a consulate. . . . Hence the basic Foreign Office perception has been a Serbian one."[76] The fact that Belgrade inherited the diplomatic and bureaucratic apparatus of the Yugoslav state meant that it enjoyed the upper hand in the diffusion of its views abroad. This explains why most of the Foreign Office connections came indeed from Serbian propagandists diffused throughout many British institutions, including the academy.

> Again and again, the things which Mr. Hurd has said, and the way he says them, actually derive from Serbian propaganda. . . . The initial lie was that this was a civil war between Bosnian villagers in which any outsiders would be quickly attacked from both sides. Once this calculated misreading of the war was accepted by Britain without question, everything else followed. It was, intellectually, already a siding with Serbia, because it was quite untrue. It simply provided the base line for the Serbian argument that they should be left to get on with their campaign of annexation. In much the same way, even at the time of the London conference, Mr. Hurd spoke of president Izctbegović not as a president of Bosnia but as a "leader of the Muslims"—exactly the way Karadžić described him.[77]

Also at stake has been the reputation of the former UN commander in Bosnia, the British Lieutenant-General Sir Michael Rose, who in May 1995 warned that Sarajevo might soon resemble Grozny, Chechnya.[78] Rose's best-known refrain was "we cannot bomb our way to peace." Robert Wright recalls an ABC News special on the UN's failure in Bosnia which "featured videotape of an unguarded conversation with a subordinate in which Rose basically calls the Muslims lazy bums who want the United Nations to do their fighting for them."[79] Rose ended his assignment on January 24, 1995, to be replaced by British Major-General Rupert Smith, of much more moderate and acceptable views.[80]

Amid the chorus of British appeasement, there have been three notable exceptions. The philosopher Sir Karl Popper (1902–1994) in one of his last public statements, called for air attacks on Serb artillery positions to end the fighting. At age ninety-one, he boldly claimed, "[Serbian aggression] has to be stopped now, because the murder is going on now. It has to be stopped because of the future of mankind, not only of Europe."[81] Only his disciple, former Conservative prime minister Margaret Thatcher, seems to have heeded the call, responding with her characteristic rhetorical prowess.

The third exception comes precisely from the opposite end of the political spectrum, the former Labour Party prime minister Michael Foot.[82] Foot produced a film for BBC called *Two Hours from London* in recognition of the geographical and cultural proximity of Sarajevo to Britain.

The Exaggeration of the Serbian-Croat Confrontation

Explanations of the war have characteristically appeared in a Russian *matrioshka* format, in which wider explanations contain derivative explanations in a concentric pattern—as bigger dolls contain smaller ones. One explanation saw the conflict as basically a Serbo-Croat clash. A derivative account saw Croatian independence as the catalyst. Within the latter, a smaller variant appeared that saw Germany's recognition of Croatian independence as the cause of the war. Yet a smaller doll—in fact, the least plausible explanation—became common currency: Germany was to blame for virtually all misdeeds in the Balkans. In the smallest doll, a Fourth Reich conspiracy thesis purported to explain the disintegration of Yugoslavia and the desire to carve the Balkans into separate spheres of influence.

However, the German recognition thesis is relatively easy to demolish. Since the first postulate of the thesis, namely, the definition of the conflict as basically Serbo-Croat, was wrong, all the subexplanations contained within it had to tumble like dominoes. Germany's recognition of Croatia was not relevant because the independence of Croatia was not the central issue and the war was not essentially a Serbo-Croat confrontation. Nevertheless, the inertia of prejudice has enticed many politicians, as well as academics, to stick to older and easier mental habits.

Because since its beginning the conflict was presented as basically a Serbo-Croat tug-of-war, several other assumptions followed. Therefore it is imperative to consider briefly this predominant position, which has been made popular by the journalist Misha Glenny.[83] If we were in search of monocausal explanations, the conflict may better be explained as being primarily between Albanians and Serbs,[84] since the initial targets were the Albanians rather than the Croats.

At a much later stage, when the pattern and plans of an unprecedently aggressive nationalism were laid out, Slovenia and Croatia became the targets. Since Slovenia was the richest region of Yugoslavia, it has been suggested that the Serbs were punishing the rebellious republic as a form of "revenge" for its effrontery. To credulous and uninformed international audiences, the conflict was presented as the poor south against the arrogant north, a classic role reversal of the Serbs' own conflict with the Albanians. But the Slovenes had also shown an unparalleled solidarity with the plight of the Albanians, who were the poorest ethnic group in Yugoslavia.[85] it was indeed the abolition of the provincial autonomy of Kosovo and Vojvodina (the latter inhabited by Hungarians, Slovaks, and other minorities) that, by revealing the regime's intentions, induced most Slovenes, hitherto staunch supporters of Yugoslav unity, to ponder openly for the first time the possibility of secession.[86]

Yet the conflict was commonly painted as Serbo-Croat at the core. Such a view has been repeated ad infinitum in several derivative interpretations of the conflict, but especially by British and American mainstream politicians. Until well after the siege of Sarajevo began, this cliché was the daily staple of the U.S. government's official interpretations of the war.

In their futile attempts to maintain the unity of Yugoslavia against powerful centrifugal trends, most Western governments de facto wedded themselves to a pro-Serbian line. Implying that the conflict was basically Serbo-Croat meant denying the harassment and persecution suffered by the other minorities. Persecution against all sorts of minorities has been well documented since before 1991.[87] In the south, Albanians, Bulgarians, Macedonians, and others were living in terror between the hammer of Serbian persecution and the anvil of their own reactive nationalisms. In the north, up to the border with Hungary—in Vojvodina, a land rich with minorities—Ruthenes, Slovaks, Ukrainians, Romanians, Hungarians, and others were subjected to increasing harassment.

Hence, the trouble did not simply stem from Croat-Serbian rivalry. The trouble lay elsewhere. It did not rest in Serbia as a whole either, but rather in Belgrade, where the destiny of Yugoslavia was mapped out many years ago. Perhaps it did not even dwell in Belgrade as such, but in that small elite of military cadres, populist politicians, organic intellectuals, and diaspora propagandists who laid the foundation for the war. Since these elites had abundant connections with the West, both in mainstream political circles and in the academy, it was not easy to attack them. Against all evidence, the Croats—and the other minorities as a corollary—were presented as "the problem" instead.

Post-Maastricht Anti-Europeanism and the Resilience of the Nation-State

Britain's attitude blended a customary British obsession over the maintenance of international borders, with an anti-European, particularly anti-German, slant. British mistrust and uneasiness over the process of European unification intervened to frame a high-handed pro-Serbian foreign policy. The belief that a strong, centralized Yugoslavia—or Serbia in its place—could restrain Germany's strength has been the pivotal concept of this ill-starred inclination. The British government "wished to maintain a large, Serb-dominated Yugoslavia. When that collapsed, it fell back instead on supporting a 'Greater Serbia' because it saw a powerful enlarged Serbia, achieved with a good deal of underhand British support, as a counterweight to German influence in the Balkans."[88]

Britain has indeed been using the Balkan War as a stepping-stone to impose its own European politics. To the cynics in Whitehall and the Foreign Office, the hundreds of thousands killed by Serbian expansionism mattered precious little. What mattered most was to coordinate the different factions of Conservative politicians, trying to keep a balance between anti- and pro-European elements, but basically sending the world a signal that the lives of Europeans killed in Bosnia were meaningless. As Hastings pointed out, "The Foreign Office remains farcically preoccupied with maintaining a 'balance of power' in central Europe and 'containing' Germany."[89]

Another fault line is the one separating the apologists of the nation-state from the defenders of supranational political aggregations which, by their nature, need to include a strong component of pluri-nationalism and multiculturalism. The former claim that national sovereignty is inviolable; the latter say that human rights, including the right to self-determination, are priorities. The former, the state-centered group, is exemplified not only by British and French attitudes, but especially by the United Nations, whose very existence is tied to the concept of state sovereignty. The United Nations is nothing more than a powerful coalition of purported "nation-states" and their ruling elites.

Bosnia and other crises have shown that the United Nations is ready to trample on the right of small peoples and small groups in the name of the principle of state sovereignty. When one of its members is attacked, the United Nations has demonstrated stern ability to react: for instance, when Kuwait was invaded by Iraq in August 1991, the United Nations, led by a firm American leadership, stood up as a single entity in the defense of the sovereignty of one of its members. Why has this been possible in Kuwait and not in Bosnia? One answer must be found in the United Nations' worship of state integrity, inviolability, and unity, more than in the popular perception of the Gulf War as a war for oil. Rather paradoxically, the issue of vital oil supplies was used to justify the war and to mobilize an international public opinion for which economic issues were far more important than territorial and humanitarian ones. In contrast, Slovenia, Croatia, and Kosovo were not full members of the United Nations when they were invaded and subjected to ferocious repression; this may explain the so-called international community's reluctance to intervene. Bosnia was attacked on its first day of independence, but the invasion plan had been drawn up long before. Bosnia was confronted with the denial of its own sovereignty as a sort of punishment for having dared to secede. The idea of a multinational Bosnia was incompatible with the prototype of the nation-state for which Serbia was fighting.

Inefficiency and indecision over Croatia and Bosnia have led to deep and perhaps irreparable splits within the European Union. There are signs of an emerging Anglo-French alliance, not only with respect to the former Yugoslavia, but also over a wide spectrum of French initiatives (support for corrupt central governments in Africa, nuclear testing in the Pacific, arms sales to client states in the Third World, resurgence of colonial ties, European economic and legislative policy, and so on). If this is the case, the very idea of European union may be threatened, since the risk of being dominated by France is no more palatable to most Europeans than the prospect of being dominated by Germany.

Moreover, the Yugoslav crisis has dealt a heavy blow to the legitimacy of the European idea. To many non-Europeans the very mention of Europe evokes complicity with and tolerance of ethnic cleansing, especially since the primary victims are Muslims. As Jean Baudrillard has pointed out, Europe now evokes spite and repugnance among ordinary Bosnians, who were previously committed to European ideals of tolerance and multiculturalism. Islamic intellectuals have denounced the ominous choice of 1992 for the celebration of Maastricht and the Act of European Union as heavily charged with symbols of genocide: five hundred years before, in 1492, the Islamic Kingdom of Granada was destroyed, while the Jews were expelled from Spain or forced to convert to Catholicism. Was not this also a historical case of ethnic cleansing? Was not this also the beginning of the genocide for hundreds of nations in the Americas? How could European leaders be so shortsighted as to discount the deep moral implications of such symbolic errors? Indeed, 1992 was the first great leap forward of European revisionism. Many raised their voice in protest but were ignored.[90] The year 1992 may well be the year that history marks as the beginning of the collapse of the moral foundation of the European Union. While ethnic cleansing moved from Croatia to Bosnia and became a widespread practice, Europeans—and Americans— were witnessing the unfolding tragedy from the comfortable opulence of their armchairs. While they were told that all sides were to blame, they became finally saturated with images of violence to the point that no emotional reaction could be discerned and no will was left to comprehend the sequence of events.[91]

Moral Relativism in Action: Equidistance and Holocaust Denial

One of the first headlines dispensing the official Serbian story that the crimes were committed by the victims, rather than the aggressors, came from the respectable London newspaper the *Independent*. The author was the daily's correspondent from the UN headquarters in New York, Leonard Doyle. Among the article's contentions was that several slaughters committed in Bosnia, including the gruesome televised one known as the bread line massacre in Sarajevo, were carried out by the Muslims "as a propaganda ploy" to win international sympathy.[92]

Like rumors and gossip, misinformation related to wars can travel far. Once something has been said to prove or disprove a particular point, even without evidence to back it up, it will indubitably be used by propagandists. Nationalists, populists, and warmongers do not need to corroborate their assertions with data. They rely on the simple authority of their position to authenticate and validate their insinuations. All they need is a name, a signature on a declaration or a statement. If the latter comes in support of their strategy and viewpoints, they will use it as evidence at any suitable time. In the end, the propagandists themselves will firmly believe in it. In the case of Bosnia, any small lie, insinuation, or innuendo was used by Serbian lobbies in the West to press their case for moral relativism. Doyle's reports in the *Independent* were later dismissed, but, as Tom Gjelten recalls, "his point has been made. Serb media still cite the *Independent* story" with great bombast in order to prove that all that fuss about the bad Serbs is pure fiction and rests only in other people's imagination.[93]

This practice of pinning the blame on the victims has found a major promoter in the United Nations. One of its most notorious exponents there has been Sarajevo's first UN commander, the Canadian Major General Lewis MacKenzie.[94] UN bureaucrats commonly repeat that the Bosnian Muslims are willing to stage attacks on themselves in an effort to grab the world's attention and trigger a military intervention on their behalf. "The argument, of course, has an appealing ring to Western government ministers always ready for reasons not to get involved in Bosnia: if the Muslims are this conniving, they don't deserve to be helped."[95] According to Gjelten, MacKenzie's case is simply the tip of the iceberg. He "merely reflects what UN service instills in its peacekeepers."[96] Bosnia has been a test case of international complicity in attempted genocide. Unfortunately, there are several signs that Bosnia's fate may not remain exceptional, that the Bosnians may share their destiny with other unfortunate peoples. During the culmination of Serbian aggression, another attempted genocide was unleashed against the Tutsi minority in Rwanda. As in the Bosnian case, genocide was accompanied by all sort of denials and connivance, as the interests of neocolonialism coincided with that of the church and various missionary groups. When in June 1994 a group of journalists tried to contact some eminent Anglican prelates, they received a chilling response:

> The two churchmen were asked if they condemned the murderers who had filled Rwanda's churches with bodies. They refused to answer. They dodged questions, became agitated, their voices reaching an even higher pitch, and the core of Rwanda's crisis was laid bare. Even the most senior members of the Anglican church were acting as errand boys for political masters who have preached murder and filled the rivers with blood. "I don't want to condemn one group without condemning the other one," Archbishop Mshamihigo said, immediately after he had condemned the RPF [Rwandan Patriotic Front, now in power]. "Our wish is not to condemn, but to show the situation that is happening in the country." The journalists walked out.[97]

This emblematic case of moral relativism shows up the most powerful nonstate organization in Africa, the church. But the occurrence was not limited to the churches. As soon as some doubts concerning the nature and extent of the Tutsi genocide were rumored about, they rapidly spread and were picked up by international government leaders. The more these leaders were in a position to do something about it, the more they tried to deny what was occurring. Denial first occurred in the main African capitals and in the Organization for African Unity (OAU). Then it inevitably reached Washington. President Clinton and his administration openly refused to use the word "genocide" in relation to Rwanda. And as if this were not enough, they also warned their staff to avoid using that word, fearing its political implications.[98] An entire population was systematically eliminated at the hands of a recognized government by a precise plan of biological homogenization, yet the U.S. administration was putting all its weight into denying what was occurring. An acknowledgment of the facts would have triggered excessive pressure for action at a moment when both Britain and the United States were trying not to get involved in international "adventures."

Similarly, British elites have repeatedly tried to deny that genocide was occurring in the former Yugoslavia. At the beginning, even the media tacitly accepted official Serbian lore. Then, forced by the tide of events and also by the sheer number of their colleagues executed at the hands of Serbian snipers, media professionals chose to reveal the tragedy in its entirety. This helped to inform the world, but not to devise new international strategies or propel major governments into action.

Bosnia: Our Future

As stated at the outset, the Bosnian conflict has often been presented as an atavistic contest in an orgy of primordial instinct. Not only is this view misleading, but the opposite prospect is far more plausible, namely, that Bosnia represents a kind of futuristic war. Bosnia *is* our future for two reasons: first, because it was a multiethnic society displaying a supreme degree of assimilation; second, because diasporas have played a central role in the conflict.

Several scholars and journalists have drawn parallels between the makeup of Bosnia and the makeup of multiracial or multiethnic societies, particularly those resulting from immigration.[99] But few have noticed that Bosnia represents an extremely advanced stage of a multiethnic society. It is a multiethnic society based on radical assimilation, where all constituent ethnic groups have lost their cultural traits and marks of distinction but have *not* lost their identities. Hence, the parallels between contemporary plural societies and prewar Bosnia are abundant.

Secularization is just an ultimate form of assimilation. Since Bosnia is (or was) one of the most secularized societies in Europe, the most commonly quoted "distinctive" marker, religion, is no more than an empty shell. Most "combatants" were secularized to the bone, and many had been for at least four generations. The conflict can be better described as one between Muslim atheists, Catholic atheists, and Orthodox atheists.[100] All existing data indicate that the level of church or mosque attendance in Serbia, Croatia, and Bosnia was low, and in Serbia even lower.[101] Hence, descriptions of the war as a religious or ethnoreligious phenomenon are tendentiously specious.

Moreover, the Bosnian War represents a particular version of a general upsurge of group identities at a time of global homogenization. As the world is rapidly becoming more integrated and interconnected, old values and principles of stability crumble. At the same time, globalization bids for planetary homogenization and the spread of a context-free and spaceless transculture.[102] Like communism and national socialism, globalism results in cultural assimilation. Assimilation may lead to the destructions of all forms of distinctiveness, but it does not have the power to erase memory and descent, which make up the pillars of ethnic identity. In other words, assimilation does not lead to an undoing of ethnonational identities. On the contrary, it may lead to their radicalization: identities remain dormant behind a smoke screen of homogeneity, until they find the opportunity to spring back with a vengeance. Identities may be assisted and rendered more evident by cultural relics and artifacts: historical buildings, places of worship, and other signs of a now blurred cultural heritage. Yet memories may linger even if outward signs of identity fall into oblivion. In other words, ethnonational identity is primarily about memories and putative descent, more than about facts and artifacts.

In a homogenized world, political violence has an aim and a function of its own. Violent conflagrations are perhaps the most effective way to remold and revitalize quiescent identities. For every assimilated group in the world there is a potential Milošević waiting to use aggression as a tool for reviving dormant identities while building up his own following. Though the Bosnian War has resulted in further destruction and homogeneity, it has been a boundary-building process. Among its most powerful results was to instill and reshape a sense of community among victims as well as among aggressors.

Few have noticed how the most appalling massacres increasingly occur between similar rather than radically distinct peoples. In Rwanda, barely any cultural divergence distinguishes the Hutus from their Tutsi victims, yet the slaughter has been one of the most vicious in this century. It has drawn a permanent line between the two groups that statesmen, alleged peace negotiators, and Rwandan "nationalists" may ignore only at their own risk. In the future, they had better not disregard this manmade chasm if they wish to avoid a repetition of the tragedy.

Bosnia is the war of the future also because of the central role played by diasporas. Diasporas reflect the ultimate stage of assimilation, yet their involvement in radical politics is undeniable. It could be said that the more diasporas are assimilated and the more they are distant and unrelated to their respective trouble spots, the more they are radical and ultranationalist. The targets of their xenophobia are not usually their immediate neighbors of ethnic competitors within the "host" country, but rather the primarily unknown antagonists of "their" distant homeland. Hence diasporas move in a double cognitive vacuum: on the one hand, the concealed ignorance of the homeland; on the other, the arrogant unfamiliarity with the enemies of the homeland. This does not deter them from expressing their group identity in more radical and fanatical terms than most "hyphenated" groups and individuals. Writing and rewriting histories and selecting and sifting all kind of data are intrinsic parts of their agenda.

Conclusion

Moral relativism is not an ideology, but a practice. In relation to Bosnia, its consequences are immediately discernible and in view of the entire world. It is a blueprint for genocide in an age of mass communication. As Thomas Cushman and Stjepan Meštrović have pointed out in the introduction to this volume, at one time we could justify our unresponsiveness by asserting that "we did not know." Today, lacking any such excuse, we see our hypocrisy revealed in its nakedness: since the media have propagated images of the Bosnian genocide on television screens across the world, we can no longer say, "we did not know." The most we can utter is "we *did not want* to know," or "we *deliberately ignored* what was going on there." In order to legitimize nonintervention, we found a face-saving rationale, suitably provided by the stratagem of moral relativism: apportioning blame to all sides became the most convenient device to justify noninvolvement. Since everybody was to blame, as a result of "Balkan savagery," the conflict became "intractable," and no clear goal was discernible ahead. Those Balkan savages are outside the realm of universal human values, and perhaps are really inhuman at heart, so peoples in the Balkans do not even deserve the most elementary human rights. Or so the story went.

In this chapter, I have attempted to show why these views prevailed in Britain, a country that exerted a crucial influence when the fate of Bosnia was at stake. If the Bosnian Muslims had been promptly and adequately armed, the situation might have produced a stalemate, which in turn might have yielded a cease-fire and then a peace agreement in a reasonably short time. The British policy of denying the Bosnians the means to secure their survival resulted from the joint pressures of two factors: pro-Serbian lobbying and the inability to recognize the consequence of British errors since the inception of the crisis.

It may be claimed that there were also objective strategic interests among Western powers to avoid any visible show of force in the settling of disputes within Europe. But French and British attitudes reflected something much stronger than apathy. In Britain, the ferocity and pervasiveness of pro-Serbian propaganda among well-identifiable groups, including the far left, suggest the presence of a factor deeper than mere indifference.

Perhaps the most important "contingent" factor has been the firm belief in a thorough Serbian victory. At the beginning, there was the belief—challenging all rationality—that Yugoslavia could survive as a unitary state. Germany's recognition was hence greeted with cries of high treason. After Germany was castigated and any further German move was prevented, the belief remained that Serbia could win militarily and reduce Bosnia to a collection of "bantustans" in the framework of a recentralized rump Yugoslavia. Both Britain and France fervently supported this option. A perspective shared by these two countries was the conceit that Yugoslavia's disintegration was a "disease" likely to "infect" their neocolonial satellites, particularly in Africa. If the international state system is naturally conservative and on guard against secession, such is particularly the case among those countries that thrive on (neo)colonial liaisons.

NOTES

In writing this chapter I benefited from the advice of several people. In particular, I wish to thank Noel Malcolm (London) for advice on the section about the "archaeology" of British attitudes and Wayles Browne (Cornell) for suggestions on the part relating to British Serbophilia in this century. Warm thanks are also due to Pamela Ballinger (Johns Hopkins), Branka Magas (London), Daniel Kofman (Oxford), Peter Marsh (Syracuse), Joze Pirjevec (Trieste), and Norman Stone (Oxford) for reading and commenting on specific aspects of this essay. Finally, the late professor Ernest Gellner (Cambridge/Prague) provided excellent feedback, especially on moral and cognitive relativism, when we met in Slovenia just a month before he died. To his memory, as an outstanding figure in the academic study of nationalism, I wish to dedicate this chapter.

1. Some valuable interpretations of the war can be found in Mark Almond, *Europe's Backyard War: The War in the Balkans* (London: Heinemann, 1994); Christopher Bennett, *Yugoslavia's Bloody Collapse: Causes, Course and Consequences* (New York: New York University Press, 1994; London: Hurst, 1994); Branka Magas, *The Destruction of Yugoslavia: Tracing the Break-Up, 1980–92* (London: Verso, 1993); and Noel Malcolm, *Bosnia: A Short History* (New York: New York University Press, 1994), 213.

2. The standard opposition in the philosophical sciences is however between moral and cognitive relativism (Ernest Gellner, personal observation). See also Ernest Gellner, *Relativism and the Social Sciences* (Cambridge: Cambridge University Press, 1985).

3. Ernest Gellner, "Anything Goes," *Times Literary Supplement,* June 16, 1995, 6–8.

4. Samuel Huntington, "The Clash of Civilizations?" *Foreign Affairs* 72, no. 3 (1993): 21–49.

5. For a critique of Huntington's thesis, see Fouad Ajami, "The Summoning," *Foreign Affairs* 72, no. 4 (1993): 2ff. The articles were republished as Samuel P. Huntington and Fouad Ajami, *The Clash of Civilizations? The Debate,* Foreign Affairs Reader (New York: Foreign Affairs, 1993). Ajami argues that "civilizations do not control states, states control civilizations." See also Fouad Ajami, "In Europe's Shadows," *New Republic,* November 21, 1994, 29–37. The front cover is dedicated to "Europe's long, vicious war against Islam in the Balkans."

6. A quote from a Serbian "propagandist," Dr. Radovanovitch, then (in 1932) director of the Press Bureau of Belgrade's Presidency of the Council, should help clarify this point: "Salonica has never been Greek; it was a Serb city peopled with Southern Serbs. Its affiliation to Greece has been its death sentence! It will not revive, it will not find again its lost prosperity, until it becomes again the great commercial port of the Balkans towards the Mediterranean and the Orient.

And it cannot become this great port unless it returns to Yugoslavia, of which it is a natural and historical dependency. It is the same with Drama, Seres, Janina, Kastoria, which have been of no importance since they were delivered to the degenerate Greek nation." Cited in Henri Pozzi, *Black Hand over Europe* (London: Francis Mott, 1935), 101; originally published as *La guerre revient* (Paris: P. Berger, 1933). In one thing Radovanovitch agreed with Greek nationalists, although his conclusion was different: "There is no Macedonian question. There isn't one because there are no Macedonian people. The regions which the Turks called 'Macedonia' are in reality purely Serb" (94).

7. Robert J. Donia and John V. A. Fine, *Bosnia and Hercegovina: A Tradition Betrayed* (New York: Columbia University Press; London: Hurst, 1994). Bosnia's pluralist heritage in terms of syncretic movements and "religious bridge building" dates back at least to the late Middle Ages and is well documented by H. T. Norris, *Islam in the Balkans: Religion and Society between Europe and the Arab World* (London: Hurst, 1994), 263–68.

8. Bennett, op. cit.

9. For France's special ties with Serbia, see Ernst Birke, *Frankreich und Ostmitteleuropa im 19. Jahrhundert* (Köln: Bohlau, 1960).

10. See Stephen Clissold, "Occupation and Resistance," in *A Short History of Yugoslavia: From Early Times to 1966,* ed. Stephen Clissold (Cambridge: Cambridge University Press, 1966), 212.

11. David Rieff, *Slaughterhouse: Bosnia and the Failure of the West* (New York: Simon and Schuster, 1995), 69.

12. See Stjepan G. Meštrović, *The Balkanization of the West: The Confluence of Postmodernism and Postcommunism* (London: Routledge, 1994).

13. Robert William Seton-Watson, *Disraeli, Gladstone, and the Eastern Question* (London: F. Cass, 1962; New York: Norton, 1972 [1st limited ed., London: Macmillan, 1935]).

14. Leopold von Ranke, *A History of Servia and the Servian Revolution* (London: John Murray, 1848), 435 ff. (reprint, New York: Da Capo, 1973). German original ed., Leopold von Ranke, *Die Serbische Revolution: Aus Serbischen Papieren und Mitteilungen,* 2. Ausg. (Berlin: Duncker and Humblot, 1844). See also Leopold von Ranke, *Serbia und die Turkei im neunzehnten jahrhundert* (Leipzig: Duncker and Humblot, 1879).

15. Mrs. Alexander Kerr, preface to von Ranke, *History of Servia,* x-xi.

16. See John Mason Neale, ed., *Voices from the East: Documents on the Present State and Working of the Oriental Church,* translated from the original Russian, Slavonic, and French, with notes (London: Joseph Masters, 1859; New York: AMS Press, 1974). The collection includes translations by Neale of Andrei Nikolaevich Murav'ev (1806–1874) and Innokentii, archbishop of Kherson and Taurida (1800–1857). His main work is in John Mason Neale, *A History of the Holy Eastern Church,* 5 vols. (London: Joseph Masters, 1847–73; New York:

AMS Press, 1976). For a good introduction to the works of Neale and on the relations between the Orthodox Eastern Church and the Anglican Communion, see in particular Leon Litvack, *John Mason Neale and the Quest for Sobornost* (Oxford: Clarendon Press; New York: Oxford University Press, 1994). On a more eulogistic level, see A. G. Lough, *John Mason Neale: Priest Extraordinary* (Newton Abbot: Lough, 1976). Neale's fascinating research also includes a copious collection of hymns and carols, biographies of Christian saints, commentaries on the Psalms, essays on liturgiology and church history, studies on the so-called Jansenist Church of Holland, the Brothers of the Common Life, the Gallican Church, the Church of Malabar, the Roman, Ambrosian, Mozarabic, Gallican, Greek, Coptic, Armenian, and Syriac rites, and the liturgies of Saints Mark, James, Clement, Chrysostom, and Basil.

17. Harold William Vazeille Temperley, *History of Serbia* (London: G. Bell and Sons, 1917; New York: AMS Press, 1970 [1st U.S. ed., New York: H. Fertig, 1969]).

18. Robert George Dalrymple Laffan, *The Guardians of the Gate: Historical Lectures on the Serbs* (Oxford: Clarendon Press, 1918).

19. Monica Krippner, *The Quality of Mercy: Women at War, Serbia, 1915–18* (Newton Abbot: David and Charles, 1980). These English women fighters began a long-lasting tradition that has provided the most celebrated accounts of unrestricted Serbophilia. Krippner mostly wrote guidebooks, on Greece, Africa, the Camargue, and, naturally, Yugoslavia. Monica Krippner, *Yugoslavia Invites: A Guide Book* (London: Hutchinson, 1954). On civilian relief during the Serbo-Turkish War, see Dorothy Anderson, *The Balkan Volunteers* (London: Hutchinson, 1968).

20. Mary Edith Durham, *Twenty Years of Balkan Tangle* (London: G. Allen and Unwin, 1920); idem, *The Sarajevo Crime* (London: G. Allen & Unwin, 1925). Durham's previous work was more "impartial": see idem, *Through the Land of the Serb* (London: Edward Arnold, 1904), 205. In her search for information, Durham narrates that she could overcome the initial mistrust only with letters of introduction from powerful notables: "Once gained some letter of introduction, I . . . received so much hospitality and kindness that Servia and the friends that helped me on my way will ever remain in a warm corner of my memory. I changed my plans from day to day and went wherever the police captains and the district engineers advised me" (205). Her views, however, changed dramatically after World War I.

21. Hugh Seton-Watson and Christopher Seton-Watson, *The Making of a New Europe: R. W. Seton-Watson and the Last Years of Austria-Hungary* (Seattle: University of Washington Press, 1981).

22. Seton-Watson's initial pro-Serbian sympathies can be discerned in his rare manuscripts and pamphlets such as *Serbia, Yesterday, To-Day, and To-Morrow: A School Address* (London: Vacher and Sons, 1916); *The Spirit of the Serb* (London:

Nisbet, 1915); and *Serbia's War of Liberation* (London: Women's Printing Society, 1916). See also idem, *Absolutism in Croatia* (London: Constable, 1912); idem, *The Southern Slav Question and the Habsburg Monarchy* (London: Constable, 1911; New York: H. Fertig, 1969).

23. For this criticism, see especially Ljubo Boban et al., eds., *R. W. Seton-Watson i Jugoslveni: Korespondencija, 1906–1941* (R. W. Seton-Watson and the Yugoslavs: Correspondence, 1906–1941) (Zagreb: Srevciliste, Institut za Hrvatskv Povijest, 1976). This is a collection of documents and correspondence by and to R. W. Seton-Watson in Serbo-Croatian, English, German, French, and Italian. See also R. W. Seton-Watson, *Sarajevo: A Study in the Origins of the Great War* (London: Hutchinson, 1926; New York: H. Fertig, 1973); idem, *The Rise of Nationality in the Balkans* (London: Constable, 1917; New York: H. Fertig, 1966). Seton-Watson was conscious of the high political implications of his research, as can be seen in a thirty-six-page pamphlet, *The Historian as a Political Force in Central Europe* (London: University of London, School of Slavonic and East European Studies, King's College, 1922).

24. Rebecca West, *Black Lamb and Grey Falcon: The Record of a Journey through Yugoslavia in 1937* (London: Macmillan, 1941; New York: Viking, 1941).

25. Ibid., 67.

26. Ibid., 99.

27. Ibid.

28. Carl Rollyson, *Rebecca West: A Saga of the Century* (London: Hodder and Stoughton, 1995) 180.

29. See Mark C. Wheeler, *Britain and the War for Yugoslavia, 1940–1943* (Boulder: East European Monographs, 1980).

30. See Philip J. Cohen, *Serbia's Secret War: Propaganda and the Deceit of History* (College Station: Texas A&M University Press, 1996).

31. Churchill had been supporting Mihailović at least since April 1941, when Yugoslavia was attacked, and until January 1944.

32. George Taylor considers the consequence of such a compromise idea in *British Policy towards Wartime Resistance in Yugoslavia and Greece,* ed. Phyllis Auty and Richard Clogg (London: Macmillan, 1975).

33. Ibid., 232.

34. Statement by Brigadier Sir Fitzroy Maclean, in Auty and Clogg, op. cit., 222. Maclean also blamed the Chetniks for collaborating with the Nazi enemy (227). His classic account of his adventures with the Partisans can be found in Fitzroy Maclean, *Eastern Approaches* (London: J. Cape, 1949; 1st U.S. ed., New York: Atheneum, 1984).

35. The Italian historian Gaetano Salvemini pointed out that monarchic institutions in the Balkans were conceived as instruments of British dominance. This was indeed Churchill's overall policy, except that he decided in the end to

support Tito. See Gaetano Salvemini, *Prelude to World War II* (Garden City, NY: Doubleday, 1954).

36. Most of the lobbyists were not Serbs themselves. As examples of this propagandist line, see Michael Lees, *The Rape of Serbia: The British Role in Tito's Grab for Power, 1943–1944* (San Diego: Harcourt Brace Jovanovich, 1990); David Martin, *The Web of Disinformation: Churchill's Yugoslav Blunder* (San Diego: Harcourt Brace Jovanovich, 1990); and idem, *The Selling of Josip Broz Tito and the Tragedy of Mihailović* (San Diego: Harcourt Brace Jovanovich, 1990). It is probably interesting to note here the central role played by the large American publishing house Harcourt Brace Jovanovich in publishing pro-Serbian propaganda.

37. See George Orwell, *Animal Farm: A Fairy Story* (London: Secker and Warburg, 1995), 164.

38. There are too many names to mention here. On E. P. Thompson's (1924–1994) own experience as a volunteer, see E. P. Thompson, ed., *The Railway* (London: British-Yugoslav Association, 1948). See also Mark Thompson, *A Paper House: The Ending of Yugoslavia* (New York: Pantheon, 1992), 118–20.

39. Again, the literature on this topic is too vast to be cited here. On self-management, see Hans Dieter Seibel and Ukandi G. Damachi, *Self-Management in Yugoslavia and the Developing World* (New York: St. Martin's, 1982).

40. *Praxis. Ed. Internationale,* 10 vols. (Zagreb: Hrvatsko filosofsko drustvo, 1965–74). The "tradition" was continued in Britain in the 1980s by *Praxis International = Praxis* (Oxford: Basil Blackwell, 1981–94). Both were written in English, French, or German, the latter with summaries in other languages.

41. Mihailo Marković and Gajo Petrović, eds., *Praxis: Yugoslav Essays in the Philosophy and Methodology of the Social Sciences,* trans. Joan Coddington et al. (Dordrecht and Boston: D. Reidel, 1979); Gerson S. Sher, *Praxis: Marxist Criticism and Dissent in Socialist Yugoslavia* (Bloomington: Indiana University Press, 1977); Mihailo Marković and Robert S. Cohen, *Yugoslavia: The Rise and Fall of Socialist Humanism: A History of the Praxis Group* (Nottingham: Bertrand Russell Peace Foundation and Spokesman Books, 1975); Julius Oswald, *Revolutionäre Praxis: Darstellung und Kritik der philosophischen Position der Grunder der Zeitschrift "Praxis" unter besonderer Berücksichtigung ihrer Religionskritik* (Dusseldorf: Patmos, 1982). The best critical analysis of *Praxis's* role in the breakup of Yugoslavia is in Magas, op. cit.

42. Marković, a former dissident and ardent antinationalist, at least in front of Western audiences, was entrusted by Milošević with the task of directing the purge of antinationalist opponents in the University of Belgrade. The reasons for his apparent "conversion" to ultranationalism seem, at the very least, enigmatic (Walker Connor, personal comment). On Marković's search for an "ethnically exclusivist state," see Norman L. Cigar, *Genocide in Bosnia: The Policy of Ethnic Cleansing* (College Station: Texas A&M University Press, 1995), 192.

43. Joze Pirjevec, *Il giorno di San Vito: Jugoslava 1918–1992: Storia di una tragedia* (Torino: Nuova ERI, 1993), 457.

44. The three most notable cases were Edward Pearce, Richard West, and Sir Alfred Sherman.

45. As Paul Garde has efficaciously pointed out, "The Serbian press affirms that the Croats are a "genocidal people" (*genocidan narod*) and speaks of the "genocidity of the Croatian people" (*genocidnost hrvatskog naroda*). . . . It goes without saying that a "genocidal people" is at every moment inclined to commit a new genocide, and that each one of its acts can be interpreted in this sense by default. There is no need for proofs." Paul Garde, *Vie et mort de la Yougoslavie* (Paris: Fayard, 1992), 347.

46. The contacts between the Italian far right and Belgrade authorities have been systematically disregarded by the British press. In May 1991, at a loud neofascist gathering in Trieste before his glorious entrance to power, the new right leader Gianfranco Fini reclaimed the return of Istria and Dalmatia to Italian sovereignty. In August 1991, he visited Belgrade to meet key figures of the regime, whom he praised for their unitarist efforts. He declared that, in case of a breakup of Yugoslavia, "Istria and Dalmatia must be handed back to Italy" (*Il Secolo d'Italia,* August 2, 1991). In Italy, the two main revisionist newspapers are the far-right *Il Secolo d'Italia* and the far-left *Il Manifesto,* which compete with each other in their anti-Croat hysteria. But the focus of the new fascist-Marxist understanding has been the neo-Stalinist and radically pro-Serb *Liberazione,* recently born with the help of conspicuous financial aid from the right. On this connection see Paolo Sylos-Labini, "Atroce demagogia," *L'Espresso,* May 26, 1995, 55–56; and Carlo Gallucci, "Insisto, quanto costa Liberazione?" *L'Espresso,* June 2, 1995, 59.

47. This unprecedented alliance between the British far right and the far left concretized in the Committee for Peace in the Balkans, a think tank founded in 1995.

48. I owe thanks to several people for this information. In particular, see Brad Blitz, "The Serbian Unity Congress and the Serbian Lobby: A Study of Contemporary Revisionism and Denial" (Stanford: Stanford University Students against Genocide), unpublished document. See also Charles Lane, "Washington Diarist: War Stories," *New Republic,* January 3, 1994, 43.

49. The "parallel" groups include the supposedly "pacifist" Campaign against Militarism (CAM) and People against War (PAW), as well as several local variants. Despite their agenda of denying ethnic cleansing and genocide, they also have an "antiracist" section, called Workers against Racism (WAR).

50. Peter Brock, "Dateline Yugoslavia: The Partisan Press," *Foreign Policy* 93 (winter 1993–94): 152–72.

51. Quoted in Lane, op. cit., 43. This has been confirmed to me personally by Roy Gutman.

52. A particularly chilling display of gruesome pictures of alleged atrocities committed against the Serbs was reproduced in an expensively formatted "special" issue of the magazine (dedicated to "The pictures they don't want you to see"): Joan Phillips, "A Selective Silence," *Living Marxism* 53 (March 1993): 19–29. Bojana Isaković, one of those responsible for the excavation of World War II mass graveyards before Belgrade's television cameras, collaborated with *Living Marxism* for the exhibition *Genocide against the Serbs* at *Living Marxism's* gallery, the Edge. Isaković is presented as working for "a project about Serbs killed in 1990, . . . [which] involved the excavation and disinterment of the bones of thousands of Serbs killed and thrown into pits by the Croatian Ustashe" (20).

53. See "Serbian Myths," *Sunday Telegraph,* September 24, 1995, 7.

54. Great Britain, House of Commons, *Parliamentary Debates,* vol. 260, no. 112 (May 31, 1995), cols. 999–1102. Great Britain, House of Lords, *Parliamentary Debates,* vol. 564, no. 96 (May 31, 1995), cols. 1117–72.

55. Noel Malcolm, "The Whole Lot of Them Are Serbs," *Spectator,* June 10, 1995, 14–18.

56. For an overview of her staunch anticommunist sentiments, see Nora Beloff, *Tito's Flawed Legacy: Yugoslavia and the West, 1939–84* (Boulder: Westview, 1985). The book is one of the many revisionist interpretations of the Allied war effort.

57. Nora Beloff, "The Third Way," *New Statesman and Society,* March 27, 1992, 26–27.

58. Ibid., 26.

59. Ibid.

60. Ibid.

61. John Zametica, *The Yugoslav Conflict: An Analysis of the Causes of the Yugoslav War: The Policies of the Republics and the Regional and International Implications of the Conflict,* Adelphi Papers, no. 270 (London: Brassey's for the International Institute for Strategic Studies, 1992).

62. Ibid.

63. Ibid., 75.

64. Ibid., 25.

65. Zametica, who is of mixed parentage and was originally a Muslim, changed his name for the third time, as previously he had cast away his birth name, Omer, for the benefit of his English audiences and colleagues.

66. Zametica's booklet has been cited again and again by supposedly unbiased Western scholars. A recent example is Susanne Woodward's detailed and voluminous research in *Balkan Tragedy: Chaos and Dissolution after the Cold War* (Washington, DC: Brookings Institution, 1995), where Zametica's comments are taken *à la lettre* at least four times (148 n. 4, 180 n. 96, 184 n. 113, 334 n. 2).

Only after the third mention are we told, in a footnote (469), that Zametica was Karadžić's advisor. In the last mention (506), Zametica's work is described as "particularly informative." Impressively, the entire book's argument is constructed on the basis of Zametica's interpretation.

67. Malcolm, "Whole Lot of Them," 16.

68. Ibid.

69. See Brad K. Blitz's chapter in this volume.

70. On Lord Carrington as a champion of moral relativism, see Almond, op. cit., 242–52, esp. 243.

71. Ibid., 247.

72. The ICFY's cochairmen were Lord Owen and Cyrus Vance—the latter on behalf of the United Nations. In May 1993 Norway's Thorvald Stoltenberg superseded Vance as cochairman of the Peace Conference and the UN secretary-general's special representative in the former Yugoslavia.

73. The role of the British government has been denounced as the "most responsible for shaping and maintaining the policy of the EC and the UN towards Bosnia. No one else has a responsibility comparable to that of Mr Hurd and Mr Major. The destruction of Bosnia has in fact been in large part an achievement of the British government. Since the London Conference and Carrington's retirement from a role he had the sense to recognize as intolerable, exactly the same policy has been carried on through Lord Owen's position in the Geneva talk." Adrian Hastings, *SOS Bosnia* (London: United Kingdom Citizens' Committee for Bosnia-Herzegovina, 1993, pamphlet), 6.

74. Ibid., 6.

75. Jacques Julliard, *Ce fascisme qui vient* (Paris: Seuil, 1994), 137.

76. Hastings, op. cit., 8.

77. Ibid., 9.

78. David Fairhall, "Hard-Hitting NATO Troops Head Rescue Team," *Guardian,* May 10, 1995.

79. Robert Wright, "TRB from Washington: Who Lost Bosnia?" *New Republic,* May 29, 1995, 6.

80. When the shelling of Sarajevo was resumed in late May 1995, General Smith ordered NATO bombing of ammunition depots near Pale, a key military target that General Rose had cautiously avoided.

81. Charles Oulton, "Political Guru Urges Balkan Air Attacks," *Independent,* March 18, 1993, 6. Popper's anti-Marxist views helped frame the ideals of Britain's Conservative government in the 1980s.

82. Michael Foot, "VE Celebrations and a Few Unfinished Battles," *Guardian,* May 6, 1995.

83. Thus, referring to the "Serbian question" in the Krajina, Misha Glenny argues that "The issue which *provoked* the war in the first place remains a matter

of seemingly irreconcilable dispute" (emphasis added). see Misha Glenny, *The Fall of Yugoslavia: The Third Balkan War,* rev. and updated ed. (New York: Penguin, 1994), 112.

84. Bennett, op. cit.; Magas, op. cit., 161, 181–89, 230–32. See also Glenny, op. cit., 35.

85. Michel Roux, *Les Albanais en Yougoslavie: Minorité nationale, territoire et développement* (Paris: Éditions de la Maison des Sciences de l'Homme, 1992).

86. On this, there is now a general accord among most Yugoslavists. See Cigar, op. cit.; Garde, op. cit.; Roy Gutman, *A Witness to Genocide: The 1993 Pulitzer Prize-Winning Dispatches on the "Ethnic Cleansing" of Bosnia* (New York: Macmillan, 1993); Magas, op. cit., 214–15, 223–25; Malcolm, *Bosnia*; Rieff, *Slaughterhouse*; Hermann Tertsch, *La venganza de la historia* (Madrid: El País, Aguilar, 1993).

87. See Hugh Poulton, "The Hungarians, Croats, Slovaks, Rumanians and Rusyns/Ukrainians of the Vojvodina," in Minority Rights Group, *Minorities in Central and Eastern Europe* (London: Minority Rights Group/TWEEC, 1993); idem, *The Balkans: Minorities and States in Conflict* (London: Minority Rights Group, 1993). On minorities in Macedonia, see idem, *Who Are the Macedonians?* (London: Hurst, 1995; Bloomington: Indiana University Press, 1995). There were also reports of sweeps and concentration camps meant to terrorize Vojvodina's Croatians, Hungarians, Ruthenes, Ukrainians, Slovaks, and Serb opponents of the genocide. See Fred Pelka, "Voices from a War Zone," *Humanist* (March-April 1995), 6–10.

88. Hastings, op. cit., 8.

89. Ibid.

90. See Fouad Ajami, "The Other 1492: Jews and Muslims in Columbus' Spain," *New Republic,* April 6, 1992, 22–25.

91. On this, see Stjepan G. Meštrović, "Postemotional Politics in the Balkans," *Society* 32, no. 2 (1995): 69 ff.

92. Leonard Doyle, "Muslims 'Slaughter Their Own People,' " *Independent,* August 22, 1992, 1.

93. Tom Gjelten, "Blaming the Victim," *New Republic,* December 16, 1993, 14–16.

94. MacKenzie's story about the Muslims who bombed themselves to attract international attention can be read in his war "biography," Lewis MacKenzie, *Peacekeeper: The Road to Sarajevo* (Vancouver: Douglas and McIntyre, 1993).

95. Gjelten, op. cit., 14.

96. Ibid., 16.

97. Mark Huband, "Church of the Holy Slaughter," *Observer,* June 5, 1994.

98. *International Herald Tribune,* June 10, 1994, 1.

99. See in particular Rieff, *Slaughterhouse*. Rieff had previously studied other immigrant societies, in particular the Cuban diaspora in Miami, Florida. See

idem, *The Exile: Cuba in the Heart of Miami* (New York: Simon and Schuster, 1993); idem, *Going to Miami: Exiles, Tourists, and Refugees in the New America* (London: Bloomsbury, 1987; New York: Penguin, 1988).

100. See Jan Hjärpe, "Islam, Nationalism and Ethnicity," in *Ethnicity and Nationalism,* ed. Helena Lindholm (Göteborg: Nordnes, 1993).

101. See Sabrina Petra Ramet, *Balkan Babel: Politics, Culture, and Religion in Yugoslavia* (Boulder: Westview, 1992).

102. See Richard J. Barnet and John Cavanagh, *Global Dreams: Imperial Corporations and the New World Order* (New York: Simon and Schuster, 1994).

James J. Sadkovich

The Former Yugoslavia, the End of the Nuremberg Era, and the New Barbarism

Although many have expressed their exasperation over the failure of the international community to act to end the carnage in the Balkans, few have seen the manner of Yugoslavia's dissolution and the response of the international community as indicators that an era characterized by the Nuremberg principles has given way to a barbaric age in international relations, in which the United Nations and other international and regional organizations act to contain and manage, not end or resolve, such phenomena as aggression and genocide in much the same way that American realtors redline decaying urban areas without addressing the causes of the decay. The past four years may have marked the victory of the proponents of state sovereignty and the practitioners of bureaucratic barbarism and power politics over the advocates of individual and collective human rights.

• • •

If we want to define an era rather than argue the law, a broad, moral approach seems most useful.[1] Morally, the Nuremberg era effected a "revolution in human affairs" by making a sovereign state's treatment of its citizens "the legitimate concern of all mankind." It followed that individual and collective rights should take precedence over the legal codes—and even the integrity—of established states. This logic led to (1) efforts to implement the principle of self-determination, which is a basic collective right; (2) the codification of human rights in international treaties and conventions, including the 1950 Nuremberg principles, in order to make international law regarding human rights uniform and enforceable; (3) the creation of multinational organizations to serve as forums for advocates of human rights, and as instruments to protect those rights; (4) the adoption of foreign policies that replaced the more cynical and egoistic goals of an earlier realpolitik with a concern for self-determination, human rights, and human progress.[2]

Legally, the Nuremberg principles and the Nuremberg tribunal overturned the Act of State Doctrine, circumscribed defenses based on the coercive power of superior orders, and asserted the right of international bodies to impose standards of behavior on citizens of national states.[3] What is more important, the international community made an effort to limit the sovereignty of states by concluding treaties containing "standards of internationally agreed, and legally binding, rules" that nominally took precedence over the laws of individual states.[4]

The Nuremberg era occurred in large part because the mass slaughter of World War I and the systematic killing of World War II made clear that modern mass warfare, or "total war," had to be regulated and that vicious domestic regimes would sooner or later become predatory imperial states.[5] Not only did statesmen begin to perceive international relations as a function of domestic politics, but during the Cold War each side used the issue of human rights to criticize the other, thereby creating higher standards for both. The need to control modern warfare and the necessary compromise between two conflicting visions of the world—the socialist, derived from such theorists as Beccaria, Rousseau, and Marx, and the capitalist, derived from thinkers like Locke, Smith, and Spencer—consequently, and perhaps ironically, resulted in a new stress on human rights. Even so, enunciating rights was one thing, applying them quite another; and the period was peppered with abuses by both superpowers and tinhorn dictatorships.[6]

The assertion of social rights such as employment, shelter, and medical care expressed a socialist ideal diametrically opposed to the often brutal practices of nineteenth-century capitalism, while the demand for such political rights as freedom to vote, own property, and move freely clashed with the often dictatorial praxis of twentieth-century socialism. Because there has been a trend to reject social rights as utopian, the new barbarism may be seen as coinciding with the recrudescence of a predatory postmodern capitalism and the acceptance of a bureaucratically managed reality that is characterized by the imposition of the culture and legal systems of powerful individuals, corporations, and states on weaker individuals, groups, and states.[7] There is a discernible enough symmetry between the bureaucracies of states, corporations, health care services, educational institutions, and military machines to suggest a generalized diffusion of the mental processes that allowed Germans to do "their jobs" and "follow orders" between 1933 and 1989. In effect, the new barbarism could be defined as a form of efficient bureaucratic indifference.

The principle that embodies the most basic clash of individual with collective rights, and of state sovereignty with both, is that of self-determination. Whether one is discussing the idealistic patriotism of Giuseppe Mazzini and Giovane Italia or the murderous chauvinism of Gavrilo Princip and Mlada Bosna, self-determination has always aimed to undo established multiethnic empires in order to create states coterminous with a particular people. Prior to 1918, the primary opposition to the principle came from conservative empires like Britain, Austria, and Russia, which sought to guarantee their interests and protect their legitimacy by containing the revolutionary potential of self-determination. The primary support for the principle came from the middle classes and elites of such embryonic states as Serbia, which stood to gain an identity, independence, *and* territory, depending on how far the principle could be stretched. By 1914, self-determination was so powerful a concept that even multiethnic empires like Russia and Britain employed it against their enemies, who returned the favor. By 1918, most expected that the "oppressed" peoples of Europe, if not those dwelling in the noncontiguous empires of the victorious powers, would be allowed to exercise their "right" to choose the state to which they would belong. This expectation and a wartime propaganda that tied self-determination to both socialist and liberal values and reiterated the idealistic goals of the belligerents laid the moral foundation for the Nuremberg era, just as the League of Nations Covenant and interwar treaties formed its legal framework.[8]

Because the principle of self-determination has subverted older multiethnic states *and* served as a means of aggrandizement for new nation-states like Serbia, it has proven to be a tricky concept to apply.[9] It has no jurisprudence; its application has never satisfied everyone involved; and in the former Yugoslavia, its use satisfied no one.[10] Ostensibly the fulfillment of south Slav self-determination, Yugoslavia was actually a disguised Greater Serbia created to contain Austria and Hungary, stymie Italy, and calm the fears of French, British, and American leaders who foresaw chaos should the Balkans be divided up into ministates—a fear resurrected by both the right and the left in the late 1980s.[11]

Non-Serbian ethnic groups were unhappy because their rights to self-determination had been abridged in favor of Serbia, which provided the military, political, judiciary, and managerial cadres for the new state. But the Serbs were dissatisfied because even the fiction of a Yugoslav state hindered their pursuit of purely Serbian interests.[12] As a result, the "first" Yugoslavia had a stormy history and in 1941 quickly disintegrated into small nationalist states sponsored by the Axis powers. Although Tito and the Yugoslav Communist Party managed to damp down ethnic rivalries after 1945, it was largely Tito's prestige (*Mi smo Tito, Tito je nas* [We are Tito, Tito is us]) and a very active police apparatus that held Yugoslavia together.[13] Following his death in 1980, the Yugoslav Communist Party's control of the regional centers of power weakened. This allowed Franjo Tudjman to employ the principle of self-determination to create a Croatian state that contained a problematic Serbian minority. It allowed Alija Izetbegović to argue for a somewhat archaic multiethnic state. And it allowed Slobodan Milošević to conquer and "cleanse" territory for a Greater Serbia. Slovenia, ethnically homogeneous and far from Belgrade, slipped away almost unnoticed, but the goals of Serbian leaders precluded an easy separation for Croatia and Bosnia.

If self-determination remains both a basic right and an imperialist ploy, the preservation of existing states now seems to take precedence over a people's right to its own state.[14] The right to secede appears to have been denied in the Helsinki Declaration; the United Nations has made defending the sovereignty and the territorial integrity of established states its highest priority; and since the early 1970s there has been a bias toward existing states, a turn away from the ideals embedded in the concept of self-determination, and a general disinclination to apply or recall those treaties seen as inconvenient or irrelevant.[15] It was thus predictable that the initial response to the crisis in Yugoslavia would be to try to salvage a Yugoslav state, even if that meant giving the Yugoslav National Army free rein and abridging certain basic civil and human rights of Serbs and non-Serbs alike.[16]

This shift was not obvious, in part because much of the rhetoric remained the same, in part because there seemed to have been so much progress toward codifying human rights in international legal instruments, and in part because so many protests were raised when rights were violated. However, the CSCE (now OSCE) and the UN Security Council were largely impotent unless the major powers agreed to act in concert, and efforts to create ad hoc tribunals similar to the one convened at Nuremberg in order to punish those who had committed war crimes and crimes against humanity in the former Yugoslavia have not had priority.[17] Not until 1993 did the United Nations reluctantly name a commission to investigate war crimes in the former Yugoslavia, and it then failed to fund the commission adequately, forcing private individuals and organizations to contribute and leading the commission to finish its work prematurely. As a result, even though a Serbian guard from the Omarska concentration camp became the first one arraigned for war crimes, the tribunal appears to be more of a token to placate a disillusioned world than a symbol of the United Nations' commitment to justice. Cherif Bassiouni, who headed the commission, has urged justice, and his report has been largely confirmed by the CIA and partially by Serbian documents implicating Milošević, but Telford Taylor, who led the prosecution at Nuremberg, has expressed a cynical view of such tribunals, and it appears that David Owen, the head of the UN negotiating team since 1992, and Boutros Boutros-Ghali, secretary-general of the United Nations, did their best to soften the commission's findings.[18]

Although such organizations as the Nuremberg tribunal and the United Nations can be viewed as fictions created and maintained to justify the dispensing of victor's justice or exclusive clubs run by cynical great powers, at least during the era from 1918 to the early 1980s, regimes of all ideological persuasions had to pay lip service to the basic ideals for which such organizations stood and make a pretense of supporting the principles embedded in such documents as the League's Covenant or the Genocide Convention of 1949.[19] Statesmen might continue to act in a cynical manner, but they had to clothe their actions in the rhetoric of human rights. If doing so smacked of hypocrisy (since there were glaring examples of human rights violations from Asia to the Americas), even a formal adherence to human rights may have prevented states from committing—and tolerating—even worse behavior, although it is obviously impossible to prove that this was so.

At the very least, the custom of appealing to international norms to judge a nation's behavior, both at home and abroad, created the illusion that progress was being made toward guaranteeing human rights, limiting the abuses of war, and ameliorating the human condition in general. The Nuremberg era was therefore permeated by a cautious optimism that things could, would, and were getting better, if not day by day in every way, at least from time to time in some places with regard to some things. Consequently, most of us were confident that never again would Europeans practice genocide, and we were certain that, barring a nuclear holocaust, nothing more serious than proxy wars would disturb the peace of the developed world to which Yugoslavia belonged by virtue of its geographical proximity to Western Europe.[20]

• • •

It is precisely the loss of this confidence in a relatively stable and increasingly humane international order that characterizes the new age of barbarism in which we find ourselves. Proxy wars have been transformed into ethnic conflicts, which now occur in Europe as well as in sub-Saharan Africa, with Bosnia and Rwanda recently providing examples that suggest the spread of barbarism rather than the progress of civilization. The reemergence of a cynical great power diplomacy that is content to contain and manage the crises that have racked Haiti, Burundi, Somalia, Bosnia, and Rwanda suggests that the bipolar absolutism of the Cold War has been replaced by a policy of "neo-realpolitik" that places the rights and interests of states above those of peoples and individuals.[21] It is not, therefore, a choice between collective and individual rights that faces us, since both are clearly subordinate to the prerogatives of states in the new era, but the problem of how to make governments respect human rights domestically and include them as a legitimate policy consideration. Vietnam made it clear that even in the United States, where the judiciary was designed to act as a check on the executive and legislative branches, the government proved incapable of objectively assessing the behavior of its own military and executive.[22]

Perhaps it is appropriate that Henry Kissinger, an admirer of Kant, Spinoza, and dispassionate calculation,[23] has been one of the most visible entrepreneurs and managers of this new age in which pundits and experts can cynically manipulate the threat of "escalation" to argue that NATO and the United States must stay out of the Balkans because we have no "national interests" there, while high-ranking military officers and well-known politicians argue that even the loss of even a few of "our boys" would be too high a price to pay to stop the killing in places like

Bosnia.[24] What, one wonders, would the experts, pundits, generals, and congressmen and congresswomen have said to the sacrifice of three hundred thousand additional Americans to avenge the death of three thousand American servicemen in 1941? Would the United States have pulled out of the Pacific and let our proxies—China, Holland, New Zealand, Australia, and Britain—do our fighting for us?

The question is not altogether specious, since the current American doctrine that its military, first, must have "clear and unambiguous objectives" and, second, must be able to deploy overwhelming force against an enemy has stripped the U.S. armed forces of any serious combat function. According to the former chairman of the U.S. Joint Chiefs of Staff, Colin Powell, the purpose of the armed forces is instead to undertake peacekeeping and humanitarian operations, support their allies, and make "any disturber of the peace" think twice about doing so.[25] Of course, a potential aggressor is unlikely to think twice when such a policy appears to hamstring the military and to hog-tie U.S. foreign policy by making it contingent on the wishes of its actual and potential allies. However, this does provide the perfect excuse for not committing U.S. forces to combat in Bosnia. Whether U.S. military leaders really fear becoming involved in another Vietnam is thus a moot point, because at most they would be called on to act as members of an international military force, as they did in Iraq. The reluctance to become involved in Bosnia compared to our previous haste to crush Iraq and our earlier willingness to wage ideological warfare in Asia and Latin America indicates, at the very least, a major change in the nature of American policy. Naked and unashamed self-interest now seems the norm, reflecting a general trend in American politics and culture of rejecting altruism in favor of more selfish virtues such as ambition. Although he has recently urged prosecution of accused war criminals, even the secretary-general of the United Nations has appeared to be more concerned with increasing the size of the organization's peacekeeping forces—and thereby the contributions of its members and the prestige of the United Nations—than with abstract concepts of justice or more concrete atrocities.[26]

• • •

If the formation of Yugoslavia was a dramatic demonstration of the limitations and contradictions of the principle of self-determination, its recent dissolution has become a "test case" for the United Nations, much as Ethiopia was for the League of Nations, and the international response to each conflict was typical of the era in which it occurred.[27] Although some believe that the United States, Britain, and France—who with Russia and China effectively control the Security Council, and hence the United Nations—"flunked" the test provided by Yugoslavia's breakup, and reporters like Peter Jennings have implied that Washington's failure to act led to enormous human suffering in Bosnia, most Western actions have been more calculated and cold-blooded.[28] International organizations no longer seem to have clear functions, and some have adopted a brutal pragmatism. Thus General John Galvin noted that in 1991 NATO decided to become a "crisis manager" rather than intervene to end the crisis in Yugoslavia; the editor of *Foreign Policy* has discerned a certain efficacy in "ethnic cleansing"; and others have advocated a return to nineteenth-century colonialism.[29]

Whereas Fascist Italy's attack on Ethiopia in 1935 elicited almost universal disapproval, Serbia's attacks on its neighbors in the early 1990s led to condemnation of those states pressing for recognition of Croatia, Slovenia, and Bosnia; they elicited criticism of the victims of Serbian aggression; and they spurred efforts to force Zagreb and Sarajevo to deal with Belgrade.[30] In 1935, movements for sanctions against Germany were undercut by France and Britain, who wished to avoid war with another great power, but who at least proposed sanctions aimed at the aggressor and not at its victim. In late 1991, the major powers placed an arms embargo on both Serbia and its victims. The arguments used to justify doing so—that the conflict was a "civil war" and that more blood would be shed if more arms were introduced—were already threadbare in 1991 and have grown more so, but they are still regularly used to justify the arms embargo on Bosnia, Croatia, and Slovenia—all sovereign states with the right to defend themselves under international usage and the provisions of the UN Charter.[31] That the great powers have *actively* denied them that right by imposing an arms embargo is the most obvious indicator that we are now in an age in which the will of the great powers takes precedence over principle, treaty, and custom.[32] Such actions are reminiscent of the Spanish Civil War, but there is a crucial difference. While Spain served as a battleground for competing ideologies and the efforts to contain the war could be seen as an effort to try to avoid a more general European conflagration, the war in the former Yugoslavia is one of territorial aggrandizement, with only a very crude racial ideology justifying Serbian aggression. The containment, therefore, would be of genocide, not of war.

There has been relatively little criticism of official policy because a pervasive ignorance of history has allowed pundits and politicians to explain, excuse, and rationalize Serbian aggression and atrocities by depicting the Serbs as historic, actual, and potential victims of their purportedly fascist, neofascist, protofascist, and fundamentalist neighbors, whose hostility to them has supposedly caused the Serbs to behave in a regrettable, but understandable, manner. Misreadings of the histories of the Balkans and World War II thus became a justification for contemporary Serbian atrocities and an excuse for the international acceptance of Serbian aggression.[33] When reporters present scenes of carnage, they objectively note that if the Serbs seem to be the worst offenders, the fault for the slaughter lies with *all* sides, because what is occurring in the former Yugoslavia is a civil war that has been raging for centuries.[34] It is thus not altogether bizarre that in April 1993 Slobodan Milošević publicly thanked Bill Clinton for refusing either to take military action or to rescind the arms embargo. At least the Serb leader knew that by not acting the American president had guaranteed that the victims of Serbian aggression would remain unarmed and unprotected.[35]

In other words, our leaders and opinion shapers are either disingenuous liars or as poorly informed as the man in the street, easily given to stereotypes, very susceptible to propaganda, and essentially befuddled by complex events—like any barbarian.

• • •

Yugoslavia was created in 1918, then re-created in 1945. It fell apart for the first time in 1941, for the second in 1991. To those familiar with its history, the recent dissolution of Yugoslavia came as no surprise, just as it was no surprise to those familiar with Balkan history that the current war was initiated by Serbia, which has been militaristic since its creation and has pursued an aggressive foreign policy for over a century. It has consequently been embroiled in numerous international crises, from the Balkan Wars to the assassination that triggered World War I, to the attacks on Slovenia, Croatia, and Bosnia by the Serbian-controlled JNA in 1991 and 1992. Indeed, when people speak of "Balkan" politics, they often unwittingly use "Balkan" as a synonym for "Serbian"—yet politicians, pundits, and diplomats have condemned the Croats as aggressors because they followed the Serbian example in Bosnia. They have scolded Croats and Slovenes for exercising their right to self-determination and "provoking" the Serbs, and they have lectured the Bosnians on their failure to give up most of their territory to mollify the Serbs.

How far we have descended into barbarism can be gauged both by our efforts to force the victims of aggression to be "reasonable" and by the extent of our tolerance of genocide, which in the former Yugoslavia has taken the form of torture and forcible expulsion as well as mass murder.[36] Initially, UN Secretary General Boutros Boutros-Ghali dismissed the carnage there as not terribly significant when compared with the problems of the Third World. Those responsible for "ethnic cleansing" have been interviewed by the hosts of ABC's *Nightline* and PBS's *MacNeil-Lehrer Newshour* as if they were run-of-the-mill politicians; and Ted Koppel has juggled statistics to make it appear that deaths occurring in African states over ten years are comparable to the slaughter perpetrated by Serbian forces in Bosnia over two.[37] Charles Maynes has noted that "ethnic cleansing" worked well in such places as Poland; and Brent Scowcroft has argued that we should accept Serbian gains in Croatia and Bosnia for the following specific reasons: "we cannot do everything everywhere"; ethnic cleansing occurs in Northern Ireland; the United States cannot restore peace where "people don't want to keep the peace themselves"; and the Serbs "have fought long and hard" to realize a Greater Serbia.[38]

Because the victims of Serbian aggression are represented as potential killers themselves, their deaths seem to be their own fault, even though the Serbs are the only minority in Yugoslavia who were *not* threatened prior to 1990, and who have lived since then among other ethnic groups with few reprisals for what has happened to members of these groups in Serbian-controlled areas. Yet the Serbs use the threat of such reprisals to justify their actions, and the international community has, until recently with NATO air strikes, refused to protect the rights of non-Serb minorities in Serbian areas.[39] UNPROFOR forces have actually helped consolidate Serbian gains, not protect human rights, because they have prevented the victims of Serbian aggression from rearming, and they have accelerated the process of ethnic cleansing by evacuating those Muslim towns and "safe havens" under attack by Serb forces. Peacekeeping has thus degenerated into protection of the aggressor, and UN forces have become accomplices to genocide.[40]

In the new age not even lip service is paid to ideal conceptions of international law and human rights. Hard-nosed realism and soft-brained conflict resolution are the order of the day; pundits and experts echo politicians and military leaders who prompt Ortega y Gasset's chorus to join in the mantra that unless a state's vital, strategic, or commercial interests are at stake, acting to enforce international agreements, intervening to assure human rights, and siding with the victim are luxuries that no government can afford. The basic documents of the Nuremberg era have become irrelevant pieces of paper, subordinate to the narrow interests of great powers. The United Nations thus presses to end apartheid in South Africa while imposing it in the former Yugoslavia, and the United States condemns Moscow for using force against breakaway republics while supporting Belgrade's right to do so.[41]

• • •

Defining the characteristics unique to the new barbarism is difficult because this has been a barbarous and brutal century. Some of the following seem familiar; the distinction is one of attitude, an Orwellian approach to reality coupled with a Bismarckian nonchalance toward the use of force, and a technician's attitude toward killing. My list is neither comprehensive nor necessarily an accurate reflection of trends. We have, after all, just entered the new era. So the best that the following observations can be is suggestive.

1. An Orwellian treatment of history is now normal. Past events are distorted to justify current policies, facilitated by media and a citizenry that are blissfully ignorant of past or present realities.[42]

2. Repeated efforts to persuade the general public that the Cold War is over have resulted in a pathetic belief that history is at an end because democracy has won out. But this victory of democracy masks the triumph of a neocapitalism whose predatory values are rapidly displacing traditional value systems, and the reemergence of a vicious, technically manipulated nationalism, every bit as deadly as its recent ancestors.

3. While elites use force to repress dissent at home and protect economic and strategic interests abroad, they refuse to use force to protect the values embedded in the basic documents of the Nuremberg era. The consequence of this is an erosion of basic individual and collective human rights.

4. There is a growing consensus that the great powers, led by the United States, will guarantee the established authorities, the territorial integrity, and the sovereignty of existing states, unless they are "failed"

states, which will need constant intervention and tutelage from the major powers and regional organizations.

5. Statesmen, academics, politicians, and pundits dismiss international treaties and law, cynically rejecting ideals in favor of policies based on and justified by a state's national (vital) interests, or by appeals to international stability (a variation on the domestic law and order theme).

6. Powerful states and their clients act unilaterally or use international organizations as surrogates to contain, validate, consolidate, and police areas where the vital *national* interests of these powers are in play.

7. There is a marked tendency to blame the victims of aggression and genocide for placing uncomfortable and inconvenient moral demands on other states, peoples, and individuals. The corollary to this is a tendency to exculpate rather than punish the guilty while forcing the victims of aggression to accommodate their attacker, save in those cases involving the national interest of a major power, such as Iraq's threat to Mideast oil fields.

8. The media have contributed to the spread of nonchalant, even voyeuristic, attitudes toward human rights violations, indifference to genocide, and treatment of war criminals as if they were regular statesmen, military leaders, and politicians. Whether this is a "postmodern" phenomenon due to misunderstandings of classic legal "texts," the result of overcrowding and high unemployment, or simply the consequence of popular indifference to corrupt political and diplomatic processes is not clear.[43]

9. While the use of force has become highly selective, it is increasingly common, evidently owing to the belief that military force can resolve political problems if applied correctly. Such a conviction coincides with a general militarizing of the languages and cultures of major societies, from that of the United States to those of the Third World. The new barbaric era is thus quintessentially a militaristic one as well.

10. Cynicism is widespread, and while most expect statesmen and politicians to lie, few expect anything decent from them.

11. There has been a growing tendency to ignore crimes committed within a state as the internal affair of the state involved, except where the interests of major powers are involved. This attitude may be rooted in a Cold War mentality that adopted a double standard as a norm. Conservatives could thus be shocked by abuses in Soviet mental hospitals, but excuse the Pinochet's excesses in Chile; and leftists were appalled at the

desaparecidos in Argentina, but intellectualized the mass murder committed by the Khmer Rouge.

12. Secret diplomacy is again in vogue; diplomatic media events are carefully managed to reassure domestic audiences or to rationalize the action or inaction of single states and coalitions of states.

In short, there has been a tendency to reassert the realpolitik of the nineteenth century without the humanistic principles of the period. So foreign policies are now less "hypocritical" in that the naked self-interest of states is repeatedly invoked to justify action or inaction, but elites have become morally insensitive. Governments will not intervene to stop aggression and genocide so long as doing so presents any risk of serious conflict. We thus extol heroes like Vaclav Havel, but refuse to act on his exhortation that our responsibility is to humanity, not to national states.[44] The strong can prey on the weak with impunity, since at most they can expect the imposition of sanctions that their patrons and friends will circumvent. Even those critical of Serbia have been willing to accept Serbian gains as faits accomplis, something the world would not concede the Italians in 1935, nor the Germans in 1939.[45] The one-dimensional heroes played by Arnold Schwarzenegger are thus our only hope in a world indifferent to justice and morality. But there is no real action hero to challenge the terminators among us. Indeed, if there has been a lesson this century, it is that fighting terror with terror makes one a terrorist, and resorting to barbarian methods to eradicate barbarism makes one a barbarian, whether one is wearing camouflage or pinstripes.

In the case of Yugoslavia, Serbia was stronger than its neighbors because it controlled the JNA and because its powerful patrons—France, Britain, Russia, and the United States—saw it in their strategic interest to avoid the creation of a *Mitteleuropa* made up of states tied to Germany and Italy. As a result, the support given Croatia, Slovenia, and Bosnia by Berlin and Rome was meaningless, because both the fledgling south Slav republics and their supporters were weaker than Serbia and its patrons. And in the new barbaric age, it is might, not right, that has the final word. To paraphrase Thomas Nagel's conclusion of twenty years ago: "We have always known that the world is a bad place. It appears that it may be an evil place as well."[46] Today it seems that the world is also a place where corrupt men and efficient bureaucrats commit barbaric acts in the name of peace.

NOTES

1. Richard Wassertrom, "The Relevance of Nuremberg," in *War and Moral Responsibility,* ed. Marshall Cohen, Thomas Nagel, and Thomas Scanlon (Princeton: Princeton University Press, 1974), 152, and 156, for his observation that criminal law, while useful to resolve conflicts, is only "a very rough guide to what is morally permissible." Not surprisingly, Wassertrom saw a moral significance to Nuremberg that overrode its legal ramifications.

2. Richard A. Falk et al., *Crimes of War: A Legal, Political, Documentary, and Psychological Inquiry into the Responsibility of Leaders, Citizens, and Soldiers for Criminal Acts in War* (New York: Random House, 1971), 50–59.

3. Wassertrom, op. cit., 134–41.

4. Paul Sieghart, *The International Law of Human Rights* (Oxford: Clarendon Press, 1983), xix, 6–7, 14. The law is essentially the codification of what is morally permissible, politically expedient, and customary in a given society. It works because it includes a specific set of procedures for resolving grievances and conflicts, but it is not synonymous with justice, which confers legitimacy to law, or morality, which is usually an absolute standard. The law is thus imperfect and practical, and it usually expresses the *minimum* standard of conduct that a community will tolerate. The law may even be immoral. The Nuremberg era therefore should be considered a period marked by a particular concept of justice informed by a morality formulated in reaction to the trends and excess of the early twentieth century, of which the tribunal's judgments were but one legal elaboration.

5. There were also countervailing tendencies, for example, those rationalizing mass destruction as normal. See Daniel Pick, *War Machine: The Rationalization of Slaughter in the Modern Age* (New Haven: Yale University Press, 1993).

6. For problems applying the Nuremberg principles, see Donald A. Wells, *War Crimes and Laws of War* (Washington, DC: University of America Press, 1984), 81–92. For basic documents, see Herbert W. Briggs, *The Law of Nations* (New York: Appleton-Century-Crofts, 1952), 1021–22. There is no space to discuss the traditions of left and right, but in broad terms those on the left stress the need to protect individuals and groups, while those on the right the necessity of assuring individual rights and freedoms. J. S. Mill, who began by focusing on the latter, ended by championing the former as a sine qua non to assure individual rights and freedoms to everyone, regardless of social standing.

7. Typical was the U.S. statement on May 24, 1991, that "U.S. policy toward Yugoslavia is based on support for the interrelated objectives of democracy, dialogue, human rights, market reform and unity." Given the power of international financial organizations, such as the International Monetary Fund, to make and break sovereign states, one of the main goals of the "breakaway" republics in

the former Yugoslavia has been to attract foreign investment by showing that they have political and social climates friendly to commerce and industry. Because democratic institutions have become linked to a predatory American form of neocapitalism whose only concern is profit, the United States is not interested in the welfare of Poles or Russians, but only in the business climate in Poland and Russia. See *New York Times*, July 1 and June 29, 1991 for Slovenia, where the same holds true. Since the end of the Cold War, the *Nation* has repeatedly pointed out the bankruptcy of a policy that makes freedom for entrepreneurs to operate synonymous with the democratic and liberal traditions of the Western world. Yet the *Nation* itself has shown tremendous confusion regarding the rights of small nations and has had a difficult time making sense of events in the former Yugoslavia.

8. A useful discussion of the principle's political ramifications can be found in Victor S. Mamatey, *The United States and East Central Europe, 1914–1918: A Study in Wilsonian Diplomacy and Propaganda* (Princeton: Princeton University Press, 1957). Lloyd Gardner's study of Wilsonian propaganda as a reaction to Leninist diplomacy is also instructive, *Wilson and Revolutions, 1913–1921* (Philadelphia: Lippincott, 1976).

9. Serbia's use of the concept should therefore not be confused with its use by Croatia, Slovenia, or Bosnia, because while Belgrade seeks to extend its state boundaries under the guise of self-determination, the other peoples of the former Yugoslavia seek only to establish theirs on a viable basis consonant with the ethnic composition of the new states of Bosnia, Croatia, and Slovenia. This may seem like hairsplitting. It is not.

10. Sieghart, op. cit., 368–70. The lack of jurisprudence is testimony to the thorny nature of the principle.

11. For example, Joseph Nye, "What New World Order?" *Foreign Affairs*, spring 1992. The breakup of Yugoslavia and subsequent military operations have been described by a number of authors, whose points of view are relatively diverse. See Sabrina Ramet, *Balkan Babel: Politics, Culture, and Religion in Yugoslavia* (Boulder: Westview, 1992); Leonard J. Cohen, *Broken Bonds: Yugoslavia's Disintegration and Balkan Politics in Transition* (Boulder: Westview, 1995); David Rieff, *Slaughterhouse: Bosnia and the Failure of the West* (New York: Simon and Schuster, 1995); and Misha Glenny, *The Fall of Yugoslavia: The Third Balkan War* (New York: Penguin, 1992).

12. For the setting of Yugoslavia's borders, see Ivo J. Lederer, *Yugoslavia at the Paris Peace Conference: A Study in Frontier Making* (New Haven: Yale University Press, 1963); and Arno J. Mayer, *Politics and Diplomacy of Peacemaking: Containment and Counterrevolution at Versailles, 1918–1919* (New York: Alfred A. Knopf, 1967). Both books tend to deal rather gently with the question of Serbian imperialism.

13. For interwar Yugoslavia, see Ivo Banac, *The National Question in Yugo-*

slavia: Origins, History, Politics (Ithaca: Cornell University Press, 1984); Branislav Gligorijević, *Parlamenti i političke stranke u Jugoslaviji, 1919–1929* (Belgrade: ISI, 1979); Ljubo Boban, *Maček i politika Hrvatske seljačke stranke, 1928–1941* (Zagreb: Liber, 1974); Atif Purivatra, *Jugoslavenska muslimanska organizacija u političkom životu Kraljevine Srba, Hrvata i Slovenaca* (Sarajevo: Svjetlost, 1974); and James J. Sadkovich, "Il regime di Alessandro in Iugoslavia: 1929–1941. Un' interpretazione," *Storia contemporanea* (1984).

14. For discussion, see Antonio Cassese, "The Helsinki Declaration and Self-Determination," in *Human Rights, International Law and the Helsinki Accord,* ed. Thomas Buergenthal and Judith R. Hall (New York: Allanhead, Osmun, 1977); and idem, "The Self-Determination of Peoples," in Louis Henkin et al., *The International Bill of Rights: The Covenant on Civil and Political Rights* (New York: Columbia University Press, 1981).

15. For example, the refusal of the United States, when found guilty of meddling in Nicaragua's affairs, to recognize the findings of a court it had pressed to establish.

16. A double standard was quickly established: Serbians in Croatia were allowed, even encouraged, to break away from Zagreb, while Croatians were censured for their desire to be free of Belgrade.

17. See Wells, op. cit., passim, for a history of such efforts. Enforcing rules of war and guaranteeing human rights have proven difficult because statesmen prefer their commitments to absolute ideals to be vaguely worded and easily repudiated. Thus, in 1928, when the great powers rejected war as an instrument of foreign policy, they reserved their "right" to wage defensive wars whenever they believed it appropriate, and few signed treaties that defined an aggressor too precisely. Similarly, most powers have decried the shedding of innocent blood and signed treaties outlawing acts such as the shelling of civilians, but the Allies systematically bombed urban areas during World War II, and if the media have deplored Serb shelling of civilians, they seldom have reported their actions as criminal, preferring to follow the lead of the diplomats who sought to rationalize Serbian atrocities in order not to antagonize Belgrade by noting that the Serbians actually intended to destroy buildings and infrastructure, not terrorize civilians. This argument of "double effect" is discussed by Thomas Nagel, "War and Massacre," in Cohen et. al., op. cit., 10–11; also Falk et. al., op. cit., 33–40, for the 1907 Hague Conventions that prohibited attacks on civilians.

18. Marc D. Charney, "Conversation with Telford Taylor: The Laws of War Are Many, but Self-Interest Is the Only Enforcer," *New York Times,* December 25, 1994; and Cherif Bassiouni's remarks in R. C. Longworth, "Peace vs. Justice," *Chicago Tribune,* September 2, 1994. See also Boutros Boutros-Ghali, "Empowering the United Nations," *Foreign Affairs,* winter 1992–93; idem, "Genocide: When Will We Ever Learn?" *International Herald Tribune,* April 6, 1995.

19. Consequently, one argument raised by fascist diplomats to justify their invasion of Abyssinia in 1935 was that the invasion was a humanitarian one because Italy would put an end to slavery in the African country. The Italian minister in Belgrade condemned the Yugoslav regime for being a brutal police state. There are various litmus tests for organizations such as the League and the United Nations. One is the way in which minority rights have been guaranteed. For discussion, see Claude Inis, Jr., *National Minorities: An International Problem* (New York: Greenwood, 1969).

20. As Justice Robert H. Jackson noted in his opening statement at Nuremberg in 1945, "the ultimate step in avoiding periodic wars" was "to make statesmen responsible to law." And if it was too much to expect that war might be banished altogether, Jackson expected the major powers to "put the forces of International Law . . . on the side of peace." Falk et al., op. cit., 78–87.

21. For example, Gerald B. Helman and Steven R. Ratner argued that states unable to manage their own affairs should be handed over to larger, more powerful states to be managed, in effect a return to the colonial era without the pretense of civilizing the colonies. See "Saving Failed States," *Foreign Policy,* winter 1992–93.

22. The last point is made by Wassertrom, op. cit., 154–55. The most glaring example was certainly the Chicago Conspiracy Trial of 1969–70; for an entertaining account, see J. Anthony Lukas, *The Barnyard Epithet and Other Obscenities: Notes on the Chicago Conspiracy Trial* (New York: Harper and Row, 1970). The vulnerability of national judiciaries to pressure is well known, and has been normal in Yugoslavia; for example, James J. Sadkovich, "The Use of Political Trials to Repress Croatian Dissent, 1929–1934," *Journal of Croatian History,* 1987–88. Robert Cullen, "Human Rights Quandary," *Foreign Affairs,* winter 1992–93, posed the question of choice and came out in favor of individual, not collective, rights, a choice that undermines the principle of self-determination.

23. Still of interest is Oriana Fallaci's portrait of Kissinger in *Intervista con la storia* (Milan: Rizzoli, 1974). Kissinger, a regular guest on such shows as *Nightline,* is one of the major power brokers in Washington and it is not a coincidence that his "associates," from Lawrence Eagleburger to Brent Scowcroft, have helped shape the new world, nor that Eagleburger's role regarding U.S. policy in Serbia should be questioned, given his links to Belgrade and Serbian business interests. See Patrick Glynn, "Yugoblunder," *New Republic,* February 24, 1992; and Lawrence C. Soley, *The News Shapers: The Sources Who Explain the News* (Westport, CT: Praeger, 1992), esp. 85–94.

24. "National interests" or "vital interests" are always either left vague or narrowly defined as commercial and mineral, and usually coupled with rhetorical questions. With regard to U.S. policy, this is clear from a sampling of the *MacNeil-Lehrer Newshour,* which is really a forum for policy makers to rational-

ize their actions to a particular segment of the American middle class. For example, on April 28, 1993, Lee Hamilton declared that the United States should stay out of Bosnia because it had no "vital interests" there, then wondered who would be willing to risk young American lives there for no reason; on February 10, 1994, John McCain labeled Bosnia a "tar baby," and Pat Schroeder and Hank Brown insisted no American lives should be risked there; on April 11, 1994, Lawrence Eagleburger warned that the United States was "dangerously close to a step-by-step escalation"; a week later, on April 18, John Warner insisted that the "lesson" was not to take risks unless clear U.S. interests were at stake; and two days after that, on April 20, William Hyland, arguing against intervention and for the arms embargo, warned that no one could predict what the Serbs might do.

25. Colin Powell, "U.S. Forces: Challenges Abroad," *Foreign Affairs,* winter 1992–93.

26. Boutros-Ghali, "Empowering the United Nations," who exulted that Yugoslavia was the biggest peacekeeping effort ever by the United Nations, noting that peacekeeping is "a growth industry."

27. The test involves the principles of ethnically pure states, which at least one Bosnian nurse dismissed as "stupid" on Radovan Tadić's documentary *Sarajevo: The Living and the Dead,* PBS, March 1, 1994, but it also involves the questions of minority rights, premeditated aggression, and state-sponsored genocide.

28. On the *MacNeil-Lehrer Newshour,* May 6, 1993, Senator Lantos claimed the great powers had "flunked"; and Jennings implied a U.S. responsibility on "While America Watched: The Bosnia Tragedy," ABC, March 17, 1994.

29. For John Galvin's remarks, see *MacNeil-Lehrer Newshour,* February 1994; also Charles William Maynes, "Containing Ethnic Conflict," *Foreign Policy,* winter 1992–93.

30. The tendency was to blame Croats, Slovenes, and Bosnian Muslims for provoking Serbia by invoking the principle of self-determination; blaming the victim is an argument often heard by the defense in rape trials in this country. There was, and continues to be, sharp criticism of Germany for pressing to recognize the "breakaway" republics. Oddly, there is little criticism of Italy and other states who favored recognition, an indication that the diplomatic clash over Yugoslavia was one that involved Germany's position in Europe. For example, Alexander Cockburn, "Beat the Devil," *Nation* August 31–September 7, 1992, argued that the Serbs were merely reacting to Croat atrocities during the early 1940s and were getting a bum rap in the Western press; or Misha Glenny and William Pfaff, who blamed all sides, especially the Croats, for the fighting. See William Pfaff, "The Shame of Bosnia," *New York Review of Books,* September 24, 1992; and Misha Glenny, "The Massacre of Yugoslavia," *New York Review of Books,* January 30, 1992. One of the more disingenuous efforts to blame the

victim was made by Alex Dragnich, who argued that Serbs had "exploited themselves for the benefit of the (Yugoslav) nation as a whole," and had repeatedly been victimized by those who had failed to appreciate their sacrifices. See Alex Dragnich, "The Anatomy of a Myth: Serbian Hegemony," *Slavic Review* 50, no. 3 (fall 1991): 559–662; for a rebuttal of Dragnich's thesis, see James J. Sadkovich, "Serbian Hegemony Revisited, or Blaming the Perpetrator, not the Victim," *Association of Croatian Studies Bulletin,* October 1991.

31. See Briggs, op. cit., 977–86; and Ian Brownlie, *Basic Documents in International Law* (Oxford: Clarendon Press, 1983), 4, 14–17. Claims that the country was involved in "civil war" effectively protected Belgrade from sanctions for attacking a sovereign state.

32. Warren Christopher warned during an interview on the *MacNeil-Lehrer Newshour* on April 5, 1993, that military intervention would mean an end to humanitarian aid and more killing and bloodshed. Less disingenuously, he added that Russia was "very reluctant" to lift the arms embargo, but did not say whether Moscow considered Belgrade its client. In an interview on the same show in March 1993, David Owen insisted that the Serbs must be offered a "carrot" in addition to being shown the "stick," so that they would talk peace and the Russians would "stay on board." More recently, Elizabeth Furse warned on the April 18, 1994, broadcast that "more people will get killed" if the arms embargo is lifted.

33. Kissinger solemnly informed Koppel's listeners that "these people have been fighting for a thousand years," on ABC's *Nightline,* April 22, 1993; the *Nation* depicted Croatia's government as "crypto-fascist" in "Bosnian Quandary," April 26, 1993; William Pfaff, "Reflections (The Absence of Empire)," *New Yorker,* August 10, 1992, argued that the peace settlements after World War I and Tito's regime after World War II had "denied" Serbs the opportunity to create an "integral Greater Serbia"; Aleksa Djilas, *The Contested Country: Yugoslav Unity and Communist Revolution, 1919–1953* (Cambridge: Harvard University Press, 1991), 43–47, 225, focused on Croatian atrocities while excusing those committed by Serbs during the war; and Robert M. Hayden, "Constitutional Nationalism in Formerly Yugoslav Republics," *Slavic Review* 51, no. 4 (1992), has implied that Croatia's president is responsible for Serbian atrocities. It is thus not surprising that John F. Burns, Stephen Engelberg, Chuck Sudetic, and Celestine Bohlen all got their history wrong and that American leaders did as well. See, for example, articles by the latter three in the *New York Times,* March 24, April 2, and May 16, 1991.

34. Typical was a National Public Radio report on November 29, 1993, that noted that Jews in Croatia were worried over the "quiet rehabilitation" of the NDH, the World War II Croatian state; and Col. Miguel Moreno's remark on an April 6, 1993, ABC *Nightline* segment that if Serbian areas had been cleansed of

Croats and Muslims, Croatian areas had also been "ethnically cleansed" of Serbs.

35. *MacNeil-Lehrer Newshour,* April 6, 1993.

36. For the relevant treaties relating to violations of human rights, see Sieghart, op. cit., 128 ff., 135 ff., 159 ff. Also see Yoram Dinstein, "The Right to Life, Physical Integrity, and Liberty," in Henkin et al., esp. 115–19, for the right to life, 122–23, for torture, 128, for liberty, and 136 for the observation that even during a war, summary execution and torture are outlawed.

37. Koppel did so on a segment of *Nightline,* compressing statistics for African states to make them seem comparable to the losses in Bosnia, and Boutros-Ghali has on several occasions played down the extent of the suffering in Bosnia, a position also taken by some members of the Jewish community, who refuse to admit any comparisons with the Holocaust, among them Erwin Knoll, editor of the *Progressive,* who in the July 1993 issue attacked those who compared Bosnia to the Holocaust and condemned "such invocation of the Holocaust as inappropriate and even offensive," agreeing with Ronald Steel that all that was under way in Bosnia was "an ugly policy of forced population transfer, intensified by a brutality endemic to Balkan wars . . . not genocide and not the Holocaust." Knoll joined those who have blamed the victims of Serbian genocide, and displayed his own ignorance of what constitutes genocide. Elie Wiesel has also been careful to distinguish between the Holocaust and what is occurring in the former Yugoslavia. But such disparate figures as George Shultz and Leon Wieseltier have found such distinctions specious, noting that genocide is not civil war and that the Holocaust should have taught us to recognize, and intervene to end, genocide. *Nightline,* April 22, 1993, for Wieseltier and April 26 for Shultz.

38. Maynes, op. cit., 11; *This Week with David Brinkley,* May 9, 1993, for Scowcroft. Also see Furse's remarks on *MacNeil-Lehrer Newshour,* above, including her suggestion that since we could not do anything in Bosnia, we should prepare for "future Bosnias." Judging by such remarks, "conflict resolution" is a euphemism for redlining military operations within the Third World, or simply an excuse for doing nothing.

39. Sieghart, op. cit., 35 ff., 72 ff., 174, 370–76. Liberty of one's person is also guaranteed, but not respected. For the rights of minorities, see Louis B. Sohn, "The Rights of Minorities," in Henkin et al., op. cit., esp. 282, for the right of minorities to preserve and develop their ethnic, religious, and linguistic characteristics, a right clearly denied non-Serbs in Serbian-controlled areas, but enjoyed by Serbs in Croatia, according to the republic's constitution. See also B. G. Ramacharan, "Equality and Nondiscrimination," also in Henkin et al., op. cit., esp. 259, 262–64, who notes the duty of states to assure freedom of thought, conscience, and religion, and to assure equality and nondiscrimination, which are affirmative aspects of the same principle.

40. UNPROFOR's role has not been a happy one. The first units arrived in

Croatia in the fall of 1991, but failed to disarm Serbian forces in Croatia and have been unable to resettle those chased from their homes by the JNA and Serbian irregulars.

41. June 28, 1991, "U.S. on Secession, Maybe."

42. Part of the problem of the *New York Times* obviously is the dominance of broadcast media, which by their nature cannot present thoughtful or thorough analyses. Not only do they tend to favor human interest stories, stress brevity, and seek out well-known personalities to interview, but deadlines and lack of penalties for being ignorant lead to superficial treatments of most news. Thus, NPR's May 7, 1994, broadcast of *All Things Considered* included a background piece on Haiti that made it seem as if the United States had tried to *save* the tiny state, whereas a great many, if not all, of the island's problems are the result of American intervention between 1915 and 1934. But then, it is unlikely that the reporters had time to read Hans Schmidt, *The United States Occupation of Haiti, 1915–1934* (New Brunswick: Rutgers University Press, 1971); David Healy, *Gunboat Diplomacy in the Wilson Era: The U.S. Navy in Haiti, 1915–1916* (Madison: University of Wisconsin Press, 1976); Hogar Nicolas, *L'occupation américaine d'Haiti: La revance de l'histoire* (Madrid, 1955); Suzy Castor, *La ocupación norteamericana de Haití y sus consecuencias (1915–1934)* (Mexico, DF, 1971), or the other scholarly works on the island's history. Similarly, it is clear that when Joseph Joffe wrote that Yugoslavia had been an "explosive concoction of warring tribes and nations," and concluded that a Greater Serbia was the second-best choice to a south Slav state, he had read relatively little Balkan history. See his "The New Europe: Yesterday's Ghosts," *Foreign Affairs,* winter 1992–93, 30–35.

43. This involves a discussion of the media and postmodernism, since a good part of the new barbarism seems to be classifiable as ennui and derives from television. Put another way, such events as the war in Bosnia exist to provide images for television audiences, and only become "real" when "mediated" through that medium. See Arthur Kroker and David Cook, *The Postmodern Scene: Excremental Culture and Hyper-Aesthetics* (New York: St. Martin's, 1986), 266–70. It is also worth noting Dana Polan's observation that the concept of a postmodernist culture implies a radical shift from a modernist's optimistic faith in technology, vision, and endeavor to a total lack of interest in reality. This has triggered a crisis of conscience (or perhaps consciousness) that has paralyzed much of the left and led Warren Montag to conclude that "On a field of conflicting forces whose balance of power shifts endlessly, we have no fixed reference points, nothing to guide us but our own errors," and Robert Stam to note the need to transcend "sterile dichotomies and exhausted paradigms." See E. Ann Kaplan, ed., *Postmodernism and Its Discontents, Theories, Practices* (New York: Verso, 1988), 45–46, 55, 142–43. The point, of course, is that our moral sensibilities have been dulled, and there are no longer any moral absolutes, even on the left.

44. *MacNeil-Lehrer Newshour,* April 22, 1993.

45. As one member of Congress noted on *This Week with David Brinkley* on May 9, 1993, the "Serbs have done pretty well here": they realized their objective of a Greater Serbia, and the "best" that the rest of the world could do was to "hold" the peace.

46. Nagel, op. cit., 24.

ELEVEN

Liah Greenfeld

War and Ethnic Identity in Eastern Europe: Does the Post-Yugoslav Crisis Portend Wider Chaos?

Editors' note: The following is the text of a speech given by Liah Greenfeld to an audience of policy-makers in the United States in 1993.

A discussion of ethnicity in the post-Cold War world, as in any other time, must begin with the definition of the phenomenon. What we mean by ethnicity in the context of East European transformations, I think, is ethnic nationalism, that is, the type of nationalism distinguished by the manner in which it defines the nation, and by the nature of its criteria for national membership. The definition of the nation in ethnic nationalisms is collectivistic and authoritarian: the nation is defined in unitary terms, as a collective individual endowed with its own will, needs, and interests, which subsume the wills, needs, and interests of its individual members, and presupposes an elite of interpreters, specifically qualified to decipher this collective will, whom the masses who are not so qualified must obey. Ethnic criteria of national membership, in turn, imply that nationality is believed to be inherent and independent of the individual choice: one can neither acquire it if one is not born with it, nor change it, if one is.

Ethnic nationalism, which is the most widespread type of nationalism, and is characteristic, among others, of East European societies, differs very significantly from other types of nationalism, and, in particular, represents the very opposite of the individualistic civic nationalism characteristic of Western liberal democracies, such as the United States or Britain. Within the framework of individualistic civic nationalisms, the nation is defined as a composite entity, an association of its members, whose aggregate—and always negotiable—wills and interests compose the interests of the nation. National membership is defined in civic terms, namely, terms identical with citizenship, which means that nationality is at least in principle open and voluntaristic: it can and sometimes must be acquired.

Ethnic nationalism has characteristic propensities in the sphere of internal politics as well as international relations that differ markedly from the parallel propensities of individualistic and civic nationalisms. For example, ethnically defined nations are more likely to engage in aggressive warfare than individualistic nations.[1] This is so for several reasons. Individualistic nationalisms are not, in principle, particularistic, for they are based on the universalistic principle of the moral primacy of the individual. This goes for any individual, whether or not he or she belongs to the national community, and as a result, the borderline between "us" and "them" is frequently blurred. One's nation is not perceived as an animate being that can nurture grievances; neither are other nations regarded as individuals harboring malicious intentions and capable of inflicting insults. The culprits and the victims in every conflict are specified, and sympathies and antipathies change with the issues and points of view. Moreover, individualistic nationalisms are by definition pluralisms, which implies that at any point in time there exists a plurality of opinions in regard to what constitutes the good of the nation. For this reason, it is relatively difficult, in individualistic nations, to achieve a consensus necessary for the mobilization of the population for war; it is especially difficult in the case of aggressive war, when no direct threat from the prospective enemy is perceived by the national population.

Ethnic nationalisms, by contrast, are necessarily forms of particularism. The borderline between "us" and "them" is relatively clear, the nations are seen as individuals capable of suffering and inflicting insults, and the national collectivity is essentially a consensual, rather than conflictual, pluralistic society. All these qualities facilitate mobilization.

In addition, during war, ethnic nationalisms are more conducive to brutality in relation to the enemy population than civic nationalisms. This is so because civic nationalisms, even when particularistic, treat humanity as one, fundamentally homogeneous, entity. Foreigners are not fellow nationals, but they are still fellow humans, and with a little effort on their part, it is assumed, they may even become fellow nationals. In ethnic nationalisms, by contrast, the borderline between "us" and "them" is in principle impermeable. Nationality is defined as an inherent trait, and nations are seen, in effect, as separate species. Foreigners are no longer fellow humans in the same sense, and there is no moral imperative to treat them as one would one's fellow nationals (in the same way as there is no imperative to treat our fellow mammals or even fellow great apes as fellow humans). The very definitions of ethnic nations presuppose a double standard of moral (or humane, decent, etc.) conduct. The tendency to "demonize" the enemy population, considered a necessary condition for "crimes against humanity," is built into ethnic nationalisms, for enemy populations within them are not necessarily defined as humanity to begin with.

According to the characteristic psycho-logic of ethnic nationalisms, in which both one's own nation and other nations are defined in terms of inherent traits, the evil other (whoever that may be) is always harboring malicious intentions ready to strike against the innocent nation at an opportune moment. For this reason, ethnic nations tend to feel threatened and to become aggressive, both to preempt perceived threats of aggression against them and because the evil nature of the adversary justifies aggression, even if no immediate threats are perceived, at the same time as it justifies brutality in relation to the enemy population. All these tendencies of ethnic nationalisms are well demonstrated by Serbian nationalism today. But they are also characteristic of other ethnic nationalisms, even though under certain circumstances they may be hidden from view.

Is there any change in the *nature* of ethnic nationalisms as a result of the end of the Cold War? I would say no. The greater salience of nationalist sentiments and the reactivation of national conflicts in Eastern Europe (which, by the way, are related to the end of the Cold War only as simultaneous but independent effects of the same cause, the collapse of the Soviet Union) cannot be attributed to the change of identity or even crisis of identity as a result of the abandonment of communism, but solely to the disintegration of imperial systems that held these sentiments and hostilities in check without modifying them in the least. The ease with which former communist bosses transform into right-wing nationalists (in the former constituent republics of the Soviet Union, as well as in

Yugoslavia—for example Milosević—and elsewhere) attests to the deep affinity between communism and ethnic nationalism. The former, as I have argued in another context, is in fact a metamorphosed variety of the latter. Ostensibly an internationalist and a universalist doctrine, communism only thinly camouflaged the nationalist character of the regimes in the Soviet bloc, particularly the regime in the Soviet Union itself. In fact there, at least since World War II, it hardly camouflaged anything at all. The main ideological premises of the Soviet regime after World War II were those of Russian great power nationalism, and if this not-so-subtle change of ideological direction or political orientation escaped the attention of the West, it was certainly felt by the hundred-million-strong non-Russian population of the Soviet Union. The great war, Vassilii Grossman wrote perceptively, "gave Stalin the possibility to openly declare the ideology of state nationalism." "Soviet, Russian people began to understand themselves in a new way, and to relate in a new way to people of other nationalities. . . . From the element of form, the national transformed into the content, and became the foundation of a new worldview [historical consciousness]."[2]

This post-World War II historical consciousness was based on the original Russian ethnic nationalism, and its perpetuation was the chief reason for the fragility of the Soviet Union, however monolithic it looked from the outside. Since nationalities were defined in terms of inherent traits, they were seen as mutually impermeable, and thus ethnic nationalism, on the one hand, made true Russification (i.e., incorporation and assimilation) of originally non-Russian populations inconceivable, and, on the other hand, prevented the integration of the constituent populations in a common new nationality, or the formation of the Soviet nation. A Soviet nation never existed (the phrase itself sounds absurd in Russian, which allows for the existence of a "Soviet state," "Soviet land," or "Soviet people"); it was a grave mistake to assume that it did, an error of perception that left Western observers and policy makers completely unprepared for the developments of the last several years and conceptually ill equipped to deal with them. The Soviet Union was a union of separate nations, held together by the might of Russia, or, in other words, an empire. The social structure of the Soviet Union reflected this political reality: immutable ethnic nationality was the basis of a rigid hierarchy, which determined people's life chances in the allegedly classless society. It is to this fact, clearly stamped in the consciousness of Soviet citizens, that the notorious fifth point in their passports corresponded.

In the framework of Russian nationalism, loyalty to the nation took precedence over loyalty to the state. The Soviet state recognized the legitimacy of loyalty to the Russian nation. Moreover, it recognized the legitimacy of loyalty to the other nations within the union as well (with one possible exception—the Jews—who, however, were defined not as a full-fledged nation, but only a nationality). This recognition was not consistent, because it went contrary to the Russian imperial interests. But, given the nature of Russian nationalism, neither could it be consistently withheld. In fact, the Soviet government sponsored the development of several inchoate non-Russian nationalities, and, in general, through its support of national cultures and bureaucracies in the republics, cultivated dual loyalties that would eventually prove so dangerous to it, and contributed to the formation of nationalist sentiments.

At the same time, the Soviet government (like any government) was often moved by instrumental, rather than ideological, considerations, and it was suspicious of the populist, antiauthoritarian, and potentially oppositional undercurrents of Russian nationalism, in the framework of which a Marxist party, or any party wielding absolute power, might look more like a foreign usurper than a legitimate government. It was also suspicious of the anti-Russian undercurrents of the non-Russian nationalisms, which it could not help but encourage. (This ambivalent position was also characteristic of the tsarist government in the days of "official nationality," and I would expect to find parallels in any nonrepresentative government in the age of nationalism.) As a result, during the Soviet period, nationalism, while by no means suppressed, was held in check: its expressions were controlled, special channels were provided for them, and the spillovers of the national sentiments outside these channels were tolerated only in certain areas (such as everyday life), where they did not threaten the interests of the ruling elite.

With the dissolution of the imperial structures, such controls became impossible. All the levees built to hold nationalism within specific channels broke down, and, with communism gone, it flooded the area. Although I know less about Yugoslavia, I have an impression that the situation there was quite similar. The reason the nationalist spillover has so far been so much more tragic in Yugoslavia may be that Russia, in contrast to Serbia, is too prohibitive in its size and strength in relation to other republics to allow events similar to the discrimination against Serbs in Croatia or in Bosnia-Herzegovina in 1990.[3] Another reason may be

that no Russian leader so far was willing to capitalize on such provocations that did take place and involve the country in military conflict, as
Milosević apparently did in Yugoslavia.[4]

The relationship between community, identity, and political change in
the new era is, I would therefore argue, very similar to what it was in the
old one, only now it is open to view, while earlier it appeared hidden.
This, however, does not mean that we should not raise this question; it is
a question of utmost importance and it is better to raise it later than never.
I already mentioned the implications of ethnic nationalism for aggressive
behavior, specifically war. I would now like to touch on its implications
for peaceful political change.

To begin with, the collectivistic and authoritarian features of ethnic
nationalism make it antithetical to liberal democracy at the same time as
they ensure its deep affinity to socialist-type regimes. Not only does this
explain the nationalist (rather than communist) character of the opposition
to democratization in the postcommunist societies, but it means that so
long as national identity and consciousness in these societies remain
ethnic, the emergence of liberal democracies in them will be highly
improbable. In other words, a successful democratization of these societies presupposes no less than a change of identity. While this is not an
impossibility, such a change of identity in societies formerly constituent
of the Soviet Union and the Soviet bloc is very unlikely. This is so chiefly
because the respective social elites of these societies have a vested interest
in ethnic nationalism, while democratization is emphatically contrary to
the interests of these elites, perhaps even more so than was communism.

The position of the social elite in East European societies belongs to
the intelligentsia, which under communism was the mainstay of dissident
movements and today represents the main pool for political leadership,
both pro- and antireform. The intelligentsia—in Russia, as much as in
Serbia, the Baltics, or elsewhere in Eastern Europe—has been the carrier
of nationalist ideas, the standard-bearer of ethnic nationalism. Nationalism, transmitted through high culture much more than through folklore,
permeates the intelligentsia's entire way of thinking and way of life,
forming the medium in which, cognitively, they exist, as fish do in water,
defining their perspectives, shaping their vision and aspirations. This
is true of the so-called democrats, as much as of the self-proclaimed
"nationalists," and it goes a long way to explain the general disaffection
of the intelligentsia today from the reform process. It should be remem-

bered that "nationalists" and "democrats" were equally opposed to communism in the past, and that, in fact, most prominent dissidents of the late Soviet period are found today among the former.

Within the framework of ethnic nationalism, culture is seen as the expression of the spirit of the nation and has the pride of place among social values. The intelligentsia, the creators and disseminators of culture, as a result enjoy immense social prestige. They are the interpreters of the nation's will, the mirror of its soul, the representatives and wielders of the supreme authority, to whom the masses owe their respect and obedience. In Russia, for example, the intelligentsia, already in the middle of the nineteenth century, assumed the place of the aristocracy, which redefined itself as "the educated class" at the same time as it embraced national identity. The social hierarchy became conceptualized in terms of the distinction between the intelligentsia and "the people." This distinction was preserved throughout the entire Soviet period—reflected in language (which conventionally distinguishes between members of the intelligentsia and the "simple" or "common" people) and in social arrangements— and became established in those of the Soviet republics in which it had not emerged independently.

Still, during the Soviet period, and in particular from the 1960s on, the Soviet intelligentsia was not satisfied with its position. While its social superiority was not challenged, it was denied political influence and prevented from assuming the role of national leadership to which, given the nature of its national consciousness and identity, it considered itself entitled. It was because of this that the Soviet intelligentsia turned away from communism and certain sectors in it became openly anticommunist. (The reasons for its disaffection with the communist regime, I should mention, were identical to the reasons that turned the Russian intelligentsia against the tsarist regime and brought the communist regime about.) The initial enthusiasm of the intelligentsia for democratic reform melted away, when it became clear that democracy, with its implication of social equality, will make the assertion of the intelligentsia's superior status at least as, if not more, unlikely. Nationalism, in distinction, implies such an assertion, and so even the "progressive" intelligentsia drifts in the direction of increasingly nationalist positions.

The chief source of nationalism's potential influence in postcommunist politics is the fact that it defines and serves the interests of the most articulate, organized, and influential class in postcommunist societies. The intelligentsia's superior status and group identity are wrapped up in ethnic nationalism and cannot be sustained outside its framework. The intelligentsia, therefore, has a vested interest in cultivating ethnic nationalism, which means cultivating exactly the complex of values that is most unfavorable for the development of liberal democracy.

In ethnically defined nations, the elites entrusted with the interpretation of the nation's will are by and large independent of the population at large and exercise disproportionate influence on the political orientation and development of their societies. The masses, in distinction, have very little say in this and are restricted to adjusting themselves to the choices made by the elites. Nevertheless, as the case of Yugoslavia makes patently clear, it is the participation of the masses that makes ethnic nationalism murderous. What is the source of appeal of nationalism to the masses? A very large role in this is played by ideological indoctrination—through literature, film, television—which gives form and direction to the people's inarticulate discontent, anger, and hopes for a better life. The intelligentsia should be held directly responsible for the ways these sentiments are expressed. At the same time, ethnic nationalism also fulfills an important independent function for the people: it guarantees them a level of dignity and self-respect that cannot be negated even by the most degrading personal circumstances. Since in ethnic nationalisms such dignity and self-respect are but reflections of the collective dignity (or prestige) of the nation, the masses have a direct interest in protecting this collective dignity. Often the easiest way to do this is at the expense of the other and through the humiliation and degradation of the other.

Nothing short of transforming ethnic nationalism into civic, which implies a change of the people's identity, can guarantee against the realization of its dangerous propensities. To effect such a transformation from without requires very strong measures, as strong as a long-term occupation or partition. Unless the international community is willing to commit itself to such measures, its efforts to restrain this brutal force in any particular case, I am afraid, will be largely in vain.

This brings us to a crucial question: does the post-Yugoslav crisis portend wider chaos? I do not think so. The Yugoslav civil war may spill over to other countries, particularly if Russians define the Serbian cause as their own, but it is unlikely that in the present conditions they would do so, and so the current Balkan crisis may well remain contained within the borders of the former Yugoslavia. This does not mean that very similar conflicts will not flare up in other East European countries and the territories of the former Soviet Union. But if they do, this will be an independent development. The Yugoslav crisis does not *portend* anything, but it gives us a clear idea of the dangers concealed in postimperial situations, when the constituent parts of the disintegrating empires are defined as ethnic nations.

NOTES

1. Some of the issues discussed below have been discussed at length in Liah Greenfeld and Daniel Chirot, "Nationalism and Aggression," *Theory and Society* 23, no. 1 (February 1994): 79–130.

2. Vassilii Grossman, *Zhizn' i sud'ba: Roman* (Moscow: Izd-vo Knizhnaia palata, 1988): 462, 464.

3. Aleksa Djilas, "A Profile of Slobodan Milosević," *Foreign Affairs* 72, no. 3 (summer 1993): 88.

4. Ibid.

TWELVE

Sheri Fink

The Anti-Genocide Movement on American College Campuses: A Growing Response to the Balkan War

> Ironically, today the students of American campuses call for arming a defender, a victim of genocide. Quite opposite, of course, the cause of 20 years ago, during the Vietnam era. I believe the cause of these students— this generation—will once again prove to be right. Why? Because youth has a way of being uncontaminated by the manipulation of politics and youth knows the truth.
>
> —Muhamed Sacirbey, foreign minister of Bosnia-Herzegovina

Violence directed against civilians in Bosnia-Herzegovina continued unabated for over three and a half years. The failure of two American presidential administrations to respond effectively when confronted with genocide in Bosnia-Herzegovina leads to a question: have dissenting voices been raised against American policy? To what extent?

This chapter provides a case study of one community of dissent in American society—the campus-based Balkan anti-genocide movement. "Balkan anti-genocide" is an appropriate name, because, as will be shown, a recognition that genocide occurred in the Balkans and a need to take action to stop it and prevent it from recurring describe the core motivations of most campus activists. Their activities range from political action, to humanitarian aid and peer education. "Movement" is appropriate, because campus groups with nearly identical ideology and actions exist nationwide and have formed a united coalition. Leaders, who coalesce in the organization known as Students against Genocide (SAGE) Coalition, provide information, facilitate intercampus communication, and lend direction to individual group actions. SAGE Coalition is closely aligned with a grassroots coordinating body, the American Committee to Save Bosnia (ACSB).

Why study the activists? Grassroots opposition to American Balkan policy has not previously been examined in detail. Aside from newspaper reports covering their demonstrations, the nature of the activist groups and the personality of the activists have remained largely unstudied. On the other hand, while ignored by the mass media and academia, the movement has accomplished much in the realms of legislative pressure, relief efforts for war victims, and education of Americans about genocide in Bosnia.

Campus-based and community-based activist organizations are the anti-genocide movement's two strong components. This chapter focuses on the campus-based groups, and is written from the perspective of an active member and leader of the SAGE Coalition since 1993. The protests, civil disobedience, teach-ins, and humanitarian projects taking place on campus in response to the Balkan situation represent a refreshing exception to the stereotypical image of the lethargic student on American college campuses in the 1990s. Rather than relying solely on observation to portray the movement, I base this chapter on written questionnaires and on telephone and videotaped interviews with the activists.[1]

The Sparks that Ignite Activists—Why They Take Action

The unfolding tragedy of the Balkans has appeared prominently in American print, radio, and televised media. In 1994 and 1995, only the O. J. Simpson trial received greater coverage on the "big three" network evening newscasts.[2]

How, then, has nightly exposure to the horrors of genocide affected the typical American viewer? How has watching the destruction of a multiethnic, multicultural society affected those who live in one themselves? The answer is surprising: few Americans claim to understand the war, and polls taken prior to the Dayton Agreement and subsequent commitment of American troops showed that most types of military involvement were thinly supported or opposed.[3]

On the other hand, for many Americans, the images of war have hit hard and have evoked a desire to understand and to act. On campuses around the country, that sentiment has found an outlet as like-minded individuals encounter one another. Concerned students seek out lectures about the war, find each other in Muslim, Croatian, Turkish, and Jewish student groups, raise the issues at Amnesty International meetings, and find ways to act after encountering Bosnia support and anti-genocide groups on campus.

An Awareness of Genocide

The broad ethnic, religious, and cultural origins of those who respond to the images of violence and suffering are remarkable. Consider these: a Haitian student at Stanford University, already sensitive to oppression and human rights abuses, a Japanese student at the University of Washington who grew up with lessons of Hiroshima, and an American student bred in the traditions of activism—all gleaned lessons from their backgrounds that encouraged them to act.

Despite their diversity, many of the activists recall experiencing nearly identical realizations leading to involvement: a sudden awareness that genocide was being committed in Bosnia-Herzegovina (or prior to that, atrocities in Croatia) and a feeling of moral obligation to respond. Jennie Davis, a University of Vermont undergraduate who founded the Vermont Committee for Peace in Bosnia and served in SAGE Coalition's elected board, had a typical response: "At first the situation was abstract and then one day it kind of hit me. I saw genocide happening today and wanted to take action. For a long time I thought, 'I should be doing something about this,' and one day I realized that I could."

A non-Jewish student living in the southern United States, SAGE Coalition activist Brent Phillips, cites lessons of the Holocaust: "The lack of action by the U.S. to halt the clear genocide in Bosnia-Herzegovina compelled me to get involved. 'Never Again' obligates us all to act (by default) if our governments are unwilling."

While quite cognizant of the differences between the Holocaust and the genocide in Bosnia, many, particularly Jewish, students nonetheless see a connection. The numbers of those killed and a myriad of other parameters might be different, but those involved in the movement perceive genocide and targeting of a religious group for expulsions, killings, or torture as intolerable anywhere and on any scale. Many of these activists, such as Stanford chemistry graduate student and SAGE-net (SAGE's electronic network) administrator Rich Green, were taught from an early age to speak out, rather than be a passive witness to such injustices: "The more that I read about Bosnia, the more I was reminded of the Holocaust. Unfortunately, it made me understand how it was possible that the world did nothing in the face of the Holocaust. I could not face looking at myself as a 'good German' who never acted."

Prior Interest in the Region: All Too Rare

Frequently, but certainly not always, those that have taken action already had a particular interest in East European affairs. This contrasts with the general student population, who, in the poll done for this chapter, indicate more interest in domestic affairs, or in the case of most foreign students, the happenings in their country of origin. Erik Nisbet, codirector of the Bosnia Support Committee at Cornell University and a SAGE Coalition activist, was previously interested in Eastern Europe and foreign affairs.

> I always had a fascination with Yugoslavia. I was planning to go to Zagreb [Croatia] to study when the war broke out. At the same time, I was involved with United Nations Association USA and Model UN—at first I thought the UN would produce a just solution. Then our group sponsored [Bosnian Ambassador to the UN] Muhamed Sacirbey to speak on campus. That's when I realized the UN's mistakes and that's what motivated me to get informed and involved.

Others became active because they shared a religious belief with the primary victims of Serbian aggression, namely, Islam. Some were from other countries in the area—particularly Turkey. Still others traced their backgrounds to the region, usually Bosnia or Croatia, or came to the United States from there to study during the war. Emira Tufo is a first-year student from Sarajevo and an active Stanford SAGE member whose reasons for involvement exemplify those of other students from Bosnia:

> I have the moral responsibility because it's my country and nobody else is doing much. I spent all my life there. I had the greatest times there. My family and friends are still there and my fondest memories are too. I spent two and a half years of war there and it seemed that no one was doing anything. Now that I'm in a position to help, I don't want to be one of the people who turned away.

An obstacle to the movement is that students whose families (or who themselves) originate from Bosnia or Croatia and who would form the logical core of the Balkan anti-genocide movement are relatively scarce. Steve Walker, a former State Department official who resigned in protest over United States policy in the Balkans, speaks frequently on campuses in his current position as director of the American Committee to Save Bosnia:

> There is no natural constituency that can provide the core of the movement. Jewish students form somewhat of a core, but Hillel hasn't taken an unambiguous pro-Bosnian, pro-arms-embargo-lifting-stance—they're more involved in education about the war. Muslim students are also a core to some extent, but not enough of them feel a strong enough connection to Bosnian Muslims—there's not the feeling that "this could be me." The anti-apartheid movement, for example, had the advantage that African Americans could more easily imagine, "this could be me."

Muslim-Jewish Cooperation

One welcome by-product of the campus-based initiatives has been the increased contacts and cooperation between involved Jewish and Muslim students. Students from these two religious groups tend to be involved in Bosnia support activities to a proportionately greater extent than others. As discussed above, this can be attributed to Jewish students' heightened awareness of the issue of genocide and the religion Muslim students share with the primary victims of the war. Haverford College's Michael Sells, a professor of comparative religions and a director of the Community of Bosnia Foundation, works closely with students on the campuses of Haverford and Bryn Mawr Colleges: "The Muslim Students Association worked with Hillel at Haverford and Bryn Mawr. The events in Bosnia got groups who usually don't communicate really actively involved in cooperating with one another."

Jewish and Muslim students learn about one another's religion and customs by working with one another. For example, holidays and prayer times need to be taken into consideration when planning demonstrations or other activities are planned. On the national grassroots level, Muslim and Jewish groups have also explored working with one another and issuing joint statements. In one example, on July 25, 1995, six prominent national Jewish and five prominent national Muslim organizations (including the Muslim Public Affairs Council, the National Association of

Arab Americans, B'nai B'rith, and the American Jewish Congress) joined other organizations and individuals in sending a letter to each U.S. Senator supporting the Dole-Lieberman bill to end the arms embargo against Bosnia.[4]

Outreach and Empowerment: Keys to Broadening Activism

Many students become involved as a result of active friends or acquaintances. Some of those most active in the anti-genocide movement started out by being sympathetic and wanting to do something, but not knowing how to take action. Mike Rothenberg is a Stanford M.D. and Ph.D. student who experienced this before joining SAGE, but then went on to serve as SAGE's legislative affairs task force director. "I felt more strongly about Bosnia than perhaps I've felt about any other issue. I never knew how to act on those feelings, though. It was only through a good friend that was thinking about ways to act that I was then able to do something about an issue that concerned me—for the first time in my life."

This willingness to act, but inability to do so alone, presents a challenge to the campus activists. Intense education and outreach efforts by the anti-genocide groups are critical to the growth of activism both on campus and nationally. This is particularly important on campuses where activist turnover is high as students graduate each spring. Outreach is also important because indications are that students familiar with Bosnia support groups on their campus, even though they might not join them, are more empowered to affect the situation than others. A Stanford premedical student said, "I know someone who's active in SAGE. Because of our conversations, I've tried to keep informed. I've also written to my senators and the president to express my concern about their lack of decisive action. I acted because 'never again' is happening again and people want to ignore it."

Individual Connections Span Oceans

Many mention news coverage of the war's atrocities as the initial impetus for their engagement. For Stanford SAGE member John Tillinghast, an article by historian Noel Malcolm clearly defined the issues. For others, the war crossed the ocean and found its way into their consciences by way of shocking, personal testimonies of concentration camp and rape camp survivors. Those stories facilitated a personal connection and understanding that broke down the abstract, intellectual construct most people have of the war. This occurred to an even greater extent when students met Bosnian refugees living in their neighborhoods or Bosnian students and faculty who came to campus during the war.

Encountering an individual affected by war evokes strong sentiments. Says Erik Nisbet: "When you see their faces, you can no longer tolerate the predominant logic of 'they're not Americans, so why should we care.' I am American and I am ashamed. Just because someone's Bosnian or Rwandan doesn't mean it's not our business. We're all human beings." Another activist puts it succinctly: "When the news makes you weep, and it doesn't seem like anyone is doing anything, you need to act to avoid losing your mind."

In summary, the students, faculty, and staff who took action tended to do so because they perceived the war in Bosnia as a human rights issue (more specifically, an issue of genocide), and they were empowered to act by both internal and external factors. As discussed below, when the activists learned more about the situation in the Balkans, their initial convictions were reinforced by the realizations that (1) stopping the appeasement of an ultra-nationalist aggressor in Eastern Europe is in America's self-interest, and (2) international law demands the prevention and punishment of genocide and supports the right of victim nations to self-defense.

The Central Issues: Genocide and the Right to Self-Defense

The movement's core ideologies from 1993 to the Dayton Agreement in late 1995 can be summarized as follows: (1) the acknowledgment and condemnation of genocide occurring in Bosnia-Herzegovina; (2) the demand that the American government act to stop the genocide (and the belief that it is in America's interests to do so); and (3) the support of the Bosnian government's right to self-defense. Following the Dayton Agreement, the movement increased its emphasis on the importance of war crimes investigations and the use of international forces to ensure that indicted war criminals are removed from power and brought to trial— particularly those accused of the crime of genocide.

Genocide

The word "genocide" is used frequently in this chapter, and is used frequently by Balkan anti-genocide activists. The choice of the word is not an emotional one, but rather a judgment based soundly on evidence of the situation in the former Yugoslavia and the legal definition of the word.

Genocide is defined under international law as "acts committed with intent to destroy, in whole or in part, a national, ethnical, racial, or religious group," including "killing members of the group" or "causing serious bodily or mental harm to members of the group." All of the following — genocide, conspiracy to commit genocide, incitement to commit genocide, attempt to commit genocide, and even complicity in genocide — are punishable under the Convention on the Prevention and Punishment of the Crime of Genocide ratified in 1948. The convention's signatories, which include the United States and Yugoslavia, have pledged to "undertake to prevent and to punish" genocide.[5] Michael Sells has considered the issue of genocide carefully and works to educate his students and other about what it means:

> The movement's focus on genocide and its definition is important. Most columnists are ignorant — they say, "this isn't genocide," but they don't know the definition of genocide set down in Geneva and the concept coined by international lawyer Raphael Lemkin after World War II. The word "genocide" was very carefully defined so it could be part of international law.
>
> Some people assume only the Holocaust is genocide or that you're making false parallels to the Holocaust when you use the word. But Lemkin defined the word specifically to avoid trivializing the Holocaust, and as a disincentive to the future occurrence of genocide.
>
> I've been amazed at columnists who claim this isn't genocide. Are they implying that they are right and a group of international jurists with a forty-year education in the subject and two years investigating war crimes in former Yugoslavia are wrong? The International War Crimes Tribunal for the Former Yugoslavia has issued indictments for genocide, including the Bosnian Serb leader Karadžić and the Bosnian Serb military leader Ratko Mladić!

While some in the media, such as *Newsday's* Roy Gutman and the *Christian Science Monitor's* David Rohde, investigated war crimes in Bosnia, others have downplayed them. Skepticism greeted the early reports of atrocities, perhaps out of a human tendency to doubt that such horrible actions could be perpetrated in the "modern world." Sadly, even after war crimes had been thoroughly documented by the investigative body of the UN War Crimes Tribunal and numerous human rights organizations, they were still being denied by Serb-nationalist lobby groups in the United States and misrepresented in the media.

Sometimes the media's mischaracterization can be blatant: for example, casting the situation as one in which "all sides are killing each other as they have been for the past six hundred years." Other times, the disbelief in genocide and the survivors of terrible atrocities can take more subtle forms. For example, in February 1996, a story ran on a San Francisco evening newscast that included painful interviews with survivors of the notorious Serb-run concentration camp Omarska now living in the San Francisco area.[6] At the time, the horrors of Omarska were universally acknowledged, having been investigated by, among others, the Red Cross and U.S. State Department; and an Omarska guard, Dusan Tadic, was about to stand trial in the Hague for war crimes. Even so, the station offered this disclaimer: "[the survivors' stories go] on and on and on. Some stories are probably exaggerations, others fabrications. In war, the truth is often the first to die."

Indeed, this lack of understanding and a failure to perceive the events in Bosnia as genocide seem to extend to the general population. On campus, perhaps the crux of the difference between activists and their fellow students is the connection they make between today's events and the lessons learned by the world community following the Holocaust. In a poll of students at Stanford in October 1995, even when prompted, respondents were least likely to say that the United States should apply the lessons of World War II or the Holocaust to Bosnia and more likely to indicate that the lessons of Somalia and Vietnam (dangers of involvement) and South Africa (rewards of limited, nonmilitary involvement) should be applied.

Perhaps those students did not realize the extent of the atrocities committed in Bosnia, or perhaps they did not want to notice. A recent Stanford graduate admitted he purposely did not follow the war:

> I think there's the issue of preferring to be ignorant rather than aware and silent or complicit in the face of genocide. It's like when you're watching TV and a documentary about hunger in Africa comes on. You just flip the channel. You don't want to feel there's something else you have to do something about.

Students who take action have a clearly different view. Like many other students involved in the Balkan anti-genocide movement, Andreas Silver of the Coalition against Genocide at UNC-Chapel Hill is concerned with genocide in multiple regions of the world:

> "Never again" does not mean "never again will Jews be slaughtered." It should be never again will Cambodians, East Timorese, Tibetans, Bosnians, and anyone else be slaughtered . . . but this has been going on steadily ever since 1945 in one place or another. The major countries which control the United Nations have fastidiously ignored their obligations under international law to prevent and punish genocide.

This sentiment, and the awareness and recognition that genocide anywhere is intolerable, has led members of the Balkan anti-genocide effort to begin responding to other cases of looming ethnic violence and genocide, for example, Rwanda, Burundi, and Chechnya. Zachary Rothschild and Jennifer Gerlach, cochairs of Drew University's SAGE chapter, emphasize the importance of broadening their work: "Our larger goal is to educate people that genocide continues to happen again and again in different places around the world. We have to take a stand against it because every life counts."

The knowledge and acceptance that events in Bosnia constitute genocide leads to the view that neutrality is no longer a valid concept. Acknowledging the occurrence of genocide forces a decision—either act to oppose it, or be its silent accomplice. At a demonstration in front of the White House after the fall of Srebrenica in July 1995, one of the placards raised by a demonstrator read, "In cases of genocide, neutrality is complicity." The fact that complicity in genocide is also punishable by international law may explain the Clinton administration's refusal to use the word.

The Right to Self-Defense

One of the key political demands of the anti-genocide movement in America has been the unilateral American lifting of the arms embargo against the Bosnian government. Following the Dayton Agreement, the activists urged that the Bosnian government be armed and trained to defend against the threat of new attacks after the withdrawal of IFOR forces. Activists justify these demands by referring to both the obligations of United Nations member states to prevent genocide and the right of a nation to self-defense, which is supported by international law. Articles 2(4) and 51 of the United Nations Charter codify this right, which may not be abridged by actions of the Security Council.[7] Furthermore, the arms embargo was imposed against Yugoslavia prior to its dissolution and thus could not be legitimately applied to Bosnia without its consent once it was admitted as a member of the United Nations.

The arms embargo also conflicted with numerous United Nations Security Council resolutions calling for the delivery of humanitarian aid, and protection of personnel delivering that aid, and protection of Bosnia's population in United Nations-declared safe areas.

Opposition: A Minor Obstacle to Action

Opposition to the activists on campus has been rather weak, but it has presented a minor obstacle to the actions of the Balkan anti-genocide groups. When opposition occurs, it tends to be in one of several forms. To begin with, it comes from some who object to making parallels with the Holocaust. For example, a Stanford professor, who noted that a forum on Bosnia was organized by Hillel, accused Jewish students of having been pushed by their connection with the Holocaust from "morality to moralizing." Perhaps he was implying that Jewish condemnation of the atrocities in Bosnia was insufficiently reasoned. However, as Brad Blitz, the organizer of the event and cofounder and former director of SAGE, put it, "the reasons behind our condemnation of the aggression in Bosnia stand well enough on their own."

Other criticism along these lines can be found within the Jewish community itself. In particular, the Holocaust survivor community appears to be split. Some, like Nobel laureate Elie Wiesel, have spoken out publicly and in the strongest terms possible about the need for a Western response to the situation in the Balkans: " 'We cannot tolerate the excruciating sights of this old new war,' Mr. Wiesel said, turning to President Bill Clinton at the opening of the Holocaust Memorial Museum in Washington DC. 'Mr. President, this bloodshed must be stopped. It will not stop unless we stop it.' "[8]

Other Holocaust survivors publicly voice concerns that the Holocaust is trivialized by comparisons with events in Bosnia. Some go further, and express an unwillingness to criticize Serbs, whom they perceive as having been friends of the Jews in World War II.[9] Some also reserve contempt for Croats, whom they consider to have been brutal puppets of the Nazis. This memory has made it difficult for many survivors to speak out on behalf of victimized Croats, and even Bosnian Muslims, today.

False Neutrality

Perhaps the most frustrating opposition the anti-genocide activists confront is the obsession of those who want to give "both sides" a platform out of a need to appear "neutral." Activists are likely to attribute such moral equivocation on the part of their peers to ignorance. "The [knowledge] gap between people who are interested and those who are not is enormous," says Shin Yasui, a Japanese student and director of the Committee for World Peace at the University of Oregon. An ABC News reporter commented in June 1995 after revealing the results of a new poll, "Few [Americans] are sure what the war in Bosnia is all about."[10]

Many of today's students go to lengths to give all sides in a conflict an equal hearing. The "default mode," then, is to not "take sides," or not to view a conflict as one between a victim and an aggressor until the situation is fully explored. Unfortunately, most students never progress past this default mode by taking time to learn about a situation and develop an educated response. "Everyone is a victim there," said a freshman biology student polled about Bosnia, who then couldn't name a single party to the conflict and said she didn't understand it well.

Wariness of Political Action

Activists are also frustrated by peers who oppose "political" types of actions. In most cases, students express willingness to attend lectures or support "humanitarian" activities for Bosnia (even though much of the humanitarian aid collected throughout the war was pillaged at Serb roadblocks and prevented from entering by dangerous skies and mined roads). Those students, however, are less likely to be willing to demonstrate or write letters to elected officials with the goal of actually ending the bloodshed. At its extreme, a few students even shy away from engaging in humanitarian aid activities, out of a perception that engaging in them would constitute taking sides. For example, the new student leader of a group that had previously sent tons of needed medical supplies to Bosnia decided to drop the program because it was "too political . . . you're making a political statement by who you send the supplies to."

On the whole, there is enormous pressure on the student groups to be more humanitarian aid-oriented than "political." Humanitarian activities are met with wider approval, provide opportunities for raising funds, and are more likely to be covered as "human interest" stories in the media. In some cases (for example, at Cornell University), activists have actually felt compelled to form separate groups—one for humanitarian activities and another for political action. This has occurred on the national grassroots level as well; a separate, nonprofit educational institute (the Balkan Institute) has been formed for public education about the situation in the Balkans. At the same time, the politically active grassroots coordinating body, the American Committee to Save Bosnia, was retained under the auspices of the Action Council for Peace in the Balkans. On campus, splitting into two organizations has the result of broadening the appeal of humanitarian aid and educational activities. Other campus organizations (such as Amnesty International) and academic departments seem more willing to work with Bosnia support groups on such "nonpolitical" projects.

At War with the Pacifists

Some students found themselves "at war" with pacifist elements on campus. While the grassroots Bosnia support movement claims among its members many who participated in the antiwar protest movements of the 1960s, there appears to be a split of opinion among traditional pacifists. The September 1995 edition of the *Progressive* highlighted this issue. It featured two articles by peace activists who argued the case for a U.S. military response in Bosnia. In the same issue, however, the editors argued, "Bombing the Bosnian Serbs . . . will certainly bring more killing and horror. And it's extremely unlikely that the Bosnian Serbs will give up." (Only days after the issue hit the newsstands, of course, the editors were proved wrong. NATO employed decisive, but militarily selective, air power; the Croats and Bosnians mounted an offensive; and the Serb forces, who could no longer shoot down on civilian populations at whim, were suddenly willing to talk peace). "Pacifists" who opposed military intervention to end the genocide in Bosnia also argued from a position of general distrust of the American military and general opposition to use of its power. Others considered themselves "noninterventionists" (however, they failed to perceive that the UN Security Council-imposed arms embargo was itself a form of intervention). Michael Sells has confronted many self-described pacifists in his Bosnia support work:

> I think there are very, very few genuine pacifists. When people claim to be pacifists I ask them, "When the ethnic cleansers come to your house and someone turns to call the police, would you take the phone out of their

hands because the police use force?" Most people wouldn't. So, I call it "pacifism for the other guy." It's in many cases a deeply cynical position.

Like much student opposition to Bosnia support activities, the "pacifist" nonresponse may be rooted in an inaccurate or uneducated view of the conflict in the Balkans. Surely, if they perceived it in terms of a nation facing genocide, most would acknowledge, at minimum, the right of that nation to self-defense. Inexplicably, the pacifist advocates of nonresponse failed to recognize that aggressive forces continued to kill innocent civilians on a massive scale (e.g., Srebrenica, Žepa, and Banja Luka) throughout the three and a half years of the Bosnian War and even after countless diplomatic initiatives. Appeals to reason and economic sanctions failed to stop the aggressors. Genocide continued unopposed and undaunted for over three and a half years because the international community failed to arm its victims or protect them.

On the other hand, some of those uncomfortable with taking political positions on the use of force took action on other levels. Sells relates,

> It's ironic, but some people with whom I disagree on political issues have gotten very involved and really accomplished things. The Quakers, for example, get involved much more than other groups. But they never want to see a bad guy and a good guy. However, once they see a documentary videotape like *Killing Memory* by Harvard's Andras Riedlmayer, there's no way people can say "everyone's to blame." Once that problem is over, then we can discuss what to do. If someone is a pacifist, then they can still help a refugee student.

This holds true of students on campus, many of whom enthusiastically participate in projects such as English- language tutoring programs for refugees, but steer clear of political demonstrations. Interestingly, some Bosnia activists who campaign for Bosnia's right to self-defense and American military involvement considered themselves pacifists at an earlier point in their lives. Rich Green was one of those:

> I read a book a number of years ago called *A Cambodian Odyssey* written by a survivor of the Khmer Rouge. This book had a profound effect on me. It made me realize that some governments are so terrible that force must be used to remove them, if necessary. This understanding contributed to the demise of my previously held pacifist beliefs . . . through studying the Holocaust on my own, my views became reinforced.

Other opposition to campus-based Balkan anti-genocide activities has come from communities of ethnic Serbs (mostly off-campus) who are organized into aggressive political lobbying groups. This subject is treated extensively in the chapter by Brad Blitz this volume. Here it is worth mentioning only that events on several campuses have been disrupted by the noisy protests of those involved with such groups.

At this point, it is interesting to note that a few of the campus activists include ethnic Serbs who are opposed to the genocide in Bosnia. Furthermore, many campus groups take pains to avoid referring to the aggressors as "Serbs" (thus accusing an entire ethnic group) and rather refer to them as "ultranationalist Serbs" or "Karadžić's Serbs." Frequently it is Bosnian refugee student members of the groups who insist on this—remarkably, after being driven from their homes by ultranationalist Serb forces, most refuse to succumb to the hatred those forces engender. "If I hate them, then I will become like them" is the way one student from Sarajevo put it. Many activists have also sought to understand the goals of the Serb-nationalists, the fears of Serbian people and what they claim incites them to seek an ethnically homogenous "Greater Serbia." None of the reasons or the goals, however, have convinced the activists that genocide is a permissible means to attain them. Says Brad Blitz: "While Serbian ultranationalists frequently frame their arguments around political concerns regarding minority status and sometimes genuine fear or uncertainty, there is a deep-seated denial as to what is actually happening on the ground. Dismembering Yugoslavia politically, by voting, is a far cry from using the military to pursue a policy of dismembering people—specifically civilians. This is what the Serb-nationalists fail to address."

The Major Obstacles: Apathy and Political Inaction

Academia's Apathy

Only at times when Bosnia features prominently in the news for one spectacular human rights atrocity or another (a Sarajevo marketplace bombed, the population of a city killed and buried in mass graves) do many people on campus briefly take notice and try to understand the situation. In attempting to capitalize on the attention, and draw more members while adding their voices to the outrage, many campus demonstrations are organized rapidly following such events. "When there is a crisis situation your phone rings off the hook," says Nader Hashemi, coordinator of the Ad Hoc Committee on Bosnia at Carleton University in Ottawa, Canada. "When there's no crisis, no one seems to care."

Thus, more than opposition, perhaps, the student activists face apathy. Some attribute it to a general sense of disconnectedness and isolation on campus. "It seems that people are reluctant to commit or get involved with anything, not necessarily just this issue," says Amy Gaglia, an activist at Syracuse University.

Add to the ambient apathy a sense of confusion and distance from events in Bosnia, and the task of organizing students around the issue grows tremendous. A Stanford biology graduate student complains, "it's hard to get involved in something you don't understand. Different papers, different reporters say different things. It's hard to get the real story." A graduate student in civil engineering adds, "the war just doesn't concern me enough to take a stand." Activist Rich Green speaks to his peers about the Balkans as often as possible. He frequently finds them uninformed and uninterested:

> People don't know the difference between the Krajina and Kosovo, between a Bosnian Croat and a Croatian Serb. The situation is complex enough that people throw up their hands and say, "I wish all those folks would just stop killing each other, but what can we do?" In short, the situation is pretty depressing in terms of people's willingness to be informed.

What does it take to overcome the students' apathy? Personal contact may be key. "To get involved I would need someone to say, 'we're having a meeting,' " said a first-year psychology graduate student who had just arrived at Stanford. "I feel like the situation is publicized but the channels to action aren't open."

This kind of response presents a challenge to activists, who realize that in order to gain support and educate the larger community, they must focus more on outreach and organizing events that will draw media coverage. The campus itself is an environment somewhat more conducive to reaching people than most. Yet activists still must work hard to be noticed. A Stanford computing staff member who expressed an interest in Bosnia had not heard of activities on campus, which had been taking place for over two and a half years: "It's hard, not being a member of any side's community. I don't have a familial attachment, and I haven't felt an organized response by our government or on the grassroots level. There probably are grassroots efforts, but I haven't heard enough about them."

Apathy on campus can drain activists' energy. Low turnouts to some events, combined with stereotyped notions about successful campus activist movements of the past, add to the problem. ACSB's Steve Walker has observed this on his campus visits, but feels that communications between the campus organizations within SAGE Coalition help counter the problem.

> It would have been easier for people to give up due to frustration over their small numbers if it weren't for SAGE. My sense is that the materials going out to students and SAGE being there to unify people has given the student activists strength and endurance. At least with SAGE and the ACSB, they are part of a living, growing coalition.

Michael Sells, the professor at Haverford College, finds himself giving pep talks to his students and explaining why they shouldn't look to the Vietnam antiwar movement as a model for their current activism efforts. He assures them that what they see as a weakness, the low proportion of students involved in anti-genocide activism, is actually an expected phenomenon:

> People tend to make a false comparison with today and the Vietnam antiwar movement. The difference is that back then people were going to get drafted. I tell the activist students here, "to compare yourself with Vietnam is a very big mistake." There's just no comparison. What's going on now fits the predominant historical pattern. People don't want to believe that genocide is happening. People are busy and don't want to accept it or feel obligated to do something about it. This is a natural phenomenon and it's natural for activists to have to find ways to confront it.

The reasons for the more widespread involvement in the Vietnam antiwar movement had much to do with the fact that students were directly affected by the war, argues Sells. In Bosnia, thus far, this has not been the case:

> In Vietnam, a minority of people were activists. But many people were willing to help shut down the university for a day. It was very easy to get a crowd.
>
> However, as soon as Nixon abolished the draft, the anti-war movement lost its major power. The numbers of people at demonstrations just plummeted dramatically. So, the difference was that at first, something was directly impinging on people's lives. This situation is not directly impinging on people's lives.

ACSB's Walker completes the thought by contrasting the proposed American troop deployment to Bosnia with that of Vietnam: "Even the U.S. sending in twenty thousand ground troops to enforce an unstable peace does not concern this generation of students. There's no draft. There's no danger of students being drawn into those troops, whereas that was a strong motivating factor in Vietnam."

In summary, the size of the current movement is commensurate with the expected response to a faraway situation, and does not warrant disparaging comparisons to the size of the Vietnam antiwar movement. That movement, however, is useful as a study of why people tend to involve themselves in activism. Today's anti-genocide campus activists are learning that to widen support for their cause, they must bring the war home by educating their peers about the risks America faces by ignoring genocide.

Lack of Faculty Interest

Apathy on campus emanates from faculty as well as students. Whereas on a few campuses, professors took the lead in educating students about Bosnia and forming activist support groups, on many others, faculty are indifferent or even hostile to such actions.[11] On a few campuses, activist professors organized in-depth courses on the war, but on many the war was either not covered, or covered as part of other courses on contemporary politics or Balkan history. In this study, most Balkan anti-genocide activists on campus described professors as only "somewhat supportive" of their groups' activities.

The relative silence of the academic community on the Balkans has surprised many. In Britain's *Times Higher Education Supplement* (August 4, 1995), Simon Targett polled leading academics in Britain and the United States on their attitudes toward the fighting. Most supported some sort of action to end the war (for example, confronting Serbian forces militarily or allowing the Bosnian government to arm itself) or else suggested the United Nations be strengthened to protect civilians. Many also agreed there were parallels between the actions of Western governments in the summer of 1995 with the appeasement of Hitler in 1938–1939. That said, some professors pointed out their disappointment with the failure of their peers to speak out about the war. Norman Stone, professor of modern history at Oxford University, was quoted as saying, "To their shame, academics have been all too silent on the Bosnian question. It's shocking."

Part of this can be explained, suggests Steve Walker, by considering that

> while the academics you'd expect to be activists are the ones who were already involved with the subject area, in this case they aren't sympathetic. The Balkan studies field is composed of a lot of people who studied Yugoslavia and spent a lot of time in Belgrade. A pro-Serb and pro-Yugoslav-unity bias predominates. The war and peace studies academics, another group you'd presume would have an interest in this area, are split on the issues.

But many others cringe at letting academia's leaders off the hook easily. Brad Blitz attempted to cajole faculty to action in several opinion pieces he penned for the Stanford Daily. In one, on April 4, 1995, he wrote,

> The faculty at this university have proven themselves intellectually and morally bankrupt. . . . [As a result of revelations about the extent of Serb atrocities] serious academics can no longer pretend that the destruction of Bosnia is the result of a civil war in which all sides are guilty. SAGE has received no support from faculty, who have refused to condemn the use of genocide against the citizens of Bosnia. Rather, in some cases, there has been a backlash from prominent faculty against such student organization. This has taken the form of a simplistic relativism which some faculty have used to criticize student protest. This relativism assumes that the University is an apolitical setting where ideas are necessarily of equal weight. It disguises a new ethic of indiscriminate moral equivalence.
>
> Stanford faculty and associates have repeatedly demonstrated their confusion between the legitimate ideal of "objectivity" and the political demand for "balance" . . . To criticize those who exclude legitimate voices [is quite different from criticizing] those who exclude the illegitimate claims of ultranationalist hate-mongers who want to be heard.
>
> A great university should be able to recognize the contradictions which the destruction of Bosnia poses to our value-system and intellectual traditions. Surely the mission of the university should be to align itself politically when necessary rather than ignoring the significance of real world events.

In sum, apathy and ignorance on campus, both from students and faculty, have constituted a serious challenge to the political action and even humanitarian aid activities of the activists. A strong focus on education and outreach, as discussed, seems the logical antidote, but cannot be expected to cure the problem entirely.

Inaction of Political Leaders

The student and grassroots movements successfully helped pressure congressional representatives and senators to vote to lift the arms embargo on Bosnia's government. After two years of effort, both houses of Congress passed the legislation in July 1995 by overwhelming margins. (Although subsequently vetoed by President Clinton, the threat of an override played an important role in pressuring the President to take action to stop the bloodshed in Bosnia-Herzegovina.) Along the way, however, activists faced opposition to lifting the arms embargo from many elected representatives.

The pacifists' argument that "more arms will bring more death and more destruction to innocent people on all sides"[12] was also employed by politicians. U.S. Congresswoman Anna Eshoo wrote to a SAGE member on August 2, 1995, "I do not support lifting the arms embargo unless a case can be made that arms sold to the Croats or Bosnian Muslims would be used only for defensive purposes and not to commit further atrocities and bloodshed."

Incredibly, this letter arrived just weeks after thousands of Bosnian Muslims from the UN-declared "safe area" Srebrenica were herded into a giant soccer stadium, killed, and buried in mass graves. The Serbs received no opposition from the West, nor were the poorly armed Bosnian fighters able to keep them at bay. The defenders of the next "safe area" to fall, Žepa, held out for weeks longer than expected—a prolonged death gasp that could have been halted by Western decisiveness.

The irony of the eastern enclaves being written off as Serb territory just weeks later in the Dayton "partition plan" for Bosnia was not lost on activists. They recognized that by allowing Žepa to fall, the West made its task of dividing Bosnia easier, at the price of thousands who were summarily slaughtered. Their blood is forever on the hands and the conscience of the Western leaders.[13]

The misleading and sometimes clearly false statements of political leaders, trying to defend their decisions to "do nothing," seem to affect the outlook of students. As Nader Hashemi puts it, "the opinions of government leaders are regurgitated by the masses." These include calling the conflict a "civil war," referring to the situation as intractable because "they've been fighting for centuries," and generally subscribing to a doctrine of moral equivalence. These platitudes are also widely cited in the mass media, contrary to the observation of many historians of the region.

The other predominant congressional argument can be encapsulated as "let's not Americanize the war." The Clinton administration was successful in convincing some that lifting the embargo meant putting United States military troops in danger. Ironically, following Clinton's veto of Congress's arms embargo legislation, American troops are now in Bosnia facing the dangers of mines and snipers to implement a plan many feel is an unjust and potentially unsustainable solution to the war. Perhaps the editors of the *New Republic* put it best when they wrote, "You Americanize the war or you Americanize the genocide."[14] That is the choice. Inaction in the face of genocide constitutes action.

The Movement's Impact

Overview: Small but Strong

While the percentage of students involved on each campus may not be overwhelming, the activists have accomplished much in the realms of peer education, humanitarian aid, refugee outreach, support for human rights, and political action. Other effective movements on college campuses have likewise made an impact well out of proportion to the numbers of those involved. At the antiwar movement's heyday in 1970, for instance, Martin Duberman quoted studies showing that activists constituted "only a small minority, though a growing one, of all college students; at Berkeley, for example, their number is put at about 15 percent."[15] More to the point, in her study of the U.S. antiapartheid movement, Janice Love highlights two successful campaigns to introduce divestment legislation that "were led and run by small groups of about six people . . . in neither state was a massive mobilization of popular support necessary for the adoption of the legislation."[16]

Indeed, while currently lectures about the war may tend to draw the most interest on campus and political activities the least, political activities are generally rated by activists as successes. A demonstration targeting a senator that, while small, lands coverage on the evening news and a picture in the newspaper makes progress in educating the public and pressuring the politician. "A few very active people on campus can help activate and motivate a large number of people," says Steve Walker, "and fortunately there are at least a handful of such people on a large number of campuses."

In the 1994–95 academic year, as a typical example, the relatively small, all-volunteer, all-student core of active SAGE members at Stanford hosted a half-dozen speakers on the war, ran a tutoring program for twenty Bosnian refugees, undertook the nearly complete financial sponsorship of a refugee family, organized five campus-based demonstrations and two demonstrations in San Francisco (all covered by local and/or national media), and raised donations for three humanitarian aid agencies. In addition, its members gave speeches, organized letter-writing campaigns to Congress and meetings with representatives, facilitated nationwide coordinated demonstrations, compiled and distributed the SAGE Direct Action Kit, ran the SAGE-net electronic network, and more. A comparable level and breadth of activity takes place on campuses around the country.

Further, most activists feel the movement enjoys the support, if not the membership, of the wider student population. Reflecting this, a January 1994 editorial about SAGE entitled "A Sagacious Group," by the editors of the *Stanford Daily* read:

> The group's approach to student activism is one to be commended. . . . And despite the thousands of miles between Stanford and Bosnia, the group's commitment has not wavered. Their attitude alone is enough to convince other students to make a similar effort on other issues . . . [and] their growing national popularity, among other things, prove[s] that student activism is far from dead.

Organizational Structure in the Electronic Age

Activist groups have been founded on American campuses at all points during the Balkan conflict—from the time of the shelling of Dubrovnik, Croatia, to the present writing. An organized movement can be traced to December 1993, when grassroots organizations, including student groups from Stanford, University of North Carolina at Chapel Hill, University of Michigan, and elsewhere met in Washington, DC, formed the American Committee to Save Bosnia, and elected Steve Walker its director. Once the ACSB was established, it began focusing on grassroots organizing, and SAGE at Stanford, under the visionary directorship of Brad Blitz, took the lead in organizing campus groups. That year, SAGE produced and/or distributed educational information, documentary videotapes, preprinted postcards addressed to congressional representatives and the president, and other materials to campuses around the country. SAGE also began distributing a newsletter with reports on campus activism, started SAGE-net, and organized several awareness-raising demonstrations that took place simultaneously on multiple campuses. The next year, the ACSB sponsored a second grassroots conference in Washington, DC. There, students from around the country organized special sessions and voted to form SAGE Coalition. SAGE Coalition's platform was derived from the platform of SAGE at Stanford, and the ACSB Call to Action.[17] Since that time, SAGE Coalition has elected officers who attend campuses around the country, and expanded its role of supporting, organizing, and facilitating communication between campus groups.

Organizing a movement that spans America's vast terrain has been helped immensely by the advent of the computer age. Rapid communication has played a key role in conveying leadership and guidance from SAGE and ACSB to foster a united political platform among the dispersed campus-based and grassroots organizations. While traditional methods of communication such as newsletters, action kits, and grassroots meetings are used by the activists, modern tools, including electronic mail, e-mail networks, and World Wide Web home pages have likewise made a great impact. The SAGE electronic mailing list (SAGE-net), moderated by Rich Green, allows activists to share information about the war, plan action initiatives, and organize humanitarian aid projects. Most college campuses provide internet services free of charge to students, faculty, and staff, and thus SAGE-net is available to most campus activists. SAGE-net participation contributes to a feeling of being part of a larger movement. Says Amy Gaglia, "with the internet connection one at least gets the feeling that there are like-minded people somewhere."

In another innovative use of the internet, SAGE Coalition leaders have instituted "e-mail meetings." From around the country, they "log on" to their e-mail accounts once every two weeks at a specified time to discuss issues. To contribute to the discussion, one need only mail his or her comment to the SAGE Coalition mailing list and each leader receives a copy within seconds, to which they may then reply.

Another internet resource that has had a powerful effect on the movement is BosNET. Over fifteen hundred direct subscribers and thousands of other receive daily, in-depth news reports concerning events in the region from a variety of news agencies and other sources, as well as activism notes, ACSB and Action Council for Peace in the Balkans publications, and much more. BosNET (also known as BosNews) has informed not only the activists, but also reporters and government officials. One reporter recently wrote, "Even with all the AP and Reuters wire and footage coming into the newsroom day and night, I still can't get the same feel for the situation [in Bosnia] as I do from BosNEWS."

The service was initiated and is run entirely by volunteers, most of whom are young people originally from Bosnia or other countries of the former Yugoslavia.[18] The volunteer BosNET moderators spend hours every day compiling the reports and sending them out.

Both SAGE-net and BosNET distribute *This Week in Bosnia,* a publication of the Boston-based Bosnia Action Coalition, written by Sharon Gartenberg. This succinct weekly electronic newsletter containing news and activism suggestions is meant to be printed out and posted in dormitories, workplaces, and places of worship to educate not only the activists, but the wider public.

The internet is used by activists in a multitude of other ways. They set up World-Wide-Web home pages to provide information ranging from maps of the region to photographs and descriptions of accused war criminals. SAGE's "web-page" encourages its visitors to send a message to the president's e-mail address—which can be done simply by clicking a button and then typing the message.

Due to the outstanding efforts of those that set up the ZaMir Transnational Net (*za mir* means "for peace"—it was organized with human rights groups in various countries of the former Yugoslavia) to provide computers, networking equipment, and system operators to people in places like Sarajevo, Tuzla, Zagreb, Belgrade, Pristina, and Ljubljana, the internet also provides an opportunity to communicate with those in the war zone (when electricity and phone lines function) and antiwar activists in other regions of the former Yugoslavia (for example, the Center for Antiwar Action in Belgrade). When Stanford SAGE helped facilitate the arrival in the United States of a Sarajevan family whose child had been injured, most of the early communication took place on the internet, using the ZaMir network. Others took ZaMir-net even further to help counter the effects of the sieges. Kenan Zahirovic, then a university student in Sarajevo, together with an American, Ed Agro, started the Sarajevo Pony Express (SPE)/PISMA. It has worked as a mail service whereby people with access to the internet pass messages from outside the war zone or across battle lines to those otherwise cut off by the war.

Using both traditional and novel tools, activists have created a range of responses to the war. The following broad categories cover most of them: humanitarian aid, education, and political action. A majority of the groups coordinate activities in all realms. Some examples follow below.

Humanitarian Aid Initiatives

The campus initiatives covered a wide range of humanitarian needs. Some groups gathered medical supplies, clothing, or money for established organizations such as the International Rescue Committee, Edinborough Direct Aid (which delivers supplies by convoy to war-torn areas), the Jewish Joint Distribution Committee, and many others. One of the most ambitious humanitarian aid collections of this type took place at Harvard University in the 1993–94 academic year. In a weeklong period, all students on the campus were visited and asked to contribute $10 toward the purchase of a truck to bring food and medicine into Sarajevo. Nearly $50,000 was raised.

Zainab Salbi, a graduate student at George Mason University, started her own humanitarian aid organization, Women for Women in Bosnia, during the war. The organization matches American women with Bosnian women who are refugees in Croatia and Bosnia. They share letters, and the Americans send financial support. A central mission of the organization is to raise public awareness among American women about what is happening in Bosnia and about the use of rape as a weapon of war.

On other campuses, students, faculty, or staff solicited scholarships for Bosnian students. These efforts were frequently coordinated with the help of the Bosnian Student Program, led by Professor Michael Sells of Haverford College, or the Bosnia Student Project of the Fellowship of Reconciliation and Jerrahi Order. Sells's group alone has solicited $3.5 million dollars in scholarships for Bosnian students.

Sells sees a parallel between such activities and those of the "sanctuary movement" of the early 1980s, which brought Central Americans who would have been targeted by death squads to America by means of underground railroads. In both, the arrival of a refugee made a huge contribution not only to that person's future, but to educating and reenergizing the movement that had organized to help him or her:

> That was one of the most mainstream protest movements in the U.S., which involved civil disobedience on the part of nuns and other church and synagogue leaders. However, the inertia was similar to today with students

on campuses. Once a refugee showed up, it made a big difference. The same thing is true with students from Bosnia. As soon as a student arrives on campus, everything changes. People are waiting for this tribal, Balkan, age-old hating, religious fundamentalist. Instead, a warm, bright student shows up and shocks them. What's amazing about these students is how rarely they do get angry about what has happened to them. The longer this goes on, though, and bright students are condemned to uncertain futures in refugee camps, the more likely hatreds will spring up and be reinforced. So, I think that anyone who is doing something with refugees is doing something beyond the humanitarian.

Some campus groups work closely with growing local Bosnian refugee populations. This takes the form of English-language tutoring and help with job and college applications. The relationships between students and refugees frequently progress to friendships, as students first-hand about the war and its effects on individuals. Mike Rothenberg spent time working with refugee children from Bosnia and Croatia at a summer camp in Croatia. He also helped bring a family with an injured child from Sarajevo to the Stanford area, and has become close with them. "Feeling I've made a difference for individual Bosnians has been the greatest reward of the work I am doing," Rothenberg said. "The positive effect of our actions on individuals is easy to see, whereas the results of our efforts regarding the larger issues, like stopping genocide, are more difficult to see."

Many Bosnians living in America choose to engage in activism and participate in student-organized demonstrations, give speeches at colleges and high schools, and speak about their painful experiences to the media. To do so clearly requires a great amount of courage.

Educational Efforts

In her study of the U.S. antiapartheid movement, Janice Love writes, "the movement's credibility, legitimacy and success depend in part on the depth and accuracy of its members' understanding of the forces they want to oppose."[19] This holds equally true in the Balkan anti-genocide movement, which places great importance on education. Activists spend a great amount of time reading newspapers, magazine articles, wire service reports (over the internet), and books to educate themselves.

This information is conveyed to peers through a variety of methods. Many campuses have held a Bosnia lecture series, teach-in, or daylong symposium. Popular speakers include Steve Walker (State Department resignee over U.S. Balkan policy and director of the American Committee to Save Bosnia); Andras Riedlmayer (Harvard librarian and Community of Bosnia member—expert on Bosnia's cultural heritage); Sven Alkalaj (Bosnia's ambassador to the United States); Muhamed Sacirbey (Bosnia's ambassador to the United Nations and former foreign minister); various visiting professors from Bosnia-Herzegovina, journalists, and humanitarian aid workers. Of all the activities that the Bosnia activists plan, these lectures seem to draw the most interest from students, faculty, and staff, and have been used as simultaneous chances to solicit new members and raise money for humanitarian aid initiatives. "Some of our most successful actions have been the numerous events with excellent speakers we were able to hold," says Tin Gazivoda, a Croatian student and a leader of Stanford University's SAGE chapter.

Educational efforts are making a difference in raising the level of awareness on campus. For instance, Steve Walker notes an improvement in the quality of questions asked at his college lectures:

> A year or two ago audiences were uninformed, and critical or skeptical at first about what I had to say. Questions now are well thought out and largely supportive of our point of view. That has to be attributed to activists on campus and public education efforts as well as events in the Balkans. It's hard for people to say all sides are to blame after watching the people of Srebrenica and Žepa be "ethnically cleansed."

Other educational efforts include "tabling" at campus events, distributing articles and information summaries (such as SAGE's "Twelve Questions on Bosnia"), and writing letters to the editor and editorials for campus newspapers. Activists tend to consider every event they plan, including demonstrations and humanitarian aid activities, as chances for education. More important, most educational efforts are geared toward empowering students to act.

Political Action

Overall, the activists maintain a strong conviction that humanitarian aid and education are not sufficient steps to stop the genocide. The groups add political activism to these activities in an effort to pressure the U.S. government to help bring a sustainable and just peace to the region and end human rights abuses.

Although there is room for debate and diverse opinion among group members, the student and grassroots organizations and their leaders have been remarkably consistent in their political demands. ACSB and SAGE Coalition affiliates subscribe to and act on nearly identical principles. These include the acknowledgment and condemnation of genocide being committed against the Bosnian people; the insistence on the Bosnian government's moral and legal right to self-defense; the support for U.S. military action (namely, air strikes) to enforce the protection of civilians and delivery of humanitarian aid; the belief in preserving a democratic, viable, and multiethnic Bosnia-Herzegovina; and the demand for war criminals to be brought to justice. Political action takes several forms, including demonstrations, letter-writing campaigns (using letters, post-cards, and petitions), calls to the "White House Comments Line," and meetings with congressional representatives and their staff members. SAGE, along with other grassroots and human rights organizations, has initiated Freedom of Information Act proceedings to release classified information the U.S. government has about genocide in Bosnia.

In April 1995, SAGE Coalition leaders debated the use of civil disobe-dience at demonstrations. This subject was considered carefully—stu-dents did not want to appear extreme, and wanted instead to ensure that they chose appropriate targets. On some campuses, the tactic was used, but on most it was not. A change came after Srebrenica fell in the summer of 1995. Extremely distressed, many decided that civil disobedience was appropriate at this juncture. Students and other grassroots activists con-verged on the White House, demonstrated, and were arrested for occu-pying a restricted area.

The activists who participated conveyed strong reasons for doing so. Joanne Trgovcich is a leader of the Coalition against Genocide at Univer-sity of the North Carolina at Chapel Hill, and she spoke about her motivations that day:

> For three years I've been doing everything a concerned citizen should be doing—writing letters, making phone calls, helping organize educational forums and peaceful demonstrations. After three years I'm left with a profound sense of disillusionment with my government and with the United Nations. I decided it was time to get arrested to make my point.

Caroline Spicer, a SAGE Coalition activist from the Bosnia Coordinating Committee and a library specialist at Cornell University, also participated. Her experience of civil disobedience brought to mind childhood memories of World War II.

It's important for me to bear witness. I remember being a kid during the Second World War and hearing about the concentration camps and what had happened to the Jews. I wouldn't have believed then that in my lifetime I would be going to jail because some people were being persecuted in the same way.

The main political message of the demonstration was to urge Congress to vote to lift Bosnia's arms embargo, which it subsequently did by a "veto-proof" majority. As Brad Blitz put it then, "We're here today because we believe the arms embargo should be lifted, because current U.S. policy in Bosnia is absolutely criminal—it is encouraging genocide and the only way forward is to ensure that the Bosnian people have the right to defend themselves."

Bosnia activists have also employed a technique used successfully by the anti-apartheid movement. Janice Love writes that those activists created a political climate in which the only antiracist option was to support the proposed legislation. "Activists were able to cast the debate so that a moral issue was at stake, and to be against the legislation was to risk a public association with racism."[20] A similar tactic was sometimes used by anti-genocide activists lobbying on the arms embargo legislation. Congressional representatives were told that failing to lift the arms ban would constitute complicity in genocide.

Indeed, it was sometimes this moral argument, rather than the strictly logical one, that won over unexpected votes. California's senator Dianne Feinstein, in the summer of 1995, was written off by the activists due to her strong opposition to lifting the arms ban. However, the events of Srebrenica apparently changed her mind. She made public statements about the effect of "the devastating photograph of a young Bosnian woman who decided she could not go on and hung herself from a tree. This anonymous image spoke eloquently to me of the desperation facing the Bosnian people as they endure rape, torture, summary execution, and a litany of war crimes."[21]

Feinstein described the photograph as "a call for change."[22] And again, once making the moral realization that "there is one thing we cannot do, and that is nothing," Feinstein found ample logical and military reasons to support her decision to lift the arms embargo. After careful consideration of the latest "Contact Group" negotiations and empty resolutions, she concluded, "It has become painfully clear now that no one will defend the Bosnians except the Bosnians themselves. If no one will defend them, we can no longer deny them the right to defend themselves. And so, I intend to support the Dole/Lieberman resolution [to lift Bosnia's arms embargo]."[23] This was another case of the ocean being spanned by a compelling picture of an individual human being. Feinstein added, "Just as the anonymous white-shirted young man facing down a column of tanks in Tiananmen Square a few years ago conveyed the unspeakable message of oppression to the world, so did this photograph point eloquently to the world's failure in Bosnia."[24]

Unfortunately, repression continues in China, and after years of compelling photographs, the genocide in Bosnia may not have permanently ended. But slowly, one by one, people are taking notice—students with the will to make their voices heard, and people, like Feinstein, who already have the power to affect political reality. Change is happening. The student and grassroots movements, their presence drawing attention to the situation, have helped convince Congress to vote overwhelmingly to grant Bosnians their right to self-defense. Although the measure was vetoed by Clinton, the threat of an override ushered in a period of intense focus and activity on the part of the Clinton administration—a dedication to American involvement in Bosnia, however flawed.

Conclusions: Looking toward the Future

Unfortunately, the story cannot end happily. Too many people have been killed under the watchful eyes of the world. Too many times those that could have stopped the slaughter looked the other way. Even while the current, tremendously unjust (and potentially unsustainable) "peace plan" was being promoted heavily by the world's most powerful country, genocide was continuing unabated in areas of Bosnia such as Banja Luka. Months into the plan's implementation, indicted war criminals are still in power. Bosnia supporters are calling the Clinton administration's solution to the war a "partition plan," and some, who have not forgotten who started the war and with what deadly goals, name it after its originator— the "Milošević plan." Whatever they call it, most of the movement's members accept the plan as the current reality and are working to ensure that important aspects of it are implemented.

These days, Bosnia activists are sticking to their guns and returning to the basic tenets of their organization—the call for "a just peace and the preservation of a democratic, viable, multiethnic Bosnia-Herzegovina." Activism for Bosnia will continue until the peace is stable, the Bosnian army is armed and able to defend civilians, war criminals are removed from power and brought to justice, and promised economic aid is fully delivered. The needs for humanitarian aid, rebuilding assistance, and justice for war criminals in the former Yugoslavia will keep the activists busy. Democracy and nonnationalist politics need to be fostered. Brilliant young Bosnians in refugee camps deserve a chance to go to college.

But what will likely motivate the Balkan anti-genocide activists far into the future will be the realization that ethnic violence looms in other areas of the world. Student activists, like Catherine Petrusz, a leader of the Coalition against Genocide (CAGE) at the University of North Carolina at Chapel Hill, feel empowered to continue working for justice: "I used to be like one of those who, today, frustrate me with their apathy. This issue has brought me into politics."

Many would like to see the establishment of a permanent war crimes tribunal. Michael Sells expresses the anti-genocide activists' challenge to the world: "The anti-genocide movement is one way the world can reenergize itself. The Cold War is over, so now let's turn our attention to abolishing genocide like slavery was abolished."

Will the movement continue to grow and gain enough power to push the world community into fulfilling this ambitious mandate? Hopefully it will, but it must first overcome some serious difficulties. These include financial limitations, which are particularly grave for student activists and the national coordinating bodies (SAGE and ACSB). Steve Walker, whose job it is, as director of ACSB, to lead the grassroots activism movement forward, is all too cognizant of the challenges:

> One glaring problem on the campus and grassroots level is the lack of resources to do a real outreach effort. We've relied instead on people that came to us and national organizations that already existed. I think that will prove to be one of our weaknesses. When a sense of crisis passes, other organizations won't care as much, and it will be harder to engage new people. The challenge will be to maintain our activists and to grow.

On the other hand, with American soldiers on the ground in Bosnia, anti-genocide groups have witnessed an upsurge of interest in their activities on many campuses. Students seem eager to understand the war and lend assistance to its victims. Some are scheduling summer trips to help with reconstruction.

This chapter presents a snapshot in the life of the campus-based Balkan anti-genocide movement. While far from exhaustive, the study carried out for this chapter was able to ascertain much about the motivations of the activists, their core ideology, the challenges they face, and the activities in which they engage. The positive and negative roles of the media in shaping both the movement and the attitudes of the larger public deserv further attention. So, too, do the innovative uses of modern computing and the internet in the political, humanitarian, and educational realms of the movement. And clearly, a broader study of the general grassroots (noncampus-based as well as campus-based) Balkan anti-genocide movement is warranted.

NOTES

1. Detailed questionnaires were distributed by electronic mail to roughly twenty-five leading activists from within the campus-based movement around the United States. They contained both open-ended and multiple-choice questions regarding the motivations of the activists, the nature of their individual organizations, the response to their efforts on campus, the major challenges of their work, and the most and least successful types of actions they have undertaken. Nine questionnaires were returned as a result of the initial distribution (nonresponding activists frequently cited a lack of time as the cause of their inability to fill out the detailed questionnaire). Therefore, a further seven interviews were conducted over the telephone with key activists, using identical questions. In addition, the questionnaire was distributed to and filled out by five leaders of the Stanford University chapter of SAGE. The returned questionnaires contained lengthy personal comments. Detailed autobiographical reasons for participation in the anti-genocide movement were provided in both written questionnaires and interviews; this resulted in a privileged view of the motivations of the activists and the challenges that face them.

In addition, a separate questionnaire was prepared and used in interviews of a random sample of twenty Stanford University students (nonmembers of SAGE) in the student union area of campus on October 10, 1995. Interviews lasted roughly fifteen to twenty minutes each and probed the students' interest in the situation in Bosnia-Herzegovina, their understandings of and attitudes about the war, their opinions about potential American involvement, and the likelihood that they would attend various activities that campus-based anti-genocide groups might sponsor. Students were not told the subject of the questionnaire when they were asked to participate; response rate (those agreeing to be interviewed as a percentage of the number asked to participate) was very high (over 90 percent); and once interviews began, they were completed in all twenty cases.

Finally, some of the information and quotations are derived from informal interviews of roughly thirty activists conducted on videotape by recent Cornell

University graduate and SAGE Coalition activist, Erik Nisbet. The interviews were recorded on July 16, 1995, during and after a demonstration in front of the White House, which campus activists, community activists, and concerned citizens from around the country attended. At the demonstration, several dozen Bosnia supporters were arrested for civil disobedience while protesting the U.S. failure to intervene and prevent the fall of the UN-declared "safe area," Srebrenica, Bosnia-Herzegovina.

2. The Tyndall Report, ADT Research; cited in the *Guardian,* October 4, 1995, and the *Washington Post,* January 3, 1996.

3. See, for example, Yankelovich poll for CNN/*Time* Magazine, conducted July 19–20, 1995 (52 percent of those polled said the United States "does not have any moral obligation to protect citizens of Bosnia against Serbian attacks"); Times Mirror Center for People and the Press poll released June 24, 1995 (61 percent surveyed opposed using U.S. forces to end the "Bosnian civil war"); in a *Newsweek* magazine poll released June 3, 1995, the majority of Americans polled (61 percent) would "support U.S. ground forces taking part in any and all peacekeeping efforts in Bosnia"; in a University of Maryland poll (report authored by Steven Kull, released May 16, 1995), a majority of adult Americans polled (64 percent) favored "large-scale military intervention to stop ethnic cleansing," holding true even assuming 3,500 American fatalities (60 percent still favored); however, a majority opposed United States unilateral lifting of the arms embargo (73 percent); *Wall Street Journal*/NBC television poll, March 11, 1994, found those surveyed favored U.S. peacekeeping forces in Bosnia (53 percent). (In many of these polls, and those taken earlier in the war, however, the majority supported U.S. ground troops to help with UN withdrawal or with enforcing a peace agreement. Perhaps this explains why President Clinton, one president to whom the polls seem to matter very much, pursued just such an intervention as elections drew nearer.)

4. The text of the letter reads as follows:

Dear Senator:

We are writing to urge you to vote yes on the Dole-Lieberman bill (S. 21) to end the U.S. arms embargo against the Government of the Republic of Bosnia and Herzegovina. We also urge you to sign on as a co-sponsor of the bill and to recruit your colleagues as co-sponsors.

The war in Bosnia is now well into its fourth year. Over 200,000 civilians have been brutally murdered by Serbian forces, tens of thousands of women raped, and almost three million people have been forced to flee their homes and villages. Serbian forces have been able to carry out their genocidal assault on Bosnia with virtual impunity because of an immoral arms embargo that denies the legitimate government of Bosnia the means to exercise its inherent right to self-defense.

The response of the United Nations to the aggression has been to send poorly armed peacekeepers, even though there is no peace to keep. In recent weeks, Serbian forces have been allowed to overrun two of the six UN-declared "safe areas," and the UN mission has approached total collapse. The lesson we must learn is that only the Bosnian Army has the will and the manpower to defend the fledgling multi-ethnic democracy and its citizens against further attacks.

It is also clear that the ultra-nationalist Serbian leaders have no interest in negotiating while they can accomplish their military and political objectives by attacking Bosnia's remaining civilian population. Until the Bosnian Army can mount a credible defense on the ground, this cowardly war of aggression will continue. And we must live in the knowledge that, at least in part, we are responsible for tying the hands of the victims.

The organizations listed below represent a wide range of religious, humanitarian, student, and citizen advocacy groups. Some of the names will be familiar to you; others have been formed in recent months by voters outraged by the genocide and our feeble and immoral response to it. We have joined together today to ask for your support for the Dole-Lieberman bill.

The U.S. and its allies, NATO, and the UN have failed to stop the aggression. Unless Congress acts—and acts NOW—thousands, perhaps tens of thousands, more innocent people will die and the price of eventually confronting this aggression will continue to rise.

By voting for Dole-Lieberman, you will be taking a clear stand against genocide, against aggression, against appeasement, and for an honorable and sustainable peace in Bosnia. You will be rejecting the failed policies of European countries that have facilitated more than three years of genocide. You will be voting for the one policy that makes moral, political, and military sense.

Vote YES on the Dole-Lieberman bill.

Sincerely,

Action Council for Peace in the Balkans, American Committee to Save Bosnia, American Council for Public Affairs, American Jewish Congress, American Muslim Council, American Task Force for Bosnia, Arab American Institute, B'nai B'rith, Federation of Reconstructionist Congregations and Havurot, Islamic Network, Muslim Public Affairs Council, National Association of Arab Americans, National Federation of Croatian Americans, National Jewish Community Relations Advisory Council, Reconstructionist Rabbinical Association, Union of American Hebrew Congregations, Academic Society of Bosnia-Herzegovina, American Bosnian and Hercegovinian Association, Americans for Bosnian Orphans, Ann Arbor Committee for Bosnia, BosNet Society, Bosnia Advocates of Metrowest,

Bosnia Briefings, Bosnia Support Committee of D.C., Bosnia Task Force, San Diego, Bosnia-Herzegovinian Help Organization, California Coalition against Ethnic Cleansing, Coalition against Genocide, Coalition for Intervention against Genocide, Free Bosnia Action Group, Friends of Bosnia (W. Mass), Friends of Bosnia, Philadelphia, Greenwich Coalition for Peace in Bosnia, Human Rights Council, USA, JACOB at B'Nai Jeshurun, Jews against Genocide/NY Committee to Save Bosnia, Jews against Genocide in Bosnia, New England Bosnian Relief Committee, New Hampshire Committee for Peace in Bosnia-Herzegovina, New York-Sarajevo Exchange, Students against Genocide (SAGE), Social Action Committee/Congregation Beth El, Stop Ethnic Cleansing, U.S. Bosnia Relief, Women in Islam.

5. See the full text of the Convention on the Prevention and Punishment of the Crime of Genocide (U.N. GAOR Res. 260A (III), December 9, 1948) in appendix 2 of this volume.

6. KRON-TV Channel 4 news, "Surviving Bosnia," February 13, 1996.

7. The arguments have been set out in a legal memorandum, "The Arms Embargo against Bosnia-Herzegovina Violates the Inherent Right to Self-Defense," by Paul R. Williams, with the support of Michael Scharf, former attorney-advisers for European and United Nations affairs, respectively, for the United States Department of State. Prepared for the Action Council for Peace in the Balkans, February 1994.

8. Quoted in D. J. Schemo, "Holocaust Museum Hailed as Sacred Debt to Dead," *New York Times,* April 23, 1993, A1.

9. See, for example, L. Katz, "Holocaust Survivors in Conflict over Bosnian War," *Jewish Bulletin of Northern California,* July 21, 1995, 1.

10. *World News Saturday,* ABC, June 3, 1995. Results of the *Newsweek* magazine poll are described above.

11. There are notable exceptions. Some faculty, such as William Hunt (St. Lawrence University) and Michael Sells (Haverford College), initiated impressive humanitarian efforts. Others, including Ivo Banac (Yale University), Thomas Cushman (Wellesley College), John Fine (University of Michigan), Stjepan Meštrović (Texas A&M University), Andras Riedlmayer (Harvard University), and Carolyn Spicer (Cornell University), primarily undertook to educate the student body and wider community. Still other faculty led efforts that included political action along with education and humanitarian aid—notably Gunseli Berik (University of Utah), Francis Boyle (University of Illinois-Champaign), Joshua Goldstein (American University), Catharine MacKinnon (University of Michigan), and John Weiss (Cornell University). This list is by no means exhaustive.

12. "The Menace of War," comment, *Progressive,* September 1995, 1.

13. These incredibly tragic events occur over and over. Citing "realpolitik," American leaders refrain from opposing and preventing the most severe atrocities. For example, on September 20, 1995, the *New York Times* published an article

indicating that paramilitary death squad leader Zeljko Raznatović ("Arkan") and his forces were being sent by Belgrade to Banja Luka. Given his extensive record of war atrocities, anyone could predict that his forces would not be used for military purposes, but rather for terror and destruction of the small remaining population of non-Serbs in Banja Luka (originally the city contained over three hundred thousand non-Serbs). Why did the Clinton administration or its chief negotiator in the former Yugoslavia, Richard Holbrooke, not pressure Milošević to recall Arkan? Why weren't air strikes threatened? At that time, the Clinton administration was preoccupied instead with pressuring Bosnian forces to refrain from liberating Banja Luka, and was rehabilitating Serbian president Milošević as a "peacemaker" and "dove" in the name of a "peace plan." Sure enough, a few weeks later the *New York Times* was reporting (October 10, 1995) that the few survivors of Arkan's latest brutal "ethnic cleansing" campaign were straggling in to Bosnian government territory. Thousands are still unaccounted for. The activists are demanding that the U.S. government be made accountable for the crime of not responding in situations like these, for failing to lift a hand and prevent the preventable.

14. "Accomplices to Genocide," *New Republic,* August 7, 1995, 7.

15. M. Duberman, "On Misunderstanding Student Rebels," in *Essays on the Student Movement,* ed. Patrick Gleeson (Columbus: Charles E. Merrill, 1970), 26.

16. J. Love, *The U.S. Anti-Apartheid Movement* (New York: Praeger, 1985), 228–29.

17. The "Call for Action," adopted January 8, 1995, by the Students against Genocide Coalition, reads,

> We are deeply concerned by the aggression and genocide taking place in Bosnia. To bring a quick and just end to the suffering of the people in Bosnia, SAGE Coalition actively supports humanitarian assistance efforts and promotes the following Call for Action:
>
> 1) The United States and other governments must acknowledge and condemn the genocide that is being committed against the Bosnian people and invoke the Genocide Convention.
>
> 2) The United States and other countries must actively support the Bosnian government's moral and legal right to self-defense and ensure that it has the means to do so.
>
> 3) The United States and other countries should lead the international community, acting through appropriate multilateral bodies—including NATO—in using all necessary means to enforce the United Nations Security Council resolutions regarding Bosnia, especially those guaranteeing delivery of humanitarian assistance and protection of civilians.
>
> 4) The United States and other governments should sponsor and mediate new negotiations with the goal of a negotiated settlement that provides for

a just peace and the preservation of a democratic, viable, multi-ethnic Bosnia-Herzegovina.

5) The United States and other countries should investigate and ensure accountability of the activities and behavior of the United Nations and its agencies in the conflict.

6) The International War Crimes Tribunal should be fully funded and supported by our governments.

18. Founders of BosNET, moderators, and others who helped with establishing and running the service include Lazer Berisha, Zeljko Bodulovic, Muris Cicic, Adnan Dzinic, Murat Erkocevic, Iztok and Stela Hozo, Dubravko Kakarigi, Dzevat Omeragic, Duško Pavlović, Naim Saiti, Zlatko Sijercic, Omer Sulejmanagich, Davor Wagner, and Nermin Zukic.

19. Love, op. cit., 13.

20. Ibid., 233.

21. D. Feinstein, "Unilaterally Lifting the Arms Embargo in Bosnia," Speech in U.S. Senate, Washington, DC, July 25, 1995.

22. D. Feinstein, "U.S. Policy in Bosnia," statement, July 19, 1995.

23. Feinstein, "Unilaterally Lifting the Arms Embargo."

24. Feinstein, "U.S. Policy in Bosnia."

THIRTEEN

David Riesman

Western Responses to the Current Balkan War

The Irish historian from Cambridge, Brendan Simms, astutely notes in this volume that the British look at 1938 not as a lesson in avoiding appeasement but rather as a lesson in isolating combatants in an area in which British self-interest is involved. He argues further that the British have applied this "lesson" to the current Balkan War.

Nevertheless I am puzzled why the French and the British remain so cruelly indifferent to Serbian aggression. Do they really fear German connections to Croatia, as the news media often suggest? That seems very farfetched indeed. Not only did the French impose a blockade following the Bolshevik Revolution, but they also sent troops, as indeed the United States did through Siberia, although briefly.

One also encounters frequently the interpretation—often implicit but sometimes made explicit—that Croatian behavior in the current Balkan War is an extension of Nazism and Ustashism, which included anti-Semitism as well as anti-Serbianism, and that the Serbs have every right to fear the Croats as well as their German backers. I am skeptical here, about the easy connections sometimes made between Nietzschean nihilism and Nazism, and even between Nazism and genocide. Anti-Semitism does not necessarily lead to genocide, and for the first years of Hitler,

Jews preferred Germany to Poland, even though Germany was not agreeable. Many accidental strains went into the linkage of anti-Semitism with the "final solution."

In contrast, it seems to me that the American left helped create a silence on the evils of communism that continued during and even after the Cold War. And indeed, the image of Germany left over from World War I is significant, when there was even more hostility to the Germans than in World War II, as an "expansionist" power. But World War I had multiple causes, and Germany was perhaps less involved than Russia, France, and Austria.

I remember a dinner of Chicago sociologists at which the former chairman, Philip Hauser, a demographer, and also Lloyd Warner, who was in sociology, were critical of those who read any "foreigners"—French would not be any better than German. This was an oblique attack on Everett Hughes, less directly on me and also on Edward Shils—in a sense, anybody who had another language or any cultivation—an all-American outlook, not more sympathetic to Franco-British than to German thought.

It is very strange that Croatia, which has suffered so much, should be blamed by many authors, along with Serbia, for the war in the Balkans. This may be a reflection of the belief that all nationalism, of whatever sort, is "inherently evil," a belief I understand very well because of my own lack of sympathy for most nationalisms. This is the case for ethnic nationalisms within the United States, and perhaps my antagonism to these has unduly influenced my attitude toward nationalisms elsewhere. I can see and even appreciate the energy behind French nationalism as I watch English become the standard language all over the world, as French had been for much of the world in an earlier day.

I find bewildering the contrast between the generosity extended to François Mitterrand, even after he admitted his Vichy connection, and the ferocious and unfair scrutiny of Franjo Tudjman, Croatia's president. Mitterrand appears strange, at once opportunistic and perhaps with a touch of idealism, in working both for Vichy and for the antifascist opposition. Mitterrand himself has been more forthcoming, as I heard on National Public Radio. One can imagine that he was opportunistic under the Vichy regime, working with the regime and at the same time, or after a time, working also with the Resistance, but then at least he deserves a certain amount of credit for imagining that the Nazis, then so all-powerful, could be defeated. By contrast, it is striking how Tudjman's strictly antifascist activities during World War II are hardly ever mentioned in the media.

What I think is really hell is to watch the situation now in Bosnia deteriorate further and further, in a kind of self-confirming welter of tragedies in which the Croats also are behaving badly — which in no way justifies the enormously greater aggression of the Serbs — and in which even some Muslims have begun to be ferocious. *It is a jailhouse created by the Serbs in which the prisoners punish each other.*

Western Inaction

I wonder to what extent defenses of the Serbs or a refusal to see the ferocity and brutality of their crimes are related to having to justify inaction. I do not see some kind of conspiracy among the Western media in promoting the image of the Serbs, Croats, and Muslims as "equally guilty" and therefore unworthy of Western resolve to pick a just side. And I do not agree with those who claim that the Western media are merely cheering on a Western collaboration with Serbia against Muslims. Rather, I see guilt leading to self-justification and then to the media reporting to a public which, fixated by the "Vietnam syndrome," does not want to get involved. Many do not want to get involved domestically either, with anybody other than their immediate circle.

Many in the American Congress seem to me cynical in wanting to lift the arms embargo against the Bosnian Muslims at this point, four years into this war, when the Serbs are all around the country and it would take a while for the new weapons to come in and for the Bosnian Muslims and others on their side, that is, cosmopolitan Bosnians, to learn to make use of them. By that time the Serbs might have taken much more territory.

On the other hand, President Clinton seems such a waverer that it is hard to imagine him sticking to any policy line to which there is any serious opposition, let alone providing opposition. Even though Clinton is punished more than he "deserves," his "I feel your pain" line is not something most people notice, actually, for they react as he did, with a false empathy where sympathy would have been appropriate. Like President Bush before him, who deflected sympathy for Bosnia onto Somalia, President Clinton deflected it onto Haiti.

What I find so dismal is Clinton's wish to invade Haiti, prompted by the Congressional Black Caucus and by Randall Robinson, a black activist who helped start the divestment movement and, that coming to an end, turned to Haiti for an outlet; he conducted a hunger strike that apparently influenced Clinton. But there did not seem to be support in the country as a whole for an attack on Haiti—and yet at the same time it was a distraction from the former Yugoslavia.

Western inaction in Bosnia is justified further by references to Rwanda, Burundi, and Haiti, with the implication that the United States cannot be the world's policeman. Haiti seems to me important because of the Black Congressional Caucus, but not of any profound importance, for there is simply another dictatorship there. I find it difficult to embrace the African slaughter of the Christians in southern Nigeria soon after Nigeria won its independence in the same framework as the former Yugoslavia, for the latter seems to me so essential, as Stjepan Meštrović[1] and Akbar Ahmed[2] have pointed out, in terms of Muslim attitudes and feelings around the world and in terms of the lessons provided further east, and further west as well. If you pile Africa on top of the Balkans, then I think most Americans will even more than at present resist any intervention, just as Clinton has not wanted to use any of his capital in order to mobilize American genuine help to the besieged Bosnians or Croatians and to make clear to the Serbs that they really run the danger of experiencing military action right at home in Belgrade. In general, as I reflect on the tortured reactions of Americans and many Europeans, it seems to me that these are excuses for not acting where it is clear that we ought to act, even at some risk to ourselves. I think Meštrović has written with clarity, eloquence, and effectiveness on this issue.

I do not understand why Republicans in the U.S. Congress, who are isolationists by tradition, suddenly seem to want to oppose President Clinton's policies and to force him to lift the weapons embargo on Bosnia. I am puzzled by the Dole-Lieberman bill to lift the arms embargo on Bosnia, and why it is conditional on the withdrawal of the UN forces from Bosnia. Why should relatively isolationist, primarily Republican senators give a damn about the United Nations, or what Britain decides? Regarding the prospect of Serbia attacking Macedonia, I am surprised that this has not already occurred.

With reference to *The Lonely Crowd,* some see this Republican movement in the Congress as part of a larger rebellion against Clinton's other-directedness into inner-directedness. But I do not see America moving toward a "conservative return to inner-directedness." This is not a way to describe the nastiness and the gullibility-paranoia of so much of the

American would-be electorate, or nonvoting "turned off" individuals. The country, frightened for its future, has turned in an ungenerous direction, hostile to immigrants and eager to respond to people who promise tax cuts. The left continues to talk about "the people," as in the pages of the *Nation*. But actually, in Massachusetts, the majority according to polls are opposed to the ballot initiative requiring a graduated rather than the flat income tax that the state has. People identify against the poor and in some measure with the rich, the corporate rich or rather the entrepreneurial rich, and they are hostile to the modest salaries paid to congressmen or public officials, or indeed to most college presidents. I do not see this sour mood as inner-directed but as a very group-oriented one of fellow talkshow hosts and fellow-people who are "turned off" and who have an incredible faith in what they know despite their ignorance.

I do think that recent Croatian and Bosnian military successes support the image of inner-directed Bosnians and Croats as people who value independence from the Serbs rather than seeing themselves only as victims.

Other Reasons for Inaction in Bosnia

In the case of the Nazis and the death camps, this was not widely known in the United States during World War II. There were ever so many Americans who loved the idea of going after "the Japs" but saw no reason to attack the Nazis, and Roosevelt was cautious to try to keep these Asia-first people on board.

It seems strange to me, knowing very little about the ethnic tensions in Yugoslavia, that so many intellectuals would be confident that war would not break out because Yugoslavs would "reason" that this was not in their best self-interest, as if the ethnic hatreds were a thing of the remote past, and as if antagonism by the more cosmopolitan and also Roman Catholic Slovenes and Croatians would be silenced by what appeared to the rest of Europe or to this country at the outset—but I think not at the present time—as "reasonable."

I have read with interest the excerpts from Slaven Letica's diary of the visit to the White House in 1990. Letica, a Croatian sociologist, was at the time President Franjo Tudjman's national security advisor. In the diary, Letica recounts how he and President Tudjman attempted to establish a Croatian federation with local Serbs so as to ease their fears, and how they both tried, unsuccessfully, to persuade President Bush as well as leading American statesmen such as Henry Kissinger to support the idea of an independent yet confederated Croatia. I also read Slaven Letica's published letter to the editor of *Newsweek*, "Missed Opportunity," drawing on his visit to the White House, learning from it, for example, how completely Croatia had been disarmed by the former Yugoslav Republic. The cynicism of Henry Kissinger's reaction does not surprise me, though at an earlier point, when we were colleagues at Harvard, and even when he first went into the Nixon administration, I had more regard for him.

But in addition to Western and particularly American inaction, I find it puzzling that Muslims in other nations are not especially helpful to Bosnia. Could it be that the active Muslims are the more "fundamentalist" ones, and they do not see the Muslims of the former Yugoslavia as their kind of Muslims? The Muslims in the United States have such inadequate representation that when there was a bombing of a federal building in Oklahoma City, some people immediately thought that it must have been the Muslims! The Jews, in contrast to the Muslims, have two groups to count on: the newspaper and media people, and the lawyers and judges. Muslims have, for the most part, neither cohort.

My wife, Evey, and I listened together to a *Talk of the Nation* broadcast where Stjepan Meštrović and Akbar Ahmed discussed the current situation in Bosnia. I thought they were remarkably effective and collaborated well. I was just waiting, as one can imagine, for the first pro-Serb voice to come—a harsh, male voice, proclaiming bias in the program. It is anxiety-provoking, I should imagine, to be on such a program, not knowing from what quarter questions may come. It seemed to me that Ray Suarez, the host of the program, was knowledgeable, as I have often found him to be on *Talk of the Nation*. I was surprised by the man who called in to express his fears of an Islamic empire and wondered about his own ethnicity. In turn, I was reminded of the willingness of George Bush to fight Iraq on behalf of Kuwait, where there might have been a settlement with just minimal concessions to Iraq, in contrast to his unwillingness, then followed by Clinton and most of this country, to get involved in the far more significant issue of Serbian aggression, first against the Croats and then against the people of Bosnia.

The views of the caller who accused Meštrović and Ahmed of bias can be found expressed in the *Boston Globe* and other newspapers about the belief of Bosnian Serbs that they are under siege, that they are victims. I found Meštrović's invention of the concept of "postemotional" to account for this line of reasoning illuminating, more so than that of "postmodern." Specifically, Meštrović claimed on the program that Serb justification of present-day atrocities on the basis of historical grievances against the Croats from World War II and against the Muslims dating back to 1389 constitutes postemotionalism. By contrast, I cannot agree with Roger Cohen's claim, in an article on the Balkan War as "postmodern," that distributing "live images of suffering . . . sap[s] whatever will or ability there may be to prosecute a devastating military campaign."[3] If there were no notice at all in the media, there would be no will at all, let alone ability. How the writer could assume that the killings in Sarajevo are a kind of fiction—all this seems desperate, indeed, a sick form of voyeurism. This reminds me of my concern that if we had not fought the Gulf War, would we have been more ready to take on this anti-Serbian conflict? I thought at the time of the Gulf War that there might have been a reconciliation between Iraq and Kuwait had the Bush administration not wanted to go to war (certainly we, that is, America, have much more interest in the former Yugoslavia than in Somalia or indeed other African countries).

Another frequently cited justification for inaction is that taking action in Bosnia would be Eurocentric. I must say I detest the notion that it is "Eurocentric" to be concerned about the Balkans and Serbian aggression. What an extraordinary self-abnegation of Americans who are, in so many ways, European and Eurocentric, and properly so.

But the most common rationalization for inaction seems to be that all sides in the conflict are somehow equally guilty. The author of a recent book review in *International Affairs,* for example, makes this argument.[4] Even if it is, as he implies, "unsophisticated" Americans who support the argument that the Belgrade regime is most responsible for the current Balkan War, that is a different picture than one sometimes has, of the Serbs having pretty wide control of public opinion in the United States. The reviewer's judgment that Croatia "mirrored Serbia's aggression in the region" is weird.

I had grave reservations about the war crimes tribunals in Germany and in Japan after World War II, which seemed to me the justice of the victor. One wonders how the international tribunal that is supposed to try war crimes from the current Balkan War will fare.

And finally, I should mention that it is also curious that the women's movements in the United States have made little response to the ethnic and cruel rapes by the Serbs. This only confirms my sense that they are entirely provincial to the situations in the United States.

NOTES

1. Stjepan G. Meštrović, *The Balkanization of the West* (London: Routledge, 1994).

2. Akbar Ahmed, "Ethnic Cleansing: A Metaphor For Our Time?" *Ethnic and Racial Studies* 18, no. 1 (January 1995): 1–25.

3. Roger Cohen, "In Sarajevo, Victims of a 'Postmodern' War," *New York Times,* May 21, 1995, Al.

4. Gabriel Patros, review of *The Balkanization of the West,* by Stjepan Meštrović, *International Affairs* 71 (January 1995): 172–73.

A Definition of Genocide

Following is a definition of genocide by Raphael Lemkin, from Axis Rule in Occupied Europe: Laws of Occupation, Analysis of Government, Proposals for Redress *(Washington, DC: Carnegie Endowment for International Peace, 1944), 79. The term "genocide" was coined by Lemkin specifically to describe the systematic murders carried out by Axis powers. Lemkin's definition was the basis for the inclusion of the term "genocide" in the UN Geneva Conventions.*

By "genocide" we mean the destruction of a nation or of an ethnic group. This new word, coined by the author to denote an old practice in its modern development, is made from the ancient Greek word *genos* (race, tribe) and the Latin *cide* (killing), thus corresponding in its formation to such words as tyrannicide, homicide, infanticide, etc. Generally speaking, genocide does not necessarily mean the immediate destruction of a nation, except when accomplished by mass killings of all members of a nation. It is intended rather to signify a coordinated plan of different actions aiming at the destruction of essential foundations of the life of national groups, with the aim of annihilating the groups themselves. The objectives of such a plan would be the disintegration of the political and social institutions, of culture, language, national feelings, religion, and the economic existence of national groups, and the destruction of the personal security, liberty, health, dignity, and even the lives of the individuals belonging to such groups. Genocide is directed against the national group as an entity, and the actions involved are directed against individuals, not in their individual capacity, but as members of a national group.

Text of the United Nations Convention on the Prevention and Punishment of the Crime of Genocide (U.N.G.C.) Resolution 260A (III), December 9, 1948

THE CONTRACTING PARTIES,

Having considered the declaration made by the General Assembly of the United Nations in its resolution 96 (I) dated 11 December 1946 that genocide is a crime under international law, contrary to the spirit and aims of the United Nations and condemned by the civilized world;

Recognizing that at all periods of history genocide has inflicted great losses on humanity; and

Being convinced that, in order to liberate mankind from such an odious scourge, international co-operation is required:

HEREBY AGREE AS HEREINAFTER PROVIDED:

Article I

The Contracting Parties confirm that genocide, whether committed in time of peace or in time of war, is a crime under international law which they undertake to prevent and to punish.

Article II

In the present Convention, genocide means any of the following acts committed with intent to destroy, in whole or in part, a national, ethnic, racial, or religious group, as such:

(a) Killing members of the group;

(b) Causing serious bodily or mental harm to members of the group;

(c) Deliberately inflicting on the group conditions of life calculated to bring about its physical destruction in whole or in part;

(d) Imposing measures intended to prevent births within the group;

(e) Forcibly transferring children of the group to another group.

Article III

THE FOLLOWING ACTS SHALL BE PUNISHABLE:

(a) Genocide;

(b) Conspiracy to commit genocide;

(c) Direct and public incitement to commit genocide;

(d) Attempt to commit genocide;

(e) Complicity in genocide.

Article IV

Persons committing genocide or any other acts enumerated in Article III shall be punished, whether they are constitutionally responsible rulers, public officials, or private individuals.

Article V

The Contracting Parties undertake to enact, in accordance with their respective Constitutions, the necessary legislation to give effect to the provisions of the present Convention and, in particular, to provide effective penalties for persons guilty of genocide or of any of the other acts enumerated in Article III.

Article VI

Persons charged with genocide or any of the other acts enumerated in Article III shall be tried by a competent tribunal of the State in the territory of which the act was committed, or by such international penal tribunal as may have jurisdiction with respect to those Contracting Parties which shall have accepted its jurisdiction.

Article VII

Genocide and the other acts enumerated in Article III shall not be considered as political crimes for the purpose of extradition.

• • •

The Contracting Parties pledge themselves in such cases to grant extradition in accordance with their laws and treaties in force.

Indictments by the International Criminal Tribunal for the Former Yugoslavia

Following is a series of indictments issued by the International Criminal Tribunal for the Former Yugoslavia against Bosnian Serbs for war crimes, crimes against humanity, and genocide. We include the indictments against Radovan Karadžić and Ratko Mladić as well as the indictments against supervisors, guards, and civilians from the Omarska concentration camp in northern Bosnia. We offer here examples of indictments that name specific crimes: there are many more defendants and many more crimes named in other indictments. These are provided to give the reader a sense of the extent to which Bosnian Serb leaders were involved in war crimes, crimes against humanity, and genocide. In addition, the specific charges laid against the individuals named in the indictments provide illustrations of the heinous and barbaric nature of the alleged crimes. It is doubtful whether such indictments will lead to actual prosecution and punishment of war criminals, since, in most cases, the defendants named in the indictments remain sheltered in Serb-controlled Bosnia-Herzegovina or in Serbia proper. Such crimes continued even as "peace talks" were being held in the United States in November 1995.

THE INTERNATIONAL CRIMINAL TRIBUNAL FOR THE FORMER YUGOSLAVIA
THE PROSECUTOR OF THE TRIBUNAL

AGAINST
RADOVAN KARADŽIĆ
RATKO MLADIĆ

Indictment

Richard J. Goldstone, Prosecutor of the International Criminal Tribunal for the Former Yugoslavia, pursuant to his authority under Article 18 of the Statute of the International Criminal Tribunal for the Former Yugoslavia ("The Statute of the Tribunal"), charges:

The Accused

1. RADOVAN KARADŽIĆ was born on 19 June 1945 in the municipality of Savnik of the Republic of Montenegro. From on or about 13 May 1992 to the present, he has been president of the Bosnian Serb administration in Pale.

2. RATKO MLADIĆ was born on 12 March 1943 in the municipality of Kalinovik of the Republic of Bosnia and Herzegovina. He is a career military officer and holds the rank of general in the Bosnian Serb armed forces. From on or about 14 May 1992 to the present, he has been the commander of the army of the Bosnian Serb administration.

Superior Authority
Radovan Karadžić

3. RADOVAN KARADŽIĆ was a founding member and president of the Serbian Democratic Party (SDS) of what was then the Socialist Republic of Bosnia and Herzegovina. The SDS was the main political party among the Serbs in Bosnia and Herzegovina. As president of the SDS, he was and is the most powerful official in the party. His duties as president include representing the party, co-ordinating the work of party organs and ensuring the realisation of the programmatic tasks and goals of the party. He continues to hold this post.

4. RADOVAN KARADŽIĆ became the first president of the Bosnian Serb administration in Pale on or about 13 May 1992. At the time he assumed this position, his *de jure* powers, as described in the constitution of the Bosnian Serb administration, included, but were not limited to

commanding the army on the Bosnian Serb administration in times of war and peace and having the authority to appoint, promote and discharge officers of the army.

5. In addition to his powers described in the constitution, RADOVAN KARADŽIĆ's powers as president of the Bosnian Serb administration are augmented by Article 6 of the Bosnian Serb Act on People's Defence which vested in him, among other powers, the authority to supervise the Territorial Defence both in peace and war and the authority to issue orders for the utilisation of the police in case of war, immediate threat and other emergencies. Article 39 of the same Act empowered him, in cases of imminent threat of war and other emergencies, to deploy Territorial Defence units for the maintenance of law and order.

6. RADOVAN KARADŽIĆ's powers are further augmented by Article 33 of the Bosnian Serb Act on Internal Affairs, which authorised him to activate reserve police in emergency situations.

7. RADOVAN KARADŽIĆ has exercised the powers described above and has acted and been dealt with internationally as the president of the Bosnian Serb administration in Pale. In that capacity, he has, inter alia, participated in international negotiations and has personally made agreements on such matters as cease-fires and humanitarian relief that have been implemented.

Ratko Mladić

8. RATKO MLADIĆ was, in 1991, appointed commander of the 9th Corps of the Yugoslav People's Army (JNA) in Knin in the Republic of Croatia. Subsequently, in May 1992, he assumed command of the forces of the Second Military District of the JNA which then effectively became the Bosnian Serb army. He holds the rank of general and from about 14 May 1992 to the present, has been the commander of the army of the Bosnian Serb administration.

9. RATKO MLADIĆ has demonstrated his control in military matters by negotiating, inter alia, cease-fire and prisoner exchange agreements; agreements relating to the opening of Sarajevo airport; agreements relating to access for humanitarian aid convoys; and anti-sniping agreements, all of which have been implemented.

General Allegations

10. At all times relevant to this indictment, a state of armed conflict and partial occupation existed in the Republic of Bosnia and Herzegovina in the territory of the former Yugoslavia.

11. All acts or omissions herein set forth as grave breaches of the Geneva Conventions of 1949 (hereafter "grave breaches") recognised by Article 2 of the Statute of the Tribunal occurred during that armed conflict and partial occupation.

12. In each paragraph charging crimes against humanity, crimes recognised by Article 5 of the Statute of the Tribunal, the alleged acts or omissions were part of a widespread, systematic or large-scale attack directed against a civilian population.

13. The term "UN peacekeepers" used throughout this indictment includes UN military observers of the United Nations.

14. The UN peacekeepers and civilians referred to in this indictment were, at all relevant times, persons protected by the Geneva Conventions of 1949.

15. The accused in this indictment were required to abide by the laws and customs governing the conduct of war, including the Geneva Conventions of 1949.

Charges

16. The charges set forth in this indictment are in three parts:

Part I of the indictment, Counts 1 to 9, charges a crime of genocide, crimes against humanity and crimes that were perpetrated against the civilian population and against places of worship throughout the territory of the Republic of Bosnia and Herzegovina.

Part II of the indictment, Counts 10 to 12, charges crimes relating to the sniping campaign against civilians in Sarajevo.

Part III of the indictment, Counts 13 to 16, charges crimes relating to the taking of UN peacekeepers as hostages.

Part I
Counts 1-2 (Genocide) (Crime against Humanity)

17. RADOVAN KARADŽIĆ and RATKO MLADIĆ, from April 1992, in the territory of the Republic of Bosnia and Herzegovina, by their acts and omissions, committed genocide.

18. Bosnian Muslim and Bosnian Croat civilians were persecuted on national, political and religious grounds throughout the Republic of Bosnia and Herzegovina. Thousands of them were interned in detention facilities where they were subjected to widespread acts of physical and psychological abuse and to inhumane conditions. Detention facility personnel who ran and operated the Omarska, Keraterm and Luka detention facilities, among others, including, but not limited to Željko Meakić (Omarska), Duško Sikirica (Keraterm) and Goran Jelisić (Luka), intended to destroy Bosnian Muslim and Bosnian Croat people as national, ethnic, or religious groups and killed, seriously injured and deliberately inflicted upon them conditions intended to bring about their physical destruction. The conditions in the detention facilities, which are described in paragraphs 20-22 hereunder, are incorporated in full herein.

19. RADOVAN KARADŽIĆ and RATKO MLADIĆ, between April 1992 and July 1995, in the territory of the Republic of Bosnia and Herzegovina, by their acts and omissions, and in concert with others, committed a crime against humanity by persecuting Bosnian Muslim and Bosnian Croat civilians on national, political and religious grounds. As set forth below, they are criminally responsible for the unlawful confinement, murder, rape, sexual assault, torture, beating, robbery and inhumane treatment of civilians; the targeting of political leaders, intellectuals and professionals; the unlawful deportation and transfer of civilians; the unlawful shelling of civilians; the unlawful appropriation and plunder of real and personal property; the destruction of homes and businesses; and the destruction of places of worship.

Detention Facilities

20. As soon as military forces from Bosnia and elsewhere in the former Yugoslavia began to attack towns and villages in the Republic of Bosnia and Herzegovina, thousands of Bosnian Muslim and Bosnian Croat civilians were systematically selected and rounded up on national, ethnic,

political or religious grounds and interned in detention facilities throughout the territory occupied by the Bosnian Serbs. These facilities include, but are not limited to:

Detention Facility	Dates of existence
Omarska	May–August 1992
Keraterm	May–August 1992
Trnopolje	May–December 1992
Luka	May–July 1992
Manjaca	Summer 1991–December 1992
Sušica	June 1992–September 1992
KP Dom Foča	April–mid-1993

21. Many of these detention facilities were staffed and operated by military and police personnel and their agents, under the control of RADOVAN KARADŽIĆ and RATKO MLADIĆ. In addition, Bosnian Serb police and military interrogators had unfettered access to all of the detention facilities and operated in conjunction with the personnel in control of these detention facilities. These facilities and personnel include, but are not limited to:

Detention Facility	Commander	Guards
Omarska	Željko Meakić (police)	police/military
Keraterm	Duško Sikirica (police)	police/military
Trnopolje	Slobodon Kuruzovic (military)	police/military
Luka	Goran Jelisić (police)	paramilitary
Manjaca	Bozidar Popovic (military)	military
Sušica	Dragan Nikolic (military)	military
KP Dom Foča	Milorad Krnojelac	military

22. Thousands of Bosnian Muslim and Bosnian Croat civilians, including women, children and elderly persons, were detained in these facilities for protracted periods of time. They were not afforded judicial process and their internment was not justified by military necessity. They were detained, in large measure, because of their national, religious and political identity. The conditions in the detention facilities were inhumane and brutal. Bosnian Serb military and police personnel in charge of these facilities, including Dragan Nikolić (Sušica), Željko Meakić (Omarska), Duško Sikirica (Keraterm) and other persons over whom they had control, subjected the civilian detainees to physical and psychological abuse, intimidation and maltreatment. Detention facility personnel, intending to

destroy Bosnian Muslim and Bosnian Croat people as national, ethnic or religious groups, killed, seriously injured and deliberately inflicted upon them conditions intended to bring about their physical destruction. Detainees were repeatedly subjected to and/or witnessed inhumane acts, including murder, rape, sexual assault, torture, beatings, robbery as well as other forms of mental and physical abuse. In many instances, women and girls who were detained were raped at the camps or taken from the detention centres and raped or otherwise sexually abused at other locations. Daily food rations provided to detainees were inadequate and often amounted to starvation rations. Medical care for the detainees was insufficient or non-existent and the general hygienic conditions were grossly inadequate.

Targeting of Political Leaders, Intellectuals and Professionals

23. Particularly singled out for persecution by the Bosnian Serb military, Bosnian Serb police and their agents, under the direction and control of RADOVAN KARADŽIĆ and RATKO MLADIĆ, were civilian political leaders and members of the primary Bosnian Muslim political party, the Party for Democratic Action (SDA), and the principal Bosnian Croat political party, the Croatian Democratic Union (HDZ), from the cities of Prijedor, Vlasenica, Bosanski Samac and Foča, amongst others. In many instances, lists identifying leaders of the SDA and the HDZ were provided

by the SDS to personnel of the Bosnian Serb military, police and their agents. Using these lists, Bosnian Muslim and Bosnian Croat political leaders were arrested, interned, physically abused and, in many instances, murdered. Some local SDA leaders who were persecuted because of their political beliefs include, but are not limited to, Muhamed Cehajić (Prijedor), Sulejman Tihić (Bosanski Samac), and Ahmet Hadžić (Brčko).

24. In addition to persecutions of Bosnian Muslim and Bosnian Croat political leaders, the Bosnian Serb military, police and their agents systematically targeted for persecution on national or religious grounds, Bosnian Muslim and Bosnian Croat intellectuals and professionals in many towns and villages including Prijedor, Vlasenica, Bosanski Samac and Foča, among others. Individuals who were persecuted include, but are not limited to Abdulah Puškar (academic), Ziko Crnalić (businessman) and Esad Mehmedalija (attorney) from Prijedor; Osman Vatić (attorney) from Brčko.

Deportation

25. Thousands of Bosnian Muslims and Bosnian Croats from the areas of Vlasenica, Prijedor, Bosanski Samac, Brčko and Foča, among others, were systematically arrested and interned in detention facilities established and maintained by the Bosnian Serb military, police and their agents and thereafter unlawfully deported or transferred to locations inside and outside of the Republic of Bosnia and Herzegovina. In addition, Bosnian Muslim and Bosnian Croat civilians, including women, children and elderly persons, were taken directly from their homes and eventually used in prisoner exchanges by Bosnian Serb military and police and their agents under the control and direction of RADOVAN KARADŽIĆ and RATKO MLADIĆ. These deportations and others were not conducted as evacuations for safety, military necessity or for any other lawful purpose and have, in conjunction with other actions directed against Bosnian Muslim and Bosnian Croat civilians, resulted in a significant reduction or elimination of Bosnian Muslims and Bosnian Croats in certain occupied regions.

Shelling of Civilian Gatherings

26. Beginning in July 1992 and continuing through to July 1995, Bosnian Serb military forces, under the direction and control of RADOVAN KARADŽIĆ and RATKO MLADIĆ, unlawfully fired on civilian gatherings that were of no military significance in order to kill, terrorise and demoralise the Bosnian Muslim and Bosnian Croat civilian population. These incidents include, but are not limited to the following:

Location/Type of Civilian Gathering	Municipality	Date	Casualties
Sarajevo (picnic)	Sarajevo	03/07/92	10
Sarajevo (airport)	Sarajevo	11/02/93	4
Srebrenica (playground)	Srebrenica	12/4/93	15
Dobrinja (soccer game)	Sarajevo	01/06/93	146
Dobrinja (water line)	Sarajevo	12/07/93	27
Sarajevo (residential street)	Sarajevo	28/11/93	11
Ciglane Market (fruit market)	Sarajevo	06/12/93	20
Alipasino Polje (children playing)	Sarajevo	22/01/94	10
Cetinjska St (children playing)	Sarajevo	26/10/94	7
Sarajevo (Livanjska Street)	Sarajevo	08/11/94	7
Sarajevo (flea market)	Sarajevo	22/12/94	9
Tuzla (plaza)	Tuzla	24/05/95	195

Appropriation and Plunder of Property

27. Shortly after armed hostilities broke out in the Republic of Bosnia and Herzegovina, Bosnian Serb forces quickly suppressed armed resistance in most villages and cities. During and after the course of consolidating their gains, Bosnian Serb military and police personnel, and other agents of the Bosnian Serb administration, under the direction and control of RADO-VAN KARADŽIĆ and RATKO MLADIĆ, systematically and wantonly appropriated and looted the real and personal property of Bosnian Muslim and Bosnian Croat civilians. The appropriation of property was extensive and not justified by military necessity. It occurred from April 1992 to January 1993 in the municipalities of Prijedor, Vlasenica, and Bosanski Samac, among others.

28. The appropriation and looting of said property was accomplished in the following manner and by the following means, among others:

A. Thousands of Bosnian Muslim and Bosnian Croat civilians were forced into detention facilities where they remained for protracted periods of time. Upon entering these internment facilities, the personnel who ran the internment facilities systematically stole the personal property of the detainees, including jewelry, watches, money and other valuables. The detainees were rarely provided receipts for the property taken from them or given their property back upon their release.

B. Civilians interned in these camps witnessed and/or were subjected to physical and psychological abuse. After witnessing or experiencing serious abuse, thousands of internees were forcibly transferred from these camps to locations inside and outside the Republic of Bosnia and Herzegovina. Before being forcibly transferred, many detainees were compelled to sign official Bosnian Serb documents wherein they "voluntarily" relinquished to the Bosnian Serb administration title to and possession of their real and personal property.

C. In many instances, Bosnian Muslim and Bosnian Croat civilian detainees were taken from internment camps to their homes and businesses and forced to turn over to their escorts money and other valuables. In other instances, they were used as labourers to load property from Bosnian Muslim and Bosnian Croat homes and businesses onto trucks for transportation to parts unknown. This occurred with the consent and approval of those in control of the detention facilities.

D. Many Bosnian Muslim and Bosnian Croat civilians who were not interned in camps were forced to stay in their communities where they were subjected to physical and psychological abuse from Bosnian Serb military and police and their agents, paramilitary forces and lawless elements of the Bosnian Serb community. Conditions for many became intolerable and they left. Before leaving, many civilians were compelled to sign official Bosnian Serb documents wherein they "voluntarily" relinquished to the Bosnian Serb administration their rights to their real and personal property. In some cases, Bosnian Muslim and Bosnian Croat civilians who left their communities were permitted to take with them limited amounts of personal property and money, but even that property was stolen from them at Bosnian Serb checkpoints or at other locations.

E. In many instances during and after the Bosnian Serb military take-over of towns and villages, Bosnian Serb military, police and their agents, entered the homes of non-Serb civilians and plundered the personal property of non-Serb civilians.

Destruction of Property

29. Persecution throughout the occupied territory by Bosnian Serb military, police and their agents, or third parties with their acquiescence, involved the systematic destruction of Bosnian Muslim and Bosnian Croat homes and businesses. These homes and businesses were singled out and systematically destroyed in areas where hostilities had ceased or had not taken place. The purpose of this unlawful destruction was to ensure that the inhabitants could not and would not return to their homes and communities. The cities, villages and towns, or Bosnian Muslim and Bosnian Croat portions thereof, where extensive destruction of property occurred include, but are not limited to the following:

Town/Village	Municipality	Approximate dates of destruction
Grebnice	Bosanski Samac	19–22 April 1992
Hrvatcka Tisina	Bosanski Samac	19–22 April 1992
Hasici	Bosanski Samac	19–22 April 1992
Derventa	Derventa	4 April 1992
Vijaka	Derventa	4 April 1992
Bosanski Brod	Bosanski Brod	3 March 1992
Odzak	Odzak	July 1992
Modrica	Modrica	Late April 1992

(cont.)

Vidovice	Orasje	29 April and 4 May 1992
Gradacac	Gradacac	mid-1992
Piskavice	Vlasenica	22 April 1992
Gobelje	Vlasenica	28 April 1992
Turalici	Vlasenica	28 April 1992
Djile	Vlasenica	1-3 May 1992
Pomol	Vlasenica	1 May 1992
Gaj	Vlasenica	1 May 1992
Besici	Vlasenica	1 May 1992
Nurici	Vlasenica	1 May 1992
Vrsinje	Vlasenica	1 May 1992
Dzamdzici	Vlasenica	8 May 1992
Pivici	Vlasenica	11 May 1992
Hambarine	Prijedor	23 May 1992
Ljubija	Prijedor	23 May 1992
Kozarac	Prijedor	24 May 1992
Biscani	Prijedor	20 July 1992
Carakovo	Prijedor	20 July 1992
Rizvanovici	Prijedor	20 July 1992
Sredice	Prijedor	20 July 1992
Zikovi	Prijedor	20 July 1992

Destruction of Sacred Sites

30. Muslim and Catholic places of worship were systematically damaged and/or destroyed by Bosnian Serb military forces and others. In many instances, where no military action had taken place or had ceased, these sacred sites were also damaged and/or destroyed. These places of worship include, but are not limited to those mentioned in paragraph 37 of this indictment. Bosnian Serb military and police forces failed to take reasonable and necessary measures to ensure that these religious sites would be protected.

31. The events described above were directed against Bosnian Muslim and Bosnian Croat civilians. Individually and collectively, these actions taken by or on behalf of the Bosnian Serb administration, have been on such a large scale and implemented in such a systematic way that they have destroyed, traumatised or dehumanised most aspects of Bosnian Muslim and Bosnian Croat life in those areas where the Bosnian Serb administration has taken control.

32. RADOVAN KARADŽIĆ and RATKO MLADIĆ knew or had reason to know that subordinates in detention facilities were about to kill or cause serious physical or mental harm to Bosnian Muslims and Bosnian

Croats with the intent to destroy them, in whole or in part, as national, ethnic or religious groups or had done so and failed to take necessary and reasonable measures to prevent such acts or to punish the perpetrators thereof.

33. RADOVAN KARADŽIĆ and RATKO MLADIĆ individually and in concert with others planned, instigated, ordered or otherwise aided and abetted in the planning, preparation or execution of persecutions on political and religious grounds or knew or had reason to know that subordinates were about to do the same or had done so and failed to take necessary and reasonable measures to prevent such acts or to punish the perpetrators thereof.

By these acts and omissions, RADOVAN KARADŽIĆ and RATKO MLADIĆ committed:

Count 1: GENOCIDE as recognised by Articles 4(2)(a), (b), (c) and 7(3) of the Statute of the Tribunal.

Count 2: a CRIME AGAINST HUMANITY as recognised by Articles 5(h) and 7(1) and 7(3) of the Statute of the Tribunal.

Counts 3-4 (Unlawful Confinement of Civilians)

34. From the outset of hostilities in the Republic of Bosnia and Herzegovina, thousands of Bosnian Muslim and Bosnian Croat civilians were unlawfully interned in detention facilities. Many of these facilities were established and operated by the Bosnian Serb military, police and their agents under the direction and control of RADOVAN KARADŽIĆ and RATKO MLADIĆ. As described in paragraphs 18 and 20-22 of this indictment and incorporated in full herein, the conditions in these facilities were inhumane. Countless civilians were abused and many perished in these internment facilities.

35. RADOVAN KARADŽIĆ and RATKO MLADIĆ individually and in concert with others planned, ordered, instigated or otherwise aided and abetted in the planning and preparation or execution of the unlawful detention of civilians or knew or had reason to know that subordinates were unlawfully detaining civilians and failed to take necessary and reasonable measures to prevent such acts or to punish the perpetrators thereof.

By these acts and omissions, RADOVAN KARADŽIĆ and RATKO MLADIĆ committed:

Count 3: a GRAVE BREACH as recognised by Articles 2(g) (unlawful confinement of civilians), 7(1) and 7(3) of the Statute of the Tribunal.

Count 4: a VIOLATION OF THE LAWS OR CUSTOMS OF WAR (outrages upon personal dignity) as recognised by Articles 3, 7(1) and 7(3) of the Statute of the Tribunal.

Count 5 (Shelling of Civilian Gatherings)

36. As described in paragraph 26 of this indictment, which is incorporated in full herein, Bosnian Serb military forces fired upon civilian gatherings that were of no military significance, thereby causing injury and death to hundreds of civilians. RADOVAN KARADŽIĆ and RATKO MLADIĆ, individually and in concert with others planned, instigated, ordered or otherwise aided and abetted in the planning, preparation or execution of unlawful attacks against the civilian population and individual civilians with area fire weapons such as mortars, rockets and artillery or knew or had reason to know that the Bosnian Serb military forces were about to unlawfully attack the civilian population and individual civilians, or had already done so, and failed to take the necessary and reasonable steps to prevent such shelling or to punish the perpetrators thereof.

By these acts and omissions, RADOVAN KARADŽIĆ and RATKO MLADIĆ committed:

Count 5: a VIOLATION OF THE LAWS OR CUSTOMS OF WAR (deliberate attack on the civilian population and individual civilians) as recognised by Articles 3, 7(1) and 7(3) of the Statute of the Tribunal.

Count 6 (Destruction of Sacred Sites)

37. Since April 1992 to the end of May 1995, in territory of the Republic of Bosnia and Herzegovina controlled by the Bosnian Serb military and police, including areas where no military conflict was ongoing, there has been widespread and systematic damage to and destruction of Muslim and Roman Catholic sacred sites. In areas such as Banja Luka, the near total obliteration of these religious sites has occurred. The sites in the Banja Luka area include the following:

Muslim Sacred Sites

Name of Mosque	Location	Date of Destruction or Damage
Sefer-Beg Mosque	Banja Luka	09.04.93
Ferhadija Mosque	Banja Luka	07.05.93
Arnaudija Mosque	Banja Luka	07.05.93
Mosque in Vrbanje	Banja Luka	11.05.93
Zulfikarova Mosque	Banja Luka	15.05.93
Behram-Efendija Mosque	Banja Luka	26.05.93
Mehidibeg Mosque	Banja Luka	04.06.93
Sufi Mehmed-Pasa Mosque	Banja Luka	04.06.93
Hadzi-Begzade Mosque	Banja Luka	04.06.93
Gazanferija Mosque	Banja Luka	04.06.93
Hadzi-Sebenova Mosque	Banja Luka	14.06.93
Hadzi-Kurt Mosque	Banja Luka	14.06.93
Hadzi-Pervis Mosque	Banja Luka	06.09.93
Hadzi-Osmanija Mosque	Banja Luka	08.09.93
Hadzi-Omer Mosque	Banja Luka	09.09.93
Hadzi-Salihija Mosque	Banja Luka	09.09.93

Roman Catholic Sacred Sites

Name of Church	Location	Date of Destruction or Damage
Church of St. Joseph at Trno	Banja Luka	24.10.91
Parish Church	Banja Luka	30.12.91
St. Bonaventura Cathedral	Banja Luka	31.12.91
St. Vincent Monastery	Banja Luka	02.12.92
Village Church	Vujnovici	05.05.95
Parish Church	Petricevac	06.05.95
St. Anthony of Padua Church and Franciscan Monastery	Banja Luka	07.05.95
Parish Church	Sergovac	07.05.95
Village Church	Majdan	08.05.95
Parish Church	Presnace	12.05.95

38. In other areas, damage and destruction to places of worship has been widespread These sites include, but are not limited to the Aladza Mosque (Foča); the Sultan Selim Mosque (Doboj); the Church of St. Peter and St. Paul, the Obri Chapel and the Sevri-Hadzi Mosque (Mostar); the parish church (Novi Seher) and the Carsijska Mosque (Konjic). Bosnian Serb military and police forces failed to take reasonable and necessary measures to ensure that these religious sites were protected.

39. RADOVAN KARADŽIĆ and RATKO MLADIĆ, individually and in concert with others planned, instigated, ordered or otherwise aided and

abetted in the planning, preparation or execution of the destruction of sacred sites or knew or had reason to know that subordinates were about to damage or destroy these sites or had done so and failed to take necessary and reasonable measures to prevent them from doing so or to punish the perpetrators thereof.

By these acts and omissions, RADOVAN KARADŽIĆ and RATKO MLADIĆ committed:

Count 6: a VIOLATION OF THE LAWS OR CUSTOMS OF WAR (destruction or wilful damage to institutions dedicated to religion) as recognised by Articles 3(d), 7(1) and 7(3) of the Statute of the Tribunal.

Count 7 (Extensive Destruction of Property)

40. After the take-over of Foča (8 April 1992), Bosanski Samac (17 April 1992), Vlasenica (21 April 1992), Prijedor (30 April 1992), Brčko (30 April 1992) and other municipalities in the Republic of Bosnia and Herzegovina, Bosnian Serb military and police forces and other elements over whom they had control, under the direction and control of RADOVAN KARADŽIĆ and RATKO MLADIĆ, systematically destroyed, or permitted others to destroy, for no justifiable military reasons, Bosnian Muslim and Bosnian Croat businesses and residences in occupied cities and villages. The areas where extensive destruction occurred include those areas described in paragraph 29 of this indictment, which is incorporated in full herein.

41. RADOVAN KARADŽIĆ and RATKO MLADIĆ, individually and in concert with others planned, instigated, ordered or otherwise aided and abetted in the planning, preparation or execution of the extensive, wanton and unlawful destruction of Bosnian Muslim and Bosnian Croat property, not justified by military necessity or knew or had reason to know that subordinates were about to destroy or permit others to destroy the property of Bosnian Muslim or Bosnian Croat civilians or had done so and failed to take necessary and reasonable measures to prevent this destruction or to punish the perpetrators thereof.

By these acts and omissions, RADOVAN KARADŽIĆ and RATKO MLADIĆ committed:

Count 7: a GRAVE BREACH as recognised by Articles 2(d) (destruction of property), 7(1) and 7(3) of the Statute of the Tribunal.

Counts 8-9 (Appropriation and Plunder of Property)

42. As described in paragraphs 27-28 of this indictment, which are incorporated in full herein, Bosnian Serb military and police personnel and other agents of the Bosnian Serb administration, under the direction and control of RADOVAN KARADŽIĆ and RATKO MLADIĆ, systematically appropriated and looted the real and personal property of Bosnian Muslim and Bosnian Croat civilians.

43. RADOVAN KARADŽIĆ and RATKO MLADIĆ, individually and in concert with others planned, instigated, ordered or otherwise aided and abetted in the planning, preparation or execution of the extensive, wanton and unlawful appropriation of real and personal property owned by Bosnian Muslim and Bosnian Croat civilians or knew or had reason to know that subordinates were about to appropriate real and personal property of Bosnian Muslim and Bosnian Croat civilians or had done so and failed to take necessary and reasonable measures to prevent this appropriation or to punish the perpetrators thereof.

By these acts and omissions, RADOVAN KARADŽIĆ and RATKO MLADIĆ committed:

Count 8: a GRAVE BREACH as recognised by Articles 2(d) (appropriation of property), 7(1) and 7(3) of the Statute of the Tribunal.

Count 9: a VIOLATION OF THE LAWS OR CUSTOMS OF WAR (plunder of public or private property) as recognised by Articles 3(e), 7(1) and 7(3) of the Statute of the Tribunal.

Part II
Counts 10-12 (Sarajevo Sniping)

44. Since 5 April 1992, the City of Sarajevo has been besieged by forces of the Bosnian Serb army. Throughout this siege, there has been a systematic campaign of deliberate targeting of civilians by snipers of the Bosnian Serb military and their agents. The sniping campaign has terrorised the civilian population of Sarajevo and has resulted in a substantial number of civilian casualties, killed and wounded, including women, children and elderly. Between 5 May 1992 and 31 May 1995, snipers have systematically, unlawfully and wilfully killed and wounded civilians

in the area of Sarajevo, including but not limited to the following individuals:

Killed

Children

Elma Jakupović, age 2, at Jukiceva Street, No 17, on 20 July 1993
Elvedina Čolić, age 4, at Kobilja Glava on 8 August 1993
Adnan Kasapović, age 16, at Dj. A. Kuna Street on 24 October 1994
Nermina Omerović, age 11, at Djure Danicica Street on 8 November 1994

Women

Almasa Konjhodzić, age 56, at the intersection of Kranjcevica and Brodska Streets on 27 June 1993
Sevda Kustura, age 50, at Spicasta Stijena on 5 August 1993
Sada Pohara, age 19, at Zarka Zgonjanina Street, No 13, on 30 August 1993
Saliha Comaga, age 38, at Mujkica Brdo, Ugorsko, on 8 September 1993
Edina Trto, age 25, at Ivana Krndelja Street on 26 September 1993
Hatema Mukanović, age 38, at Obala 27 July 89 Street on 11 January 1994
Radmila Plainović, age 51, at Vojvode Putnika Street on 7 February 1994
Lejla Bajramović, age 24, at B. Boris Kidric Street, No 3, on 8 December 1994

Elderly

Hajrija Dizdarević, age 66, at Ivo Kranjcevic Street 11 on 17 July 1993
Marko Stupar, age 64, at Zmaja od Bosne No 64 Street on 12 January 1994
Fadil Zuko, age 63, at Stara Cesta Street, on 2 February 1994
Dragomir Čulibrk, aged 61, at Prvomajska BB on 16 June 1994

Men

Adnan Mesihović, age 34, at Hasana Brkica Street on 3 September 1993

Junuz Campara, age 59, at Milutin Djuraskovic Street on 6 September 1993

Augustin Vucić, age 57, at Ante Babica Street on 13 March 1994

Jasmin Podzo, age 23, at Mala Berkusa Street 10 on 4 March 1995

Wounded

Children

Boy, age 2, at Stara Cesta Street on 26 June 1993

Boy, age 12, at Kupalista swimming pool on 5 August 1993

Girl, age 9, at Kobilja Glava on 8 August 1993

Boy, age 14, at Dzemal Bijedic Street on 3 September 1993

Girl, age 8, at Ivana Krndelja Street on 3 September 1993

Boy, age 15, at X transverzale Street bb on 4 October 1993

Boy, age 13, at Donji Hotonj II Street on 10 November 1993

Boy, age 12, at Petra Drapsina Street on 28 November 1993

Boy, age 17, at Dzemala Bijedica Street on 10 January 1994

Boy, age 5, at Zmaja od Bosne Street on 19 June 1994

Girl, age 16, at Senada Mandica-Dende Street on 26 June 1994

Boy, age 13, at Miljenka Cvitkovica Street on 22 July 1994

Boy, age 7, at Zmaja od Bosne Street on 18 November 1994

Girl, age 13, at the cross-roads of Rogina and Sedrenik Streets on 22 November 1994

Boy, age 14, at Sedrenik Street on 6 March 1995

Women

Female, age 20, at Hotonj on 5 August 1993

Female, age 52, at Franca Rozmana Street on 6 August 1993

Female, age 55, at Spanskih Boraca Street 011 30 August 1993

Female, age 35, at Ivana Krndelja Street on 3 September 1993

Female, age 32, at Nikola Demonja/ Grada Bakua Street area on 6 January 1994

Female, age 46, at Olimpijska Street, No 15, on 18 January 1994

Female, age 42, at 21 Maj Street on 9 May 1994

Female, age 50, and female, age 62, at Nikole Demonje Street on 25 May 1994

Female, age 45, at Mojmilo Dobrinja Road on 13 June 1994

Female, age 46, at Zaim Imamovic Street, No 15 on 20 July 1994

Female, age 54, at Baruthana Street on 8 November 1994

Female, age 28, at Zmaja od Bosne Street on 9 November 1994
Female, age 28, at Zmaja od Bosne Street on 18 November 1994
Female, age 24, at Franca Lehara Street, No 3 on 8 December 1994
Female, age 49, at Sedrenik Street on 10 December 1994

Elderly
Female, age 71, at "Ciglane" Market on 17 September 1993
Female, age 72, at Nikole Demonje Street on 2 October 1993
Female, age 60, at Lovcenska Street on 7 December 1993
Male, age 63, at St Anto Babić on 13 March 1994
Male, age 62, at Omladinskih Radnih Brigada Street on 16 June 1994
Male, age 61, at Prvomajska BB on 16 June 1994
Male, age 67, at Senad Mandic Denda Street, on 17 July 1994
Male, age 63, at Sedrenik Street on 11 December 1994
Male, age 62, at Sedrenik Street on 13 December 1994
Female, age 73, at the intersection of Zmaja od Bosne and Muzejska
   Streets on 18 December 1994

Men
Male, age 36, at Trg of Zavnobih on 1 February 1993
Male, age 52, at Kobilja Glava on 25 June 1993
Male, age 29, at Stara Cesta Street on 7 October 1993
Male, age 50, and male, age 56, at Brace Ribara Street on 2 November
   1993
Male, age 36, at Stara Cesta Street on 14 December 1993
Male, age 27, at Zmaja od Bosne Street on 19 June 1994
Male, age 20, male, age 27, male, age 39, and male, age 34, at Zmaja
   od Bosne Street on 9 November 1994
Male, age 29, at Sedrenik Street on 8 December 1994
Male, age 46, and male, age 33, at intersection of Franje Rackog and
   Marsala Tita Streets on 3 March 1995
Male, age 52, at Sedrenik Street on 6 March 1995

45. RADOVAN KARADŽIĆ and RATKO MLADIĆ individually and in
concert with others planned, ordered, instigated or otherwise aided and
abetted in the planning, preparation or execution of the sniping of civilians or knew or had reason to know that subordinates were sniping
civilians and failed to take necessary and reasonable measures to prevent
such acts or to punish the perpetrators thereof.

As to the deliberate attacks by sniper fire against the civilian population and individual civilians, which resulted in death and injury to said civilians, and acts and omissions related thereto, RADOVAN KARADŽIĆ and RATKO MLADIĆ committed:

Count 10: a VIOLATION OF THE LAWS OR CUSTOMS OF WAR (deliberate attack on the civilian population and individual civilians) as recognised by Articles 3, 7(1) and 7(3) of the Statute of the Tribunal.

As to the killing by sniper fire of these civilians, among others, and acts and omissions related thereto, RADOVAN KARADŽIĆ and RATKO MLADIĆ committed:

Count 11: a CRIME AGAINST HUMANITY as recognised by Articles 5(a) (murder), 7(1) and 7(3) of the Statute of the Tribunal.

As to the wounding by sniper fire of these civilians, among others, and acts and omissions related thereto, RADOVAN KARADŽIĆ and RATKO MLADIĆ committed:

Count 12: a CRIME AGAINST HUMANITY as recognised by Articles 5(i) (inhumane acts), 7(1) and 7(3) of the Statute of the Tribunal.

Part III
Counts 13-16 (Hostages/Human Shields)

46. Between 26 May 1995 and 2 June 1995, Bosnian Serb military personnel, under the direction and control of RADOVAN KARADŽIĆ and RATKO MLADIĆ, seized 284 UN peacekeepers in Pale, Sarajevo, Gorazde and other locations and held them hostage in order to prevent further North Atlantic Treaty Organisation (NATO) airstrikes. Bosnian Serb military personnel held the UN peacekeepers throughout their captivity by force or by the threat of force. In some instances, the UN hostages were assaulted. During and after protracted negotiations with Bosnian Serb leaders, the UN hostages were released in stages between 3 June 1995 and 19 June 1995.

47. After seizing UN peacekeepers in the Pale area, Bosnian Serb military personnel, under the direction and control of RADOVAN KARADŽIĆ and RATKO MLADIĆ, immediately selected certain UN hostages to use

as "human shields," including but not limited to Capt. Patrick A. Rechner (Canada), Capt. Oldrich Zidlik (Czech Republic), Captain Teterevsky (Russia), Maj. Abdul Razak Bello (Nigeria), Capt. Ahmad Manzoor (Pakistan) and Maj. Gunnar Westlund (Sweden). From on or about 26 May 1995 through 27 May 1995, Bosnian Serb military personnel physically secured or otherwise held the UN peacekeepers against their will at potential NATO air targets, including the ammunition bunkers at Jahorinski Potok, the Jahorina radar site and a nearby communications centre in order to render these locations immune from further NATO airstrikes. High level Bosnian Serb political and military delegations inspected and photographed the UN hostages who were handcuffed at the ammunition bunkers at Jahorinski Potok.

48. RADOVAN KARADŽIĆ and RATKO MLADIĆ, individually and in concert with others planned, instigated, ordered or otherwise aided and abetted in the planning, preparation or execution of the taking of civilians, that is UN peacekeepers, as hostages and, additionally, using them as "human shields" and knew or had reason to know that subordinates were about to take and hold UN peacekeepers as hostages and about to use them as "human shields" or had done so and failed to take necessary and reasonable measures to prevent them from doing so or to punish the perpetrators thereof.

In regard to UN peacekeepers seized and held hostage between 26 May 1995 and 19 June 1995, RADOVAN KARADŽIĆ and RATKO MLADIĆ, by their acts and omissions, committed:

Count 13: a GRAVE BREACH as recognised by Articles 2(h) (taking civilians as hostage), 7(1) and 7(3) of the Statute of the Tribunal.

Count 14: a VIOLATION OF THE LAWS OR CUSTOMS OF WAR (taking of hostages) as recognised by Articles 3, 7(1) and 7(3) of the Statute of the Tribunal.

In regard to the UN peacekeepers used as "human shields" on 26 and 27 May 1995, RADOVAN KARADŽIĆ and RATKO MLADIĆ, by their acts and omissions, committed:

Count 15: a GRAVE BREACH as recognised by Articles 2(b) (inhumane treatment), 7(1) and 7(3) of the Statute of the Tribunal.

Count 16: a VIOLATION OF THE LAWS OR CUSTOMS OF WAR
(cruel treatment) as recognised by Articles 3, 7(1) and 7(3) of the Statute
of the Tribunal

24 July 1995

Richard J. Goldstone
Prosecutor

THE INTERNATIONAL CRIMINAL TRIBUNAL FOR THE FORMER
YUGOSLAVIA
THE PROSECUTOR OF THE TRIBUNAL
AGAINST
ŽELJKO MEAKIĆ
MIROSLAV KVOĆKA
DRAGOLJUB PRČAC
MLADEN RADIĆ a/k/a "KRKAN"
MILOJICA KOŠ a/k/a "KRLE"
MOMČILO GRUBAN a/k/a "CKALJA"
ZDRAVKO GOVEDARICA
GRUBAN
PREDRAG KOSTIĆ a/k/a "KOLE"
NEDELJKO PASPALJ
MILAN PAVLIĆ
MILUTIN POPOVIĆ
DRAŽENKO PREDOJEVIĆ
ŽELJKO SAVIĆ
MIRKO BABIĆ
NIKICA JANJIĆ
DUSAN KNEŽEVIĆ a/k/a "DUČA"
DRAGOMIR ŠAPONJA
ZORAN ŽIGIĆ a/k/a "ŽIGA"

Indictment

Richard J. Goldstone, Prosecutor of the International Criminal Tribunal
for the former Yugoslavia, pursuant to his authority under Article 18 of
the Statute of the International Criminal Tribunal for the former Yugoslavia ("The Statute of the Tribunal"), charges:

1. From about 25 May to about 30 August, 1992, Serb forces collected
and confined more than 3,000 Bosnian Muslims and Bosnian Croats from
the opstina of Prijedor, Bosnia-Herzegovina, in the former Yugoslavia, in
inhumane conditions, under armed guard, in the Omarska "camp", located
in a former mining complex approximately fifteen kilometres from the
town of Prijedor. As set forth below, the Serb forces killed, raped, sexually
assaulted, beat and otherwise mistreated the prisoners at Omarska.

Background: Omarska Camp

2.1. In May, 1992, intensive shelling of Muslim areas in the opstina Prijedor caused the Muslim residents to flee their homes. The majority of them then surrendered or were captured by Serb forces. As the Serb forces rounded up the Muslims and any Croat residents, they forced the Muslims and Croats to march in columns bound for one or another of the prison camps that the Serbs had established in the opstina. The Serb forces pulled many of the Muslims and Croats from the columns and shot or beat them on the spot.

2.2. On about 25 May 1992, about three weeks after Serbs forcibly took control of government authority in the opstina, and two days after the start of large scale military attacks on Muslim population centres, the Serb forces began taking prisoners to the Omarska camp.

2.3. During the next several weeks, the Serb forces continued to round up Muslims and Croats from Kozarac, Prijedor town, and other places in the opstina and interned them in the camps. Many of Prijedor's Muslim and Croat intellectuals, professional and political leaders were sent to Omarska. There were approximately 40 women in the camp, and all the other prisoners in the camp were men.

2.4. Within the area of the Omarska mining complex that was used for the camp, the camp authorities generally confined the prisoners in three different buildings: the administration building, where interrogations took place and most of the women were confined; the garage or hangar building; the "white house," a small building where particularly severe beatings were administered; and on a cement courtyard area between the buildings known as the "pista". There was another small building, known as the "red house", where prisoners were sometimes taken but most often did not emerge alive.

2.5. Living conditions at Omarska were brutal. Prisoners were crowded together with little or no facilities for personal hygiene. They were fed starvation rations once a day and given only three minutes to get into the canteen area, eat, and get out. The little water they received was ordinarily foul. Prisoners had no changes of clothing and no bedding. They received no medical care.

2.6. Severe beatings were commonplace. The camp guards, and others who came to the camp and physically abused the prisoners, used all manner of weapons during these beatings, including wooden batons, metal rods and tools, lengths of thick industrial cable that had metal balls affixed to the end, rifle butts, and knives. Both female and male prisoners were beaten, tortured, raped, sexually assaulted, and humiliated. In addition to regular beatings and abuse, there were incidents of multiple killings and special terror. Many, whose identities are known and unknown, did not survive the camp.

3. The persons accused in this indictment were commanders, guards and others responsible for the conditions and mistreatment of prisoners in Omarska camp or otherwise assisted the accused.

The Accused:

4. Željko MEAKIĆ also known as (hereinafter a/k/a Mejakić, a/k/a Meagić), was in charge of Omarska camp beginning in late June, 1992, and was in a position of superior authority to everyone else in the camp. Before he took command of the camp, he was chief of security and had full authority over all the guards and any visitors. Before the war began in Bosnia-Herzegovina, he was a police official in Omarska village.

5. Miroslav KVOČKA and Dragoljub PRČAC were deputies to Željko MEAKIĆ and were in positions of authority superior to everyone in the camp other than MEAKIĆ. For most of the first month of the camp's operation, KVOČKA was the commander of the camp. Prior to the start of the war, both KVOČKA and PRČAC were officials at the Ministry of the Interior in Prijedor.

6. Mladen RADIĆ a/k/a Mlado RADIĆ a/k/a Krkan; Milojica KOŠ a/k/a Krle; and Momcilo GRUBAN a/k/a Ckalja were shift commanders who each supervised one of the three shifts of guards that operated the camp. As shift commanders, when they were on duty, they were in positions of superior authority to all the camp personnel, second only to the camp commander and his deputies.

7. The following accused were among those who acted as guards in the Omarska camp:

   a. Zdravko GOVEDARICA
   b. first name unknown GRUBAN
   c. Predrag KOSTIĆ a/k/a KOLE

    d.   Nedeljko PASPALJ
    e.   Milan PAVLIĆ
    f.   Milutin POPOVIĆ
    g.   Draženko PREDOJEVIĆ
    h.   Željko SAVIĆ

8. In addition to the above-listed accused, who regularly performed duties in Omarska camp, other Serbs entered the camp, subject to the authority of Željko MEAKIĆ, Miroslav KVOČKA, and Dragoljub PRCAC, where they killed, beat or otherwise physically abused prisoners. Among those who entered the camp were the following accused:

    a.   Mirko BABIC
    b.   Nikica JANJIC
    c.   Dusan KNEŽEVIĆ a/k/a DUCA
    d.   Dragomir SAPONJA
    f.   Zoran ZIGIC a/k/a ZIGA

General Allegations:

9. At all times relevant to this indictment, a state of armed conflict and partial occupation existed in the territory of Bosnia-Herzegovina.

10. All acts or omissions set forth as grave breaches recognised by Article 2 of the Statute of the Tribunal occurred during that armed conflict and partial occupation.

11. All of the prisoners at the Omarska camp, and the Bosnian Muslims and Croats of the opstina of Prijedor referred to in this indictment were, at all relevant times, persons protected by the Geneva Conventions of 1949.

12. All of the accused in this indictment were required to abide by the mandate of the laws and customs governing the conduct of war, including the Geneva Conventions of 1949.

13. Unless otherwise set forth below, all acts and omissions set forth in this indictment took place between 24 May and 30 August 1992.

14. In each paragraph charging torture, the acts were committed by, or at the instigation of, or with the consent or acquiescence of, an official or person acting in an official capacity, and for one or more of the following

purposes: to obtain information or a confession from the victim or a third person; to punish the victim for an act the victim or a third person committed or was suspected of having committed; to intimidate or coerce the victim or a third person; and/or for any reason based upon discrimination of any kind.

15. In each paragraph charging crimes against humanity, a crime recognised by Article 5 of the Statute of the Tribunal, the alleged acts or omissions were part of a widespread or large-scale or systematic attack directed against a civilian population, specifically the Muslim and Croat population of the Prijedor district.

16. Paragraphs 4 through 15 are realleged and incorporated into each of the charges described below.

17. The term "Serb" refers either to Bosnian citizens of Serbian descent or to individuals for whom it is unknown whether they were Bosnian Serbs or citizens of Serbia proper.

Charges:
Accused: Zeliko Meakić

18.1. Željko MEAKIĆ, intending to destroy, in whole or in part, the Bosnian Muslim and Bosnian Croat people as national, ethnic, or religious groups, was complicit with other persons in the killing of Bosnian Muslims and Bosnian Croats from the opstina Prijedor at the Omarska camp, thereby committing GENOCIDE, a crime recognised by Article 4(a) of the Statute of the Tribunal.

18.2. Željko MEAKIĆ, intending to destroy, in whole or in part, the Bosnian Muslim and Bosnian Croat people as national, ethnic, or religious groups, was complicit with other persons in causing serious bodily or mental harm to Bosnian Muslim and Bosnian Croat people from the opstina Prijedor in Omarska camp, thereby committing GENOCIDE, a crime recognised by Article 4(b) of the Statute of the Tribunal.

18.3. Željko MEAKIĆ, intending to destroy, in whole or in part, the Bosnian Muslim and Bosnian Croat people as national, ethnic, or religious groups, was complicit with other persons in the deliberate infliction of conditions of life on Bosnian Muslim and Bosnian Croat people from the opstina Prijedor at the Omarska camp calculated to bring about their physical destruction in whole or in part, thereby committing GENOCIDE, a crime recognised by Article 4(c) of the Statute of the Tribunal.

19.1. With respect to the allegations in this indictment, Željko MEAKIĆ, Miroslav KVOČKA, Dragoljub PRČAC, Mladen RADIĆ, Milojica KOŠ and Momcilo GRUBAN knew or had reason to know that persons in positions of subordinate authority to them at Omarska camp were about to commit those acts, or had already committed those acts, and failed to take the necessary and reasonable steps to prevent those acts or to punish the perpetrators after the acts had been committed.

19.2. During the operation of Omarska camp, camp guards and others who were subordinate to Željko MEAKIĆ, Miroslav KVOČKA, Dragoljub PRČAC, Mladen RADIĆ, Milojica KOŠ and Momcilo GRUBAN regularly and openly killed, raped, tortured, beat, and otherwise subjected prisoners to conditions of constant humiliation, degradation, and fear of death.

Accused: Zeliko Meakić, Miroslav Kvočka, Dragoljub Prčać, Mladen Radić, Milojica Koš and Momcilo Gruban in their capacity as superiors

19.3. Željko MEAKIĆ, Miroslav KVOČKA, Dragoljub PRČAC, Mladen RADIĆ, Milojica KOŠ and Momcilo GRUBAN are criminally responsible for the acts of their subordinates in the wilful killing of Omarska prisoners, including those described in paragraphs hereunder, GRAVE BREACHES OF THE GENEVA CONVENTIONS OF 1949 (hereinafter GRAVE BREACHES) recognised by Articles 2(a) and 7(3) of the Statute of the Tribunal, or;

19.4. Alternatively, Željko MEAKIĆ, Miroslav KVOČKA, Dragoljub PRČAC, Mladen RADIĆ, Milojica KOŠ and Momcilo GRUBAN are criminally responsible for the acts of their subordinates in the murder of Omarska prisoners, including those described in paragraphs hereunder, VIOLATIONS OF THE LAWS OR CUSTOMS OF WAR recognised by Articles 3 and 7(3) of the Statute of the Tribunal and Article 3(1)(a) of the Geneva Conventions.

19.5. Željko MEAKIĆ, Miroslav KVOČKA, Dragoljub PRČAC, Mladen RADIĆ, Milojica KOŠ and Momcilo GRUBAN are criminally responsible for the acts of their subordinates in the murder of Omarska prisoners, including those described in paragraphs hereunder, CRIMES AGAINST HUMANITY recognised by Articles 5(a) and 7(3) of the Statute of the Tribunal.

19.6. Željko MEAKIĆ, Miroslav KVOČKA, Dragoljub PRČAC, Mladen RADIĆ, Milojica KOŠ and Momcilo GRUBAN are criminally responsible for the acts of their subordinates in the torture of Omarska prisoners, GRAVE BREACHES recognised by Articles 2(b) and 7 (3) of the Statute of the Tribunal, or;

19.7. Alternatively, Željko MEAKIĆ, Miroslav KVOČKA, Dragoljub PRČAC, Mladen RADIĆ, Milojica KOŠ and Momcilo GRUBAN are criminally responsible for the acts of their subordinates in the torture of Omarska prisoners, VIOLATIONS OF THE LAWS OR CUSTOMS OF WAR recognised by Articles 3 and 7(3) of the Statute of the Tribunal and Article 3(1)(a) of the Geneva Conventions.

19.8. Željko MEAKIĆ, Miroslav KVOČKA, Dragoljub PRČAC, Mladen RADIĆ, Milojica KOŠ and Momcilo GRUBAN are criminally responsible for the acts of their subordinates in the torture of Omarska prisoners, CRIMES AGAINST HUMANITY recognised by Articles 5(f) and 7(3) of the Statute of the Tribunal.

19.9. Željko MEAKIĆ, Miroslav KVOČKA, Dragoljub PRČAC, Mladen RADIĆ, Milojica KOŠ and Momcilo GRUBAN are criminally responsible for the acts of their subordinates in the rape of Omarska prisoners, including those described in paragraphs hereunder, CRIMES AGAINST HUMANITY recognised by Articles 5(g) and 7(3) of the Statute of the Tribunal.

19.10. Željko MEAKIĆ, Miroslav KVOČKA, Dragoljub PRČAC, Mladen RADIĆ, Milojica KOŠ and Momcilo GRUBAN are criminally responsible for the acts of their subordinates in wilfully causing great suffering to Omarska prisoners, including those described in paragraphs hereunder, GRAVE BREACHES recognised by Articles 2(c) and 7(3) of the Statute of the Tribunal, or;

19.11. Alternatively, Željko MEAKIĆ, Miroslav KVOČKA, Dragoljub PRČAC, Mladen RADIĆ, Milojica KOŠ and Momcilo GRUBAN are criminally responsible for the acts of their subordinates in the commission of outrages upon personal dignity, including humiliating and degrading treatment of the Omarska prisoners, VIOLATIONS OF THE LAWS OR

CUSTOMS OF WAR recognised by Articles 3 and 7(3) of the Statute of the Tribunal and Article 3(1)(c) of the Geneva Conventions.

19.12. Željko MEAKIĆ, Miroslav KVOČKA, Dragoljub PRČAC, Mladen RADIĆ, Milojica KOŠ and Momcilo GRUBAN are criminally responsible for the acts of their subordinates in the unlawful confinement of civilians, including those listed in paragraphs hereunder, GRAVE BREACHES recognised by Articles 2(g) and 7(3) of the Statute of the Tribunal, or;

19.13. Željko MEAKIĆ, Miroslav KVOČKA, Dragoljub PRČAC, Mladen RADIĆ, Milojica KOŠ and Momcilo GRUBAN are criminally responsible for their own acts or omissions and for the acts of their subordinates in the unlawful imprisonment of the prisoners of Omarska, including those listed in paragraphs hereunder, CRIMES AGAINST HUMANITY recognised by Articles 5(e) and 7(3) of the Statute of the Tribunal.

Accused: Zeliko Meakić

20.1. Around 20 July 1992, the last remaining pocket of Bosnian Muslims and Bosnian Croats was captured from the area west of Prijedor town known as the Brdo. Many were taken to Omarska camp. When they arrived, Željko MEAKIĆ and camp guards beat them severely with batons and other weapons.

20.2. Željko MEAKIĆ wilfully caused these prisoners great suffering or serious injury to body or health, a GRAVE BREACH recognised by Articles 2(c) and 7(1) of the Statute of the Tribunal, or;

20.3. Alternatively, Željko MEAKIĆ wilfully subjected these prisoners to cruel treatment, a VIOLATION OF THE LAWS OR CUSTOMS OF WAR recognised by Articles 3 and 7(1) of the Statute of the Tribunal and Article 3(1)(a) of the Geneva Conventions.

20.4. Željko MEAKIĆ committed inhumane acts on the Brdo prisoners, a CRIME AGAINST HUMANITY recognised by Articles 5(i) and 7(1) of the Statute of the Tribunal.

21.1. About 25 June 1992, during an interrogation on the first floor of the administration building, two guards beat Saud BESIĆ repeatedly with batons and kicked him. Željko MEAKIĆ entered the room, kicked Saud

BESIĆ in the chest and the two guards continued to beat him until he lost consciousness.

21.2. Željko MEAKIĆ subjected Saud BESIĆ to inhumane treatment, a GRAVE BREACH recognised by Articles 2(b) and 7(1) of the Statute of the Tribunal, or;

21.3. Alternatively, Željko MEAKIĆ inflicted cruel treatment on Saud BESIĆ, a VIOLATION OF THE LAWS OR CUSTOMS OF WAR recognised by Articles 3 and 7(1) of the Statute of the Tribunal and Article 3(1)(a) of the Geneva Conventions.

21.4. Željko MEAKIĆ subjected Saud BESIĆ to inhumane acts, a CRIME AGAINST HUMANITY recognised by Articles 5(i) and 7(1) of the Statute of the Tribunal.

Accused: Mladen Radić

22.1. During June and July, 1992, Mladen RADIĆ repeatedly subjected "A" to forcible sexual intercourse. The first occasion was on or about the night of 25 June 1992. Mladen RADIĆ took "A" to a room downstairs in the administration building, forced her on a table and subjected her to forcible sexual intercourse. Two or three nights later, RADIĆ again called "A" out of the room where she slept and again subjected her to forcible sexual intercourse. On at least three more occasions during June and July 1992, Mladen RADIĆ called "A" out of the room in the administration building where she slept and subjected her to forcible sexual intercourse. These crimes are charged separately below:

First Incident

22.2. Around 25 June, 1992, Mladen RADIĆ wilfully caused "A" great suffering by subjecting her to forcible sexual intercourse, a GRAVE BREACH recognised by Article 2(c) of the Statute of the Tribunal, or;

22.3. Alternatively, around 25 June 1992, Mladen RADIĆ subjected "A" to cruel treatment by forcible sexual intercourse, a VIOLATION OF THE LAWS OR CUSTOMS OF WAR recognised by Article 3 of the Statute of the Tribunal and Article 3(1)(a) of the Geneva Conventions.

22.4. Around 25 June 1992, Mladen RADIĆ raped "A", a CRIME AGAINST HUMANITY recognised by Article 5(g) of the Statute of the Tribunal.

Second Incident

22.5 Around 27 June 1992, Mladen RADIĆ wilfully caused "A" great suffering by subjecting her to forcible sexual intercourse, a GRAVE BREACH recognised by Article 2(c) of the Statute of the Tribunal, or;

22.6. Alternatively, around 27 June 1992, Mladen RADIĆ subjected "A" to cruel treatment by forcible sexual intercourse, a VIOLATION OF THE LAWS OR CUSTOMS OF WAR recognised by Article 3 of the Statute of the Tribunal and Article 3(1)(a) of the Geneva Conventions.

22.7. Around 27 June, 1992, Mladen RADIĆ raped "A", a CRIME AGAINST HUMANITY recognised by Article 5(g) of the Statute of the Tribunal.

Third Incident

22.8. During July, 1992, Mladen RADIĆ wilfully caused "A" great suffering by subjecting her to forcible sexual intercourse, a GRAVE BREACH recognised by Article 2(c) of the Statute of the Tribunal, or;

22.9. Alternatively, during July, 1992, Mladen RADIĆ subjected "A" to cruel treatment by forcible sexual intercourse, a VIOLATION OF THE LAWS OR CUSTOMS OF WAR recognised by Article 3 of the Statute of the Tribunal and Article 3(1)(a) of the Geneva Conventions.

22.10. During July, 1992, Mladen RADIĆ raped "A", a CRIME AGAINST HUMANITY recognised by Article 5(g) of the Statute of the Tribunal.

Fourth Incident

22.11. During late July, 1992, Mladen RADIĆ wilfully caused "A" great suffering by subjecting her to forcible sexual intercourse, a GRAVE BREACH recognised by Article 2(c) of the Statute of the Tribunal, or;

22.12. Alternatively, during late July, 1992, Mladen RADIĆ subjected "A" to cruel treatment by forcible sexual intercourse, a VIOLATION OF

THE LAWS OR CUSTOMS OF WAR recognised by Article 3 of the Statute of the Tribunal and Article 3(1)(a) of the Geneva Conventions.

22.13. During late July, 1992, Mladen RADIĆ raped "A", a CRIME AGAINST HUMANITY recognised by Article 5(g) of the Statute of the Tribunal.

Fifth Incident

22.14. During late July, 1992, Mladen RADIĆ wilfully caused "A" great suffering by subjecting her to forcible sexual intercourse, a GRAVE BREACH recognised by Article 2(c) of the Statute of the Tribunal, or;

22.15. Alternatively, during late July 1992, Mladen RADIĆ subjected "A" to cruel treatment by forcible sexual intercourse, a VIOLATION OF THE LAWS OR CUSTOMS OF WAR recognised by Article 3 of the Statute of the Tribunal and Article 3(1)(a) of the Geneva Conventions.

22.16. During late July, 1992, Mladen RADIĆ raped "A", a CRIME AGAINST HUMANITY recognised by Article 5(g) of the Statute of the Tribunal.

Accused: Zoran Žigic, Dusan Knežević, Dragomir Šaponja, and Nikica Janjić

23.1. In about July 1992, Zoran ŽIGIĆ, Dusan KNEŽEVIĆ and a third unknown person savagely beat Becir MEDUNJANIN on two occasions over a two day period in the "white house." The accused assaulted Becir MEDUNJANIN with a club, a chair, a baton and kicked him. The morning after the second assault Becir MEDUNJANIN died in the room and his body was removed from the camp immediately.

23.2. Zoran ŽIGIĆ and Dusan KNEŽEVIĆ participated in the wilful killing of Becir MEDUNJANIN, a GRAVE BREACH recognised by Article 2(a) and 7(1) of the Statute of the Tribunal, or;

23.3. Alternatively, Zoran ŽIGIĆ and Dusan KNEŽEVIĆ participated in the murder of Becir MEDUNJANIN, a VIOLATION OF THE LAWS OR CUSTOMS OF WAR recognised by Articles 3 and 7(1) of the Statute of the Tribunal and Article 3(1)(a) of the Geneva Conventions.

23.4. Zoran ŽIGIĆ and Dusan KNEŽEVIĆ participated in the murder of Becir medunjanin, a CRIME AGAINST HUMANITY recognised by Articles 5(a) and 7(1) of the Statute of the Tribunal.

24.1. On or about 10 June 1992, Zoran ŽIGIĆ, Dusan KNEŽEVIĆ, Dragomir ŠAPONJA, and Nikica JANJIĆ went to the Omarska camp. ŽIGIĆ, KNEŽEVIĆ, ŠAPONJA, and JANJIĆ were not regular guards at the camp, but were allowed into the camp to murder, beat or otherwise physically abuse the prisoners. On that particular day, they called four prisoners at the Omarska camp, Emir BEGANOVIĆ, Rezak HUKA-NOVIĆ, Asef KAPETANOVIĆ, and Sefik TERZIĆ into the "white house" and severely beat them. The accused used metal batons and cables, a knife, their fists and kicked the victims with their military-style boots.

Victim: Emir Beganović

24.2. Zoran ŽIGIĆ, Dusan KNEŽEVIĆ, Dragomir ŠAPONJA, and Nikica JANJIĆ participated in wilfully causing serious injury to the body or health of Emir BEGANOVIĆ, a GRAVE BREACH recognised by Articles 2(c) and 7(1) of the Statute of the Tribunal, or;

24.3. Alternatively, Zoran ŽIGIĆ, Dusan KNEŽEVIĆ, Dragomir ŠA-PONJA, and Nikica JANJIĆ participated in subjecting Emir BEGANO-VIĆ to cruel treatment, a VIOLATION OF THE LAWS OR CUSTOMS OF WAR recognised by Articles 3 and 7(1) of the Statute of the Tribunal and Article 3(1)(a) of the Geneva Conventions.

24.4. Zoran ŽIGIĆ, Dusan KNEŽEVIĆ, Dragomir ŠAPONJA, and Nikica JANJIĆ participated in subjecting Emir BEGANOVIĆ to inhumane acts, a CRIME AGAINST HUMANITY recognised by Articles 5(i) and 7(1) of the Statute of the Tribunal.

Victim: Rezak Hukanović

24.5. Zoran ŽIGIĆ, Dusan KNEŽEVIĆ, Dragomir ŠAPONJA, and Nikica JANJIĆ participated in wilfully causing serious injury to the body or health of Rezak HUKANOVIĆ, a GRAVE BREACH recognised by Articles 2(c) and 7(1) of the Statute of the Tribunal, or;

24.6. Alternatively, Zoran ŽIGIĆ, Dusan KNEŽEVIĆ, Dragomir ŠA-PONJA, and Nikica JANJIĆ participated in subjecting Rezak HUKA-

NOVIĆ to cruel treatment, a VIOLATION OF THE LAWS OR CUSTOMS OF WAR recognised by Articles 3 and 7(1) of the Statute of the Tribunal and Article 3(1)(a) of the Geneva Conventions.

24.7. Zoran ŽIGIĆ, Dusan KNEŽEVIĆ, Dragomir ŠAPONJA, and Nikica JANJIĆ participated in subjecting Rezak HUKANOVIĆ to inhumane acts, a CRIME AGAINST HUMANITY recognised by Articles 5(i) and 7(1) of the Statute of the Tribunal.

Victim: Asef Kapetanović

24.8. Zoran ŽIGIĆ, Dusan KNEŽEVIĆ, Dragomir ŠAPONJA, and Nikica JANJIĆ participated in wilfully causing serious injury to the body or health of Asef KAPETANOVIĆ, a GRAVE BREACH recognised by Articles 2(c) and 7(1) of the Statute of the Tribunal, or;

24.9. Alternatively, Zoran ŽIGIĆ, Dusan KNEŽEVIĆ, Dragomir ŠAPONJA, and Nikica JANJIĆ participated in subjecting Asef KAPETANOVIĆ to cruel treatment, a VIOLATION OF THE LAWS OR CUSTOMS OF WAR recognised by Articles 3 and 7(1) of the Statute of the Tribunal and Article 3(1)(a) of the Geneva Conventions.

24.10. Zoran ŽIGIĆ, Dusan KNEŽEVIĆ, Dragomir ŠAPONJA, and Nikica JANJIĆ participated in subjecting Asef KAPETANOVIĆ to inhumane acts, a CRIME AGAINST HUMANITY recognised by Articles 5(i) and 7(1) of the Statute of the Tribunal.

Victim: Sefik Terzić

24.11. Zoran ŽIGIĆ, Dusan KNEŽEVIĆ, Dragomir ŠAPONJA, and Nikica JANJIĆ participated in wilfully causing serious injury to the body or health of Sefik TERZIĆ, a GRAVE BREACH recognised by Articles 2(c) and 7(1) of the Statute of the Tribunal, or;

24.12. Alternatively, Zoran ŽIGIĆ, Dusan KNEŽEVIĆ, Dragomir ŠAPONJA, and Nikica JANJIĆ participated in subjecting Sefik TERZIĆ to cruel treatment, a VIOLATION OF THE LAWS OR CUSTOMS OF WAR recognised by Articles 3 and 7(1) of the Statute of the Tribunal and Article 3(1)(a) of the Geneva Conventions.

24.13. Zoran ŽIGIĆ, Dusan KNEŽEVIĆ, Dragomir ŠAPONJA, and Nikica JANJIĆ participated in subjecting Sefik TERZIĆ to inhumane acts, a

CRIME AGAINST HUMANITY recognised by Articles 5(i) and 7(1) of the Statute of the Tribunal.

Accused: Gruban

25.1. Between early June and 3 August 1992, a guard at the Omarska camp with the surname GRUBAN, who was a member of Mladen RADIĆ's shift, repeatedly forced "F" from the room where she was sleeping, took her to another room on the first floor of the administration building in the Omarska camp and subjected her to forcible sexual intercourse.

25.2. GRUBAN wilfully caused "F" great suffering by subjecting her to forcible sexual intercourse, a GRAVE BREACH recognised by Article 2(c) of the Statute of the Tribunal, or;

25.3. Alternatively, GRUBAN subjected "F" to cruel treatment by forcible sexual intercourse, a VIOLATION OF THE LAWS OR CUSTOMS OF WAR recognised by Article 3 of the Statute of the Tribunal and Article 3(1)(a) of the Geneva Conventions.

25.4. GRUBAN raped "F", a CRIME AGAINST HUMANITY recognised by Article 5(g) of the Statute of the Tribunal.

Accused: Predrag Kostić a/k/a Kole

26.1. Between early June and 3 August 1992, Predrag KOSTIĆ, a guard at the Omarska camp, forced "F" from the room where she was sleeping, took her to another room on the first floor of the administration building in the Omarska camp and subjected her to forcible sexual intercourse.

26.2. Predrag KOSTIĆ wilfully caused "F" great suffering by subjecting her to forcible sexual intercourse, a GRAVE BREACH recognised by Article 2(c) of the Statute of the Tribunal, or:

26.3. Alternatively, Predrag KOSTIĆ subjected "F" to cruel treatment by forcible sexual intercourse, a VIOLATION OF THE LAWS OR CUSTOMS OF WAR recognised by Article 3 of the Statute of the Tribunal and Article 3(1)(a) of the Geneva Conventions.

26.4. Predrag KOSTIĆ raped "F", a CRIME AGAINST HUMANITY recognised by Article 5(g) of the Statute of the Tribunal.

Accused: Milutin Popović, Draženko Predojević, Zeljko Savić and Nedeljko Paspalj

27.1 Around 6 July 1992, on the "pista", the victim Rizah HADZALIĆ, in response to a comment by a guard, used a common polite Bosnian Muslim expression, "Bujrum". The accused Milutin POPOVIĆ, together with the co-accused Draženko PREDOJEVIĆ, Željko SAVIĆ, Nedeljko PASPALJ and a guard known only as "Nedo", went to Rizah HADZALIć and beat him for using this Muslim expression. The four accused and "Nedo" beat Rizah HADZALIĆ until he fell to the ground in a sitting position. About half an hour later, Rizah HADZALIĆ died as a result of the beating.

27.2. Milutin POPOVIĆ, Draženko PREDOJEVIĆ, Željko SAVIĆ and Nedeljko PASPALJ participated in the wilful killing of Rizah HADZALIĆ, a GRAVE BREACH recognised by Article 2(a) and 7(1) of the Statute of the Tribunal, or;

27.3. Alternatively, Milutin POPOVIĆ, Draženko PREDOJEVIĆ, Željko SAVIĆ and Nedeljko PASPALJ participated in the murder of Rizah HADZALIĆ, a VIOLATION OF THE LAWS OR CUSTOMS OF WAR recognised by Articles 3 and 7(1) of the Statute of the Tribunal and Article 3(1)(a) of the Geneva Conventions.

27.4. Milutin POPOVIĆ, Draženko PREDOJEVIĆ, Željko SAVIĆ and Nedeljko PASPALJ participated in the murder of Rizah HADZALIĆ, a CRIME AGAINST HUMANITY recognised by Article 5(a) and 7(1) of the Statute of the Tribunal.

Accused: Milan Pavlić

28.1. In early June, 1992, a large group of prisoners were confined in the canteen area of the administration building of the Omarska Camp. One night an elderly man, Mehmedalija NASIĆ, stood up and shouted in apparent protest over the prisoners' confinement. He was, at the time, distressed and possibly mentally disturbed by the conditions that he had been forced to endure. The accused, Milan PAVLIĆ, a regular guard at Omarska, ordered him to sit down. NASIĆ did not sit down, and after a few minutes PAVLIĆ fired his rifle, killing the victim and wounding several other prisoners sitting nearby.

28.2. Milan PAVLIĆ wilfully killed Mehmedalija NASIĆ, a GRAVE BREACH recognised by Article 2(a) of the Statute of the Tribunal, or;

28.3. Alternatively, Milan PAVLIĆ murdered Mehmedalija NASIĆ, a VIOLATION OF THE LAWS OR CUSTOMS OF WAR recognised by Article 3 of the Statute of the Tribunal and Article 3(1)(a) of the Geneva Conventions.

28.4. Milan PAVLIĆ murdered Mehmedalija NASIĆ, a CRIME AGAINST HUMANITY recognised by Article 5(a) of the Statute of the Tribunal.

Accused: Zdravko Govedarica

29.1. On or about 17 June 1992, Zdravko GOVEDARICA, a guard in the Omarska camp, with four other guards whose names are not known, took Serif VELIĆ, a prisoner in the camp, to a room in the Administration Building where they stripped him to his underwear, kicked him in the testicles, repeatedly beat him with a baton and rifle, and kicked him in the ribs, causing him to lapse in and out of consciousness.

29.2. Zdravko GOVEDARICA wilfully subjected Serif VELIĆ to great suffering, a GRAVE BREACH recognised by Article 2(c) of the Statute of the Tribunal, or;

29.3. Alternatively, Zdravko GOVEDARICA subjected Serif VELIĆ to cruel treatment, a VIOLATION OF THE LAWS OR CUSTOMS OF WAR, recognised by Article 3 of the Statute of the Tribunal and Article 3(1)(a) of the Geneva Conventions.

29.4. Zdravko GOVEDARICA subjected Serif VELIĆ to inhumane acts, a CRIME AGAINST HUMANITY recognised by Article 5(i) of the Statute of the Tribunal.

Accused: Mirko Babić

30.1. "F" was taken to the Omarska camp as a prisoner in early June 1992. Sometime between early June and 3 August 1992, "F" was taken to the Separcija building at the entrance to the Omarska camp and placed in a room where Mirko BABIĆ subjected "F" to forcible sexual intercourse.

30.2. Mirco BABIĆ wilfully caused great suffering to "F" by subjecting her to forcible sexual intercourse, a GRAVE BREACH recognised by Article 2(c) of the Statute of the Tribunal, or;

30.3. Alternatively, Mirko BABIĆ subjected "F" to cruel treatment by forcible sexual intercourse, a VIOLATION OF THE LAWS OR CUSTOMS OF WAR recognised by Article 3 of the Statute of the Tribunal and Article 3(1)(a) of the Geneva Conventions of 1949.

30.4. Mirko BABIĆ raped "F", a CRIME AGAINST HUMANITY recognised by Article 5(g) of the Statute of the Tribunal.

Accused: Dusan Knežević

31.1. Around the latter part of June or first part of July 1992, near the building known as the "white house," a group of Serbs from outside the camp, including DUSAN KNEŽEVIĆ, ordered prisoners, whose names are not known, to drink water like animals from puddles on the ground, jumped on their backs and beat them until they were unable to move. As the victims were removed in a wheelbarrow, one of the Serbs discharged the contents of a fire extinguisher into the mouth of one of the victims.

31.2. Dusan KNEŽEVIĆ participated in wilfully causing a group of Omarska prisoners, whose names are not known, great suffering or serious injury to body or health, a GRAVE BREACH recognised by Articles 2(c) and 7(1) of the Statute of the Tribunal, or;

31.3. Alternatively, Dusan KNEŽEVIĆ participated in subjecting these unknown Omarska prisoners to cruel treatment, a VIOLATION OF THE LAWS OR CUSTOMS OF WAR recognised by Articles 3(1)(a) of the Geneva Conventions.

31.4. Dusan KNEŽEVIĆ participated in subjecting these unknown Omarska prisoners to inhumane acts, a CRIME AGAINST HUMANITY recognised by Articles 5(i) and 7(1) of the Statute of the Tribunal.

Richard J. Goldstone
Prosecutor

Contributors

Michael N. Barnett is associate professor of political science at the University of Wisconsin at Madison and is currently a MacArthur International Peace and Security Fellow. He has published widely in the areas of international relations, the Middle East, and the United Nations, and is the author of *Confronting the Costs of War: Military Power, State, and Society in Egypt and Israel.*

Jean Baudrillard is Jean Baudrillard.

Brad K. Blitz is a Ph.D. candidate at Stanford University.

Philip J. Cohen, M.D., currently practices medicine and writes and lectures on the Balkans. He is the author of *Serbia's Secret War: Propaganda and the Deceit of History.*

Daniele Conversi received his Ph.D. at the London School of Economics and Political Science and has taught at Cornell University. He is the author of several publications, including *The Basques, the Catalans, and Spain: Alternative Routes to Nationalist Mobilization.* He is the cofounder of the Association for the Study of Ethnicity and Nationalism (ASEN).

Thomas Cushman is associate professor and chair of the department of sociology, Wellesley College. He is the author, most recently, of *Notes from Underground: Rock Music Counterculture in Russia* and has written extensively on communist and postcommunist societies and cultures.

Sheri Fink is a Ph.D. candidate at Stanford University. Since September 1994, she has been president of Students against Genocide (SAGE), an organization coordinating joint anti-genocide activities on campuses nationwide, and providing educational and activist materials to groups on those campuses. She has written numerous briefings on the Balkan situation, given invited speeches, as well as edited three editions of *SAGE Update,* the organization's newsletter.

Liah Greenfeld teaches in the University Professors Program, Boston University, and is the author of *Nationalism: Five Roads to Modernity.*

Daniel Kofman has published numerous articles in the Israeli and foreign press on the war in Bosnia and other political issues. In 1993 he founded the Israel Public Committee for Bosnia. He is currently writing his doctoral dissertation in the philosophy sub-faculty of Oxford University on the subject of national rights and self-determination.

Slaven Letica is professor of sociology at the University of Zagreb, a former principal advisor to President Franjo Tudjman, and author of numerous books and articles on intellectuals, politics, ethnic conflict, and war in the former Yugoslavia.

Stjepan G. Meštrović is professor of sociology at Texas A&M University. The author of many books on social theory, his works include the edited volume *Genocide after Emotion: The Postemotional Balkan War* and *The Coming Fin de Siècle.*

David Riesman is Henry Ford II Professor of Sociology, Emeritus at Harvard University.

James J. Sadkovich is associate professor of history at the American University in Bulgaria. He is widely published in scholarly journals on the topics of fascism and the history of World War II.

Brendan Simms is a Fellow of Peterhouse, University of Cambridge, and the author of numerous articles on the crisis in the former Yugoslavia.

Index

Academy of Humanism, 55
ACSB. See American Committee to Save Bosnia
Adžić, General Blagoje, 44, 121 n.
Africa, 287
Albania, 40, 54, 176, 262–63
Ambivalence, 4–6, 20; of intellectuals, 5, 6–7; and postmodernism, 11. *See also* Western intellectuals
American Association for Advancement of Slavic Studies, 25
American Civil War, 168
American Committee to Save Bosnia (ACSB), 35 nn., 41, 314, 325, 335, 339–40, 343. *See also* SAGE (Students Against Genocide)
American Philosophical Association, 55
Amnesty International, 37; reports of Croatian atrocities against Serbs, 16, 315; reports of Yugoslavian war killings, 59–60, 93
Anti-Genocide Campaign: campus grassroots activism, 22
Anti-Islam, 26
Arkan. See Ražnatović, Željko
Arms: Israeli-made, Serb use of, 115–16; Israeli sale of to Serbia, 112, 114, 117. *See also* Arms embargo
Arms embargo, 4; Dole-Lieberman bill to end, 318; policy makers against lifting of, 23; U.S., against Bosnia-Herzegovina, 20, 23, 30–31, 44, 118, 289–90, 325, 341
Atrocities: committed by former Yugoslavia; 23; Croat and Bosnia Muslim acts against Serbs, 122 n.; in Croatia and Bosnia-Herzegovina, 47; proof of Serbian atrocities, 96; Serbian acts against Bosnia, 1, 5–6, 10, 15, 45, 93, 120 n.; Serbian and Bosnian Serbian acts against Bosnian Muslims, 122 n. *See also* Belgrade
Auschwitz, 6, 9

Austria, 122 n., 284–85
Auty, Phyllis, 123 n.

Bacon, Francis: quoted, 65
Baker, James, 183–84
Balkan War: root cause of, 17, 25, 29; use of term, 3, 5
Baram, Haim, 106
Barbarism. *See* New Barbarism
Barnett, Michael N., 23
Bassiouni, Cherif, 15, 286, 297 n.
Baudrillard, Jean, 10, 11, 29–30, 79–89; as postmodernist, 12
Belgrade, 4, 12, 14–17, 23–24, 29, 31, 42–43, 51–54, 76, 97–98, 109, 113–14, 117, 167, 184, 193, 195, 254–55, 258, 289, 292, 296–98 nn., 301 n., 336; condemnation of Belgrade-sponsored aggression, 22; emigration psychosis alive in, 56; newspaper reports of Serbian atrocities in Croatia and Bosnia; 16; political establishment, 55; propaganda against Croats, 18; sanctions against, 20; supplier of fuel and money to Bosnian Serbs, 36 n.; war raged by proxies of Belgrade regime, 3, 4, 6, 287
Belgrade regime, 4, 6, 15–16, 29, 42, 52, 54, 56, 63 n., 114; responsible for Serb guerrilla attacks against Croatia, 55. *See also* Belgrade
Bentley, Congresswoman Helen Delich: support of Serbia, 197–203
Binder, David, 13
Blitz, Brad K, 18, 25, 277 n., 327, 341
Block, Robert, 13
Bosnia, 3, 4, 6, 24, 26–27, 29–31, 53–54, 68–70, 73–74, 76, 87, 89; comparison to Vietnam, 68; right to self-defense, 187–88; West abdicates responsibility for, 75
Bosnia-Herzegovina, 50–54, 61–62 n., 94, 103, 188–90, 313–14, 344 n.; depicted as

405

Bosnia-Herzegovina *(Continued)*
civil war; 26, 44–45, 47; Serbian concentration camps in, 45; Serbian war plan, 39; war against, 3, 6, 43; weapons embargo, 20
Bosnian Muslims, 5, 14, 16, 20, 27–30, 46, 52, 85, 92, 98–99, 103–5, 108, 123 n.; atrocities of, 122 n.; ethnic cleansing of, 2, 98, 294; European sites of genocide, 8; formation of Muslim-Croat federation, 3; mass killings, 7, 8, 10; mass rape of women and young girls, 99. See also *Islam between the East and West* (Izetbegović)
Bosnian Serbs, 10, 23, 27, 79, 96, 191–92, 195; attacks of, on UN-declared safe areas Srebrenica and Žepa, 1; portrayal as victims of Croat-Muslim aggression, 25; reactivate concentration camps, execute civilians and arouse mass terror, 2; right of to self defense, 4, 10–11
Bosnians, 30, 81, 86, 105
Boutros-Ghali, Boutros, 1, 143–44, 151–52, 154, 159 n.; quoted, 286, 291, 297 n., 301 n.
Britain, 48, 75–76, 119 n., 243–71, 284, 288–89, 294
Brzezinski, Zbigniew, 8, 22, 35 nn.
Bulgaria, 3

Cambodia, 10, 72
Cancar, Petar, 99
Carrington, Lord Peter, 190, 269; blaming of violations on Muslim Slavs, Serbs and Croats, 20
Carter, Jimmy, President, 24, 223; peace mission to Herzegovina, 36 n.
Chetnik movement, 70, 253–54, 255; militia campaigns of massacre, 54; Serbian irregulars, 54; slaughtering of Muslims, 103. *See also* Mihailović, Draža; Partisans
China, 288
Chomsky, Noam, 10, 32 n.
Christopher, Warren, Secretary of State, 77, 155, 300 n.
Churches and houses of worship: destruction of. *See* Genocide
CIA, 97–98; report on atrocities of Belgrade regime, 15, 46, 97, 286; report on genocide, 15
Cigar, Norman, 17, 34 n., 64 n., 120–21 nn., 160 n., 230 n.; as former Pentagon analyst, 93–94, 96, 98

Civic Nationalism. *See* Nationalism
Civilized federalism, 22
Clinton administration, 33 n., 98, 142, 220, 333, 348
Clinton, Bill, President, 153, 155–56, 161 n., 290, 323, 332, 345; inaction on Bosnia, 68. *See also* Dole-Lieberman bill
Cohen, Philip J., 14, 18, 123 n.
Cohen, Roger, 10, 13, 161 nn.
Cold War, 106, 117, 118, 134–51, 254, 283, 287, 292, 293, 343
Collective guilt: as pretext for mobilizing against a population, 18; doctrine of, 25, 27
Collective security, 75
Communist Party, Yugoslav, 40, 49, 285. *See also* Tito, Marshal Josip Broz
Concentration camps, 52, 190, 192; in Bosnia-Herzegovina, 112; Nazi camps, 53; Serbian camps, 45, 52–53, 95; Western responses to Auschwitz and Dachau, 6. *See also* Auschwitz; Dachau; Omarska (Serbian concentration camp)
Conversi, Daniele, 18–19, 244–81
Cosic, Dobrica, 40, 55
Croatia, 5, 13, 23–27, 29, 31, 36–37 n., 41, 50, 53–54, 76, 92, 96, 122 n., 177–83, 248, 255, 258–59, 262, 302 n., 316, 323, 325, 334, 337–38; Croatian offenses against Bosnian Muslims in Mostar, 16; Croatian Serbs, 4, 18, 27; Croat-Muslim drive to recapture territory, 2; declaration of independence, 43–44; fascist Ustasha regime in World War II, 25; formation of Muslim-Croat federation, 3, 4, 6; free election held in, 41; invasion of, 43; police and local militia, 42, recapturing of Krajina, 16; Serbian plan for war in, 39
Croatian Democratic Union (HDZ), 18
Croats, 35 n., 39, 40, 46, 49–52, 54, 72, 74, 92, 98; in Bosnia, 75, 105; role of in Partisan resistance, 49
Čubrilović, Vaša, 56, 57 nn.; "Expulsion of the Albanians" memorandum, 40
Cultural determinism, 247–48
Cultural monuments, destruction of. *See* Genocide
Cultural relativism, 246
Cushman, Thomas, 1–38

Dachau, 6

Dawidowicz, Lucy, 6
Dayton Accord, 2, 24, 117–18, 314, 322; and genocide, 319–21; partition plan, 332; right to self-defense, 319
Diaspora groups, 187–243
Diaspora Jews, 110
Dindić, Zoran, 55
Diždarević, Zlatko, 10
Djilas, Milovan, 104
Dole, Senator Robert, 22, 183–84. *See also* Dole-Lieberman bill
Dole-Lieberman bill: Clinton veto of, 332–33, 345 n.; to end arms embargo against Bosnia, 318, 342, 345 n., 346 n.
Drašković, Vuk, 166
Dubrovnik, 14; shelling of, 166

Eagleburger, Lawrence, 119 n. 166, 183–84; names suspected war criminals, 298–99 nn.; ambassador to Belgrade, 91; secretary of state, 23, 45
East Timor, 10
Embassy of the Federal Republic of Yugoslavia, 97
Emigration psychosis, 40
Enlightenment project, 8–9, 11, 22, 29; enlightened civility, 11
Equivocation: role in Western non response to Bosnia, 19, 27
Erne, David, 48, 51–52; inflammatory report to UN commission, 48
Ethnic cleansing, 2, 4, 6, 14–15, 25, 29–30, 36 n., 45–46, 52, 82, 88, 94, 108, 117, 149–50, 256, 291; campaigns of, 53; misuse of term, 14–16. *See also* Rape
Ethnic conflict, 14; between Croats and Muslims, 18
Ethnic nationalism. *See* Nationalism
Ethnic partition, 24. *See also* Dayton Accord
Europe, 16, 26–27, 29, 66, 71–72, 82–83, 88, 122 n., 150; genocide and atrocities in, 20–21; the new Europe, 79; "real" Europe as a white Europe, 82; U.S. withdrawal from, 69
European Commission on Human Rights: reports of Croatian atrocities against Serbs in Krajina, 16
European Community, 2–3, 44, 48, 75, 244–45, 265; imposes arms embargo, 44

Falk, Richard, 295

Fascism, 5
Federal Defense Ministry: Serbian controlled, 43
Federation of Yugoslav Immigants; opposing lift of arms embargo, 341–42, 349 n.
Ferdinand, Archduke Franz: assassination of, 40
Finci, Predrag: quoted, 56
Fink, Sheri, 7, 22
Foca, 99
Former Yugoslavia, 2–3, 5, 8, 14, 16, 23, 37 n., 52, 72–73, 92, 96, 101, 110–13, 149, 176, 282–303, 316, 343; dissolution of Yugoslavia, 14; war crimes in, 8; war in, 90
Frames of reference: as rationalizations, 28; importance of, 28; rationalization for nonintervention in Bosnia, 20, 24; sociological study of, 26; sociological term for rationalization, 20, 25–26, 30; tolerance by Western nations of genocide in Bosnia, 27
France, 38 n., 75, 117, 119 n., 244, 248, 265, 271, 288–89, 294
Frankfurt School, 16

Gajić-Glišić, Dobrila, 113
Galvin, General John, 289
Genocide, 1, 3–6, 8–15, 17–19, 22, 25–27, 29–30, 46–47, 56, 79, 102, 108, 119, 123 n., 297 n., 301 n.; adequacy of UN definition of, 19–20, 230 n.; complicity of Serbian intellectuals in, 14–15; definition of, 16, 320, 359; deliberate instrument of Serb policy, 52–54; European, 8, 68, 287, 291–94; European state policy in World War II, 4, 6; in Bosnia, 7–11, 13, 19–20, 24, 27–28, 60 n., 79, 120 n., 149; in Bosnia-Herzegovina, 16; involvement of Serbian leaders and intellectuals, 36 n.; Serbian, 26–27, 47; vs. other war crimes and atrocities, 18; Western elite ignorance of, 20. *See also* Media (electric); Media (print)
Genocide Convention of 1948 (1949), 43, 286, 348 n., 360
Gentile, Louis, 8
Germany, 6, 13, 24, 27, 29, 72, 101, 106, 121 n., 123 n., 248, 256, 262, 264, 271, 284, 289, 294; recognition of Slovenia and Croatia, 13
Gligorov, Kiro, 166
Greater Serbia, 72, 76, 189, 195; propaganda

of, 180–81
Greece, 3, 119 n., 244, 247–48; Greek-Turkish model for Bosnia, 69
Greenfeld, Liah, 22
Gutman, Roy, 57 n., 60 n., 77 n., 93–94, 99, ll9–22 nn., 256, 320

Hamilton, Congressman Lee: recipient of Balkan lobbying efforts, 214–21
Helsinki Commission, 48
Helsinki Declaration: denying right to secede, 285, 297 n.
Helsinki Watch, 15, 48, 60 n., 120 n.; reports of, 95, 98, 112, 121 n.; reports of Croatian atrocities against Serbs in Krajina, 16
Herzfeld, Michael 131–34, 147, 158 n.
Historical determinism, 19, 247–49
Historical parallels: to Bosnian war, 65–68
Hitler, Adolf, 24, 29, 48, 51 68 72, 76; expulsion of Jews, 39–40
Holocaust Jewish, 6–9, 29–30, 40, 45, 56, 68, 72, 111, 119 n., 122–23 nn., 149, 315–16, 320–21, 323; as instance of genocide, 7, 19; difference from genocide in Bosnia, 7–8; European site of, 8, 9; memorial in Washington, DC, 68; Steven Spielberg and *Schindler's List,* 8; the "we did not know" rationalization, 6. *See also* Western intellectuals
Hungary, 285; Hungarians in Croatia, 45
Hussein, Saddam, 85–86
Hyperreality: concept of portrayal of death, 10, 79; world of the simulacrum, 10

Indicted war criminals, 4, 19
Indonesian government, 10
Instrumental rationality, 9
International Court of Justice, 48; demands Serbia and Montenegro prevent genocide in Bosnia, 20
International Humanist and Ethical Union, 55
International Law of Human Rights, The (Sieghart), 283, 295
International Tribunal for the Prosecution of Responsible Persons for Serious Violations of International Humanitarian Law Committee in the Territory of Former Yugoslavia since 1991 (UN commission), 48
International War Crimes Tribunal, 15, 17, 320; charges Serbs with genocide and

crimes against humanity, 20; indicts Bosnian war criminals, 2, 20, 363; indicts Bosnian Croats, 16
Iran, 29
Islam between East and West (Izetbegović), 28
Islamic fundamentalism, 26–29, 108
Islamic terrorism, 28
Israel, 25, 29–30, 90–127
Israeli Communist Party, 102
Italy, 285, 294
Ivanko, Alexander, 21
Izetbegović, Alija, 28, 103, 109, 166, 285; *Islam Between East and West,* 28

Jews, 10, 25, 40, 45, 92, 104, 107, 114, 124; European, 24–25, 30; Zionist federation, 68. *See also* Diaspora Jews
Judas, Miloš, 58 n.

Karadžić, Radovan, 2, 5, 24, 27, 35 n. 49, 51, 73, 76, 93, 98–99, 105, 108, 166, 169, 191–96, 221, 259; International War Crimes Tribunal indictments against, 363–401
Kaufman, Michael T., 3
Kenney, George, 28
Kofman, Daniel, 9, 25, 29
Kollek, Teddy (former mayor of Jerusalem), 92, 107, 117
Kosovo, 40–41, 59, 76, 198; Serbian attacks, 59 n.; Serbian defeat by Turks, 41; Serbs terminate autonomy of, 41
Kostović, Ivan, 58 n.
Krajina, 14, 17, 41; blockade of roads, 41–42; Croat recapture of, 16; Serbian revolt, 25, 41
Kuristan, 10

League of Nations, 73, 75; Covenant, 284
Letica, Slaven, 14, 31 n., 35 n.
Lewis, Anthony, 8

MacKenzie, General Lewis, 63 n., 91, 96, 119 n.
Major, John, Prime Minister, 96, 119 n., 260
Maksimović, Vojislav, 99
Marković, Ante, 166–67, 169–70
Marković, Mihailo, 55, 64 n., 253–54; denounces U.S. role in Persian Gulf War, 55
Martić, Milan, 50, 124 n.
Masaryk, Thomas, 22
Mazowiecki, Tadeusz, 45, 60 nn.

Media (electronic), 79; bias in reporting Croat and Muslim acts against Serbs, 17; bias in Israeli reporting, 105; Bosnia as media spotlight, 9–10; globalization of information, 6; "second media age of postwar era", 7

Media (print), 7, 79; American, 106; bias in reporting Croat and Muslim acts against Serbs, 17; coverage in Bosnia, 9; on genocide in Bosnia, 10

Mesić, Stipe, 43

Mihailović, Draža, 48–49, 51, 55 n., 76, 108, 113, 116

Military forces: International Rapid Reaction forces, 85, 88; Slovenian Territorial Defense Forces, 43–45; Yugoslav Federation Army, 53–54; Yugoslav Federation Army defeated by Slovenian defense forces, 44, 48; Yugoslav National Army capture of Croatian territory, 4

Milošević, Misha, 191–94

Milošević, Slobodan, 5, 16, 40–43, 51, 55–56, 64 n., 68, 72, 76, 91, 93, 108, 114, 116, 121 n., 125 n., 166, 170–71, 175–76, 193, 255, 258, 285, 290, 342

Mladić, General Ratko, 35 n., 38 n., 223, 259; indicted war criminal, 2; list of indictments against, 13, 363–401

Moljević, Stevan, 59

Montenegro, 3, 20, 40–41; Serbian ally, 41; UN imposed sanctions against, 193

Moore, Patrick, 17

Moral equivocation, 18, 19; equivalency of Serbs, Bosnian Muslims, Croats as perpetrators of war crimes, 53

Moral relativism, 11–13, 18–19, 22–23, 231 n., 244–46, 256, 258–59, 266–67, 270–71; definition of, and role in postmodernism, 111

Moral universalism, 246

Mostar, 16

Moynihan, Senator Daniel, 31

Multiculturalism: 11–12; and treatment of Serbia, 11–12

Muslims, 25, 27, 35 n., 50, 53, 68, 72, 74, 92, 96, 98, 103, 105; fate of, compared to Armenians, 68

Nagel, Thomas: quoted, 294

National Council of the Republic of Serbia: declaration of Krajina as Serbian, 43. See

also Yugoslav Federation, constitution of 1974 and violations of

Nationalism, 23, 175; civic and ethnic, differentiation between, 22–23; ethnic, 302–12; federalist (unitarism), 169; pro-Serbian, 106; separatist, 169. See also Tudjman, Franjo

NATO, 28, 118, 153–55, 166, 177, 255, 286–87, 291, 325, 346; air strikes against Bosnian Serbs, 1–2, 10, 131, 154, 291

Nazis, 4, 6, 9, 24–28. 45, 48–49, 53, 56, 72, 76, 92, 94–95, 108–9, 122

Nedić, General Milan (Nazi puppet ruler), 26

Neo-isolationism, 23, 69

New Barbarism, 2, 8, 148, 302 n.; Orwellian approach to, 292–93

New European Order. See New World Order

New Intellectual Order, 82

New World Order, 82–83, 87

New York Review of Books, 13, 121 n.

New York Times, 8, 13, 20, 25, 32 nn., 36–37 nn., 48, 55 n., 58–59, 96, 119 n., 159–61 nn., 191, 296–97 nn., 300 n., 302 n., 347–48 nn.

New York Times Magazine, 19, 28

Nuremberg: contrast with Bosnia in principles, 282–83, 295 n.; Western ignorance of principles of, 20

Nuremberg era: post-World War II trials, 8, 46, 284, 286–87, 292, 295 n., 298 n.

Omarska (Serbian concentration camp), 32, 45, 94–95

Opačić, Jovan, 50

Open Media Research Institute, 17

"Orientalism," 26

Orr, Ori, 114, 116–17

Orwell, George, 5, 11–12, 292; contempt for fascism, 5; critic of evil, 11

Ostojić, Veelivor, 99

Owen, David, 286

Pale, 97

Partisans, 103, 253–54. See also Tito, Marshal Josip Broz

Pavelić, Ante, 18. See also Croatian Democratic Union (HDZ)

Peace talks: Dayton Accord, 2; negotiated settlement, 24. See also Dayton Accord

Peres, Shimon, Foreign Minister, 102, 114

Perry, William, Secretary of Defense, 155
Persian Gulf War, 55, 86–87
Petovar, Tanja, 52
Poland, 291
Popović, Pero, 63 n.
Porat, Yehoshua, 105
Poster, Mark, 7
Postmodernism: as intellectual movement, 12; culture of, 302 n.; definition and characteristics of, 11–12; media and postmodernism, 11–12, 302 n.; as rebellion against the Enlightenment project, 11; voyeuristic tendencies of, 79. *See also* Moral relativism
Powell, General Colin (chairman of U.S. Joint Chiefs of Staff), 288, 299 n.
Public information: information "super highway," 9; relationship to moral intervention, 7

Rabin, Prime Minister, 111, 116, 124 n.; assassination of, 115
Radic, Stjepan, 174
Rape, 5–6, 15, 44, 52–53, 93, 106, 108; as Serbian method of terror, 46–47, 61 n., 99; gang, of pregnant women by Serbian soldiers, 47; mass, 6, 15, 17; as part of ethnic cleansing, 47; of young girls, 106; camps, for forcibly impregnating non-Serbian women, 47; systematic, of Muslims, 20
Rašković, Jovan, 4, 14, 42, 49–50, 55; *Luda zemlja,* 50. *See also* Serbian Democratic Party
Rationalization. *See* Frames of reference; Typifications
Rav-Ner, Tsvi, 97
Ražnatović, Željko, 93, 106; as "Arkan," 4, 106
Red Cross: reports of Croatian atrocities in Krajina, 16
Relativism. *See* Moral relativism
Republic of Serbia, 41
Revisionism, 232 n.
Rieff, David, 4, 95, 98–99, 120 n., 160 n., 296 n.
Riesman, David, 22, 31
Rifkind, Malcolm, 71–73, 75, 91, 96
Root causes of Bosnian war, 67
Rorty, Richard, 11, 32 n.
Russia. *See* Soviet Union, 247–48
Rwanda, 10, 24, 128–62, 287, 322

Sadkovich, James J., 20, 282–303
SAGE (Students Against Genocide), 256, 314–15, 329, 334–35, 339– 40, 343, 348 n.
SANA (Serbian Academy of Science and Art), 76; 1986 memorandum, 39–41, 55, 56– 57 nn.
Sarajevo, 1–2, 10, 21, 29, 37, 47, 49, 56, 79– 84, 88, 100–2, 105, 109, 151, 155, 190–91, 256, 289, 316, 336; shelling of marketplace and bombing of schools, 27
SCIC. *See* Serbian Council Information Center
Secular theodicy, concept of, 133
Self-determination, principle of, 285, 290, 298 n. *See also* Tudjman, Franjo
Serbia, 3, 39–41, 53, 83, 91–92, 100, 177; leadership named as suspected war criminals, 45; sanctions against, 68; war effort of, targeting civilian Croats, 54; military juggernaut of, 4, 8, 14, 20, 23, 25, 29, 41, 43; supports Yugoslavian weapons embargo, 44
Serbian Academy of Science and Art. *See* SANA
Serbian aggression, 26–27, 29, 47, 56, 75, 84– 86, 91, 119 n., 124 n., 126 n.; blitzkrieg of rape, looting, mutilation and civilian murder, 44; genocide in Balkan War, 17; pan-Serbian, 173; use of Western troops to check aggression, 67; military inability of the West to react to, 87
Serbian Council Information Center (SCIC), 194
Serbian Democratic Party, 42, 50–51, 55, 193
Serbian expansionism: threat to European security, 76
Serbian Information Initiative, 236 n.
Serbianization, 11, 84; Baudrillard's definition of, 11, 84–86
Serbian labor camps. *See* Concentration camps
Serbian nationalism, revival of, 40
Serbian Orthodox Church, 188; issues "Proposed Serbian Church National Program," 41–42
Serbian program of genocide. *See* Atrocities; Genocide
Serbian propaganda, 25, 41, 44; nature of, 91

Serbian Radical Party, 6, 16, 5–52. *See also* Seselj, Vojislav
Serbian Socialist Party, 55
Serbian Unity Congress (SUC), 52, 194, 200–14, 217, 221–29, 238 nn., 241 n.
SerbNet: Serbian American lobby group, 91, ll9 n., 200–203
Serbophilia, 245, 250, 252, 256; after collapse of Titoism, 255–62; British Serbophilism and toleration of war crimes, 19. *See also* West, Rebecca
Serbs, 5, 11–20, 23–26; 28–29, 40, 43, 46, 52, 67, 70, 74–75, 82, 84–86, 88, 91, 98, 101, 105; and killing of Bosnian Muslims, 10; of Croatia seek autonomy, 41; propaganda of, created by Serbian intellectuals, 18; exodus of, from Bosnian control, 14; superiority of, 50
Šešelj, Vojislav, 16, 52, 106
Sieghart, Paul, 295 n.; *The International Law of Human Rights,* 283, 295
Silajdžić, Harris (prime minister of Bosnia), 73
Simms, Brendan, 17, 19, 65–78
Simulacrum: concept of, 10, 79
Slovenes, 92, 101, 168
Slovenia, 13, 27, 52, 54, 106, 258, 263; declaration of independence, 43, secession of, 13, 44; 1991 war against, 3, 6
Socialist Party, 16. *See also* Milošević, Slobodan
Soviet Union, 48, 109, 151, 284, 294
Spanish Civil War, 5, 73, 289, 290
Srebrenica, 1, 17, 106, 125 n.
Stalin, 72; expulsion of Jews, 40
Stefanović, Mirko (charge d' affaires for Embassy of the Federal Republic of Yugoslavia), 97
Stojanović, Svetozar, 55
Strasbourg, 80
Students Against Genocide. *See* SAGE
SUC. *See* Serbian Unity Congress

Teitelbaum, Raoul, 105
Telford, Taylor, 286, 297 n.
Thatcher, Margaret Prime Minister, 71, 75; accuses Britain of complicity in genocide, 72
Third Reich, 68, 72; practices of, 68
Tito, Marshal Josip Broz, 27, 40, 123 n., 175, 198, 253–55, 258, 285, 300 n.

Toholsi, Mieoslav, 28
Trevelyvan, G.M.: quoted, 66, 76–77
Tudjman, Franjo, 16, 18, l09, 114, 117, 122 n., 165–66, 170–85, 255–56; participation in antifascist Partisan movement, 173; principle of self-determination, 16, 18, 285;
Twain, Mark, 19
Typifications, 20

United Kingdom. *See* Britain
United Nations, 20, 48, 52, 73, 75, 88, 95, 102, 114, 117, 128–31, 261, 264–65, 267, 285–86, 288–89, 294, 298 n., 330; accused of corruption in Bosnia and Croatia, 21, 23–24; definition of genocide, adequacy of, 19–20; Charter of, 15, 30–31, 35 n., 134–38, 289, 322; Charter, Article 51 of, 15, 30–31, 322; Commission of Human Rights and Misha Milosevic, 45, 60 n., 192; commission investigating war crimes, 48; documentation of Serbian war crimes, 15, 46; and genocide, 15, 129–31, 134, 141, 145–46, 147; in Bosnia-Herzegovina, 8; resolutions of, 23; sanctions, 113;
United Nations Commission of Experts, 48, 51–53, 55 n.
United Nations Convention on Genocide, 60 n.; Article 2, definition of genocide, 46
United Nations General Assembly: adoption of Article 2, 46
United Nations Protection Force. *See* UNPROFOR
United Nations Security Council, 60 n., 101, 128–30, 138–55, 159 n., 245, 286; adopts resolution banning weapons sales to Yugoslavia, 44
United States, 11, 44, 48, 93, 117, 118, 129–30, 134, 145–47, 150, 294, 302 nn., 348 n.; imposes arms embargo, 44
United States Congress: attributes war crimes to Serbs, 15; Commission of Security and Cooperation in Europe, 33 n. *See also* Dole-Lieberman bill
United States Department of State, 45, 97, 121–22 n.; attributes war crimes to Serbs, 15; reports atrocities and war crimes in Former Yugoslavia to the UN, 46
UNPROFOR (United Nations Protection Force), 63 n., 88, 149–57, 160 n., 162 n., 291

Ustasha, 13, 18, 26, 36 n., 255; crimes of regime, 104–5

Vance-Owen plan, 261
Veil, Simone: quoted, 10
Verstehen: definition of, 15, 33 n.
Vietnam War, 30, 68
Vojvodina, 76; Serbian province of, 100; Serbs terminate autonomy, 40–41
von Ranke, Leopold (German historian): quoted, 2
Vukovar, 14

War crimes, 1–2, 4, 23, 111; crimes committed by Nazis, 6; Serbian, 4, 15–16, 18–19, 53. *See also* CIA; Helsinki Watch; United States Congress; United States Department of State
War criminals, 2, 4, 13; Western negotiations with indicted criminals, 23. *See also* Karadžić, Radovan; and Mladić, General Ratko
Washington Post, 48, 58–59, 161 n., 345 n.
West, Rebecca, 252, 255
Western elites, 118; definition of, 3; agreement with Serbian views, 5; ambivalence of, toward Bosnian genocide, 5, 11
Western intellectuals, 4–5, 11, 15, 21, 79; change in the habits of, 5; Eurocentric response to Bosnian genocide, 10, 18, 19; failure to respond to genocide and rape, 19; guided by ambivalence, 22; response to European genocide, 8, 23, 26, 29–30; silence on genocide, 22

Western policy: rationalizations for lack of, in Balkans, 21
Western role in Balkan War: analysis of, 3; ambivalence of Western intellectuals, 4; comparison of Western intellectual response to the Holocaust and Bosnia, 8; silent witness, 3; view of war as Civil War, 67; ineffective response before air strikes, 1, 13
Wiesel, Elie, 9, 22, 68, 95–96, 323
World War I, 40, 69
World War II, 2–4, 6–7, 16, 18–19, 24–30, 36 n., 40, 49–50, 56, 67, 72, 91–92, 96–97, 104, 109, 114, 116–17, 122–23 n., 283, 290, 294; lesson of, 68; post-World War II era, 18

Yugoslav Communist Party See Communist Party, Yugoslav
Yugoslav Federation, 26; constitution of 1974 and violations of, 41–43
Yugoslav Federation Army. *See* Military Forces
Yugoslavhood, 174–76
Yugoslav National Army. *See* Military Forces

Zagreb, 52, 95, 289, 316; cluster bomb shelling, 14
Zametica, Jovan, 104, 123 n., 259, 278 nn.
Zelenbaba, Suzana, 50
Žepa, 17, 21
Zimmerman, Warren (U.S. ambassador to Yugoslavia), 22, 35 n., 165–72, 177–78